Changing Dimensions of Social Justice in the New Global Era

Indian Experiences

CHANGING DIMENSIONS OF SOCIAL JUSTICE IN THE NEW GLOBAL ERA

Indian Experiences

Foreword by

Prof. M P Dube
Dean, Faculty of Arts and
Director, Institute of Gandhian Thought and Peace Studies
University of Allahabad

Editors

Kamlesh Gupta
Trivikram Tiwari
Nandini Basistha

RAJIV GANDHI CHAIR IN CONTEMPORARY STUDIES
ALLAHABAD UNIVERSITY, ALLAHABAD

PENTAGON PRESS

Changing Dimensions of Social Justice in the New Global Era: Indian Experiences
Kamlesh Gupta, Trivikram Tiwari, Nandini Basistha (Eds)

Technical Support:
Praveen Kr. Pandey
Anupam Kumar

ISBN 978-81-8274-655-8

First Published in 2013

Published by
PENTAGON PRESS
206, Peacock Lane, Shahpur Jat,
New Delhi-110049
Phones: 011-64706243, 26491568
Telefax: 011-26490600
email: rajan@pentagonpress.in
website: www.pentagonpress.in

Printed at Chaman Enterprises, Delhi.

Contents

PART III
PUBLIC POLICY AND INCLUSIVE GROWTH

PART IV
JUSTICE, GENDER AND DEMOCRACY

PART V
MARGINALITIES AND JUSTICE

Foreword

Justice is the most central concept to politics. John Rawls, the most important and influential liberal theorist of justice in recent decades, maintained that Justice is the first of virtues of Social Institutions in the way that truth is of scientific theories. It has been the subject of intense argument during the last quarter of 20th century and onwards. The idea of justice is generally distinguished between formal and substantive senses. In the formal sense, Justice is correct weighting and proportion in judgments. The core element of the idea of justice is that like cases should be treated alike. It is a rule of logical impartiality. On the other hand, what counts as like cases and what involves equal treatments are domains of substantive principles. What substantive principles are appropriate in particular situations and what they imply has been debated since ancient times. Today the most significant species of justice are: Procedural or un-patterned and distributive or patterned or Social Justice. Procedural theories of justice uphold the 'rule of law'; justice is concerned with rule-following. The main concern of justice for proceduralists is not a teleocratic order, rather maintaining procedural rules to provide conditions for individual freedom. The most important procedural justice theories are Friedrich Hayak's commutative account of justice and Nozick's entitlement theories. But distributive justice has become the principal normative concern of modern political life. It has been defined as a question of equity in the distribution of social goods. Brighouse rightly claims that "the fundamental question is this: how and to what end, should a just society distribute the various benefits. (resources, opportunities, and freedoms) it produces, and the burdens, (costs, risks, and unfreedoms) required to maintain it?"

Distributive Justice deals with the distribution of benefits and burdens 'to each according to his due or fare allocation of burdens and benefits in society.' There are various principles that determine 'due'. Each principle can be formulated in the form of rights, deserts, needs, services, work, moral worth, ability, skill, or status, and so forth. These principles can be sub divided into desert and non-desert oriented distributive principles. There is no problem with desert oriented distributive principles because a person with merit worthy activity or a valuable quality should be rewarded in relation to that activity or quality. But most contentious are non-desert oriented distributive principles. Since 1970s much attention has fallen to these principles of which a larger bulk of contemporary justice theorizing is based on contractarian claims—wide ranging agreement or consensus on a rational procedure—and empirical assumptions (needs).

In theorizing distributive justice, Gauthier and Buchanan advance a sophisticated form of rational choice argument. To them justice is an outcome of a mutual bargaining process among individuals in an initial position. They regard justice as mutual advantage. On the other hand, John Rawls, Barry and Scanlon regard Justice as impartiality. In Rawls justice is not seen as a bargaining position as in Gauthier. It is the outcome of rational agreement between discrete individuals. To him justice is 'the appropriate division of social advantages'. However, Michael Walzer and Miller attempt to establish a plural concept of justice.

John Rawls develops a fair way of developing such principles of distribution. The basic idea in Rawls is 'to identify a fair arrangement in society for all parties to agree to without knowing how it will affect them.' It will cut out the possibility of arbitrariness in decision about justice. For Rawls, justice should not reflect or re enforce arbitrary chance or interests, but rather should aim to nullify them for the sake of basic fairness. Rawls initial task, and his primary innovation, was to evolve a device to achieve this nullification. For this he conceives an 'original position'—a form of rational disinterestedness. Thus the principles of justice for basic structure of society are the object of the original agreement.

Rawls maintains that justice regulates the distribution of primary goods. The primary goods include basic rights and liberties, powers and offices, income and wealth, the bases of self-respect and leisure. The distribution of these goods is regulated by two principles, the first of which has lexical priority over the second. The first principle holds that basic rights and liberties are distributed in a suitably fair way, income and wealth and the rest should be distributed equally unless the unequal distribution would increase the share going to the least well off.

The views of Rawls have been attacked both by Robert Nozick and F A Von Hayak. In their view, justice is not a matter of how benefits or burdens are distributed, but a matter of protecting individual rights to resources. They maintain that the concept implies an agency entitled to achieve it, which is incompatible with the individual liberty. To them goods and opportunities are justly distributed when they are in the hands of their rightful owners.

The traditional distributional approach has been challenged by various theorists during the 1990s and onwards; the sole emphasis on distribution without an examination of the underlying causes of the maldistributions was not acceptable to several contemporary political theorists. Iris Young, Nancy Frazer, Axel Honneth and Charles Taylor argue that while justice must be concerned with classic issues of distribution, it must also address the process that constructs mall distribution. To them individual and social recognition, rather than simply fair process for the distribution of goods and benefits, are the key elements of attaining justice. In fact, they are influenced by the real world of political injustice. Their central concern is recognition and participation in the decision-making.

Amartya Sen and Martha Nussbaum expand the conception of justice beyond John Rawls (distributive justice) by advancing capability approach. They have developed a theory of justice that focuses on the capacities necessary for individuals and groups to function and flourish. Along with distribution of goods, focus is on how those goods are transformed into functioning and flourishing of individuals and communities; focus is to judge how those distribution affect our well being and how we 'function'.

Traditionally questions of justice have been central to political life. But in recent years issues of environment have become integral part of the discourse of justice. Today environmental and ecological justice have become very important themes of discussion for social and political theorists and movements. Central to the environmental justice is distribution of goods and bads, but at the same time it is tied with some discussion of recognition, political participation and capabilities at both the individual and community level. The neo-liberal model of globalisation and development has made inequity from bad to worse, both between the North and the South, and between rich and the impoverished in Southern nations; there is an enormous growth in the fortunes of a rich minority at the expense of the majority of the population. It creates threat to food security and sustainable livelihood of deprived sections, specially tribals, women and children. It drains of natural resources for economic gains. Current development process has devastated natural resources and habitats, created environmental refugees and is posing a serious threat to continuation of life on planet earth itself. Impact of globalisation on society, polity, economy, environment and ecology has made theorizing and realisation of justice much more complex.

Analysis on these lines may help to refine the process of social justice realisation. The book, Social Justice in the Era of Globalisation pursues this line of inquiry by providing students, scholars and policy makers with an extensive review of research on social justice. The book is written for a wide audience that includes academics, policy makers, social activists and students concerned with social justice issues. I hope that the book contributes to public understanding of the most important social justice problems, issues, and policies that society now faces and with which it must deal.

M.P. Dube
Dean, Faculty of Arts and
Director, Institute of Gandhian Thought and Peace Studies
University of Allahabad

Acknowledgement

This volume is an outcome of a two-day National Seminar on *Social Justice in India: Emerging Issues* organized by the Rajiv Gandhi Chair in Contemporary Studies of University of Allahabad in September 2010.

We thank to our Vice-Chancellor and university administration for their support and cooperation. We must thank Prof. M.P. Dube, Dean Faculty of Arts, Allahabad University who always extended his guidance as well as academic and administrative support in organizing this event. This book could not have been possible without his constant support and encouragement. We also must thank him for writing such an outstanding foreword on our request. The Indian Council of Social Science Research (ICSSR), New Delhi, deserves special thanks for co-sponsoring the event. Rajiv Gandhi Chair Staff worked with complete dedication and zeal to make the gathering of distinguished scholars and policy makers to a grand success. We must thank these scholars from different parts of India for taking all troubles in coming over to Allahabad and lighting the way ahead for us.

Two of the essays in this collection have already been published earlier, in draft form, in *Journal of Social and Political Studies*. We thank the Editorial Board of consulting Journal for permitting us to reprint these articles from their journal. Finally, Mr. Rajan Arya, the Chief Executive Officer of Pentagon Press, deserves thanks for bringing the book within a short span of time.

About

About the Editors and Contributors

- **Prof. Debasis Guha,** is currently teaches Philosophy in the Department of Philosophy, University of Allahabad. Prof. Guha specializes in Ethics apart from other interests in the field of Ethics. He has more than 35 papers published in different national and international Journals of Philosophy, Political Sciences and Business Management. He has written six books on Applied Ethics apart from a book on *"Pain and Sufferings, An Analytic Study of the Concepts"*.
- **Prof. M.T. Desai** (Retd), Former Head of Political Science Department, Gujarat University, Ahmedabad. His area of specialisation International Relation Thought. His publication included; *Concept of Internationalism of Jawaharlal Nehru, Ravindra Nath Tagore and Shree Aurobindo*. He has seven research paper published in reputed journal in his credit.
- **Dr. J.P. Mishra,** is currently Reader, Faculty of Law, University of Allahabad. His specialisation is in Constitutional Law (India & UK), IPR, Jurisprudence and Environmental Law. He had published 15 papers in reputed national and international journals, in seminar proceedings (national/international), and as Chapters in edited books. He had also written several books, like *'An Introduction to Intellectual Property Law' (Third Edition 2012), 'Bauddhik Sampada Adhikar-Ek Parichaya' (Second Edition 2010, won Raj Puraskar of from Ministry of Justice, Government of India in 2006)* and *'An Introduction to Cyber Law' (First Edition 2012).*
- **Prof. C.P. Barthwal** (Retd), Former Vice Chancellor, Kumaun University, Nainital, he has 38 years of experience of teaching, training, research evaluation and administration. Prof Barthwal is winner of U.P. State Government Dr. Ganesh Shankar Vidhyapith Award for his book on Local Self-Government, NIPM/LBS Best Research Paper Award, Parvat Gaurav Samman, 2007 (awarded by Parvatiya maha Parishad, Lucknow) and Uttarkhand Ratan, 2007 (awarded by All India Intellectual Conferences).
- **Dr. Subhash Shukla** is currently Lecturer, Centre for Globalisation and Development Studies, University of Allahabad. His works include *Foreign Policy of India* (New Delhi, 2007); *Issues in Indian Polity* (New Delhi, 2008); co-author of *Antar Rashtriya Rajneeti ke Siddhanta* (New Delhi, 2010) and *Theory in International Politics* (New Delhi, 2011) and has co-edited *India's Foreign Policy: Emerging Challenges* (New Delhi, 2012). To his credit, he has

15 papers published in various journals, of national and international repute.

- **Dr. Pradeep Sharma** is currently Lecturer, Centre for Globalisation and Development Studies, University of Allahabad. His areas of academic interest include globalisation, development, social justice, civil society, public policy, social movements, democracy and decentralisation. He also taught at Centre for Political Studies, Jawaharlal Nehru University, New Delhi, and published work on *Dalit Politics and Literature* in addition to research papers and articles.
- **Ms. Nandini Basistha** is currently working as Senior Research Fellow at Rajiv Gandhi Chair in Contemporary Studies, University of Allahabad. She has done M.A. and M.Phil. in South and Southeast Asian Studies from University of Calcutta. She has presented paper in various seminars, including Southampton (UK), Singapore, Gwalior, Kolkata, Lucknow, Siliguri, Shillong, Guahati, Dibrugarh, Allahabad and many more places. She has written many articles in international and national journals and books.
- **Mr. Trivikram Tiwari** is currently working as Senior Research Fellow at Rajiv Gandhi Chair in Contemporary Studies, University of Allahabad. He has done M.A. in Political Science from University of Allahabad. Presently working on Nationalism and Multiculturalism, Trivikram has keen interest and command over classical and contemporary political theory and political thought. He has presented stimulating research papers in various seminars at places including Southampton (UK), Veraval (Gujarat), New Delhi, Allahabad and various other locations.
- **Ms. Santwana Pandey** is Assistant Professor of Political Science at the Guru Ghasidas Vishwavidyalay, Bilaspur, Chhattisgarh. She specializes in the issues of social justice and sensitive issues regarding our society and its tender fibre as women and children and more recently she has written about other political issues related to state and regional politics, growth and structural changes that are occurring here. She is a research fellow of the Department of Political Science, Babasaheb Bhimrao Ambedkar University, Lucknow, U.P., India.
- **Prof. Sudha Pai**, Centre for Political Studies, Jawaharlal Nehru University, New Delhi. Since joining the Centre she has taught Courses and guided research in the field of Indian Politics and Comparative Politics. Her research interests include Dalit Politics, State Politics in India, Agrarian Politics, Globalisation and Legislative Governance. She has been member of many Research Projects including SIDA (Sweden) and the UNRISD. She was Senior Fellow at the Nehru Memorial Museum and Library, Teen Murti, New Delhi for a period of three years to work on a project Developmental State and the Dalit Question in Madhya Pradesh: Congress Response (January 2006-09).

- **Dr. Kamlesh Gupta** presently working as a Post Doctoral Research Associate at Rajeev Gandhi Chair in Contemporary Studies, University of Allahabad, Allahabad. He has eight years Teaching Experience at SOS Political Science & Public Administration, Jiwaji University, Gwalior (MP). His research area includes; Contemporary Issues of Public Administration, Issues of Public Policy and Development, Democratic Decentralisation. His major Publications include; *Teaching and Research Aptitude* (2006), *Shri Aurovindo: Mentor of New Society* (2007), *Recent Trends in Decentralisation* (2009) and several Research Paper published in various journals of national and international repute.
- **Dr. Rakesh Kumar** is an Assistant Professor in the Post-graduate Department of Economics at S.K.M. University, Dumka, Jharkhand. Dr. Kumar availed a JRF of the UGC and did his D.Phil from the University of Allahabad. He has keen interest in issues related to social justice, environment and sustainable development and has presented several papers in national and international seminars.
- **Mr. Pragyanshu Amaoni** is the Doctoral Candidate in the Centre for International Politics, Organisation and Disarmament (CIPOD), School of International Studies, Jawaharlal Nehru University (JNU), New Delhi. His research interests include international politics, particularly the dynamics of international organisations as well as the interface of social stratification with modernity in Indian society.
- **Dr. Lalima Singh** is Currently Reader, Department of Sociology at S.S. Khanna Girls' Degree College, Allahabad. She has done her Ph.D. in "Reservation Policy in India: A Socio Economic Perspective". She has contributed paper in National and International Seminars/Journals.
- **Prof. S.V. Pande (Retd),** Former Pro Vice-Chancellor and Director, Institute of Social Science, Dr. B. R. Ambedakar University, Agra. His area of specialisation is Social Stratification and Indian Society. He has published four books and twenty three research paper in foreign and national journal.
- **Dr. Archana Srivastava** is currently Assistant Professor, Institute of Social Science, Dr. B.R. Ambedakar University, Agra. His area of specialisation is Woman Studies and Sociological Theories. He has published ten research papers in foreign and national journal.
- **Dr. Sushil Pande** is currently Assistant Professor, Northern India Engineering College, Lucknow (U.P.). His area of specialisation is Human Resource Management. He has published seven research paper reputed journal.
- **Prof. Sumita Parmar** is teaches in Department of English and European languages, University of Allahabad. She was awarded the Senior Fulbright Fellowship and worked on Black Feminist Criticism as part of her post-doctoral work with Prof Barbara Christian, the eminent Black

Feminist scholar and Critic at Berkeley, University of California. She has traveled widely in the United States of America, Canada and Australia, as well as the Fiji Islands. She is Director of the Centre for Women's Studies of the University of Allahabad. She is also the Editor of the bi-annual *Journal of Women's Studies.* Prof Parmar has contributed articles and chapters to various journals and books and serves on the editorial board of several journals of Women's Studies.

- **Dr. Sonal Shankar** is a Guest Lecturer at Allahabad University, Law Department, and Allahabad. She has completed Ph.D. on the topic "Domestic Violence and Sexual Harassment of Women at Workplace in India—A Critical Study" from Department of Law, University of Allahabad. She has also been assigned the position of the convener of the moot court society and placement adviser of the placement cell of the said course.
- **Prof. S.N. Chaudhary**, former Dean, Faculty of Social Science is currently Rajiv Gandhi Chair Professor at Barkatullah University Bhopal, Madhya Pradesh. He has also been a fellow of the A.N. Sinha Institute of Social Studies, Patna, Indian Institute of Advanced Study, Shimla and SMH Paris. He has also conducted field work among Red Indians in British Columbia (Canada). Dr. Chaudhary produced 30 Ph.Ds., completed 27 research projects and published 27 books and 57 research articles. Currently Prof. Chaudhary is working on Tribal Indebtedness, Impact of Technology on Society, Suicide among Tribal Farmers and Tribal Development
- **Prof. Rajatsubhra Mukhopadhyay** teaches Sociology at the North Bengal University, West Bengal. His areas of research interest are Sociology of Family and Kinship, Social Movements and Agrarian Social Structure. He has contributed many scholarly articles to reputed periodicals and edited volumes.
- **Mr. Sumit S. Srivastava** is currently Lecturer, Centre for Globalisation and Development Studies, University of Allahabad. He is editorial assistant Indian Anthropologist, peer reviewed journal of Indian anthropological association, New Delhi. His areas of academic interest include Gender Studies and Political Sociology. He has published two research papers and two articles in edited book.
- **Prof. S.N. Tripathy**, Director, Centre for Social Exclusion and Inclusive Policy, Gokhale Institute of Politics and Economics, Pune (Maharashtra). He was awarded D. Litt degree in Economics on the topic, "Tribal out-migration in Orissa: a study in KBK districts" from Berhampur University (Orissa) and Post-doctoral Award from the Ministry of Tribal affairs, Government of India, New Delhi. Prof. Tripathy has to his credit authored, co-authored and edited 51 books, 150 research papers, guided 14 PhD scholars and completed dozens of research projects/evaluation studies funded by UGC, New Delhi, ICSSR, New Delhi , Ministry of

Tribal Affairs, Ministry of Social Justice and Empowerment, Ministry of Agriculture, Govt. of India, etc.

- **Ms. Uma Tripathi** is a Guest Lecturer, Department of Law, University of Allahabad. At present she is pursuing research in criminology. Her research topic is "Challenges of Female Criminality and its Preventive Mechanism". Being an avid reader and writer she has several research papers on social issues to her credit.
- **Mr. Dhananjay Rai** is currently Assistant Professor at Central University of Gujarat, Gandhinagar (Gujarat). He holds doctorate from Centre for Political Studies, Jawaharlal Nehru University, New Delhi. Previously, he was Research Fellow at the Centre for Policy Analysis, New Delhi.
- **Dr. Anshuman Mishra** is an Assistant Professor in the Department of Law, University of Allahabad. His areas of academic interests are constitutional law, administrative law, and election law. He has written a book on Election Law and several research papers and articles in various reputed journals.
- **Dr. Santosh Kumar** is currently Lecturer, Centre for Globalisation and Development Studies, University of Allahabad. He obtained his Ph.D. from SIS, Jawaharlal Nehru University, New Delhi. He has worked for DFID-PMO project, consulted Plan India-International, VVGNLI on ILO project. He was in Washington, D.C., United States of America during (2008-09) and worked on the issues of Population, Health and Environment. He has published a book titled *"Epidemiology of HIV/AIDS in South Africa"* in 2011.

Introduction

In the era of globalisation, the State changes its nature according to global forces, becoming more regulatory and controlling. So the nature of the state have been changed now from welfare state to transformative state. The state, as an institution, guarantees social welfare and social justice to the deprived groups but globalisation has not only threatened it but also made it weak. In the contemporary context, the social justice agenda is taken over by non-state organisations that is critical. The older theories of social justice, which are either inadequate or inapplicable today, cannot cover the new developments that have taken place and, therefore, they have to be reviewed, specifically in the Indian context. Globalisation has not only affected all aspects of human life but also influenced social institutions to a great extent. It operates in an uneven and unequal manner. The neo-liberal economy has further compounded the unevenness and inequality in society. The small minority of world's population holds maximum resources while the majority of people grapple with poverty. Today, there are various contemporary challenges in front of the state to attain social justice, these are inequality, gender injustice, disparity, failure of public policy, marginality and environmental issues etc. Social justice is an important issue and therefore there is an urgent need to rethink on it in contemporary perspective.

The concept of justice has occupied a high ground in philosophical discussions in India from time immemorial. The Gita, which contains the substance of the Vedas and the Upanishads, for instance, proclaims, "Only those who perceive all living creatures of the world irrespective of their caste, creed, etc., as manifestations of the God, are real scholars". Western philosophers also contributed immensely towards the evolving the concept of social justice while adding different connotations to the concept. Viewing social justice in the contemporary context, John Rawls, in his book, *A Theory of Justice* (1972), revived interest in the substantive questions of political theory in the concept of Social Justice and connected it to an individual's pursuit of the good life. In this book, Rawls attempts to reconcile liberty and equality in a principled way, offering an account of "justice as fairness." Central to this effort is his famous approach to the seemingly intractable problem of distributive justice. The work of Nozick and Hayek too needs a mention here. Their contribution added new dimensions to the then existing notions of social justice. On the other hand, the recent work of Amartya Sen, *Idea of Justice* opens up a whole new spectrum of looking at the concept of justice. In present global perspective, the changed nature of the state effects the nature of social justice as well.

Indian society is passing through a crucial and transformative stage. As is evident from the ever growing presence and global impact of Indian brains and work force, the country has made remarkable progress in all spheres. However, there are still certain areas where we have failed to match the aspirations of founding fathers of the our nation. Though our country is the largest democracy in the world, but social exclusion has remained its chronic problem. We have set landmarks in world trade but the gap between rich and the poor and gender inequality has widened to magnitudes never seen before. Thus we can witness various forms of social justice in reality—social claim as justice, attainment and restoration of dignity as justice, end to discrimination as justice, retribution as justice, conciliation of claims as justice, social idea of minimal justice, positive discrimination as justice, protection of the vulnerable sections of society as justice, and finally autonomy as justice. One also finds Social justice as having strong gender implications. However, a process of rethinking on the concept of social Justice and its emerging contemporary issues in the changing scenario would definitely prove futile in probing its different contours for a deeper and in-depth analysis.

The need was felt to have a discussion on various concerns raised and themes releating to the contemporary issues of social justice in India for better understanding of the facts. So therefore, Rajiv Gandhi Chair in Contemporary Studies, University of Allahabad organised a two-day National Seminar on "Social Justice in India: Emerging Issues" during September 2010. This book is an outcome of the papers presented by academic experts during this seminar which were later revised and edited for this book. The book focuses on various dimensions of social justice in India, including theoretical, philosophical and constitutional aspects of the theme.

Accordingly, the volume discusses contemporary issues of social justice in India, visions of social justice in the era of globalisation, hurdles of the public policy and implementation, marginalized sections, various dimensions of human security, gender equality and democracy. Against this backdrop, the book brings out contemporary perspectives on social justice specific to Indian context, challenges for social justice, conceptualisation in the era of globalisation and understanding the praxis of social justice in India.

Part-I: Social Justice in the New Global Era

The beginning with a conceptual analysis and philosophical concern of the social justice in the era of globalisation, *Prof. Debashis Guha* started his paper "Philosophers' Concern with Social Justice" with a skeptical note. He asks few questions like: Why should philosopher discuss Social Justice?; Why should they enter into the problem of Social Justice with their peculiar method of inquiry? etc. and tries to address all these in his article. In his search for answers, he analyses the term "Social Justice" very critically and discusses different aspects of social justice in relation to individuals, groups, castes and classes of the society. Finally he ends his article with a neutral analysis of affirmative action.

"Global Justice in Rawls' The Law of Peoples" is an article written by *Prof. M. T. Desai* about global justice with special reference to Rawls' *The Law of Peoples.* He discusses how the meaning of justice is contentious even within a domestic society. It becomes more so when we talk about "international justice" or "global justice". Then there is the other question of justice as 'fairness' or 'impartiality' as a matter of procedural justice as against 'substantive justice' involved in issues of social justice at global level. International justice deals with states. In the Westphalian order, it means nothing but an ethic of co-existence. It is therefore procedural. In the article, Prof. Desai has dealt with all the spheres of justice. With an in-depth analysis of Rawls' theory he finally concludes that Rawls was more a protagonist of 'international justice' rather than of 'global justice'. Even his concept of international justice involves peoples rather than states. *The Law of Peoples* can be defended most importantly in terms of political culture and community autonomy. Goal of human welfare may seem to some more important. How much of what is to be sacrificed for what, can be determined only by experience consequences, and one's political values. The initiatives taken by the law makers in India to keep social justice intact in the soul of India can be viewed as a positive sign of democracy but adopting a reservation policy based on caste or religion has a deep rooted negativity in itself. In this article *Dr. J P Mishra* has critically explained Indian efforts to sustain social justice by means of protective discrimination. The article highlights the harmful effects of reservation policy adopted in the Indian Constitution. The article thoughtfully discusses the ignorance of the Indian Government regarding the failure of the reservation tool in achieving the objective of social equality and hence inability to preserve social justice among the Indian citizens and manipulating the same for political benefits. Thus, caste based reservation not only resulted in widened gap between various classes but also the power game involved with it has kept the needy ones out of the sphere of its benefits. The author also views caste census as dangerous for the concept of social justice and suggests certain measures to achieve social justice through social equality in the true sense.

Part-II: Constitutional Vision and Reality

Part second deals with the constitutional aspect of social justice and indian reality. *Prof. C.P. Barthwal,* in his paper, "Social Justice in India: an Analysis" analyses various aspects of social justice in India. After introducing the subject, he defines justice through various definitions and highlights some facts of social justice from the theoretical point of view. Prof. Barthwal states that nearly sixty years have elapsed since the Constitution came into force. The question arises how far have we been able to achieve social justice in India? Do we still lag behind? If yes, to what extent? What more needs to be done so that we can achieve social justice as early as possible? Nobody can question the need for uplifting the down-trodden, the weak and the impoverished both horizontally and vertically, but to make reservation a political issue, vying with each other for being included into net, even to the extent of including those who belong to the creamy layer and have enjoyed the concession twice, would only make a mockery of it. It is equally necessary that those who have enjoyed certain facilities and privileges should make room for others—following the dictum of the greatest good of the greatest number.

In the article, "An Analysis of the Constitutional Vision of Social Justice in India", *Dr Subash Shukla and Dr Pradeep K. Sharma* to make an in-depth study of the constitutional vision of social justice in India as envisaged during the Constituent Assembly Debates and as enshrined in the Preamble of the Constitution. In the opening paragraphs, they analyze the vision of social justice in the Indian Constitution while in the later sections, they discuss the means that have been employed to attain this goal and its success in implementation. In conclusion, they opine that though the Indian Constitution ensures legal and procedural safeguards, and substantive measures have been taken by the Indian State to establish social justice, the biggest challenge still remains in ensuring cultural justice establishing a secular Indian identity far removed from the present caste based identity of Indian society. In their article, "Social Justice and Multiculturalism: The Indian Experience" *Nandini Basistha and Trivikram Tiwari* discuss the relationship between social justice and multiculturalism in Indian perspective. After giving a short note on the concept of 'multiculturalism' and 'justice', they elaborate the notion of multiculturalism in India from ancient days. Then, coming back to the post-independence era, they figure out the constitutional vision of multiculturalism and the Nehruvian idea of assimilation. Elaborating on the different problems in implementation, in conclusion, they suggest some ways for attaining justice in the Indian multicultural scenario. *Santwana Pandey* points out the vulnerability of a big marginalized section of Indian society, viz., working children, in her article, "Constitutional Provision and Social Reality: Perspective of Child Labour". She discusses Indian constitutional provisions and legislations for eradicating child labour and their limitations in implementation. After elaborating Indian constitutional provisions regarding child labour in India, she compares them with the international standards of organisation like ILO and UNICEF. In the later section she discussed social practices in the promotion of child labour in all parts of the world and the inefficiency of the State and Central Government in eliminating the stigma of child labour from our society. In conclusion, she suggests some ways for eliminating this practice.

Part-III: Public Policy and Inclusive Growth

The third part contains papers that make on overview of Public Policy and Inclusive Growth related to Social Justice. In her paper *Prof. Sudha Pai* focuses on the debate on affirmative action on reservation. She argues that globalisation questions have been raised about the continued usefulness of the policy of Protective Discrimination or reservations for dalits. There is a growing feeling that in the changed context it does not contribute to the agenda of Social Justice. Two developments are responsible for this—first with the shrinking of the State and use of new forms of governance, employment opportunities in the public sector have gradually declined. Second, the emergence of a small, but influential generation of young, educated, and politically conscious, middle class of dalits who strongly feel they should receive a 'fair share' in the fruits of globalisation which has resulted in higher growth rates, a strong private sector, highly-paid professional occupations and business opportunities. A significant fallout has been the rise of a contentious debate—among both dalit and non-dalit scholars/activists—on the working of the policies of reservation in the post-Independence period, the benefits that have accrued to them, and the new types of preferential policies that are required so that dalits can also reap the benefits of globalisation. Prof Pai, analyzes this debate. The focus here is on policies based on affirmative action such as 'Supplier Diversity'—first discussed at the Bhopal Conference, 2002—that could lead to 'democratisation of capital' which, its supporters argue, would enable them to participate in the new market economy, removing in the long run the need for reservations. To understand the rationale underlying these policies, the paper briefly draws upon two Supplier Diversity programmes implemented by the Madhya Pradesh Government. The author argues that, in a globalizing economy, such policies hold considerable latent possibilities to create, over time, an entrepreneurial business/industrial dalit class, so far lacking. In recent years dalits have obtained political empowerment i.e. entered the political arena, formed political parties and governments, but remain conspicuously absent in the business/industrial sector. Such policies would provide economic empowerment and end the marginalisation that this disadvantaged group faces in this sector.

Dr Kamlesh Gupta emphasize, in his paper, entitled "Social Justice: Policy Initiatives and Implementation," the importance of policy initiatives and their implementation for ensuring social justice. He advocates that policy initiatives by the government and their proper implementation are the chief solutions to the problem of social justice in the present perspective. He focuses on policy initiatives for social justice after independence and compares them with the present situation and also analyses the present status of social justice. The paper focuses on contemporary perspectives of social justice, challenges of policy concern and implementation and suggestions for policy concern and implementation. *Dr Rakesh Kumar,* in his article, "Extent of Inclusiveness during the Post-reform Period", discuss the new inclusive approach of the Indian economy, which establishes new linkages—global to local and local to local—across international boundaries. After defining the term "inclusive growth", he discusses the debate in India about whether the country's economic reforms fulfilled the objective of inclusive growth and helped India's poor through the so-called trickle down mechanism. Then he logically proves that lack of inclusiveness is borne out by data on several dimensions of performance. In conclusion, he suggests that for a competitive system to be in equilibrium the value of both must be equal. *Pragyanshu Amaoni* focuses on the theoretical understanding of affirmative action with respect to such policies of other countries. The pre-constitutional and post-constitutional provision along with the debates from the perspectives of proponents as well as opponents is analysed. He argues for better policy designs in affirmative actions in the rapidly changing environment. He also argues that caste-based reservation in not about 'appeasement' but eliminating the historical disadvantages in an unequal and unjust society. The extension of reservation to the private sector should alter the socio-economic profile of job-holders in the neo-liberal capitalist economy in India. The utmost requirement of developing India is the 'nation-building' which should be based on an egalitarian society so that it can provide a leadership at the global level. In her article, *Dr. Lalima Singh* "Child Labour in India: Present Status and Policy Analsysis" describes the plight of child labourers in India and critically analyses the policies adopted by the Government of India. The author also discusses the role of international organisations in tackling the problem of child labour mostly prevalent in developing countries like India. The article give great importance to the role of society in eliminating child labour. Awareness and a sense of responsibility along with effectively formulated and implemented can remove the phenomenon of child labour and make children educated and healthy, contributing to the development of a nation.

Prof. S.V. Pande and others briefly examine the origin and the current meaning of the concept of Social Justice as the rational basis of democratic values and the aims to establish how and why it is a pre-requisite to all social development which implies a lot more than mere economic development or growth. Thereafter attention has been drawn to the contribution of Ambedkar, particularly in the context of Indian society, in respect of establishing a socially-just society in India after its independence in 1947. Ambedkar's opposition to the exploitative castes through his social and political activism and the crucial role played by him in the process of writing of the Constitution of India is specially highlighted. It is throughout maintained that till the stage of a just social order is established, Ambedkar's relevance will not wone, be it 21st century, or even thereafter.

Part-IV: Justice, Gender and Democracy

The fourth part of the book throws light on Justice, Gender and Democracy. It begins with the paper of *Prof Sumita Parmar*. She discusses justice within the framework of the nation and its laws and its implications and ramifications vis-à-vis women. Women continue to be treated as a single largest under-privileged group in India. In such a context, the role of justice becomes specially vital and significant. In her paper she tries to answer some basic questions as; to the ordinary person what does the word justice denote? In every day life what is the role of justice? Is there a distinction between mere punishment and justice or are the terms synonymous? Or is punishment always the consequence of the enforcement of justice? More important and significant, how does the mechanism of the implementation of civil justice function? In conclusion she suggests some precondition for women to access justice. Without education, awareness of rights and decision-making power, women are often unable to claim their rights, obtain legal aid or go to court. The Government has to display some political will and make concerted efforts in consonance with NGOs, activists, and all those who are stakeholders in the empowerment of women, before some impact, however small, is made. *Sonal Shankar* discusses Indian constitutional perspectives on gender justice in her article, "Constitutional Vision and Gender Justice". After discussing Indian constitutional endeavors of generating justice though the Preamble, Fundamental Rights and Directive Principles of the Indian Constitution, she raises the fundamental question—"Have the women been able to reap the benefits provided for them under the Constitution of India?" Citing different cases she describes the vulnerable position of women. To prove that Indian Constitutional vision is in favour of gender justice, she refers to Article 14 (Equality before Law), Article 15 (Prohibition of discrimination on grounds of sex), Article 16 (Equality of opportunity in matters of public employment), Article 19 (Freedom of Trade and Occupation), Article 21 (Protection of life and Personal Liberty), Article 23 (Right against exploitation and prohibition of traffic in human beings), and the Role of Directive Principles of State Policy in Protecting the Rights of Women. She also enumerates the fundamental duties towards women enshrined in the Constitution. In conclusion, she suggests that the responsibility of upliftment of women has to be shared by the State, community organisations, legislators who frame the laws and a gender sensitive judiciary which interprets the Constitution and other laws in order to give effect to the legal reforms in the field of gender justice and to cultivate, dignity and opportunity for both the sexes equally.

In his paper entitled "In Between Tradition and Democracy: The Status of Land Ownership to Rural Women in Madhya Pradesh", *Prof. S.N. Chaudhary* discusses the status of land ownership of rural women in Madhya Pradesh. The opening part deals with the status of land rights of women in India in the historical perspective, efforts made by the constitution, state through policies and schemes and civil societies to extend land rights to women. In Part II, Prof Chaudhary elaborates on the insight of the social sciences to map the current state of land rights for women in different parts of Madhya Pradesh. Towards the end, the role of patriarchy has as a barrier to the process of extending land entitlement to rural women been explained. In conclusion Prof Chaudhry argues that because of the continuation of the tradition of patriarchy with the help of particularistic culture only a small number of women are associated with land as owner in the villages. Even constitutional provisions, land reform measures and civil society organisations and a host of other democratic forces have largely failed to extend land rights to maximum number of women. There are other inhibiting factors, both local and non-local which also enforce women to remain dependent, deprived and voiceless.

In his article, "Interrogating Social Justice from Gender and Kinship Perspective", *Prof. Rajatsubhra Mukhopadhyay* examines some of the aspects of social justice from the gender and kinship perspective in a more comprehensive frame. After illustrating gender disparity in society, he describes different governmental initiatives for women's empowerment. Then he highlights some of the facts which make us anxious about the status and plight of women in India particularly with reference to social justice. He describes how, in Indian society, entitlement for familial resources including food, health, nutrition etc., are based largely on kinship rules, and in this regard patriliny is in balanced and works for disadvantage of women. He opiniones that what the masses of Indian women want today is social justice, economic justice and political justice. In this context the concept of 'empowerment' of women is a *sine qua non* for bringing about a harmonious, sustainable and equalitarian society. However, while devising strategies to bring about changes in social, cultural, economic, political and legal aspects in the interests of women, one needs to understand the limits within which women function, and why certain measures have not succeeded to deliver the expected goods. Here the sociologists could provide necessary inputs from their research and show how gender equality could be achieved and where the impediments lie. In his article *Dr Sumit S. Srivastava* broadly discusses incidences of gender discrimination against women in Indian society. He focuses on power differentials between men and women resulting from the lack of availability, affordability and accessibility of resources to women. The author presents gender discrimination not only in terms of health, knowledge and decent standard of living but also in terms of opportunity and decision making power in the political, public and private realms. The author highlights violence against woman as an obstacle in her development and social equality. The increasing cases of dowry deaths, rapes, female feticide/ infanticide, domestic violence etc. lead to the huge mobilisation of women resulting in mass movements that had very crucial and significant roles in safeguarding women against violence and inequality. The mass movements resulted in formulation of needed legislations, required amendments in existing laws and appropriate changes in policy plans. He concludes that women's movements have had a positive and forceful impact on securing gender equality for women.

Part-V: Marginalities, Human Rights and Justice

The last part of the book focusses on Marginalities, Human Rights and Justice. The article of *Prof. S.N. Tripathy* presents the studies on migrant labourers in Maharashtra. The study is focussed on seasonal migration in the state, its causes and impact. It depicts the plight of migrant labourers in terms of wages, shelter, food, education for children, medical facilities, working conditions etc. The article also discusses the legislations enacted to protect migrant workers from the exploitation of contractors and employers but finds that no particular emphasis has been given to improve the conditions of seasonal migrant workers. In her article, *Uma Tripathi* states that there is a hard felt need for reservation in the vast and increasing private sector primarily because according to our constitutional mandate we need a level playing field even there too. Privatisation of public sector units has already adversely affected the majority of urban dalits . Since there is nothing private about the private sector, providing reservation can be a remedy against market discrimination as well as means of fulfillment of political democracy. We can very well observe that where there is no reservation, dalit representation is entirely nonexistent. The two compelling factors to justify reservation in the private sector are backwardness and inadequacy of representation. If the weaker classes are not given a preferential treatment in the form of positive discrimination it would be grossly unjust and derogatory to the concept of social justice. The latter can solely be fulfilled by creating a spirit of accommodation for the brothers, keeping in view their legitimate aspirations and rightful demands.

In his paper "Dalits and Social Justice: A Perusal of Electoral Politics", *Dhananjay Rai* treats social justice as a process not as an end. This formulation extricates social justice from various imposed attributions such as it being a state-driven mechanism to redress the causes and grievances of dalits, static and passive formulations of empowerment and circumvention of transformative politics. After discussing the introduction, he describes dalit, expansion principle and transformation principle, then he talkes about core political formulations and expansion principle for dalits through political parties. The analysis indicates that expansion of dalit participation through core political formation is reduced, significantly. In the conclusion, he said that without augmenting and strengthening the transformation principle, the future and nature of expansion principle through electoral politics is difficult to discern and predict. He suggests that social justice has a transformative role and redistribution of resources is one of the components.

The paper titled "Compensatory Discrimination in Favour of Members of Scheduled Tribes in Panchayats in Scheduled Areas" by *Dr. Anshuman Mishra,* gives a legal insight of the dimensions that affirmative action policies have acquired. Relevant provisions of the Constitution of India as well as other statutes along with case laws have been thoroughly discussed in order to prove that how policy making is different from its implementation. The Courts are bound to interfere as guardians of the Constitution in a social order whole the country has got to protect the deprived sections of the society. *Dr Santosh Kumar* discusses the linkages between health and human rights in his article, "Health and Human Rights in the era of Globalisation: An Indian Perspective". After referring to different international laws related to health and human rights, he narrated the condition of health and human rights in India. Touching upon different sensitive issues—like health challenges of safe drinking water, sanitation, right to food, entitlement to challenged personnel

(HIV/AIDS patients, the old and the homeless, infirm, destitute and street children), malnutrition, tobacco hazard and environment pollution, health care expenditure, feticide, gender gap, honor killing, trade in human organs and violation of ethical norms—he concludes with the present scenario of health and human rights in the era of globalisation. He opinions that there are a few successes but many challenges remain to be met. The legal protection and enactment of laws to any such challenges are imminent to safeguard the human rights.

The above mentioned contributions focussing on contemporary dimensions of social justice in India. We hope that this volume will help in enriching academic debates as well as quality research in the future. We also hope it will provides guidelines to those who want to study new dimensions of social justice, further, we are glad to present this to you. We do not claim all-inclusiveness of the book but we surely want it to be a serious and thought-provoking attempt in the field of social justice.

PART I

SOCIAL JUSTICE IN THE NEW GLOBAL ERA

1

Philosophers' Concern with Social Justice

Debashis Guha

Let us start the discussion with a skeptical note because all skeptical questions are not 'false' in nature, many of them are rather meaningful and do a lot of service to the field of knowledge: Why should philosopher discuss Social Justice when they have their Gods and Souls and every queer concepts and issues in hand? Why should they enter into the problem of Social Justice with their peculiar method of inquiry to put Social Sciences in shambles? Is it not true that the problem concerning social justice is a social scientific problem? Is it not true that social justice belongs to official sociology, political science, history, economics and anthropology? Why should there be an official philosophy of social issues? Truly, metaphysics, epistemology, ethics, and logic belong to official philosophy. There appears to be no sign of social scientific concern in philosophy. Then the real skeptical question is: Why should there be a philosophy of social science or social philosophy, to be precise? This paper takes up this skeptical question seriously and tries to show that first of all, philosophy is rightly concerned with social scientific issues or that there is a social philosophy having a great sense. Second, this can be instantiated by "social justice" as a pertinent issue in social philosophy. Wonder of all wonders is the fact that while discussing these things, we come to know what is the *meaning* of "social justice" as a concept and what philosophers are concerned with when they consider the case of "social justice". The last thing first, the philosophers are absolutely *not* fit and just in *doing* social justice. However, they are equally apt in telling us what it consists in and what the logic of the *models* of social justice is, that is, whether that is sound or unsound, and what the ethics of social justice is even if social philosophers have argued that social justice is so needed in our society. There is thus a meta-inquiry on the part of philosophers concerning justification of social justice by the social scientists. Obliquely therefore, philosophers have entered into the discussion that they should be allowed to validly pass into the social scientific territory.

Social justice as a philosophical problem truly speaking falls in the realm of social philosophy wherein philosophical reflections on social issues are justified. When we make this sweeping remark, we know well that "social" in social philosophy is "what pertains to social phenomena". In this sense, philosophically relevant reflections on social matters constitute social philosophy that in turn covers political, economic, anthropological and historical matters. Thus social philosophy takes on many issues that cut across economics, politics and so on. For instance, social philosophy considers the perceptions of economics and politics regarding social justice and from independent philosophical standpoints reflect on what the social scientists think about such justice. In this sense, there is philosophical economics and political philosophy as sensible inquiries within philosophy, which among many issues, takes on the considered perceptions of economists and political scientists for philosophical analysis covering social justice. For instance, philosophers' inquiry extends to what economists propound as models for social justice or what political scientists propound as model of social engineering because in any case, the logic of models or grounds or justifications (pertinent or impertinent reasons so to say), should be scrutinized for their soundness. And more reasonable is that justifications should be scrutinized for the *humane* features. This is why "affirmative action" as an aspect of social justice should be scrutinized for its logical soundness (for or against arguments, that is, pro-con logical arguments), and such actions should be scrutinized for their ethical soundness (pro-con ethical arguments).[1] If social sciences on the whole and social justice as an issue for the science is concerned with human affairs in our societies, no such affair can be left unscrutinized logically and ethically. Social philosophy thus considers the case of social justice most importantly because it emphasizes individual and group decisions that influence other members and groups in societies. Such influences are amenable to logical and ethical inquiries as said before. Moreover, when we inquire into absolute or finalistic thesis of social justice, we are inquiring into the *metaphysics*[2] of social justice. From all this we have came to justify the very basis of social scientific interest like social justice, in which, the philosophers now take keen interest because certain individual and group behavior that influences other individuals and groups are amenable to a number of sensible philosophical inquiries such as logical, ethical and metaphysical.

We have said that apart from the above mentioned philosophically relevant inquiries, one of the most important aspects of philosophical social inquiry is the clarification of *meaning* of the concept "social justice". Philosophers make it a point that before entering into complex logical, ethical and others philosophically relevant inquiries, we must take on *language clarification*,[3] that is, clarification of the meaning of concepts under consideration. We must know what it amounts to when we speak of "social justice," for instance.

First, "social" in "social justice" refers to human society and not animal society because we do not really know whether animals have a society and whether we have a role or an exact role in that society. There is no doubt that when we want justice in human society we cannot close our eyes towards animal well-being or we can neglect them or become unjust to them. We just mean to say that we want to be just to our fellow beings, those very close to us or those distantly related or those who are remotely related as humans. In a catholic sense, "social" in "social justice" is justice for those who participate in a social way of life, which is to say that whether in our own person or any in other, at this time or times to come, those having unique social form of life demand some justice. When we take "social" in a relatively narrow sense, it amounts to a *particular* society in which we thrive. This may be further qualified in a numbers of senses, such as, the country in which someone lives or the state in which one is or the section, caste, and class in which one belongs, each identifiable by unique social form of life having intricate social relations and interactions. In this sense, we mean to say that *our* or *their* society demands some basic justice for reasons unique to us and them, which includes that animals and trees and the entire biotic community that mingles in and with our being, cannot be handed injustice. In this sense, social justice goes well with the idea of non-human well-being or non-human justice but that is only an aspect of our society's (human so to say), justice and not primarily justice for the non-human beings. Let us take an example. A particular section of society demands justice economically, politically, legally and so on, among other things; suppose, that society owing to their unique social ways or form of life demand snakes or other reptiles in their society to be protected for overall restoration of their way of life because that may be respect to an important taboo. Now, this call for justice in a particular human society for restoration of reptiles in the name of restoration of taboo should be better called, "social justice" and not animal justice because being just to reptiles (an animal) is *means* to do justice to humans of a particular society having a unique way of life. Hence, the *end in itself* is justice to humans than animals. Being just to animals (reptiles) is only of contributory value or valuable as means. Hence, broad spectrum social justice is a body of enhancement of many contributory goods, economic, political, material, and animal and so on. In these ways, justice is done to one or more human society or societies having their ways of life, their specific demands and unique ideas of a good life.

If "social justice" primarily refers to justice in human society, we can now find out what primarily "justice" refers to. Justice in "social justice" is understood as a necessary or associate ground for a just state or country. A state or a country on the whole is called "just" when the body is an *ideal system* or a coherent system wherein individuals or citizens cohere in a more or less harmony not disharmony or anarchy. A society is just when it refers to individuals contributing through their behavior, thought and actions to maintain best harmony in society. Not only this, it refers to a system of laws, rules and administrative and political regulations. It refers to political, mechanism and constitution that enables an ideal harmony in a state. A just society thus refers to a system of humans having identifiable form of life coexisting in a more or less harmonious system which is more the less rule-guided, wherein self-fulfillment, self-satisfaction, self-protection and wish fulfillment of common men are possible through self-sacrifice and community well being. The *internal checks* by individuals and the *external mechanism* of authorities in a society complement for community well being and the formation of greater balance of good than evil in a society. It is a state of "social justice". Clearly, in "social justice", the general rules for individual and community well being has been *voluntarily* or intentionally accepted and assimilated by each owner seeking agents. When we put checks on our owner-seeking nature by accepting community rules after deliberation and scrutiny, and when community regulates not for its own sake, we have a state of "social justice". This unique form of life, that is, a "socially just form of life" is identifiable in the midst of numerous wishes, aspirations and owner seekingness, and most importantly, balance or harmony at multiple levels, political, economic, distributive, fiscal, legal and many more so that greater balance of good over evil in human society prevails. Hence, "social justice" is a *covering concept*, the meaning of which is clearer when a number of goods that are contributory or extrinsic in nature are clear to us. Simply put, the nature of "social justice" bears a *universal* sense, much like natural justice, because it is the universal social ideal for us to realize as an intrinsic good, which is the ideal for every society. The realization of this ideal enables society to realize their own self for which a number of extrinsic goods are of great importance.[4]

Social justice thus refers to a unique balance of owner seekingness and social well being—a unique way through which individual and society have come to their own selves, not at all tending to be an authority. We can thus say that social justice is a state of balance of individual and community rights, duties and obligations. In a sense social justice from individual standpoint is a *station of life* in social unities wherein she find an internal relation between her and the society at large; wherein her rights, duties and obligations are amenable to greater balance of social good over evil. From the standpoint of the community self, social justice refers to a state of *non-differentiation* between individual and society because it refers to "whole good over evil produced in the individual and social life". Social justice in an important sense is thus a state of personal and communal welfare. This further refers to *freedom* of individual and social agency because bereft of freedom of will, intention and decision, we cannot conceive of any agent to strive for well being in which self regarding and other regarding attitudes are of utmost value. As said before, external and internal checks and freedom of social agents, enable us to harmonize self and other regarding attitudes.[5]

We have seen that "social justice" is a spectrum concept, the meaning of which is clearer to us when we analyze the bands of the spectrum. Each band of color enables us to grasp the meaning of the otherwise extremely broad and at times not so clear concept. If we take the *political* use of the word "social justice," for the clarification of meaning, social justice is in the main "fairness". Hence, when we speak of social justice, we must conceive of a state of affair in human society wherein some human agencies feel responsible for 'fairness" in distribution of goods and evils to fellow citizens for their legitimate needs and misdeeds. Political justice as participant in the board spectrum of social justice is thus, disregard to individual favors and regard to communal harmony for the respect of harmonious coexistence. Negatively, social justice refers to lack of favor or for individual wish-fulfillment. It bears the sense of "prohibitions" of wish-fulfillment on any arbitrary ground by an individual or group or groups. If this be the case, social justice through political intervention is also "equality", that is, despite individual differences, fortunes and advantages in society, social justice refers to "egalitarian" attitude on the part of a fair political agency in the distribution of goods. Nevertheless, these ideals of fairness and equality are *formal* in nature than material. It is important to note that the *first order fairness* is evident in "ideal political principle" which is applied by agencies for social good, such as the principle of basic rights. *Second order fairness* principles are certain "political maxims" such as, right to election campaign though checked a few hours before voting takes place. These first and second order political principles are principles of fairness for social unity, peace and harmony.

Social justice through political fairness refers to some *institutional authoritative power*, by virtue of which certain regulative sweeping powers are able to control social disruptions. The regulative powers to balance good over evil enable the political authority to be good rather than evil. It is due to this that despite political power to frame fair laws for punishment, the authority are deemed to be good rather than evil.

Not only this, the spectrum of social justice contains the economic color. There is social justice through economic justice, wherein justice or fairness in distribution is most important. Whether we speak of production or distribution of goods and service we do speak of fairness and when the economic fairness happens at the social level, we speak of social justice. In this case a society is just when there is proportionate justice in the distribution of social goods and services. In the main, social justice through economic fairness is just distribution of assets and money. A just society is that wherein natural resources and produced goods are equitably distributed. Wherein the transaction of assets and money as well as expenditure and savings of what people earn are in accordance with a civil regulation that is fair and equitable. The economic services demand fulfillment and deserts (prize) are thus not arbitrary and authoritative. There is a proper market, whose economy is identifiable by just transaction laws and control as well as free and fair competition. Social justice as economic fairness is thus having a just business mechanism as well as just business control. When market based economy is harnessed through fair regulation and laws, there is justice is society. However, this is not to say that only open market economy is fair or just and free economy gives us just society. When the openness and freedom of economy goes on ethical holiday, that is, uncontrolled by political machinery, where every party is guided by the ethos of gluttony egotism, there is neither freedom nor justice. Hence, social justice refers to equitable dynamics of the market and money. The beacon light should be wish-fulfillment and well being of the community at large than individual based good. Hence, a society is just when community utility and community's overall good is well in view and regulative mechanisms are strong enough to quell the sporadic egotism. While cooperation and social welfare rules supreme, social justice cannot close eyes to community welfare or in a sense altruistic good.[6]

This further takes us to another aspect of social justice which is *fiscal justice*. The central point in such justice is whether or not a community enterprise is able to shoulder welfarist strategies and how far is it able to do so and in what ways. This takes us to the taxation system in a given community that imposes its powers to swap the needed amount of money to do justice at different levels of society for well being, irrespective of religion, caste and class. This is needed to check and balance individual and corporate earnings so that the overall health of the exchequer is good enough to shoulder monetary responsibilities and to do widespread social good that the people and government conceives to be so important. This takes us to the justice through direct and indirect taxes, a system of earning by governments for social good. A society is thus just wherein a just taxation policies go along with a defendable conception of welfare. A society is just wherein the revenue earning and its expenditure on social good is so tuned that individual aspirations and social goods, fortunes of few and communal welfare do not clash. There is no clash of interests and advantages among social strata that rather than bridging gaps among social classes, are widened.

A close ally to political justice is administrative justice, and we say that social justice is conceivable where there is administrative justice. The social institutions and organization have to run well for overall good of the society. This is done by administrative machinery in our society. Administration is at the grass root level of family to the upper crust of government institutions. Its role in judiciary, executive, fiscal, educational, production units and political organizations are, felt. If there is no justice at the administrative levels of society, the society cannot be just. Administrative justice is thus an important aspect of social justice. The crux of such justice is that there is some" authoritative justice", though "authority" itself is wrongly conceived as arbitrary and imposing in nature. Rather than being undesirable, an authority is desirable if it is pro-community. All authorities are not egocentric, they should be and they are in many cases other centered. The administrative authority is thus the most wanted social agency that stands for the social and political perception and will to do good. It is the most needed social agency for social development and social control. If this be the goal of authority, it is neither arbitrary nor egocentric. However, all administrative authorities must be "free" to decide and act in favor of desire fulfillment of social agents and social agencies irrespective of all social stigmas. When authority displays its controlling powers freely but in a regulated manner, they become *trustees* to the society. This is exactly when there is a chance for social justice. Truly, administrative justice is often legally backed and it appears to be bossing than welfarist. Nevertheless, when social agreement and acceptability of law is for social good, authoritative acts are good themselves. Hence, social justice conceives justice at the level of administration.

Thus far we have discussed that philosophers have a task cut out to clarify what it amounts to when we speak of "social justice." We have done this by looking into the different aspects of social justice in relation to individuals, groups, castes and classes of the society. If fair and equitable treatment is given to the safeguard of rights of individuals and groups with respect to certain unique enjoyment of duties and obligations, we speak of social justice. Further, when we speak of enjoying particular customs, rites, religious ceremonies, social ceremonies, social customs and traditions without official intervention, that is, laws that forcibly prevent them, we have a just society. Even the one having heterodox way of life, iconoclastic zeal and atheistic way of life, must be given ample scope to enjoy those ways of life without any official hindrance. However, that does not mean that any agent or agency can force others to his or her way of life. Social justice requires official intervention when freedom of people is breached and legitimate rights are taken away. However, there are a number of serious social rights we enjoy. We have the right to live, educated, get sufficient information, earn a respectable living, settle in peace, and marry and so on. A just society does not breach these rights if that does not breach community interests and well being. Many important issues in social justice come up when we consider these rights. Philosophers take interest in the pro and con arguments regarding affirmative action, population control and many such social actions that seriously affect community's life. We have said that going through the logic of such arguments and justification of social mechanisms, models and decision making are good cases for philosophers to inquire. We now turn to the most important philosophically relevant inquiry, that it, ethical scrutiny of so called justice done in the society. More often than not what is in the name of social justice are questioned for ethical validity. This takes us to *social ethics*. An interesting philosophical inquiry of social matters like, social justice is within social ethics.

Let us take the case of affirmative action, an important mechanism for social justice. The basic point is that for scientific or social scientific grounds available to us, affirmative action has been deemed either just or unjust. This is peculiar! How can scientist claim some action to be both socially just and unjust? There must be some reasons for such contrary claims. Most interesting fact is that the said sound reasons available to both parties are anchored to scientific basis or hard facts. On the one hand those who deem it just speak of "historical injustice" done to some sections of society since a long time that needs correction or revision at the present time. To do so, some special favors have to be given to the historically deprived class or caste. The "favor" in itself is not wrong because the end or goal of it is social well being, not partisan welfare. Who can ignore the hard fact of the said historical injustice? On the other hand, the contrary stand is that, what if there were injustices at a remote past? At the present time, injustice has vanished by virtue of civil society's constitutional remedies. In the eye of law there is no caste or class based injustice needing any special treatment. Moreover, how far should we go if the said deprived class is already well-off? Then there is another view based on hard fact that the well-off can be done away with as creamy layer so that justice percolates deeper to churn more cream at the top. Is everything fine with contesting claims? Philosophers say that not at all, because questions like these are extremely complex because they are *open ended* in *nature.* The open-ended questions like: Is affirmative action socially just? Does not give a pertinent answer based on hard facts alone. The historical, anthropological, sociological, economic and political replies are in fact *open-ended* because those replies soon face a nagging question: Why at all social scientific justice be justified? This is justification of scientific justification or *meta- justification,* which is available with the philosophers in what we call ethics, or more precisely, in social ethics. Let us be clearer on this account. Even if we say that social remedy of historical injustice is good, we still ask: Why at all remedy of such injustice be good? A circular answer is not needed but there is an answer to it. We can think deeper to find that the said "good" of scientific remedy is *justifiable* on grounds beyond science. We can say (we do say in fact, if we think carefully), that such remedy is good or just because it creates *greatest balance of good over evil* in our society. Or, it is tantamount to *social welfare.* Or it is *intrinsically valuable* and thus our duty. In any case, we are basing our scientific reply on ethical grounds of either utilitarianism or welfarism or deontology. Affirmative action for social justice despite being scientifically justified, a meta-inquiry leads to further ethical justification. What utilitarianism justifies may be refuted by deontologists. If utilitarianism is a *pro-argument* for affirmative action, the ethics of deontology can advance *con-argument.* Then what is the way out? Well, there is no final true answer in ethical parlance. Philosophy does not have right and wrong answers. It only has *logically* strong or weak answers. The best way is again available to the philosophers because now they transcend ethics to adopt *logical scrutiny* of contesting arguments and find the logical strengths of some arguments to take sides. This might well end up in some logic of affirmative action that do not take either sides to take a different side altogether. Philosophers are thus argumentative but they are not babbles.

Endnotes and References

1. In the philosophical parlance, 'pro and con arguments' are of great value. These arguments are for justification or refutation of some considered positions. More often than not philosophers speak of logic of justifications meaning thereby either strict formal proofs or non-formal justifications. Arguments used by philosophers are either formal in nature or non-formal in nature. Philosophers are neither concerned with baseless guess work or subjective feelings used as arguments. Hence, they are interested in scrutiny of the arguments in favor or disfavor of the contention. They are thus equally interested in logical and illegal justifications. Hence, arguments in favor of disfavor of social justice and/or how to do social justice (its models) are under logical scanner. We will all agree that the underlying formal logical structure of arguments must be valid and conclusion should be drawn correctly or soundly. This takes logic to the core of all pro-con arguments and discussion of justification of models and methods.
2. At times, like philosophers, social scientists have a peculiar habit to fall back on metaphysical rumblings. This is in the main due to our search for sacrosanct and fundamental truths or absoluteness of ideas. If we believe that social justice is possible *if and only if* there is no class-struggle or alienation of class on grounds of economic exploitation, we are advocating a metaphysical social scientific thesis.
3. In the recent times philosophers have strongly argued in favor of a "curative" task of philosophy. Analytic philosophers like Ludwig Wittgenstein have argued that a majority of philosophical problems are due to ambiguities in our use of language. Hence, the language of philosophical discussions must be cleared of all ambiguities. Even on this basis, it is extremely important for philosophers to find out what the expression "social justice" amounts to when used in social scientific discussions as well as social philosophical discussions.
4. In moral philosophy or ethics we speak of good and evil in non-spiritual terms in most of the cases. In such cases "good" refers to "valuable" or of "worth: whereas "evil" refers to "bad" or "disvalue" or "worthless" In ethics we speak of intrinsic good and extrinsic good (also bad), meaning thereby what is of value all by itself and for that reason is good or end or ideal of our moral life. External or intrinsic good things (or goods) are those contributing to or are instrumental in achieving the goal. In this sense, "welfare of society" is "intrinsic good", distribution of goods in equal and fair way are extrinsic good things.
5. In professional ethics it is said that people having a "profession" are different from those having an "occupation" because professionals have needed ethical acumen to reflect on value and disvalue of decisions and actions before they really do something. They are also people who can thus put internal checks on them and work under external checks as well. Hence, they have regard for valuable regulations imposed by authorities. It is these social agents who are able to harmonize self and others by way of having a quality of life and quality of work life. This must be crucial for a social engineer as a professional.
6. In ethics we speak of a number of overreaching normative thesis or ideals (mostly metaphysically absolutist), such as, teleology and deontology. The former is better known for its numerous types like, egoism, egotism, altruism and Welfarism. Egoism speaks of satisfaction or fulfillment of one's own self as the ideal. Egotism speaks of satisfaction of one's own self provided it is by means of "pleasure." Altruism speaks of pleasure- satisfaction of other selves. Welfarism speaks of overall wellbeing of social being that counts wellbeing of non-human beings and things among other things and holds that wellbeing is a cluster concept that does not only contain pleasure rather many non-hedonic goods as ideals of life.

2

Global Justice in Rawls' The Law of Peoples

M.T. Desai

Justice, according to John Rawls, is "the first virtue of social institutions, as truth is of the systems of thought."[1] It is true that injustice taints social and political institutions and makes their reform imperative as other vices like inefficiency do not. The question is, whether this makes justice as the first virtue debatable. There are other virtues like security, order and welfare which are equally important. There is even a view that political institutions can not provide these virtues without being just, so that justice is not only the 'first virtue' but the 'master virtue'—the sum of all the most important virtues that social institutions can manifest.[2] Hedley Bull gives priority to order as compared to justice, in case of conflict of objectives of states. Quakers would attach highest value to the goal of peace.

Further, justice being a function of society's structure raises two other questions. A wider focus would involve consideration of justice to international level. Moreover, justice as virtue of social institutions assumes discontinuity between a theory of justice and a theory of morality for individuals.

Concept of Global Justice and International Justice are differentiated on the basis of their reference to justice in relation to which units. Here three concepts are important. Bull refers to concept of International System, International Society and World Society. International System consists of states. It is said to be formed, 'where states are in regular contact with one another and where in addition there is interaction between them, sufficient to make the behavior of each a necessary element in the calculation of other, then we may speak of them, forming a system'.[3] This is distinguished from International society, which is constituted, 'when a group of states, conscious of certain common interests and common values, form a society in the sense that they conceive of themselves to be bound by a common set of rules in their relations with one another, and a share in working of common institutions'.[4] World society, presumes a 'world common good' which identifies 'common ends or values of the universal society of all mankind'[5]. According to Bull, there is not yet a world society in existence. But according to Shaw, 'there is a global system of social relations in which all human beings are, to some extent, connected, and which covers the entire globe'.[6] Although many points in Bulls' contention have become debatable such as, distinction between International system and International Society; essential components of International Society; existence or non-existence of World Society; relationship between International Society and World Society. This is not the place to go into detailed discussion of these issues. Suffice is to say International system refers to minimal international interactions between states. On the other hand, International Society presumes greater integration in terms of values, norms. World Society would expand horizons of interactions to include individuals and presumably keep the individual or human good as the central consideration.

Justice can be talked about within a society. Rawls, in his 'A Theory of Justice', talks about justice within a liberal democratic society and provides principles on the basis of which this society can be structured. His attempt to talk about international justice comes about by way of formulating principles of foreign policy for democratic liberal societies. These are referred to in 'Law of People'. Rawls believes that a consensus can be formed about these principles between liberal democratic states, although Rawls prefers to use the term 'Peoples' instead of 'States', for which he gives reasons. But what about 'non-liberal', 'non-democratic' societies. After all, one has to deal with them, simply because they co-exist. Whether, there is a theoretical basis for dealing with them or with what that means are controversial issues. Firstly, there is the issue of legitimacy. A state has a right to rule. Is it because it is recognized as a state by international law, irrespective of nature of regime or policies that regime follows and is thus entitled to enjoy rights of sovereignty, both internal and external. In this sense, no other state has right to intervene in affairs of even a repressive state. As per this view, all states are legitimate and can be dealt with as per norms of international law. On the other hand, according to another view legitimacy of state depends upon its ability to give protection to individuals, internally and externally, ability to defend certain human rights and satisfy certain needs. According to this view, not all states would be legitimate and a regime may lose legitimacy or gain legitimacy, depending upon circumstances. Thus a state which loses its legitimacy and becomes incapable of self help is likely to invite help by others, whether the illegitimate state likes it or not, in what form, under what circumstances, and to what degree and by whom, these are the issues for the theorists of humanitarian intervention, but for them humanitarian intervention is definitely legitimate. Those who define legitimacy of state as a by-product of international law, believe that liberal democratic states should co-exist with non-liberal or even repressive regimes as a matter of law. There are some who would advocate co-existence of liberal and non-liberal states as a matter of expediency. Rawls differs from all these views and believes that he can produce rules of behavior in foreign policy, which will be acceptable both to liberal as well as non-liberal but decent hierarchical societies, not as a matter of expediency, not even because they are rational but because they are reasonable. Initially accepted rules of behavior, will be imbibed by matter of habit (it is natural for liberal democratic societies to practice this code of conduct in relation to non-liberal societies. For liberal societies, practice of code of conduct springs from liberal belief, gives them assurance of their identity and because they have contented citizens governed according to principles of Justice domestically, prescribed by Rawls, therefore liberal societies have nothing to fear from non-liberal but decent hierarchical societies (although liberal societies have something to fear from other types of non-liberal societies).

'The Law of Peoples' was preceded by *'Political Liberalism'* which in turn was preceded by *'A Theory of Justice'*. *'A Theory of Justice'* provided principles of justice within a domestic liberal democratic society. These principles of justice would get rid of several ills of society and become basis of a stable polity. It is necessary to refer to them to find out as to whether Rawls finds them to be useful in relations between societies as well.

Rawls refers to three principles : (1) 'Equal Liberty' principle (2) (a) 'Fair Equality of Opportunity' principle, which states inequality is to be attached to positions open to all under conditions of fair equality of opportunity (b) 'Difference Principle' under which inequalities is to be so arranged that it benefits least advantaged. According to Rawls first principle is more important than second principle. As far as second principle is concerned, (2) (a) is to be given greater weightage than (2) (b).

Rawls uses the old instrument of social contract to formulate his view. He is like social contract theorists like Hobbes, Locke and Rousseau in describing the 'State of Nature' as fictional rather than historical but is original in stating that contract takes place behind 'a veil of ignorance' in which the contractors do not know many things.

Actual contracts reached by people in real life may reflect, bargaining, strength of parties and other circumstances. Rawls' notable innovation is to try to ensure that the agreement that defines principles of justice is fair by depriving parties of agreement of any information that might corrupt or bias the choice of principles.[7] Parties choose under 'Veil of Ignorance'. In this original position, 'no one knows his place in society, his class position or social status, nor does any one know his fortune in distribution of natural assets and abilities, his intelligence, strength and like ... not even their conceptions of good or their special psychological propensities.'[8] This symmetry produces a sense of justice in rational human being.[9] The original position is 'appropriate initial status'.[10] Then Rawls describes 'justice as fairness'. It conveys the idea that principles of justice are agreed to in an *initial situation that is fair.*[11] This does not mean that justice and fairness are same. Further, principles of justice agreed upon are not renegotiable. The society thus constituted is voluntary (comes close to), created for mutual advantage and its members are autonomous, rational and mutually disinterested.[12] According to Rawls, ideally speaking, 'original position' behind a 'veil of ignorance' would at least create principles, which satisfy the traditional conceptions of social justice.[13] According to Rawls, although contractors in initial situation may consider various bases of principles of justice, situated as they are, behind 'a veil of ignorance' they will most likely choose principles recommended by Rawls. They have some rational plan of life but they do not know the details. How then are they to decide? A rough guidance is given by Rawls. Even in a 'veil of ignorance' situation, people expect primary social goods like rights, liberties, opportunities and income and wealth and they want more of it rather than less, as whatever their ultimate intensions, they can be carried out with the help of primary social goods.[14] When one compares Rawls' social contract and the state of Nature with that of Hobbes, Locke and Rousseau a striking distinction is that men in their state of nature knew themselves, knew each other, had certain weaknesses and had very specific expectations. Rawls' men in original position where under a 'veil of ignorance' and their expectations from social (which includes political) structures where to have an enforcer of principles of justice. Who are the parties to the first original position? In domestic society, they consist of citizens. The principles are decided by deliberation. But as Rawls puts it, 'the original position is not to be thought of as every one who will of some time; or much less, as an assembly of every one, who could live at some time. It is not a gathering of all original or actual persons .... ' since the differences among the parties are unknown to them, and everyone is equally rational. Similarly situated, each is convinced by same arguments. Therefore we can view the agreement in the original position from the one person selected at random. ... Persons are required to communicate through a referee ... (who) forbids the attempt to form coalitions. ... The veil of ignorance makes possible a unanimous choice of a particular conception of justice'. (*Theory of Justice*, pp. 120)

Rawls extends the idea of social contract to society of peoples. 'I first chose the name "Peoples" rather than "Nations" or "States" because I wanted to conceive of peoples as being different from those of states, since the idea of states as traditionally conceived with two powers of sovereignty was unsutaible.'[15]

Rawls describes "Law of Peoples" as a particular political conception of right and justice that applies to principles and norms of international law and practice.[16] He believes that same procedure which is followed in 'Theory of Justice' would also produce principles of justice for creating a well-ordered society of 'liberal' and what he describes as 'decent' peoples. He describes his vision as 'a realistic utopia'.[17] The central ideas behind this are two: (1) many of ills of today result from political justice, (2) once injustice is removed, these evils would disapper.[18] Rather than assuming as Hobbes, Locke and Rousseau did, that human nature shapes institutions, Rawls assumes that good institutions will create good citizens.[19] Then these citizens (reasonable and just) will work to make those institutions enduring. Rawls thinks such a scenario is possible and desirable. Therefore he describes it as a 'realistic utopia.'[20] Rawls thinks that under such a realistic utopia, foreign policy problems like war, immigration, nuclear weapons proliferation will disapper.[21]

The Rawlsian reason for discussing foreign policy principles of liberal peoples in relation to non-liberal principles, is not prescription but self-assurance that non-liberal people will also consider these principles reasonable. 'The question of how far are non-liberal peoples to be tolerated is an essential question of liberal foreign policy'.[22]

The first agreement is between citizens of liberal people, the second between representatives of liberal peoples. Here liberal societies would have five features: (a) fair equality of opportunity; (b) a decent distribution of income and wealth; (c) society as employer of last resort; (d) basic health care; and (e) public financing of elections (Rawls, *A Theory of Justice*, p. 50). All liberal societies would have them. Their citizens would therefore be contented and would not want war. Finally there is an agreement between liberal people and non-liberal but decent peoples. 'Each of this agreement ... is entered into by equal peoples symmetrically situated in the original position behind an appropriate veil of ignorance. Hence the undertaking between peoples is fair'.[23]

The question for Rawls is, 'what can be the basis of society of peoples, given the reasonable and expected differences of peoples from one another?' (*The Law of Peoples*, pp. 54-55). Peoples have differences in language, religion. They are also exposed to different geographical and historical experiences. When finding out public reason for society of liberal principles, there was a family of liberalisms, there was a menu of principles. When the question of Law of Peoples is considered, citizens of liberal countries talk of advantages of association with other peoples. They consider two things, principle of equality of peoples and of reciprocity. According to Rawl's, people have a moral nature (whereas states do not have). What people want is self-respect. (*The Law of Peoples*, p. 62.) The society which can be tolerated by liberal democratic constitutional society is described by Rawls as 'decent' society which has a decent consultation hierarchy of groups composed of citizens. An original position of decent consultation hierarchical peoples fairly symmetrically situated with a 'veil of ignorance' can be imagined. A decent society would not have aggressive aims, secures some human rights and perform certain moral duties. There is a common good idea of justice and officials believing that law must have that objective in view. All reasonable citizens, at least must in liberal society will find such people acceptable.

'The Law of People' is realistic because it takes account of plurality of peoples, is not prescribed but voluntarily accepted and with experience may prove to be part of culture of peoples and become enduring but is also utopian and does not rule out change. The reason as Rawls puts it is 'limits of possible are not given by actual, for we can to a great or lesser extent change political and social institutions and much else'.[24] Citizens in this utopia, act according to concept of justice, fairness; tolerance, reciprocity and show willingness to meet others half way.

The 'Law of Peoples' is also utopian in the sense that such peoples do not exist. "The idea of a reasonably just society of well ordered peoples will not have an important place in a theory of international politics until such peoples exist and have learned to co-ordinate the actions of their governments in wider forms of political, economic and social co-operation.[25] Liberal democratic peoples (decent also) have an accountable (reasonable) government, common sympathies and moral nature which formulate reasonable law of peoples. Rawls prefers peoples as actors rather than states because states go to war and have autonomy in dealing with their own people which are not to the liking of Rawls. Two international developments, states' right to go to war only for self-defence and concept of human rights is in harmony with Rawls' view.

When representations of liberal peoples meet behind a veil of ignorance, they are not aware of comprehensive doctrines which will help develop political conception of justice that can be focus of overlapping consensus. When they meet for formulating 'Law of Peoples', they do not know size of country, population, relative strength of people, natural resources or level of economic development though they do know what makes democracy successful. The difference with domestic case is that citizens in a liberal democratic system have a comprehensive conception of good but a liberal society does not have.

The most important expectation of peoples is desire to be treated as equal to others, although certain functional inequalities as prevailing in UN may become acceptable. People should treat other peoples with due respect and terms of co-operation should be based on reciprocity.

The principles which constitute basic charter of *'The Law of Peoples'* include implementation and obligations on the part of people : to observe freedom and independence; observation of treaties and undertakings; equality and people being parties to agreement, duty of non-intervention; right of self-defense; honoring human rights; restrictions in conduct of war; duty to assist peoples under un-favorable conditions. More principles might be added. Interpretations of principles between societies might differ.

What type of features would a 'decent' society have ? Firstly, although a non-liberal society may be treated equally but the principle of equality may not hold when the non-liberal society's government treats its citizens. A decent society should have a consultant hierarchy, of groups, but not of individuals. Government in this type of society is not elected by people consisting of individual citizens. It would be a society in which certain rights would be there, such as; liberty of conscience and freedom of religion and thought (not extensive and equal) permitting its practice in peace and without fear, although one religion may be a favoured religion and followers of that religion may hold upper positions of political authority and are influential in vital issues like foreign affairs.

Followers of other religion are otherwise treated equally and may even be part of armed forces and serve in higher ranks of authority. The society is non-expansionist (Even Jihad is interpreted in moral and spiritual terms and not in military terms). Society vested with human rights is a necessary condition of decency. Human rights exclude forceful and justifiable intervention by other peoples and set a limit to pluralism among people.[26] Basic rights of a decent society, according to Rawls, are (1) rights protecting life and integrity of the person; (2) rights to liberty of a person; (3) rights of formal equality and protections of rule of law; and (4) as already stated some degree of liberty of conscience.[27]

The meaning of justice is contentious even within a domestic society. It becomes more so when we talk about "international justice" or "global justice". Then there is other question of justice as 'fairness' or 'impartiality' as a matter of procedural justice as against 'substantive justice' involved in issues of social justice at global level.

International justice deals with states. In the Westphalian order, it means nothing but an ethic of co-existence. It is therefore procedural.[28] Here the concept is that of international system which is 'anarchial' but is also a society which follows certain norms or rules. The situation here in comparison with domestic society is different. A national or a domestic society is a co-operative venture for achievement of certain common ends, whereas a society of states (societies) is not a scheme of co-operation for achievement of certain common goals. Therefore the norms of justice, as advocated by Rawls in *'A Theory of Justice'*, applies in domestic society but same principles do not apply when issue of justice between societies is involved. A reason why this happens is 'unlike a civil society, international society is without a superior to define and enforce, the rights of its members.'[29] Those who believe that international society consists only of rules may be described as 'Pluralists', whereas those who believe that there are common goals may be described as 'Solidarists'. Rawls thus believes in pluralistic conception of international justice. For Rawls this is appropriate. The liberal democratic principles may constitute comprehensive doctrine'. But by way of principle, just as liberal democratic principles society respect for non-liberal persons and groups internally, provided that they obey the law. So political liberalism at international level prescribes respect for non-liberal societies, provided these societies, are reasonably just internally and obey international law'.[30] Political liberalism rests on idea of 'public reason' which involves, finding a common ground with others while formulating arguments. In theoretical terms, the issue involved is that of moral legitimacy of states or peoples.

Realists are of two types. There are some who regard morality as irrelevant and others who regard morality as justifiable only for purpose of state. For this purpose violating moral norms may be justified. Even if they do not disregard morality but believe in situations of necessity, morality may be put aside (war, defense) or more coherently justice must be put aside for expediency or prudence.

According to some who believe in liberal democratic conviction, only democratic states or societies are legitimate and therefore can not tolerate non-liberal societies as legitimate because of their treatment of their citizens. Thus the principle of 'domestic jurisdiction' and 'non-interference' would not apply in liberal societies' treatment of non-liberal societies. Thus, according to these, liberals norms of international law would not apply. Those who believe in humanitarian intervention face objections from protagonists of international law. However, there are valid questions: does a state not lose its legitimacy when it fails to protect its citizens? Does it not lose immunity from intervention under these circumstances? Does that duty not fall on others? Does it fall on a state or states or international organization? How does the general duty become duty of a special agent? "International justice requires not only that states treat other states justly, as the domestic analogy would imply but also that they concern themselves with well-being and rights of people everywhere."[31] Thus international justice can be defended on cosmopolitan basis as well. What are Rawl's views on this issue?

For Rawls, domestic society does exist but not World Society. An international society is possible but not of states but of peoples. International society of states would require—'a co-operative venture of shared goals'. Within a state, such society does exist. It can be a just society as well if formulated on the basis of Rawls's principles of justice. On the basis of same principles an international society of states can not be created as there is no basis for that. At the same time an international system is not the only thing that human being can create, according to Rawls. A liberal and 'decent' society of peoples (well ordered societies) is possible. The 'decent' society would not be just like liberal democratic one. The society would not have full political participation of all citizens, may not treat all its citizens equally and would not allow comprehensive range of human rights but it is 'decent' and has a right to be treated equally. Thus a 'decent' society is legitimate and should not be an object of intervention. According to Rawls, 'decent societies' should also not be subjected to global intervention, on the basis of distribution or redistribution of social goods, because global distributive justice requires 'shared meanings'. Not all cultures may embody idea of such a justice. Rawls is a pluralist. 'Thus principles of economic redistribution are a matter of choice, not of justice'.[32] It may represent a desirable goal but not an enforceable duty. Thus Rawls does not believe in global justice as far as distributive justice is concerned. However, this statement should be qualified. Rawls does talk of giving assistance to 'burdened societies'. Even here the 'duty of assistance' is to societies, not to individuals (who may benefit indirectly). The qualification for assistance is that such societies are not aggressive or expansive and may respect human rights in a limited way. They 'lack political and cultural' societies, human capital and knowhow, and often the material and technical resources. The goal is to bring them into well-ordered societies. Such societies need not be poor or wealthy. Economic redistribution or equality is not the goal. The assistance is not a permanent basis. The objective is to help people live their lives decently, rationally, reasonably, help society live its life on the basis of self-determination. Rawls as pluralist believes that on this basis, there exists 'duty of assistance'. Cosmopolitans, on the other hand, believe in goal of equality as an end in itself and therefore in global distribution principle on a continuous basis keep individual in focus. Rawls would be satisfied with 'duty of assistance' to 'burdened societies' and individuals would benefit only indirectly.

However, Rawls does not treat 'outlaw states' in the same way, although the objective is again to bring these states into 'well ordered societies'. Outlaw state is one where the regime acts to advance its own (rational and not reasonable) interests and not for self defense. Well ordered peoples can go to war in self-defense against such a state. Of course 'decent' society and 'benevolent despotisms' too have right to self-defense. 'Liberal' and 'decent' societies will have to use political wisdom to make decisions about correct means of bringing other societies in society of well-ordered peoples.

Thus as far as outlaw societies activities like war or violation of human rights are concerned, the duties of well ordered societies are enforceable but the objective is not to create immediately a global society of well ordered peoples but the ultimate goal is that.

The Law of Peoples raises the issue of whether such a law can be enforced by state (Rawls has raised doubts) or form other than state is needed. Talk about 'New International Economic Order' in 1970s was state centric. Rawls did not believe in distributive justice beyond state. Critics allege that Rawls considered societies as closed, whereas globalization and economic interdependence are creating a global economy. Thus principles of distributive justice between societies must be considered, specially when it is alleged that inequalities in world society are created by international economic order. Pogge argues that poverty, malnutrition, starvation, environmental degradation are suffered in Third World for benefit of wealthy countries. However, how to change the situation, may invite different type of suggestions.

Relationship between different parts of humanity need not be thought only in terms of justice. Care for weak, duty to relieve poverty can be other ways of thinking about it. Conceptually we all are part of humanity. Many issues can be tackled by involving states. We are witnessing erosion of norms of sovereignty and non-intervention. Other non-state actors; emerging civil Society; better global governance may also help.

Rawls was more a protagonist of 'international justice' rather than of 'global justice'. Even his concept of international justice involves peoples rather than of states. *The Law of Peoples* can be defended most importantly in terms of political culture and community autonomy. Goal of human welfare may seem to be some more important. How much of what is to be sacrificed for what, can be determined only by consequences experienced, and one's political values.

Endnotes and References

1. John Rawls, *A Theory of Justice*, rev. ed., Cambridge, MA : Harvard University Press, 1999, p. 3, (Sec. ch-1, n.9)
2. A. John Simmons, *Political Philosophy*, Oxford University Press, 2008, p. 67.
3. Hedley Bull, *The Anarchical Society* : A study of order in World Politics, Macmillan, 1977, p. 10.
4. Ibid., p. 13.
5. Ibid., p. 84.
6. Shaw, 'Global Society and Responsibility : the theoretical, historical and political limits of 'international society' in *Millennium Journal of International Studies*, 21(3) pp. 421-434.
7. Richard J. Arneson "Justice after Rawls" in J. Dryzek, B. Honig and A. Phillips (edi.), *The Oxford Hand book of Political Theory*, Oxford University Press, 2006 (Paper book, 2008), p. 48.
8. Rawls, op.cit., p. 11.
9. Ibid., p. 11.
10. Ibid., p. 11.
11. Ibid., p. 11.
12. Ibid., p. 12.
13. Ibid., p. 16.
14. Ibid., p. 79.
15. John Rawls, 'The Law of Peoples', Harvard University Press, Cambridge, Massachusetts, 1997, Paper book, 2001, preface.
16. Ibid., Introduction p. 3.
17. Ibid., p. 6.
18. Ibid., p. 6-7.
19. Ibid., p. 7.
20. Ibid., p. 7.
21. Ibid., p. 8-9.
22. Ibid., p. 10.
23. Ibid., p. 10.
24. Ibid., p. 12.
25. Ibid., p. 19.
26. Ibid., p. 80.
27. Samuel Freeman, *Rawls*, Routledge, London, 2007, Indian Edition, 2008, pp. 429-430.
28. Chris Brown, "From International to Global Justice", J. Dryzek, B. Honig and A. Phillips (edi.) in *The Oxford Handbook of Political Theory*, Oxford University Press, 2006 (Paperbook 2008), p. 523.
29. Terry Nardin, "International Political Theory" in Burchill and Others (edi.), *Theories of International Relations*, Palgrave, Macmillan, Fourth Edition, 2009, p. 294.
30. Ibid., p. 296.
31. Ibid., p. 298.
32. Ibid., p. 303.

3

Social Justice: The Affirmative Negative

J.P. Mishra

The Indian Constitution, says Granville Austin, is a social document. The Constitution envisages several measures, and opens up immense possibilities for the policy makers to realise social justice through various measures, the reservations to the Scheduled Castes, Scheduled Tribes and other backward castes being one of these. Of late, the government has decided to embark on a mission to know the caste and religion wise exact number of people living below the poverty line.

The present paper makes a modest attempt to examine the efficacy of the affirmative action of the state in the form of reservations, as also the possible implications of the proposed census, in realisation of the goal termed social justice.

PROLOGUE

Justice lies in equal protection of the rights of parties seeking justice. The administration of justice results into rights and duties both. If it gives A a right, or if it upholds A's right; it alternatively gives B a duty to respect that right. B is duty bound or, sometimes, so is the entire world if the right in question happens to be a *jus in rem*.

However, social justice is a more complicated concept as it addresses the groups of individuals and protects their interests in such a way that justice to individuals does not loose its meaning. A slight error committed in the balancing exercise may ruin the individual prospects, hamper the group interests or, worst, may become an instrument of social disintegration. In either case, the balancing agency has to have a cautious treading.

Equality, thus, is the essence of justice. The present paper attempts to identify the dominating trends in the realisation of social justice in India, and hints that the affirmative action adopted for bringing about social justice is in fact likely to induce, in the long run, an inequality in the society. That is to say, the state's affirmative action is negative in its impact on the society.

SOCIAL JUSTICE IN ANCIENT INDIA

Equality in India has always been a cherished value, so has been justice. The picture of justice, however, remains incomplete unless there is glow of equality in it. The equality that reigned supreme in philosophy somehow could not translate itself as effectively at the real plane; and it proved a fertile ground for growth of inequality in the society. The worst sufferer was social justice. The characteristics, which derived their classification from the innate relationship of man with nature and were to remain as open and dynamic as nature, got metamorphosed into classes with rigid boundaries of their own. The theory that a man was as good as his deeds became the thing of the past; and the human actions began to be judged by the class the doer belonged to.

The said myopic view favoured few and degraded the rest in the society. The varying cannons of individual justice ultimately prepared a ground for social injustice. This was a stage where social justice was dispensed in a way that looked hardly any better than injustice. It led to the division of the society on planes physical as well as mental. As equality faded away from social life, the gap was filled up by injustice; and after a few centuries, one could find the social fabric weakened by the gaps which had acquired unbridgeable dimensions. This division was seen at its very best when India saw herself converted into hundreds of 'sovereign republics'; making the climate most suited for invasions.

THE INDEPENDENCE AND AFTER

With the dawn of the independence, the things started moving favourably for social justice. The Constitution that followed in a couple of years and a half's time, provided for the promotion of educational and economic interests of Scheduled Castes, Scheduled Tribes and other weaker sections.[1] To obviate legal hurdles in this regard, as had arisen from the observations of the Court in the *State of Madras v. Champakam Dorairajana*[2], there was introduced the first amendment to the Constitution to protect their interest by means of providing reservations.

The reservations for SC/ST continued to be in force for about forty-two years only to witness another dose of reservation for the Other Backward Classes. Both reservations continue till date. In the year 2009, the OBC reservation completed a period normally regarded as representing one generation.

However, there is no signal that the reservations are going to be done away with in the near future. Instead, we see more and more 'discoveries' in the form of SC/ST/OBC and the sphere of these categories keeps on burgeoning with several castes making a bee-line to be blessed with reservation in one or the other categories.

That with the advancing age and society more and more sections of society are getting poorer and more downtrodden than they were hitherto fore, is simply baffling for a reasonable man.

SOCIAL JUSTICE: AFFIRMATIVELY NEGATIVE

It is a very peculiar way of looking at things which does not regard a person poor unless he belongs to a certain caste in the society. Let us, with full honour to the Supreme Court's observation in the *Indra Sawhney case*[3], call the castes the classes. But does it really make a difference if we say that Mr 'so and so' shall be regarded poor only if he comes from 'such and such' class of society, no matter how hunger-stricken he is, in real sense of the term?

As the things stand at present, a person becomes ineligible for state's affirmative action even if his economic condition is weak; while another person becomes eligible even if he may be in a better financial condition. The only reason forwarded for this unusual treatment is the presence or absence of that all pervading factor: the caste-factor. The fact that the presence or absence of the caste-factor does do this miracle tells enough of the version of social justice we have adopted. The decision of the Central Government on May 19, 2011 to conduct caste-wise census in order to know the exact number of families living below poverty line in each caste is the latest in this regard.

Like the proverbial lion who pounced upon the dear standing downstream saying, 'if it is not you who have polluted my water, it must have been your father or your father's father...'; the present Indian state appears to be punishing a great majority of hunger-stricken mass of humanity just because "their fore-fathers might have perpetrated injustice against the so called 'backward classes'. This, if any thing, will lead to another society where there is a reversal of status: the forwards of today becoming backwards/downtrodden tomorrow and vice versa. Is it the sort of society the framers of our Constitution would have dreamt of? Is this exactly what we want to achieve in the name of social justice?

Social justice must have its end in social equality; and, therefore, simple logic will tell us that something which produces an opposite effect, something that results in social inequality can not have social justice at its root.

The affirmative action of the State appears to have several such negative points some of which shall be hinted at here. Let it be noted at the very outset that the said negativity of the affirmative action is adversely affecting not only those that are outside the reservation frame as has been noted above, but it also jeopardises equally negatively the prospects of those who lie inside the said frame and stand in a greater need of the affirmative action.

Owing to the peculiar way in which we have allowed the social justice to be administered to the weaker sections of the society, they helplessly see their share of state's protective discrimination being high jacked by their brethren who are better off.

THE CREAMY LAYER

Contrary to its objective of weeding out from amongst the Other Backward Classes those who are well off, and pave the way for speedy progress of those that lie at the lowest ladder of social order; the creamy layer concept has, to a great extent, only favoured the former and worked to the disadvantage of the latter. It, thus, amounts to allowing the fat-bellied increase their waist by a few more inches while their hapless brothers who really deserve (if one can use the term) reservation become all the more emaciated.

Official and unofficial (that is independent) data put the figure of people below poverty line between 270 and 330 million in this country. Of these, a few million (because fixing the number is both difficult as well as likely to create dispute and deviate us from the real point at issue) may belong to the so called upper-caste who, according to the view prevailing at present, do not have a right to be regarded as poor. The rest of this hunger stricken mass of humanity has to compete—if they have to ever have the benefit of affirmative action—with others of their class who are above poverty line. Worst, they are cursed to see their children compete with the children of those who are just below the creamy layer.

The creamy layer limit that was rupees one lakhs in 1993 was enhanced to rupees 2.5 lakhs in 2004 and rupees 4.5 lakhs in 2008. It means that presently an OBC person earning up to 37500 rupees per month is entitled to get the reservation benefits. It may be mentioned here that this move on the part of the government did not go well with the Supreme Court which went to the extent of saying that it would "try to take the cream out of the creamy layer" if a petition was filed.[4]

With all the inflation and other such factors that may be brought to one's aid in calculation of 'real' worth of the above scales of income, it still is crystal clear that such persons as have been declared to be below creamy layer, stand to get the lion's share of this affirmative action.

Viewed thus, the upper substratum of the OBC will always be walking away with the cake, in the face of hungry hundreds of the same class. Not only this, whenever the overall income increases or the value of the rupee decreases, the said upper substratum will use its presence in the corridors of power to get the creamy layer enhanced so that they continue to snatch the share of their less 'privileged' OBC brethren. The situation is no better in case of SC/ST where there is no applicability of the creamy layer concept. Here too, instances are not very rare where affluent SC/STs are, on the financial scale, miles ahead of others in the category. A recent observation of the apex court to extend creamy layer concept to SCs/STs in promotions could not have the desired effect as the lawmakers described it as 'politically unacceptable'.[5]

Things have become more than clear in several parts of India that, at least in some areas, only a particular caste (or, at any rate, only a few castes) among the OBC, or as the case may be, SC/ST, are continuously high-jacking this cream of affirmative action to give a glow to their already shining prospects; even as the rest of the persons in the class are left in a state of perpetual neglect.

The only difference that the affirmative action has made is that it has shifted the point of blame. Earlier, the poor would curse the landlords and other elite for the sorry state of affairs; now, they curse their misfortune or bad luck. With the slogan shouting of social justice by the government and their OBC/SC/ST leaders these hapless people have so far been kept in dark about this negative game of affirmative action. With so much sloganeering for social justice in our favour, think they, it is sure to benefit us too some day, little knowing that that 'someday' will never be translated into a 'today'.

NOW, THE CASTE-BASED CENSUS!

So far the Government has cut a sorry figure when it comes to providing any data on how the reservation facilities extended to the downtrodden for the past 15 years (or, for the past 50 years) have bettered the lot of those who really stood in the need of state patronage.

The latest move by the Central Government to start a census based on caste with an avowed aim to determine the number of families in each caste living below the poverty line may well become a powerful database to assess whether and, if yes, up to what extent the reservations have benefited the target groups. To this end, the Government's move must be welcomed by everybody who believes in social justice.

This apparently pious move, however, is not free from blemishes altogether; for reasons more than one. Firstly, it is likely to perpetuate the caste stigma which may prove to be a great hindrance in social transformation:[6]

> "Though colonial administrators attempted to map caste, the post-independence establishment recoiled at a record of caste identity in the national census. However, after the Mandal Commission inaugurated a phase of competitive politics around caste, for electoral mobilisation and policy benefits, there seemed to be a new rationale in knowing the real numbers. Given how much rides on caste classification, in terms of education, employment and welfare, even political office, some argue that there is a need to assess the dimensions of each claim. *However, this argument fails to recognise that officially assigning caste categories can harden these identities (emphasis added).*"

This could be a retrograde step for a society willing to move forward. The Supreme Court majority judgement underlined the social reality that the caste stigma remained even after the socially backward classes became financially well off. The apex Court made these observations to reject the economic backwardness as a criterion for reservations. Justice Krishna Iyer went to the extent of saying that such caste-stigma should be done away with by intermingling of various social groups through inter-caste marriages etc. Hardening the caste blocs, through the caste census is likely to work against such a vision for future envisaged by the judges of the Supreme Court.

Secondly, it may result in newer demands for reservations for the castes who might feel quota wise under-represented, plunging the society into another caste-war. This may hardly be looked into as a healthy sign for realisation of social justice. The fact that the census in question is also to take note of one's religion may only add fuel to the fire; so far as reservation demands are concerned. For example, the demand of reservations for backward Muslims which has been raised in several states may be gaining a firm ground in days to come courtesy the proposed census.

On the other hand, there is also a danger underlying such an exercise; and that is that if such a database comes into existence, it will expose the 'real' beneficiaries, and display the plight of those who really needed these benefits but somehow could not get it. This will be renaissance of sorts for the less privileged classes and will force the powers to reconsider their present version of social justice as well as its functioning. The vested interests in the OBC/SC/ST themselves would least like to think of such a situation. That this is more than a mere hypothesis is clear in the echo that we get in the latest concept of extremely backward classes (EBCs). It is only a matter of days when one may see a bitter clash of interests between OBC and EBC.

In spite of all this, it must be noted that the government's decision to have a caste-based Census, which is only the first of its kind in the independent India(the last time it was done was in the year 1931 by a regime whose political ideology was entirely different from the present government of the people, by the people and for the people, does mark a realisation on the part of political leadership that poverty remains a great hurdle in the way of social justice and equality. This is so because alleviation of poverty is certainly a very positive step towards the objective of a society marked by justice and equality.

THE LEGISLATURE

As all men can not be one and the same, so can not be their interests. In a society, there is always a variety of interests nurtured by various individuals or groups of individuals. These interests are competing and clashing with each other. The law-maker has to see which interest is to be given priority over which and to what extent. Also, he has to try to harmonise the conflicting interests with an eye on satisfying as much of interests as can be and compromising the least amount of interests.

Also, things are not as easy as they might otherwise appear to be; particularly when the society in question is a heterogeneous in more than one respects. Indian society presents such an example where diversity is omnipresent: be it in life-styles, rituals, culture, community, language, and the level of development. Thus to achieve equality and justice proves to be an uphill task for the law-maker; particularly because the society is under a constant revolution. It is here that the intention of the legislature acquires utmost importance in the law that it enacts.

At times, however, the intention of the legislature is far from clear. On the one hand they extend reservation to central universities/institutions, but on the other hand, they invite foreign universities and institutions to open their branches in India. At one breath it okays reservations in government jobs, but in the same breath it also welcomes with red carpet every multinational that is ready to invest money in India. With the number of government jobs decreasing fast and job opportunities in private sector increasing day-by-day, the affirmative action, visible in the form of reservations, will become empty slogan devoid of substance in the near future.

Similarly, with increasing participation of foreign institutions in education sector in India, it will only benefit the elite-whether they come from so called forward class or backward classes; because they have nothing to offer to the children of those families who can't afford to pay lacs of rupees as fees.

The intention of the legislature is not easily understandable also in case of allowing reservations in promotions[7]. If a person gets recruited courtesy affirmative action and continues to get promoted till he gets the top post, again by dint of affirmative action, he will be the last person to think of innovation and excellence on his part. As a human being if he is getting everything on the basis of something other than his merits, he may not think of anything more, as every human conduct is governed by a because[8] (meaning, purpose) and since he has got all the incentives ipso facto (by virtue of belonging to a particular class) he will not strive for excellence. It would appear that the fundamental right to get reservation[9] benefits runs counter to one's fundamental duty to strive for excellence.[10]

THE POLITICS

While there is no denying the fact that it is the politics which opened up the gates of development to the millions of downtrodden, it is equally true that the same politics is trying to make the most of reservation card for petty political gains. Having once opposed tooth and nail the application of economic criterion in determination of backwardness, our political leaders are now all out to lure the so called forward classes by advocating reservation facilities to backwards among forwards. It is not easy to understand this change of heart except for the fact that the vote plank is what the parties care for the most; otherwise, if it is not the application of economic criterion in determination of backwardness, nothing else is.

It is not less interesting to note that having tasted the political benefits, in 2010 Assembly elections, of playing EBC (Extremely Backward Class) Card and providing 50 per cent Women's Quota in local bodies, the Bihar Chief Minister Nitish Kumar has announced his government's decision to set up a Savarna Commission almost on the lines of Backward and SC/ST Commissions. This in all probability is sure to open up a new phase in Indian politics where one is likely to see the political parties trying desperately to brow-beat one another in their attempts to lure the 'backward' forwards through the lollypop called reservation.

However, nothing more can characterise the double speak of our political parties vis-à-vis social justice than the fact that despite there being two governments of entirely different political hues, the women's reservation bill is still biting the dust in Parliament. The year 2010 has witnessed it being passed by the Upper House; but the ruling United Progressive Alliance is yet to muster enough courage to get it okayed by the Lower House. If anything, it reflects the stark difference in the various versions of social justice that these political parties seem to espouse.

If the injustices of the past were any criterion to let one qualify for the affirmative action, one may argue, it would be the womenfolk who deserve it the most—at all levels of political and governmental participation. Because women, save in rarest of the rare circumstances, had been kept outside the mainstream—at the lowest it was the deprivation, while at the higher level it was their isolation from the tides of times that made their situation in the society vulnerable.

Invoking the past injustices as reason to shower reservation benefits on one class of people, and, forgetting to take note of another class (the women) that is similarly situated; reflects poorly on the wisdom and farsightedness of the Indian legislator. This is also a severe blow to sincere efforts for social justice; and another negativity of the affirmative action.

SOCIAL ENGINEERING

The most abused term in this regard is the social engineering. Of late this most celebrated concept of the preceding century is being openly used for any which calculation that has the enough poll-potential. The politicians almost shamelessly see the pros and cons of caste populations in a constituency and field candidates who are likely to benefit the most by the caste—criterion. The most recent example was the Brahmin—Bahujan chemistry in UP which again was not a social engineering as it stood on the ground of de-recognition of a sizeable portion of our population, namely other backward classes.

Roscoe Pound, the father of the concept of social engineering, had laid emphasis on the fact that the legislator, like an efficient engineer, should try to satisfy maximum interests in the society with the least friction.[11] Today's legislators are least bothered about this 'least friction' factor as long as they are sure of winning elections.

But one thing can hardly escape one's notice. Those who make it to the legislature either by purchasing caste-loyalties or by adopting any means other than the parliamentary ones, can never take the concept of social engineering in its true spirit. They may use the caste-chemistry and the population arithmetic to grab the power but they simply can not come to terms with social engineering because it is an inclusive formula rather than an exclusivist one.

CONCLUSION

The idea of ensuring social justice to those who had stood marginalized and downtrodden for no fault of theirs is the most welcome one because without this democracy will lose its meaning for us; and therefore no sane person would oppose this weapon of social engineering. The fact needs no exaggeration that one can realize one's freedom and exercise one's rights in the best possible way only when there is an overall social equality; for the simple reason that every such freedom and right may become a reality for all only through social justice.

But as has been noted above, the social justice can not be realised by promoting one section at the cost of the other, or by ignoring the importance of an individual in a society. Also, the powers should not try to impose social justice in a way that eats into the very vitals of the society because doing so will prove self annihilating for the society.

So long as our vision of society reflects in the form of Brahmin Samaj, Kurmi Samaj, Kshatriya Samaj, and such other 'societies'; and so long as our leaders continue to patronize such societies by getting a sword here and getting weighed against gold/silver coins there; there is almost no chance of emergence of a society in the real sense of the term. And, with so many caste-based groups projecting themselves as 'their' societies, the concept of 'our society' may well remain on papers. Social justice, then, may become a distant dream.

There was a long felt need to do some survey on the impact of governmental measures to make social justice a reality. However, the wisdom of the government to conduct such a survey with the colours of caste and religion is likely to adversely affect the cohesive and secular fabric of the society: "Just as we need accurate data on numbers of the poor for more useful welfare schemes, we should also avoid imposing a fixity on their caste identity by putting this information in the official census."[12]

Therefore, to make social justice a reality in our society, at least the following minimum measures need to be taken:

1. The rights and dignity of an individual must be given equal weight and protection and should not be allowed to be curtailed on the basis of caste, creed etc. Any criterion applied for the purpose of providing protective discrimination should be as far as possible universally applicable. Thus the economic and other such criteria should be applied irrespective of an individual's caste and creed etc.
2. Efforts must be directed to ensure that the minimum discriminatory protection is given to any section of society or any individual, and making him duty bound to expedite his journey in life with this 'capital' rather than depend always on state's bounty. Presently, there is only a clamouring for right to get reservation and an unwillingness to ever become independent. Reservations must provide an individual a take off point after which he/she must utilise his/her

time, resources and energy to shape his/her career.

3. Government must set the limits of creamy layer in such a way that it corresponds to the prevailing social and economic conditions; otherwise the purpose of protective discrimination may not be achieved easily and may even prove counterproductive. Setting limits disproportionate to the existing socio-economic conditions may prove counter productive.
4. Efforts must also be made to focus on other means to help the deprived and the downtrodden e.g. providing them basic minimum facilities of food, nutrition, teaching aid, scholarships and the like so that they get an opportunity to develop their personality and are in a position to get jobs with the minimum push up in the form of reservation. This will undoubtedly contribute to overall increase in efficiency of administration etc.
5. Finally, the idea must be to apply the reservations in their best spirit so that the process to achieve social equality, which is the principal objective of social justice, is accelerated. Reservations must be regarded as exception rather than norm. To try to accord a kind of perpetuity to reservation policy will be fatal for the very existence of the society. Because, in the prophetic words of Justice Krishna Iyer:[13]

   "To lend immortality to the reservation policy is to defeat its raison deter; to politicize this provision for communal support and Party ends is to subvert the solemn undertaking of Article 16(1)."

Endnotes and References

1. Article 46, Constitution of India, Central Law Agency, Allahabad, 2011.
2. AIR 1951 SC 226.
3. *Indra Sawhney vs. Union of India*: AIR 1993 SC 477. It is otherwise known as the Mandal Commission case.
4. An IANS report from New Delhi dated October 14, 2008 stated it thus: "The Supreme Court on Tuesday scoffed at the central government's recent decision to raise the annual income limit to Rs. 450,000 for deciding who are the better off-forming "creamy layer"—among the other backward classes (OBCs) and not eligible for various quotas. A five-judge constitution bench headed by Chief Justice K G Balakrishnan also indicated that the government's decision may face a severe scrutiny by the apex court, if the same is challenged through an appropriate lawsuit."
5. It was on October 19, 2006 that the Constitution Bench headed by the then Chief Justice of India, and comprising Justice K G Balakrishnan, S H Kapadia, C K Thakker, and P K Balasubramanyan delivered a judegment on some 70 petitions filed from several States challenging the validity of 77th, 81st, 82nd, and 85th amendments to the Constitution which had the effect of overruling the decision in Mandal Commission case that there would be no reservation in promotions. The Court upheld the validity of all these amendments, but emphasized the principle of creamy layer would strictly apply in their promotions.
6. See, the Indian Express, Lucknow, may 21, 2011 the editorial entitled 'Stay Sharp: We should be wary of bundling caste and religion information with the BPL lists'.

7. Once a person is granted protective discrimination, say, as a matter of right; he should also be asked to take it upon himself as his/her duty to strive for his betterment so that he may not stand always in the need of the same protective discrimination. Unequal treatment may be an exception which must not be allowed to crystallize in to a norm. Sometimes, it appears as if the intention of the legislature is to provide incentive for backwardness rather than remove it.
8. For example, consider Jhering's view of law, who says that every human conduct is governed by a 'because' (meaning, purpcse), and since law is all about conduct it too should have a purpose. a law with no purpose is, according to him, no (valid) law.
9. Articles 14-16, Constitution of India.
10. Article 51-A(j), ibid.
11. See, Pound's book, *An Introduction to the Philosophy of Law* published by Yale University Press/Universal Law Publishing Co. Pvt. Limited, Second Indian Reprint 1998; particularly at p.47.
12. See, the *Indian Express*, Lucknow, May 21, 2011 *op. cit.*
13. See, ABSK Sangh case: AIR 1986 SC 298 at p. 306.

PART II

CONSTITUTIONAL VISION AND INDIAN REALITY

4

Social Justice in India: An Analysis

C.P. Barthwal

INTRODUCTION

For centuries, India persisted with a social order which was marked by elaborate hierarchies. It was basically organised on the principle of inequality of men. Modem India, however, was to be different and better than its historical past. This could be achieved only by attaining "social justice".

The quest for social justice is a continuing pursuit of absorbing interest in societies with marked social, educational and economic inequalities. The advent of democratic form of government, and socialism as a guiding political philosophy in these societies, has increased the interest in the articulation of issues relating to social justice. In all such societies, social justice prominently figures on the agenda of governmental action, infused and inspired by constitutional provisions, special legislations, court verdicts, and state-initiated programmes for general well-being of the weaker and vulnerable sections of the society.

In India, the academic discourses on social justice issues are becoming more commonplace now, than ever before. The reasons for the resurgence of interest in the subject lie in the fast changing political milieu where under the proclamations are made on issues concerning the development of the disadvantaged sections of the society. These proclamations are not new; they had been there since independence. What is new today is that every political party, irrespective of its political ideology, wants to project itself as the most potent protector of the poor, not always for genuine reasons, but for increasing its influence in the arena of caste-politics. The increasing ascendancy of intermediate and lower castes in the political power structure has overturned the nature of 'political-promise-making', leading the main players, in the political game, to realise the danger of pursuing the old agenda of populist proclamations. The change in the caste-characteristics of upcoming politicians has also caused another inevitable development, i.e. the need for change in the rhetoric of political activism. The emergence of highly vocal and more aggressive politicians belonging to the Scheduled Castes, Scheduled Tribes and Other Backward Classes has altogether changed the priorities of political agenda, resulting in an increased emphasis on justice-related issues.

In such a changed political scenario, poverty alleviation programmes, policies of protective discrimination and the welfare packages for the weak and vulnerable, especially those belonging to Scheduled Castes, Scheduled Tribes and Other Backward Classes, have received a new urgency to materialise the constitutional commitment of securing JUSTICE—social, economic and political- to people who have been traditionally dispossessed and disadvantaged. The retrieval of the Mandal Commission Report from the woods sparked off a national debate on what the term social justice means, who does it specifically refers to, what philosophy it entails and policies, programmes and strategies it envisages to promote the important ingredients of the concept. Since then, social justice has become a buzzword, a term too frequently used in the manifestoes of all political parties; a concept keenly and contestingly discussed in an overwhelmingly large number of academic and administrative discussions. Large number of writings and multitude of views expressed by the academics some how keep the confusion intact and do precious little by way of clarifying the conceptual cobwebs, explaining the essence of the idea and delineating the broad parameters of the policies and programmes being pursued in the name of social justice. The result is that the meaning of the concept and the message subsumed under it continues to be problematic. Little wonder, many people suspect that the idea has been hijacked by politicians and given a new and narrow twist. This seems to be true in view of the fact that many debates on social justice seem to drum up the propagandist views which often imply a kind of hate campaign.

WHAT IS JUSTICE

Justice, in a broader perspective, eludes proper definition. Aristotle defines it as a "virtue of the soul distributing that which each person deserved". Its origin, according to Cicero, is to be sought in the divine law of eternal and immutable morality. Holiness toward God and justice toward men usually go together. It is equally said to be the sum of all moral duty. According to Benjamin Disraeli, "It is truth in action." John Stuart Mill talks of justice as "a name for certain classes of moral rules which concern the essential of human well-being more nearly, and are therefore, of more absolute obligation than other rules for the guidance of life". Justice is supposed to bring in both harmony and holiness in people. Truth is its handmaid, freedom its child, peace is its companion, safety walks in its steps, victory follows in its train. In fact, according to Sydney Smith, "It is the brightest emanation from the Gospel: it is the attribute of God". Another writer J.B. Bosanquet in his *Sermon on Justice* suggests that "if justice prevails, good faith is found in treaties, truth in transactions, order in government, the earth is at peace, and heaven itself sheds over us its beneficent light and radiates down to us its blessed influence". Justice comprises the whole of virtue and complete conformity with the approved pattern of moral conduct.

Justice ultimately means the active process of preventing or remedying that which would arouse the sense of injustice. The experience of the sense of injustice provokes people to join hands together in resisting the danger posed before them, and in exciting over an achieved success. Justice, as such, is more than a static equilibrium or a quality of the human will. It is, in fact, an active process of agenda or exercise for public good. The meaning of the term comes alive whenever one confronts injustice or 'does' justice.

One definition of justice is "giving to each what he or she is due." The problem is of knowing what is "due".

SOCIAL JUSTICE

Social justice generally refers to the idea of creating an egalitarian society or institution that is based on the principles of equality and solidarity, that understands and values human rights and that recognises the dignity of every human being. The term and modern concept of social justice was coined by the Jesuit Luigi Taparelli in 1840 based on the teachings of St. Thomas Aquinas and given further exposure in 1848 by Antonio Rosmini-Serbati. The idea was elaborated by the moral theologian John A. Ryan, who initiated the concept of a living wage. Father Coughlin also used the term in his publications in the 1930s and the 1940s. The concept was further expanded upon by John Rawls and John Stuart Mill in the 1860s. The liberal political philosopher John Rawls drew on the utilitarian insights of Bentham and Mill, the social contract ideas of John Locke, and the categorical imperative ideas of Kant. His first statement of principle was made in *A Theory of Justice* where he proposed that "each person possesses an inviolability founded on justice that even the welfare of society as a whole cannot override. For this reason justice denies that the loss of freedom for some is made right by a greater good shared by others." His views are definitively restated in *Political Liberalism* where society is seen "as a fair system of co-operation over time, from one generation to the next."

The progress of human civilization has been marked by unending quest for social justice. Every society has aimed at establishing a good and just social order, though opinions have differed at different times and places about what constitutes a good and just social order. The concept of social justice is a normative concept and unavoidably involves moral judgement. As an objective of social policy it underlines the gap between what is socially desirable and the prevailing social situation at any given time.

The idea of equality is central to the concept of social justice. Though complete equality is not regarded as an attainable or even a desirable goal, extreme inequalities of income, wealth and power are not considered as compatible with a just social order. Again the ideas about the permissible degree of inequality would vary.

If the idea of equality is central to the concept of social justice, that of equality of opportunity is central to the concept of equality. Equality of opportunity is today regarded as a fundamental value in the modern world. However, scholars accept that exclusive stress on formal equality of opportunity may not lead to a socially desirable state given the initial differences in natural abilities and social circumstances (R.H. Tawney & John Rawls). Hence the principle of equality of opportunity has to be modified by the principle of redress to correct the "bias of contingencies in the direction of equality" (Rawls). The principle of redress now guides widely the social policy in various countries and is termed as 'protective discrimination' in India and 'affirmative action' in the U.S.

In a highly stratified and inegalitarian society as India is the principle of redress or protective discrimination has a special justification. The legalistic principle of equality of opportunity in the Indian context has to be subordinated to overriding consideration of social justice. Thus interpreted, the concept of social justice would mean that the social and economic disadvantages from which large sections and social groups in our country have been suffering from generations are removed through state action and that they are enabled to compete with the other well placed groups to avail the equality of opportunity in the real sense on an equal footing. This would mean raising the educational levels and income earning capacities of the socially disadvantaged groups. This would, in the Indian context, also mean that their social status is uplifted so that they can live with dignity and self-respect. A further aspect of social justice in the Indian Constitution that needs to be stressed is that the principle of equality of opportunity is not merely to be seen in an individual context, but in the context of larger social groups and communities which have been relegated to a position of subordination and deprivation for long.

Social justice is based on the concepts of human rights and equality and involves a greater degree of economic egalitarianism through progressive taxation, income redistribution, or even property redistribution. These policies aim to achieve what developmental economists refer to as more equality of opportunity than may currently exist in some societies, and to manufacture equality of outcome in cases where it is not there.

The expression 'social and economic justice' involves the concept of 'distributive justice' demanding removal of economic inequalities and rectifying the injustices resulting from dealings or transactions between unequals in the society. In this context, the concept of equality necessitates consideration. It is defined as the condition of having 'equal dignity, rank or privilege with others', as also the condition of being 'equal in power, ability, achievement or excellence'. Another definition in the lexicon implies fairness, impartiality, equality and due proportion of share. These three definitions are not consistent with each other. There is also the dichotomy of all men being unequal in power, ability and excellence. As such, a certain amount of inequality is a pre-requisite in any award of justice. Thus inequalities are natural and inevitable in all situations and these have to be redressed.

SOCIAL JUSTICE IN INDIA

A quick glance at the ancient Indian social and political thought reveals that the term 'social justice', as understood today, did not figure prominently in many of the early writings of justice-related issues. If it did figure in at all, it only embellished the charter of reforms initiated by the social reformers of the eighteenth and nineteenth centuries. Then, the social reform agenda hinged heavily upon the elimination of social evils that plagued the Indian society. Elimination of social evils concerning the status of women and the untouchables, no doubt, fell in the domain of social justice that did not cover the entire gamut of issues concerned with social justice as we are made to understand them now.

The question then is where to find the roots of the concept of social justice and the ideas associated with it? The opinion on the sources may vary, but the overwhelming response, however, remains in favour of the Constitution of India. The concept of social justice forcefully enters through Article 38 of the Constitution which says that "the State shall strive to promote the welfare of the people by securing and protecting, as effectively as it may, a social order in which justice, social, economic and political shall inform all the institutions of life".

While there is general agreement that the roots of the modern conception of social justice in India lie in the sprawling constitutional terrain, certain commentators complain that the Constitution has left the term social justice undefined. This is why, they think, the conceptual confusion prevails and the interpretational problems arise. Viewed rationally, the lament is without substance. The complainers obviously forget the fact that Constitution is neither a dictionary, nor a thesaurus, and hence, cannot define each and every key-concept it uses in the text. The Constitution is basically a political document, a testament on national ideals and aspirations. Let us also admit that definitions are more important for class-room academics than for statesmen who were assigned to draft the Constitution. Let us probe into the matter further. Our constitution-makers were well aware of the fact that there is no universally recognised single concept of justice; the concept is made of several conflicting principles, and that relative weight attached to each principle varies from one type of society to another. Varying conceptions foreclosed for them any easy option of defining the concept. Likewise, the constitution-makers did not attempt to define several other key concepts they used; for example, secularism. Being the men of letters and learning they were fully familiar with the western notions of justice, as reflected in the western social and political thought. They were well-aware of the fact that social justice is a dynamic concept that varies from society to society, system to system and culture to culture, at different points of time. Further more, they knew that the ideological differences in the conceptualisation of social justice have produced varying conceptions of social justice with little similarity and much less consensus. Precisely for this, they had their own vision of social justice commensurate to and in conformity with the given social, cultural and economic context of the country. They endeavoured to tailor the idea in a manner as to suit to the basic ethos of the Constitution, namely, socialism, secularism and democracy. Without attempting any dogmatic definition they incorporated several Articles of far-reaching significance, which, when taken together, constitute the country's social justice agenda. Without rejecting the western notions of social justice, our Constitution-makers accepted only those notions which were ideally suited to build a new social order in which justice-social, economic and political-shall enthuse and inspire all the institutions of life. They were sensitive to the demands of social justice, suitable to the elimination of social, economic and political injustices in-built in the system.

Thus social justice, constitutionally accented but left undefined, is by now a common phrase. The Constitution of India, in its Preamble, refers to justice in its various forms, i.e. social, economic and political. Further, Art. 38(1) of the Constitution directs the state to strive for "a 'social order' in which justice, social, economic and political shall inform all the institutions of the national life". As interpreted, from time to time, by experts and the law courts, the term social justice includes three aspects:

1. Removal of economic inequalities;
2. Provision of a decent standard of living to the people; and
3. Protection of the interests of the weaker sections of the society.

Part IV of the Constitution, containing Directive Principles of State Policy, includes provisions aimed at removing economic inequalities: For example, Art. 38 (2) directs the state "to strive to minimize the inequalities in income". Art. 39(c) says "the operation of the economic system should not result in the concentration of wealth and the means of production to the common detriment". The Directive Principles also recommend a decent standard of living by making provision for "adequate means of livelihood" (Art. 39), "equal pay for equal work for both men and women" (Art. 39), and "to all workers, a living wage, conditions of work ensuring a decent standard of living and full enjoyment of leisure and social and cultural opportunities" (Art. 43).

The main emphasis of social justice, however, is on the protection of the interests of the weaker sections of the society, which means, taking care of the interests of the Scheduled Castes, Scheduled Tribes, Other Backward Classes, women and children. The Constitution of India makes a number of provisions for protection of the interests of the weaker sections of the society. Art. 15(3) empowers the state to make any special provision for women and children. Art. 15(4) enables the state to make any special provision for the advancement of any socially and educationally backward classes of citizens or for the Scheduled Castes and the Scheduled Tribes. Under Art. 16(4) reservation can be made in various services and posts in favour of any backward classes of citizens. Art. 39 directs the state to prevent the misuse of children by forcing them in undertaking vocations which are not suited to their age. Art.46 directs the state to promote with special care the educational and economic interests of the people and in particular of the Scheduled Castes and the Scheduled Tribes and protect them from social injustice and all forms of exploitation. Seats are reserved for SCs and STs in Parliament and State Legislatures (Art. 330). Seats have also been reserved, by the Constitution 73rd and 74th (Amendment) Acts, in urban and rural local bodies and in favour of SCs, STs, OBCs and women. The Constitution, in Art. 335, provides for the reservation of seats for SCs and STs in services and posts at the Union and State level. Reservation in services has now been extended to OBCs also.

To give effect to the concept of social justice, as enshrined in the Constitution, a number of laws have been passed by the Central & State Governments. Further, there is a Ministry of Social Justice Empowerment at the union level and Social Welfare Departments at state levels to take up various schemes for bringing about social justice. Finally, there are a number of Boards & Commissions at the central and state levels to help people who belong to weaker sections.

AN OVERVIEW

Nearly sixty years have elapsed since the Constitution came into force. The question arises how far have we been able to achieve social justice in India? Do we still lag behind? If yes, to what extent? What more needs to be done so that we can achieve social justice as early as possible?

Nobody can question the need for uplifting the down-trodden, the weak and the impoverished both horizontally and vertically, but to make it a political issue, vying with each other the demand for expanding its net, even to the extent of including those as well who belong to the creamy layer and have enjoyed the concession twice, would only make a mockery of it. It is equally necessary that those who have enjoyed certain facilities and privileges should make room for others—following the dictum of the greatest good of the greatest number.

ENDNOTES AND REFERENCES

C.P. Barthwal, *Social Justice in India*, 1998.
Donna Riley, *Engineering and Social Justice*, 2008.
David I. Smith and Terry A., *Spirituality, Social Justice and Language Learning*, 2007.
F.A. Hayek, *The Mirage of Social Justice*, 1973.
J. Zajda and S. Majhanovich, V. Rust, *Education and Social Justice*, 2006.
John Rawls, *A Theory of Justice*, 2005.
John Rawls, *Political Liberalism*, 2003.
R.H. Tawney, *Equality*, 1931.

5

An Analysis of the Constitutional Vision of Social Justice in India

Subhash Shukla and Pradeep K. Sharma

ABSTRACT

This paper tries to make an in depth analysis of the constitutional vision of social justice in India as visualized during the Constituent Assembly Debates and as enshrined in the Preamble of the Constitution. It makes a threefold analysis as to what is the vision of social justice in the Indian Constitution; what are the means that have been employed to attain this goal and; how far the vision has been realized so far. The paper maintains that the constitutional vision of establishing social justice in India primarily involves three aspects: (i) provision of equal political and socio-economic rights in the form of Fundamental Rights and the Directive Principles of State Policy; (ii) adoption of a socio-economic model of development to attain the socialistic goal of equal opportunities for all and the reduction of the disparities between the rich and the poor and; (iii) provision of special safeguards in the Constitution and policies of positive affirmation for the disadvantaged sections of the Indian society. By way of conclusion, the paper argues that though the Indian Constitution ensures legal and procedural safeguards and substantive measures have been taken by the Indian State to establish social justice, however the biggest challenge still remains in ensuring cultural justice and as to how to establish a secular Indian identity far removed from the present caste based identity of the Indian society.

I

The Constitutional Vision

The establishment of a just society had been the mainstay of all political discourses since ancient times and same was the case with the members of the Constituent Assembly while framing the Constitution of India. The Preamble, which embodies the philosophy of the Indian Constitution, states that the people of India constitute a sovereign, democratic republic, which is socialist and secular, as incorporated by the 42nd amendment of the Constitution, and thereby secures to its citizens justice; social, economic and political; along with liberty, equality and fraternity. It has to be pointed out that priority given to the concept of justice as compared to liberty, equality and fraternity, and to social and economic justice as compared to political justice, was deliberate.[1] The order of the words indicates that the concept of social and economic justice was perhaps considered the most fundamental norm of the constitution of India.[2]

Thus, it could be said that the constitution makers envisaged a concept of social justice, which involved the establishment of an egalitarian social order where there was no discrimination among individuals on the basis of caste, religion, race, sex or place of birth and everyone enjoyed equality of status and opportunity. During the Constituent Assembly Debates, it was argued by some that these social changes were to be effected through the mechanism of political democracy and individual liberty.[3] On the other hand, other members were of the view that mere political democracy would not suffice but economic democracy was required to effect the desired social change.[4] These goals of political and economic democracy have been sought to be implemented through certain political and socio-economic rights. The political and civil rights have been guaranteed through the Fundamental Rights whereas the socio-economic rights are to be secured over a period of time through the Directive Principles of State Policy. We can say that the core of the social revolution, required to bring about the social change, lies in the Fundamental Rights and Directive Principles of State Policy, which could be termed as the conscience of the Constitution.[5] According to Granville Austin, the Directive Principles foster this social revolution by establishing the conditions necessary for its achievement.[6] These conditions were to be established by adopting a socio-economic model of development through a policy of socialism, which involved initially to establish a socialistic pattern of society and gradually it was incorporated in the Preamble of the Indian Constitution through the 42nd amendment.

Besides this, the Constitution makers have provided certain necessary safeguards by making certain provisions, which make a positive discrimination in favour of the weaker and disadvantaged sections of society, so that they could be able to avail the same opportunities as being availed by the well-off sections of the society.

Thus, the constitutional vision of establishing social justice in India involves three aspects:

(i) Provision of political and socio-economic rights in the form of Fundamental Rights and Directive Principles of State Policy respectively;

(ii) The adoption of such a model of socio-economic development which goes on to attain the goal of socialism by reducing the disparities between the rich and the poor and provides for equalization of opportunities for all; and

(iii) Provision of special safeguards and policies of positive affirmation for the disadvantaged sections of Indian society.

II

Fundamental Rights and Directive Principles of State Policy

Though the Indian Constitution in Part III guarantees certain political and civil rights to all its citizens, even then certain rights have been clearly and explicitly mentioned in it so as to secure and protect the interests of the weaker and the disadvantaged and so that they have an equal footing in society. Such rights are as follows:

(a) Though under Article 14 equality before law and equal protection of laws to all its citizens within the territory of India, Article 15(1) provides for that the State shall not discriminate against any citizen on grounds only of religion, race, caste, sex, place of birth or any of them. Under Article 15(2), it is mentioned that no citizen shall, on grounds only of religion, race, caste, sex, place of birth or any of them, be subject to any disability, liability, restriction or condition with regard to: (a) access to shops, public restaurants, hotels and places of public entertainment; or (b) the use of wells, tanks, bathing ghats, roads and places of public resort maintained wholly or partly out of State funds or dedicated to the use of the general public.

(b) Similarly under Article 16, while guaranteeing equality of opportunity for all citizens in matters relating to employment or appointment to any office under the State, it is mentioned that there shall be no discrimination against any citizen on grounds only of religion, race, caste, sex, descent, place of birth, residence of any of them, in respect of any employment or office under the State.

(c) Under Article 17, untouchability is abolished and its practice in any form is forbidden. Parliament is authorized to make a law prescribing the punishment for this offence (Article 35) and in exercise of this power, it has enacted the untouchability (offences) Act, 1955, which has been amended and renamed in 1976 as the Protection of Civil Rights Act, 1955.[7]

(d) Under Article 18, the State shall not confer any title, not being a military or academic distinction.

(e) Under Article 23, traffic in human beings and beggar and other similar forms of forced labour are prohibited and any contravention of this provision shall be an offence punishable in accordance with law.

(f) Under Article 29(2), no citizen shall be denied admission into any educational institution maintained by the state or receiving aid out of State funds on grounds only of religion, race, caste, language or any of them.

Part IV of the Constitution relates to the Directive Principles of State Policy, which are to secure the social and economic rights of the citizens, in general, by the State. These principles have been declared to be fundamental in the governance of the country and it shall be duty of the State to apply these principles in making laws (Article 37). Through these principles, the state tries to secure economic and social justice over a period of time as the economy developed and social change took place. The following Directive Principles of State Policy under the Constitution are particularly important from the point of social justice:

(a) Under Article 38(1), the State shall, in particular, strive to promote the welfare of the people by securing and protecting as effectively as it may a social order in which justice, social, economic and political, shall inform all the institutions of the national life.

(b) Under Article 39(b) and (c), the State shall direct its policy towards securing that the ownership and control of the material resources of the community are so distributed as best to subserve the common good and that the operation of the economic system does not result in the concentration of wealth and means of production to the common detriment.

(c) Under Article 39A, it is mentioned that State shall secure that the operation of the legal system promotes justice on the basis of equal opportunity.

(d) Under Article 46, there is a provision that the State shall promote with special care the educational and economic interests of the weaker sections of the people, and, in particular, of the Scheduled castes and the Scheduled Tribes, and shall protect them from social injustice and all forms of exploitation.

However, herein it has to be mentioned that the implementation of these Directive Principles of State Policy was not an easy task. In the initial years not only did it conflict with the Fundamental Rights, particularly the Right to Property, but the Supreme Court of India till 1967 took the view point that the Directive Principles have to conform and run subsidiary to the chapter on Fundamental Rights. The First Constitution Amendment Act and the Fourth Constitution Amendment did lead the Supreme Court to give some importance to the Directive Principles of State Policy. However, while developing the doctrine of harmonious construction, it reiterated that the Directive Principles of State Policy were subordinate to the Fundamental Rights.[8]

However, the 24th and 25th Constitutional Amendments in 1971 reversed the position. They not only established the supremacy of the Directive Principles vis-à-vis the Fundamental Rights, it also made laws giving effect to Article 39(b) and (c) shall be called in question in any court. Though the Supreme Court upheld the validity of the 24th and 25th Constitutional amendments in Keshvanand Bharti case[9] but it struck down the clause giving judicial immunity to the implementation of Article 39 (b) and (c) on the ground that judicial review is a basic feature of Indian Constitution which could not be altered.

The Indira Gandhi Government tried to arrest the implications of the Keshvanand Bharti case by the 42nd amendment act, whereby it was declared that there shall be no limitation on the constituent power to amend the Constitution and that the validity of any Constitutional Amendment Act shall be questioned in any court on any ground. But in the Minerva Mills case[10] the Supreme Court struck down these provisions of the 42nd Amendment Act. In this case, the Supreme Court held that both the Fundamental Rights and Directive Principles are equally important and one cannot be sacrificed for the other.

Special Safeguards and Affirmative Action

The Indian democracy, in search of both formal and substantive equality, had to address on an urgent basis the cause of the historically disadvantaged groups. Whereas the requirements of formal equality meant the equal protection of law against discrimination on morally invidious grounds, the requirements of substantive equality meant recognizing the needs of the more disadvantaged.[11] Both these commitments run parallel to in the constitution. In order to fulfill these requirements, the following provisions have been made in the Indian constitution:

(i) Though Article 15 provides for prohibition of discrimination on grounds of religion, race, caste, sex or place of birth, Article 15(4), added by the First Constitution Amendment Act in 1951, provides that nothing in the Article 15 or in clause (2) of Article 29 shall prevent the State from making any special provision for the advancement of any socially and educationally backward classes of citizens or for the Scheduled Castes and the Scheduled Tribes. Similarly, under Article 15(5), inserted by the 93rd Amendment Act, 2005, it is mentioned that nothing in Article 15 or in sub-clause (g) of clause (1) of Article 19 shall prevent the State from making any special provision, by law, for the advancement of any socially and educationally backward classes of citizens or for the Scheduled Castes or the Scheduled Tribes so far as such special provisions relate to their admission to educational institutions, whether aided or unaided by the State, other than the minority educational institutions referred to in clause (1) of Article 30.

(ii) Though the right of free movement and residence throughout the territory of India and of acquisition and disposition of property are guaranteed to every citizen under Article 19(1)(e), however special restrictions may be imposed by the State as may be required for the protection of their interests, for instance to prevent the alienation or fragmentation of their property under Article 19(5).

(iii) Under Article 330, there is a provision for reservation of seats for Scheduled Castes and Scheduled Tribes in the House of People. The number of seats reserved in any State or Union Territory for the

Scheduled Castes and Scheduled Tribes shall be in same proportion to the total number of seats allotted to the State or Union Territory in the House of the People, as the population of the Scheduled Castes in that state or union territory or the Scheduled Tribes in the State or Union Territory as the case may be, in respect of which seats are so reserved, bears to the total population of the State, or the Union Territory.

(iv) Under Article 332, there is the provision for reservation of seats for Scheduled Castes and Scheduled Tribes in the Legislative Assemblies of the States, in the same proportion as their population is to the total population of the State.

(v) Under Article 335, the claims of the members of the Scheduled Castes and the Scheduled Tribes shall be taken into consideration, consistently with the maintenance of the efficiency of the administration, in the making or appointments to services and posts in connection with the affairs of the Union or of a State. After the Eighty-second Amendment of the Constitution in 2000, it has been provided that nothing in this Article shall prevent making of any provision in favour of the SC/ST for relaxation in qualifying marks in any examination or lowering the standards of evaluation, for reservation in matters of promotion to any class or classes of services or posts in connection with the affairs of the Union or of a State.

(vi) Under Article 338, there shall be a National Commission for the Scheduled Castes and Scheduled Tribes to be appointed by the President. It shall investigate all matters relating to the safeguards provided for the Scheduled Castes and Scheduled Tribes under the Constitution and to report to the President upon the working of those safeguards and the President shall cause all such reports to be tabled before each House of the Parliament.

(vii) Under Article 339, the President may appoint at any time, after ten years of the commencement of the Constitution, a Commission to report on the administration of the Scheduled Areas and the welfare of the Scheduled Tribes in the States. The Union can also give directions to the State as to drawing up and execution of schemes specified in the direction to be essential for the welfare of Scheduled Tribes in the State.

(viii) Though Article 16 guarantees equality of opportunity in matters of public employment and prohibits discrimination on grounds only of religion, race, caste, sex, descent or place of birth in respect of any employment or office under the State; however, special provisions have been made for the socially and educationally backward classes and Scheduled Castes and Scheduled Tribes. While the Constitution of India has abolished representation on communal lines, it has included safeguards for the advancement of the backward classes among the residents of India (irrespective of their religious affiliations), so that the country may be ensured of an all-round development and they fulfill the assurance of social justice held out by the Preamble of the Constitution.[12] Under Article 16(4), it has been provided that nothing in this Article shall prevent the State from making any provision for the reservation of appointments in favour of any backward classes of citizens, which in the opinion of the State, is not adequately represented in the services under the State.

The Constitution does not define backward classes in India. However, in Article 340 of the Constitution, it is mentioned that a Commission can be appointed to investigate the conditions of backward classes, which could propose measures to be taken by Central or State Governments in order to improve their condition. Such a Commission was appointed in 1953 under the chairmanship of Kaka Saheb Kalelkar. This Commission was to suggest the following:[13]

(a) to determine the tests by which any particular class or group of people can be called backward,
(b) to prepare a list of such backward communities for the whole of India; and
(c) to examine the difficulties of backward classes and to recommend steps to be taken for their amelioration. Though this Commission submitted its report in 1955, but the tests recommended appeared to be vague and wide to be of much practical value, hence the State Governments were authorized to give assistance to the backward classes according to the lists prepared by themselves.

The second Commission appointed under the chairmanship of B.P. Mandal submitted its report in 1980. This report, on the basis of 1931 census, identified 3743 castes as backward. Using a controversial toolkit of caste backwardness, it favoured proportional equality between those that it considered as backward and the rest that were fortunate enough to be forward.[14] Since the Supreme Court in the *Balaji v. State of Mysore* case (1963),[15] had fixed an upper ceiling of 50 per cent as the limit on reservations, therefore it recommended 27 per cent of reservation for OBCs. The Mandal Report made a tripartite distinction between equality of opportunity, and equality of treatment and equality of results, following the work of Herbert J. Gans.[16] Accordingly, it says that Article 16(1) is not an egalitarian principle, but it is in fact a libertarian principle, as it does not give due consideration to the needs of the disadvantage. Similarly, equality of treatment by its implication of uniformity of justice doesn't differentiate between the advantaged and disadvantaged. Hence, the only true egalitarian ideal that ensures justice to the disadvantaged, according to this report, is the idea of equality of results.

The V.P. Singh Government accepted the recommendations of the Mandal Commission Report in 1990. This raised a political storm countrywide. This led to the challenging of the Government decision of givng 27 per cent reservation to the OBCs in the Supreme Court as unconstitutional. However, in the *Indira Sawhney v. Union of India* Case (1992),[17] Supreme Court set aside the challenge and upheld the recommendations of the Mandal Commission Report for 27 per cent reservation in government jobs to the OBCs (other backward classes). Thereafter, 27 per cent reservation for OBCs in Government jobs has been implemented since 1993.

III

By Way of Conclusion

The Indian Constitution makers had envisaged a social revolution that would establish a new and just social order, which would be free from casteist discrimination so that every citizen of India could be able to lead a life of respect and dignity and could enjoy equal opportunities for their moral and material development.

For this provisions were made in the form of Fundamental Rights and Directive Principles of State Policy with the objective of ensuring both formal and substantive equality. It has to be said that with the provisions of equal rights to all its citizens it has ensured formal equality before law and equal protection of law for them. Herein, special mention has to be made about the steps taken to abolish untouchability. The passing of the Untouchability (Offences) Act, 1955 made preaching and practicing untouchability an offence and was applicable to the practice of untouchability in public places. It is radical in the sense that it treats caste presumptions as the basis for filing First Information Reports.[18] On the other hand, the 1989 Act, which is called the SC/ST Prevention of Atrocities Act, is more comprehensive and stringent. It does not limit itself to the human rights; it in fact goes beyond this and includes in its framework the issue of humiliation as crime. Thus, insulting anyone, outraging the modesty of women and scavenging has been treated as serious offence. Though the strict legal provisions have made the upper castes conscious about the penalties involved about practicing of untouchability, however these constitutional provisions tend to achieve only a limited success in extracting upper caste compliance with cultural justice. This is because the upper castes have failed to take the moral lead in offering unconditional recognition to those social groups deprived of this recognition. But it is the Dalit assertion for self respect wherein they have taken the lead and forced the Central and State Governments to implement these constitutional provisions in order to ensure cultural justice to them and force the upper castes to acknowledge their comparative worth.[19]

The Constitution while ensuring formal social equality through the prevention of discrimination on the grounds of caste, sex, religion, race or place of birth, it tries to ensure socio-economic equality by taking into account the weaker position of the disadvantaged sections of the society and providing for special safeguards in terms of public employment. Provisions of 22.5 per cent reservation for SC/ST in government jobs and 27 per cent reservation for the Other Backward Classes has gone a long way in the economic and social empowerment of the disadvantaged sections of the society. However, it has to be said that now the time has come to review the fact whether they are benefiting a particular elite class within these disadvantaged sections. The implementation of the 'creamy layer' in reservation of jobs for OBC was a necessary step to ensure that the benefits of the reservation policy become score board based. It is also time to reflect upon such a 'creamy layer' concept among the SC and ST so that it benefits the ordinary SC/ST of the villages of this country and not the wards of bureaucrats or powerful politicians who have availed the benefits for more than two generations; or to a particular tribe like the Meenas of Rajasthan. Despite their disadvantaged socio-cultural position, it is high time that we evolve a 'creamy layer' concept in reservation in jobs for SC/STs if we have to make the benefits more inclusive within the SCs and STs itself. Then, we have to ask the question as to what should be the limits of reservation or where should the process of reservation see the beginning of its end. Probably, it is high time that policies are so evolved that the disadvantaged sections are provided such socio-economic opportunities that they can compete with the best without requiring the protective discrimination of reservation.

Furthermore, it has to be mentioned that the goal of the Constitution was to establish an egalitarian order where there was no distinction between higher and lower castes or wherein the discrimination present in the Indian society against certain lower castes got abolished so that they could lead a life of respect and dignity along with the upper castes. Initially, Jawaharlal Nehru acknowledged the pernicious influence of the caste system. He regretted the divisive effect of the social structure, based on caste, at a time when he wanted to build a strong and united India, and was not so much concerned about the need to fight caste as a priority objective for social change. For him, economic modernization would have eventually eradicated caste feelings. However, there were sections that argued that caste was the factor in determining social and educational backwardness. According to B.R. Ambedkar, all these infinite divisions that had grown up in our social life have been because of the caste system or caste religious divisions etc.[20] Therefore, he made it clear that, for him, what were called backward classes were 'nothing else but a collection of certain castes.'[21]

Such unique social system requires a critical inquiry and reconsideration of caste as an analytical category that played and continues to play an important role in the functioning of the Indian democracy and thereby the Indian polity. Scholars like Rajni Kothari and D.L. Sheth view caste and its relationship with politics with more integrated and sociological sense where they explained that caste has, at least, three dimensions: secularization of politics (in terms of governmental aspects like caste councils and so on and that of political aspects like inter caste authority and alignment), differentiation and integration dimension and consciousness dimension. As explained by Rajani Kothari, it is not politics that gets caste-ridden, it is caste that gets politicized.

There are other scholars like M.N. Srinivas and Sathyamurthy who analysed caste in sociological terms like that of Sanskritisation and Westernisation, where caste is invoked for achieving higher status in the highly rigid varna system. The course of the 20th century in India also witnessed strong Dalit movements that envision an egalitarian society ensuring dignity and respect of all human beings. Though caste identity was seen as a category for integration and consciousness, Dalits movement aims always for a society based on equity and dignity. Recently, in North India, caste has emerged in its various new forms: a descriptive category, identity category and mobilisational instrument, which has traditionally been there in the Indian society, but has assumed new forms in the democratic polity. With OBC agitations spreading all over the North India amidst economic liberalization package, the role of caste in the coming decades is yet to be properly analysed. In this regard, it would be appropriate to mention M.N. Panini who established that the country today stands at the crossroads of development and the path of liberalization opens up a genuine possibility of breaking the strangle hold of caste over the economy. Sudha Pai also emphasizes upon the fact that India's global polity and economy must create new opportunities and better avenues for the deprived so as to achieve the constitutional vision of social justice based upon equality and liberty.

Endnotes and References

1. Bipin Chandra, Mridula Mukherjee, Aditya Mukherjee, India since Independence, Penguin Books, New Delhi, 2008, p. 54.
2. Subhash C. Kahsyap, 'The Framing of the Constitution and the Process of Institution Building;' in B.N. Pande (ed.), Centenary History of the Indian National Congress, Vol. IV (1947-64), Vikas Publications,New Delhi, p. 50.
3. M.R. Masani, Constituent Assembly Debates, Vol. I, Lok Sabha Secretariat, New Delhi, 1999, pp. 92-93.
4. B.R. Ambedkar, Constituent Assembly Debates, Vol. I, pp. 99-100.
5. Granville Austin, The Indian Constitution :Cornerstone of a Nation , Oxford University Press, New Delhi, 1966 p. 50.
6. Ibid., pp. 50-52.
7. D.D.Basu, Introduction to the Constitution of India, Wadhawa and Co. Nagpur, 2002, p. 96.
8. Subhash Shukla, Issues in Indian Polity, Anamika Publishers, New Delhi, 2008, p. 19.
9. AIR 1973, S.C. 1461.
10. AIR, 1980, S.C. 1789.
11. Ashok Acharya, Affirmative Action For Disadvantaged Groups : A Cross Constitutional Study of India and the U.S., in Rajiv Bhargave (ed.), Politics and Ethics of the Indian Constitution, Oxford University Press, New Delhi, 2008, p. 269.
12. n. 8, p. 392.
13. Ibid., p. 394.
14. n, 19, p. 283.

15. Balaji V. State of Mysore, A. 1963 S.C. 649.
16. n. 19, pp. 283-284.
17. Indira Sawhney v. Union of India, (1992) Supp. (3) S.C.C. 217.
18. Gopal Guru, Constitution Justice : Positional and Cultural, in Rajiv Bhargava (ed.), op. cit., p. 236.
19. Ibid., pp. 236-237.
20. Parliamentary Debates, Vol. xii, 13 (Part–II), column 9616.
21. Ibid., col. 90006.

6

Social Justice and Multiculturalism: The Indian Experience

Nandini Basistha and Trivikram Tiwari

If one asks to all what is the most serious problem of this era, what will be the answer? In Indian perspective, the answer may be 'separatism'. From fourteen in 1950, India is now a Union of twenty-eight states. Still the autonomy and statehood demands are not decreasing but increasing day by day and, thus, making the unity of India at stake. Most of the time, the demand of separation arise out of suppression or, in other words, social injustice, which ultimately pose serious threat to the multicultural notion of Indian identity. The political demands for self-determination are centrally linked to the idea of a distinct identity of an ethnic group. Behind identity politics there is always some hidden issue of justice. In this paper, we will try to establish a co-relation between multiculturalism and social justice in Indian perspective. Our focus will be on:

- Notion of Multiculturalism;
- Multiculturalism in India in Past;
- Nehruvian Idea of Assimilation;
- Movements for Separation;
- Justice in the Indian Context;
- Guarantee on 'Multiculturalism' and 'Justice' in Indian Constitution;
- Hiccups in Implementation;
- How to Attain Justice in the Indian Multicultural Scenario.

Recent decades have witnessed an enormous increase in the magnitude of state versus community conflict.[1] To ascertain their cultural rights in the political arena, different communities are waging struggle against the state authority. In spite of the serious efforts to safeguard freedom and liberty to the minorities in maintaining their cultural identity, Indian government fails to control this separatist mentality of the communities. Most of the time, the demand of separation arise out of suppression or, in other words, social injustice, which ultimately pose serious threat to the multicultural notion of Indian identity. In the following paragraphs, we will try to discuss the relationship between social justice and multiculturalism in Indian perspective.

One can ask why we are using the term 'multiculturalism' instead of 'pluralism'. According to Bhikhu Parekh, a multiculturalist perspective is composed of the creative interplay of three important and complementary insights—namely the cultural embeddedness of human beings, the inescapability and desirability of cultural plurality, and the plural and multicultural constitution of each culture.[2] While the term 'multiculturalism' originated in Sweden in 1957, Canada was the first country to recognize that multiculturalism was integral to its national identity and adopted it as its national policy in 1960.[3] But, actually, all societies of today are culturally heterogeneous in different degrees for some forces as industrialisation, the easy mobility of goods and people, and the global reach of the multinational media, members of even the most traditional and isolated societies are daily exposed to new ways of life and thought.[4] However, in some societies cultural heterogeneity is not a result of contingent external influences but communally grounded. These societies include several more or less well-organised cultural communities, each held together by a distinct body of ideas concerning the best ways to organise significant social relations and lead individual and collective lives. Such societies are rightly called 'multicultural'.

Being the second most populous country with social and cultural diversity multiculturalism is obvious in India. It has prevailed here through tolerance in different spheres of culture, like religion, language, race, ethnicity and so on. Unlike in the West, where it is virtually equated with atheism, multiculturalism in India is a celebration of religions not their denial. The edicts of Ashoka, himself a convert from Hinduism to Buddhism in the third century B.C.E., promulgate a norm of mutual respect and toleration.[5] Even the Mughal emperors observed Diwali and Nauroz. Until the early twentieth century, Hindus routinely took part in the Mohuram processions. To emphasize this aspect Gandhi had passages read from the holy books of all the major religions before his prayer meetings. When the Zoroastrians of Persia felt that their religion was in danger from the invading Muslims, where else could they go but to India! The Tibetans felt similarly in their homeland, they chose India.

Although the term 'multiculturalism' is never used in the Indian constitution, India has emerged as a model of pluralism and secular democracy in the post-colonial world. Nehru was not, however, opposed to assimilation because without it a nation could never be built, particularly in a society like India.[6] But his idea of assimilation[7] was not a forced or externally imposed one.[8] He said that such an assimilation process would develop of its own accord through education and contacts, without any special effort.[9] In such a process, he emphasized, every care should be taken to retain the individuality of cultures, much of which was, for him, retainable. Further clarifying his ideas on this issue, he said that people living in India should feel that they have perfect freedom to live their own lives according to their wishes and genius, and that India should signify for them a protecting as well as a liberating force. He pointed out that the policy of the state was not to interfere with tribal affairs but to offer the largest measure of autonomy. He also attached great importance to the valuable customs of ethnic groups. Nehru believed that the legal guarantee of equality of citizenship regardless of religion, caste, creed or other social attributes would render communalism obsolete.[10] Nehru's approach to the problem of the management of ethnic conflicts, and to the issue of nation- and state-building, thus was at once democratic and multicultural.

But, in spite of the efforts of national integration we see statehood demands for ascertaining different cultural identities - like language, religion, or ethnicity. Starting from the creation of Andhra Pradesh in 1956 on the basis of Telegu language, we see an array of new states was established on the linguistic and ethno-regional grounds. Following this trend, the Union of India is now a federation of twenty-eight states in place of fourteen states in the 1950. Even now there are ongoing struggle prevails in different places, like Harit Pradesh in Western Uttar Pradesh, Vindhyachal in Madhya Pradesh, Telengana in Andhra Pradesh, Vidarbha in Maharashtra, Kodagu in Karnataka, Gorkhaland and Kamtapuri in West Bengal, and Bodoland in Assam. Most of the political demands for self-determination are centrally linked to the idea of a distinct identity of an ethnic group. Identity politics will always be bound by differences; but it is also important to look at the broader aspect of democratic setup beyond the realm of identity politics. While the state has its rules, statutes and the Constitution as a means of guaranteeing justice, we are forced to perpetrate a sense of identity and tell others to do what they want to, within that. They seek justice within it, but basically that means beyond it. This inexhaustibility of justice is a historical product. So, there is no denying that behind identity politics there is always some hidden issue of justice.

The discussion on marginality producing pleas for justice led to following observation on the contested idea of justice.[11] Will Kymlicka also advocates for a liberal framework for the just treatment of minority groups.[12] Now the question is what is justice? Aristotle describes justice as treating all equal things equal and all unequal things unequal. Following this dictum, the post-traditional democratic theorists said that all humans have equal value and should therefore be treated as equals. But, according to John Rawls, justice is about the way the major social institutions distribute fundamental rights and duties and determine the division of advantages from social cooperation.[13] Thus, negating the utilitarian concept of 'the greatest happiness for greatest number', Rawls has preached the idea of 'greatest benefit to the least-advantaged members of society'. But criticizing Rawls' theory of justice, Amartya Sen argued in his book, 'The Idea of Justice', that social justice should not be evaluated in binary terms, as either achieved or not.[14] Rather, he claims that justice should be understood as existing to a matter of degree, and should correspondingly be evaluated along a continuum.[15] Furthermore, he argues that we do not need a fully-established abstract ideal of justice to evaluate the fairness of different institutions. He claims that we can meaningfully compare the level of justice in two institutions without positing an ideal, transcendental idea of justice. He names the opposite position institutional transcendentalism. Speaking on the Indian context of justice, Justice K. Subba Rao, a former Chief Justice of India identified, 'In its larger sense it seeks to remove the imbalance in the political, social and economic life of the people. As the three activities are interconnected, there cannot be social justice unless the society progresses in all directions.[16] Therefore, social justice generally refers to the idea of creating an egalitarian society or institution that is based on the principles of equality and solidarity, that understands and values *human rights*, and that recognizes the dignity of every human being.

The Indian Constitution which is the source of many state policies can be said to be a basic multicultural document, in the sense of providing for political and institutional measures for the recognition and accommodation of the country's diversity.[17] Moreover, Dr. B.R. Ambedkar recognizes 'liberty, equality, and fraternity' as the 'principles of justice'.[18] Mahatma Gandhi advocated for the welfare of the untouchables and tribal of India. Following the dictum of these two father-figures, it is written in the Preamble of Indian Constitution that, 'WE, THE PEOPLE OF INDIA, having solemnly resolved to secure to all its citizens: JUSTICE, social, economic and political; LIBERTY of thought, expression, belief, faith and worship; EQUALITY of status and of opportunity; and to promote among them all.'[19] Indian constitution- makers tried to incorporate idea of justice and multiculturalism in different articles: 'The State shall not deny to any person equality before the law or the equal protection of the laws within the territory of India' (Article 14); 'The State shall not discriminate against any citizen on grounds only of religion, race, caste, sex, place of birth or any of them' [Article 15(1)]; 'There shall be equality of opportunity for all citizens in matters relating to employment or appointment to any office under the State' [Article 16(1)]; 'Subject to public order, morality and health and to the other provisions of this Part, all persons are equally entitled to freedom of conscience and the right freely to profess, practice and propagate religion'[Article 25(1)]; 'Any section of the citizens residing in the territory of India or any part thereof having a distinct language, script or culture of its own shall have the right to conserve the same'[Article 29(1)].[20] The aforesaid provisions are not merely constitutional. The executive has also established elaborate enforcement mechanisms. The National Commission for Minorities Act (1992) was passed by parliament in 1992 to monitor the working of the constitutional safeguards in union and state laws. The alertness of the constitution to this question is beyond doubt. It not only provides for the protection of minority interests, but seeks to ensure that individuals belonging to minorities do not suffer from discrimination.[21]

In spite of this genuine notion of Indian policy-makers, we see hiccups in the implementation of a just-multicultural society in India. National ruling parties sought to promote economic development within the framework of an elite-dominated representative democracy. They have taken the policy of socialism, abolition of traditional privileges, reform and reservation of certain rights of the Scheduled Castes and Schedule Tribes for attaining social justice and economic equality. But Cultural majoritarianism creates dissatisfaction among groups. The upper caste Hindu culture has been presented in deities, icons, rituals, folklore and religious symbols as representative of mainstream modern India. Even sometimes the ruling party tries to console the major minority group, like Muslims, but not the minor minority groups. Thus the gods and customs of Sudras, Dalits and Tribes are marginalized, and the cultural integrity of these groups is pushed further into the background. Unjust social structure and social relation creates disgruntlement amongst people, which ultimately unite them to start identity politics.

Thus, the reality of multiculturalism in India not only challenges the ideology of the unitary nation-state, but also raises problems for the concept of majoritarian democratic rule by putting demands for group-diffenciated rights on the political agenda.[22] The real meaning of democracy was located in reversing the discrimination and cultural marginalization that groups had suffered in Indian society. But the assumption that the pursuit of social justice requires the creation of a more egalitarian society has been challenged by the new political-economic realities. Pluralism becomes a fact of life, and so is cultural conflict. But there cannot be democracy if any section of the society is discriminated on the basis of religion and inequality.

For India the problem is how does the modern state deal with indigenous multiculturalism within one culture in terms of concepts and perceptions.[23] Since most Indians define themselves as both individuals and members of particular communities and demand both individual and collective rights, there is no reason either why the Indian state should not have both liberal or non-liberal features and reflect its citizens' dual political identity. Today, we need to think more clearly about long-term goals. We need to think about the enduring conflicts that arise in multination states, about the institutions that can manage those conflicts in a peaceful manner and about the underlying assumptions and beliefs that allow citizens to debate them in a free and democratic way.[24] So, when different communities have different needs and are not alike in relevant respects, it is unjust to insist on treating them alike. Like Quebec, Kashmir has a distinct history, identity, tradition and so on, and needs powers not demanded by or necessary for other Indian states, this is equally true of the Punjab with its distinct Sikh identity, and the North-Eastern states with their tribal identities. Muslims, Christians, Parsis and other national minorities have their distinct ways of life, and a common civil code either cannot be easily out of their different systems of personal laws or runs the risk of enshrining the views of the powerful Hindu majority. Since the state cannot remain indifferent to the inequities of some of these laws and needs to insist on certain basic principles of justice, the only just and practicable course of action is to aim a unified rather than a uniform civil code. Such a code lays down common principles of gender equality, individual liberty and social justice and leaves the minorities free to follow their suitably revised personal law. Following to Bhikhu Parekh, we can say, 'India is not a narrow band of cultural nationalism. India is nothing if it is not an open society.'[25] For securing multicultural identity of India we have to take not the way of coercion but giving proper space to flourish and make India a safe haven of all cultures. Although there may be differences in practices, castes and tribes share concepts and perceptions that are fundamental to the Indian knowledge system, we have to establish a 'just society'.

Endnotes and References

1. 'Indo-Myanmar Cross-border Insurgency', by Nandini Basistha, in *'Asteriskos, Journal of International & Peace Studies'*, ISSN 1886-5860, 5/6/2008, p. 151.
2. 'What is multiculturalism?', by Bhikhu Parekh, retrieved from http://www.india-seminar.com/1999/484/484%20parekh.htm
3. 'Multiculturalism', retrieved from 'EconomistSubscriptions.com'
4. 'A Commitment to Cultural Pluralism', by Bhikhu Parekh, retrieved from http://www.krachtvancultuur.nl/uk/archive/commentary/parekh.html
5. 'Frontiers of Justice', by Martha C. Nussbaum, Oxford University Press, New York, 2007, p. 303
6. 'Multiculturalism in Contemporary India', by Harihar Bhattacharyya, in the International Journal on Multicultural Societies (IJMS), Vol. 5, No. 2, 2003, p. 156
7. Nehru had used the word 'assimilation' in the sense of 'integration' in his speeches. We know in present both the words have different connotations but we still used the speech in original form.
8. Ibid., p. 156
9. Ibid., p. 156
10. 'Social Cleavages, Multiculturalism and Emerging Space for State in India under Globalization Regime', by Dr Sarojini Mishra , Dr Nirod Palai, Dr Kumar Das, presented in the International Economic History Congress, Session 22, held at Helsinki, August 2006, p. 7.
11. 'Injustice invites Insurgency: Story of Rajbangshis', by Nandini Basistha, from the book 'Social Justice, Politics and Anomie', ed. by Prof. Bhawani Singh, Gatam Book Company, Jaipur, 2010, p. 111.
12. 'Will Kymlicka', retrieved from http://en.wikipedia.org/wiki/Will_Kymlicka
13. 'A Theory of Justice', by John Rawls, Oxford: Clarendon Press, 1971, p. 7, quoted in the essay 'Class, Democracy and Conceptions of Justice in India', by Vidhu Verma, from the book, 'Justice Political, Social, Juridical', eds. Rajeev Bhargava et. al., p. 257.
14. 'The Idea of Justice', by Amartya Sen, Allen Lane & Harvard University Press, 2009, retrieved from http://en.wikipedia.org/wiki/The_Idea_of_Justice
15. Ibid.
16. 'Social Justice and the Social Process in India', edited by N.R. Madhava Menon, Indian Academy of Social Sciences, India, 1988, p. viii.
17. Ibid. p. 3.
18. 'Annihilation of Caste with a Reply to Mahatma Gandhi', in Dr, Babasaheb Ambedkar: Writings and Speeches, Vol. 1, compiled by Vasant Moon, Bombay: Education Department, Government of Maharashtra, 1989, p. 57.

19. The Constitution of India (As modified up to the 1st December, 2007), Government of India, Ministry of Law and Justice, p. 1.
20. Ibid., pp. 6-15.
21. Bhattacharyya, *op. cit.*, p. 159.
22. 'Democracy and the Limits of Minority Rights', by Nalini Rajan, Sage Publications, New Delhi, 2002, p. 118.
23. 'Multiculturalism as a Modern and an Indigenous Concept in India', by Jan Brouwer, from the book, 'Mapping Multiculturalism', ed, by Kushal Deb, Rawat Publications, Jaipur and New Delhi, 2002, p. 290.
24. *Multiculturalism and Minority Rights: West and East*, by Will Kymlicka, retrieved from www.ecmi.de/jemie/download/Focus4-2002_Kymlicka.pdf
25. Quoted in the essay, ' India's Unity Originates from Diversity', written by Soumi Das, from the journal, 'West Bengal', December 2006, p. 22.

7

Constitutional Provision and Social Reality: Perspective of Child Labour

Santwana Pandey

Child Labour is a severe problem in India and world wide. No country claims to be free from child labour. According to the International Labour Organization (ILO) a new generation of children is being deprived of the chance to take their rightful place in the society and economy of the 21st Century. The ILO has proposed that 'child labour' will disappear in a decade. But in reality the situation is worsening. One in eight children in the world is exposed to the worst forms of child labour which endanger children's physical, mental health and moral well being. Our constitution provides the regulations against child labour but in society you will find everywhere flouting of such provision. It is not sufficient only to make legislations a remedy of any social problem. We will have to create the social circumstances and environment accordingly. The socio-economic conditions of the common man should be such that they send their children to school for education and development in a healthy environment and not to any hazardous workplace.

INTRODUCTION

Child labour keeps children out of school and is a major barrier to development. The children under the age of fourteen in India constitutes than the entire population of the United States. The great challenge before the India state is to provide nutrition, education and health care to these children. Children under the age of fourteen constitute around 3.6 per cent of the total labour force in India. Of these children, nine out of every ten work in their own rural family settings. Nearly 85 per cent are engaged in traditional agricultural activities. Less than 9 per cent work in manufacturing, services and repairs.

In the present study we are going to discuss this crucial problem of child labour in the wake of current scenario. We will discuss what the constitutional provisions and legislations are and how much they have been successful in achieving their goal. The whole paper is divided into three sections. In the first section we will discuss what provision our constitution provides regarding child labour in India and what the international standards like International Labour Organization and UNICEF are. The second section clears the picture about the social practices in the promotion of child labour in every corner of the world and the third section discusses the inefficiency of the government and state as well in eradicating this stigma from the society. In the concluding section, we will discuss how we can get rid of such evil practices to make our world really beautiful place to live in.

CHILD LABOUR STUDY

According to the Indian census of 1991, there are 11.28 million working children under the age of fourteen years in India. Over 85 per cent of this child labour is in the country's rural areas, working in agricultural activities such as farming, livestock rearing, forestry and fisheries. There is a three dimensional process of child labour: The Child, The Employer and Child's family. So there is an urgent need to take steps from all these three angles altogether.

The ILO defines 'child labour' as "work that deprives children of their childhood and their dignity, which hampers their access to education and the acquisition of skills, and which is performed under deplorable conditions harmful to their health and their development." In the initial years, MVF volunteers taught children in bridge camps apart from mobilizing the community to send their children to school. The MVF strategy is not just to push for the right of the child to get equal quality education, but also to ensure that there is a consensus on this issue amongst all key stakeholders.[1]

According to a recent UN report, the problem of child labour in agriculture is extremely acute. According to experts, "... some 70 per cent of the estimated 218 million world total of child labourers are employed in agriculture, and of these 132 million are between the ages of 5 and 14." There are some other heart rending figures as follows:

- More than 75 per cent of working children aged 10-14 are female.
- More than 80 per cent of the working children are between 10 and 14 years of age.
- More than 70 per cent were unpaid family workers, working in a family business.
- Of those children working for wages, between 80-90 per cent are engaged in sales and service activities and a very small percentage in farming activities.
- All enterprises which employed young persons are privately owned, with the majority in the services sector.

WHAT DOES THE CONSTITUTION AND LEGISLATION SAY?

The Indian Constitution has consciously incorporated provisions to secure compulsory universal elementary education as well as labour protection for children. Labour Commissions in India have gone into the problems of child labour and have made extensive recommendations. The Constitution of India in Article 39 of the Directive Principles of State Policy pledges that "the State shall, in particular, direct its policy towards securing ... that the health and strength of workers, men and women, and the tender age of children are not abused, and that citizens are not forced by economic necessity to enter avocations unsuited to their age or strength, that children are given opportunities and facilities to develop in a healthy manner, and in conditions of freedom and dignity, and that childhood and youth are protected against exploitation, and against moral and material abandonment."

The Child Labour (Prohibition and Regulation) Act, 1986: The Act prohibits the employment of children below the age of 14 years in 16 occupations and 65 processes that are hazardous to the children's lives and health. These occupations and processes are listed in the Schedule to the Act. In October 2006, the Government has included children working in the domestic sector as well as roadside eateries and motels under the prohibited list of hazardous occupations. More recently, in September 2008 diving as well as process involving excessive heat (e.g. working near a furnace) and cold; mechanical fishing; food processing; beverage industry; timber handling and loading; mechanical lumbering; warehousing; and processes involving exposure to free silica such as slate, pencil industry, stone grinding, slate stone mining, stone quarries as well as the agate industry were added to the list of prohibited occupations and processes;

The Factories Act, 1948: The Act prohibits the employment of children below the age of 14 years. An adolescent aged between 15 and 18 years can be employed in a factory only if he obtains a certificate of fitness from an authorized medical doctor. The Act also prescribes four and a half hours of work per day for children aged between 14 and 18 years and prohibits their working during night hours.

The Mines Act, 1952: The Act prohibits the employment of children below 18 years of age in a mine. Further, it states that apprentices above 16 may be allowed to work under proper supervision in a mine.

The Juvenile Justice (Care and Protection) of Children Act, 2000: This Act was last amended in 2002 in conformity with the UN Convention on the Rights of the Child covers young persons below 18 years of age. Section 26 of this Act deals with the Exploitation of a Juvenile or Child Employee, and provides in relevant part, that whoever procures a juvenile or the child for the purpose of any hazardous employment and keeps him in bondage and withholds his earnings or uses such earning for his own purposes shall be punishable with imprisonment for a term which may extend to three years and shall also be liable for fine. In some States, including Karnataka and

Maharashtra, this provision has been used effectively to bring to book many child labour employers who are otherwise not covered by any other law and to give relief and rehabilitation benefits to a large number of children.

The Minimum Wages Act, 1948: Prescribes minimum wages for all employees i n all estabilishments or to those working at home in certain sectors specified in the schedule of the Act. Central and State Governments can revise minimum wages specified in the schedule. Some consider this Act as an effective instrument to combat child labour in that it is being used in some States (such as Andhra Pradesh) as the basis on which to prosecute employers who are employing children and paying them lower wages.

The Right of Children to Free and Compulsory Education Act, 2009: Provides for free and compulsory education to all children aged 6 to 14 years. This legislation also envisages that 25 per cent of seats in every private school should be allocated for children from disadvantaged groups including differently abled children.

The Child Labour (Prohibition & Regulation) Act 1986 of India was the culmination of efforts and ideas that emerged from the deliberations and recommendations of various committees on child labour. Significant among them are the National Commission on Labour (1966-69), Gurupadaswamy Committee on Child Labour (1979), and the Sanat Mehta Committee (1984).

As a follow-up of this commitment, and being a party to the UN Declaration on the Rights of the Child 1959, India adopted the National Policy on Children in 1974. The policy reaffirmed the constitutional provisions and stated that "it shall be the policy of the State to provide adequate services to children, both before and after birth and through the period of growth to ensure their full physical, mental and social development. The State shall progressively increase the scope of such services so that within a reasonable time all children in the country enjoy optimum conditions for their balanced growth."

Under Section 5 of the Child Labour (P&R) Act 1986, the Government of India is empowered to constitute a Child Labour Technical Advisory Committee for the purpose of addition of occupation and processes in the Schedule to the Act. The Committee consists of a Chairman and members not exceeding ten. The Committee has been reconstituted on February 5, 1996 under the chairmanship of Director General of Indian Council of Medical Research.

It should also be mentioned that India is second to none in its commitment to and in the upholding of the core international labour standards such as freedom of association, collective bargaining, non-discrimination, etc. India is signatory to a record 36 ILO labour conventions. The Child Labour (Prohibition & Regulation) Act, 1986 of India prohibits the employment of children below the age of 14 in factories, mines and in other forms of hazardous employment, and regulates the working conditions of children in other employment. India has announced a National Policy of Child Labour as early as 1987, and was probably the first among the developing countries to have such a progressive policy. Through a notification dated May 26, 1993, the working conditions of children have been regulated in all employment not prohibited under the Child Labour (Prohibition and Regulation) Act. Further, following up on a preliminary notification issued on October 5, 1993, the government has also prohibited employment of children in occupations such as abattoirs/slaughter houses, printing, cashew de-scaling and processing, and soldering.

Farmers also recruit children because they can make them work longer hours. Children are easier to control and can be cajoled with inexpensive treats. Children work uncomplainingly and are not aware of the hazardous conditions they are working in. They are unaware of the high quantities of pesticides used in cottonseed cultivation. According to Venkateswarulu and Lucia Da Corta, "A new system of employing female children as 'bonded labourers" has come into practice in recent years in ... rural South India. ... Female children are employed on long-term contract basis in return for loans advanced to their parents by local seed producers who have agreements with the national and multinational seed companies."[2]

The authors estimate that there are nearly 400,000 female children in the age group of 7 to 14 years who are employed in the cottonseed fields. Out of these, 250,000 are employed in the state of Andhra Pradesh. This figure is greater than the total number of children working in the so-called 'hazardous' industries sector such as carpet-weaving, glass bangles, diamond polishing, gem polishing and limestone put together. An interesting point being made by the authors is that while child labour does not exceed 25 per cent in any of the industrial sectors, child labour in the cotton seed production accounts for 90 per cent of the labour force.[3]

Hybrid seeds are produced through cross-pollination, which has to be done manually. Each individual flower bud has to be emasculated and pollinated by hand by a large labour force. Cross-pollination requires 90 per cent of the total labour days employed and 45 per cent of the capital investment. According to the authors, "It is estimated that, while nearly 2,200 labour days are required for cultivation of one acre hybrid cottonseed crop, cross pollination work itself accounts for nearly 2000 labour days."[4]

SUPREME COURT DIRECTIONS ON CHILD LABOUR

The Supreme Court of India, in its judgement dated 10th December, 1996 in Writ Petition (Civil) Number 465/1986, has given certain directions regarding the manner in which children working in the hazardous occupations are to be withdrawn from work and rehabilitated, and the manner in which the working conditions of children working in non-hazardous occupations are to be regulated and improved. The judgement of the Supreme Court envisages:

(a) Simultaneous action in all districts of the country;

(b) Survey for identification of working children (to be completed by June 10, 1997)
(c) Withdrawal of children working in hazardous industries and ensuring their education in appropriate institutions;
(d) Contribution of Rs.20,000 per child to be paid by the offending employers of children to a welfare fund to be established for this purpose;
(e) Employment to one adult member of the family of the child so withdrawn from work, and if that is not possible a contribution of Rs.5000 to the welfare fund to be made by the State Government;
(f) Financial assistance to the families of the children so withdrawn to be paid out of the interest earnings on the corpus of Rs.20,000/ 25,000.00 deposited in the welfare fund as long as the child is actually sent to the schools;
(g) Regulating hours of work for children working in non-hazardous occupations so that their working hours do not exceed six hours per day and education for at least two hours is ensured. The entire expenditure on education is to be borne by the concerned employer;
(h) Planning and preparedness on the part of Central and State Governments in terms of strengthening of the existing administrative/ regulatory/enforcement frame-work (covering cost of additional manpower, training, mobility, computerization etc.) implying additional requirement of funds.

In the event of any child labour being found employed in any such process, simultaneous action would be taken to recover an amount of Rs. 20,000/from the offending employer.

The UN Convention on the Rights of Children (CRC) (Article 38) has explicitly prohibited person under age of 18 being recruited into the armed forces or direct participating in hostility. In spite of this special provision under CRC, many countries still involve children below 18 years in hostilities. In India (Areas surveyed: Two districts of the State of Gujarat-Surat, half urban and half rural, and Surendranagar, with a nearly two-thirds rural population):

- In the areas covered by the survey, one of every ten paid rural workers was a child. The proportion of children in the paid workforce is much lower in urban areas.
- Around 25 per cent of the children worked in both urban and rural areas, taking into account primary and secondary activities.
- Child workers in rural areas were mainly unpaid family workers and causal labourers.
- In urban Surat, nearly one-third of children working were engaged in the formal sector.
- More girls undertook agricultural activities than boys.

- In urban Surat about one-third of child workers were engaged in sales and around one in 10 (mainly boys) worked in diamond polishing.
- In enterprises, children were paid less than the adult workers, with the differential being less in the case of children working in tea or snack stalls.
- Nearly 20 per cent of the child employees of urban Surendranagar and 15 per cent of those in rural and urban Surat reported that they were paid lower wages than the rate prevalent in those localities.

M.V. Foundation was told by a cottonseed field supervisor in Madaaram village, Parigi mandal of Rangareddy district in Andhra Pradesh, the reason for giving advances to parents.[6] Many middle and upper class families do not hesitate to engage young boys and girls to help them with household cores. The middle class family feels by employing a child below 14 years they are helping poor families to increase their earnings for daily livelihood. There is a wide range of child employment in different areas and different circumstances. Most of them work in forced conditions. This could be understood as follows:

(A) Street Children: Children living on and off the streets, such as shoeshine boys, rag pickers, newspaper-vendors, beggars, etc. The problem of street children is somewhat different from that of child labour in factories and workshops. For one thing, most children have some sort of home to go back to in the evenings or nights, while street children are completely alone and are at the mercy of their employers. They live on the pavements, in the bus stations and railway stations. They are at the mercy of urban predators as also the police. They have no permanent base and are often mobile. So their problem is more acute than that of children working in a factory and living at home.

(B) Children in Industrial Setting: Children working in various industries, such as carpet industry, glass industry, fireworks industry etc. These children are mostly faced with the most hazardous work and inhuman working conditions. They are easily exploited as they are totally at the mercy of their adult employers. It has adverse effects on their health. Though they exist in large numbers they are invisible due to inaccessibility of such factory units. They can even be bonded child labourers sometimes.

(C) Bonded Children: Children who have either been pledged by their parents for paltry sums of money or those working to pay off the inherited debts of their fathers. Bonded children are in many ways the most difficult to assist because they are in accessible. They will spend their life in servitude till they get married and can, in turn, sell their children.

(D) Working Children: Children who are working as part of family labour in agriculture and in home-based work. If children are working 12-14 hours a day along with their parents at the cost of their education, their situation is similar to that of children working for other employers.

(E) **Migrant Children**: Studies reveal that the majority of migrant labour is to be found is states like Andhra Pradesh, Rajasthan, Karnataka, Gujarat, Tamil Nadu and Maharashtra. Almost all major states appear to be affected by migration, although to varying degrees. Many industrial and agro-industrial sectors like brick-making, salt manufacture, sugar cane harvesting, stone quarrying, construction, fisheries, plantations, rice mills and so on run largely on migrant labour.

(F) **Children used for commercial sexual exploitation**: Directs links between commercial sexual exploitation of children and other forms of exploitative work of children are numerous. Factories, workshops, street corners, railway stations, bus stops and homes where children work are common sites of sexual exploitation. Children are especially powerless or resist abuse by employers, either as perpetrators or intermediaries. The pimps often act as procurers for city brothels, lending money to the family, which must be paid back through the daughters work. The physical (health, danger of HIV/AIDS, sexually transmitted diseases) and psychological damage inflicted by commercial sexual exploitation makes it one of the most hazardous forms of child labour.

The Dakshini Rajasthan Mazdoor Union (DRMU) has prepared a separate report based on primary data on the number of children working on BT cotton fields, which shows that out of 604 labourers, 199 or 32.9 per cent were children below the age of 14 years.[6] According to the authors of the DRMU report, "With regard to spread, except for two farms, the team found CL (Child Labour) on all the farms. The survey thus undoubtedly confirms that CL continues to be used on cottonseed farms and indeed, the use is widespread this year (2007).[7] The DRMU survey team found that boys outnumber girls. They also found that 9.5 per cent of the farms did not employ any boy and 28.6 per cent farms did not employ any girl child. Girls seem to be concentrated in some farms. In four farms, the survey team found seven to ten girls each. None of the farms employed more than six boys. Eighty-nine per cent of the farms employed upto three boys.[8] The survey report says "on the basis of the current survey we may safely assert that the incidence of CL in total labour force in the year 2007 ... in the state of Gujarat on cottonseed farms was around one-third of the total labour force. Earlier we had observed that the total area under CSP (cottonseed production) in Gujarat is over 25,000 acres. We had also noted that for each acre about ten labourers are required. This has been substantiated by many farmers in response to a specific question on labour requirement. Accordingly this year the total estimated labour requirement was to the tune of 2.5 lakh labourers."[9] In the informal sector a large number of children were exposed to dangers. For example, some children spend the night in workshops or cars, while others handle potentially dangerous materials, without adult supervision.

This paper covers the significant aspect of India's constitutional and legislative provisions relating to child labour, the enforcement of these provisions, and programs being undertaken nation-wide to eliminate child labour. In the context of the historic Right to Education Act (RTE) guaranteeing compulsory elementary education to all children in the age group of 6 to 14, Save the Children launched a 45-day campaign on April 30 to raise public awareness about the reality of child labour in India and to lobby the Government to ensure that the millions of children now engaged in child labour are included in the implementation of the RTE Act. Arindam Roy writes about the Kol tribes of Shankargarh, a block just 50 kms from Allahabad where he says almost every person in the area is a bonded labourer, forced to work for silica sand mining sub-lessees. The major occupation in the area is mining of silica. The rate is Rs. 150 per tractor load. Two persons can be expected to mine and load a tractor in 3 or 4 days. According to Roy, "The slavery of kols is complete. Their children, eight years upwards are not spared either. When children are not breaking the stones, they are made to carry headloads ('taslas') to the waiting trucks or tractors. For each head load, they are given a pebble ('kauri'). They are paid Rupee 1 for carrying 40 head loads, at the rate of 2.5 paisa per head load. After running endlessly, carrying some 400 head loads, these little children are paid about Rs. 10."[10] Existing estimates vary widely partly because they relate to different source districts of migration, different destinations and probably also because of different methodologies used. However, whether the proportion of child labour is 33 per cent or 25 per cent is not the issue. The fact is that significant numbers of children are working in hazardous conditions on BT cotton farms. This has been widely recorded by agricultural workers' unions and NGOs working for the abolition of child labour.[11]

The Government of India is determined to eradicate child labour in the country. The world's largest child labour elimination program is being implemented at the grass root level in India, with primary education targeted for nearly 250 million. In this, a large number of non-governmental and voluntary organizations are involved. Special investigation cells have been set up in states to enforce existing laws, banning employment of children in hazardous industries. The allocation of funds by the Government of India for the elimination of child labour was $10 million in 1995-96 and $16 million in 1996-97. The allocation for the current year is $21 million.

The child labour program in India is a national concern that involves the Government of India, the governments of the States and the Union Territories of India, as well as such tripartite fora as the Indian Labour Conference and the Standing Labour Committee. A massive national and regional media campaign has been launched to sensitize society against child labour. Funds have been allocated to districts identified as child-labour endemic for surveys to identify child labour, and for awareness generation programs among employers, parents and the working children themselves.

Jayachandran in her study of brick kilns in Thane and Nashik districts reports that there were huge problems in getting migrant children back into school. Important among these were the reluctance of employers to let children study, reluctance of employers to let schools be set up in the vicinity of the workplace as well as lukewarm response of the district administration. In some cases the brick owners did not allow the child labourers to sit for the final exams and forced them to work at the kilns on examination days.[12] Even in progressive states like Maharashtra and Gujarat, in the high-migration pockets, which lie in the backward districts, school functioning is less than satisfactory. Poor education possibilities push children further into migration. Ironically, with large-scale enrolment drives, the names of most migrant children are on school rolls; but in reality they are out of school, getting absorbed into labour at worksites, and falling irreversibly into the vicious annual cycle."[13] A major program was launched on 15th August 1994 for withdrawing child labour working in hazardous occupations and for rehabilitating them through special schools. The National Authority for the Elimination of Child Labour (NAECL) was constituted on 26th September, 1994 under the Chairmanship of the Minister for Labour, Government of India. The functions of NAECL are:

- to lay down policies and programs for the elimination of child labour, particularly in hazardous employment
- to monitor the progress of the implementation of programs, projects and schemes for the elimination of child labour;
- to coordinate the implementation of child labour related projects of the various sister Ministries of the Government of India (to ensure convergence of services for the benefit of the families of child labour).

India's National Policy on Education, 1986 gives the highest priority to the program of universal elementary education, and recommends that free and compulsory education of sufficient quality be provided to all children up to the age of 14 years before we enter the 21st century. Compulsory Education Acts have been enacted in 14 states and 4 Union Territories viz. Assam, Andhra Pradesh, Bihar, Delhi, Gujarat, Haryana, Jammu & Kashmir, Karnataka, Madhya Pradesh, Maharashtra, Punjab, Rajasthan, Tamil Nadu, Kerala, West Bengal, Chandigarh, Pondicherry and Andaman and Nicobar Islands.

A recent report in *The Hindu* quoted a study, which said "nearly 80 per cent of girl child labourers in Bidar and 52 per cent of such children in Chamarajanagar were agricultural labourers. The study found that a significant number of children were paying off their parents' debts." The same report said that 49 per cent of child labourers in Bidar and 42 per cent of those in Chamarjanagar are involved in agricultural labour.[14] In absolute terms, the number of girl child workers has increased from 2.8 million to 3.5 million since 1971. Over 80 per cent of these girls are still caught up in the agricultural sector, mostly as full-time agricultural labourers."[15]

The International Program on the Elimination of Child Labour is a global program launched by the International Labour Organization in December 1991. India was the first country to join it in 1992 when it signed a Memorandum of Understanding with the ILO. The long-term objective of IPEC is to contribute to the effective abolition of child labour. Its immediate objectives are:

- Elimination of the capability of ILO constituents and Non-Government Organizations to design, implement and evaluate programs for Child Labour Elimination;
- To identity interventions at community and national levels which could serve as models for replication; and Creation of awareness and social mobilization for securing elimination of child labour.

State-wise Projects under IPEC and Number of Children Covered (1992-97)

State	Projects approved	No. of Children
Andhra Pradesh	15	15455
Bihar	3	1340
Delhi	6	4200
Gujarat	5	1350
Haryana	1	300
Karnataka	2	1320
Kerala	2	2000
Madhya Pradesh	6	2050
Manipur	1	500
Maharashtra	7	1750
Orissa	4	1500
Rajasthan	7	5800
Tamil Nadu	17	6710
Uttar Pradesh	11	13939
West Bengal	19	22890
Regional	2	NA
All India Institutions	11	NA
Total	120	81154

Source: MOU between the Government of India and the ILO, the IPEC program December 31, 1996.

CONCLUSION

Children are blooming flowers in the garden of society. It is, therefore, a duty on the part of the members of society to protect these flowers from the damaging effects of excessive exposure to heat, cold and rains and also not to pluck them to satisfy their momentary whims. In spite of taking all these initiatives, the million dollar question before us is that why child labour is not getting eliminated at a much faster pace. It can be said that it is not sufficient to implement legislation but at the same time circumstances and atmosphere is also essentially required to accomplish such goals. When the capitalist class will always seek to maximize their gains at the cost of the future of generation next how these blossoms can will be able to bloom properly. Secondly, the state should not limit itself to the work of enacting legislations only but take a step further in creating conducive environment that may provide the capitalists enough space to flourish their business with keeping in mind the pathetic condition of the poor. While child labour is a complex problem that is basically rooted in poverty, there is unwavering commitment by the Government and the people of India to combat it. Success can be achieved only through social engineering on a larger scale combined with national economic growth. International policies and actions, therefore, must support and not hamper India's efforts to get rid of child labour.

To make the anti child labour law a reality, poverty and unemployment need to be eliminated. Unless the standard of living improves at the lower levels of the society, children will be forced to work. If we do not take necessary steps to curb this problem, we not only lose the present manpower but also our generation next would be in danger as they will not be getting the chance of their all-round development and growth. After seeing this unhappy picture, we are compelled to think once again on our own propaganda of INDIA SHINING.

Endnotes and References

1. For a more detailed analysis of MVF's strategy see Shantha Sinha (2005) "Emphasizing Universal Principles towards Deepening of Democracy. Actualising Children's Right to Education" in *Economic and Political Weekly*, Vol. XL, No. 25, June 18-24, pp. 2569-2576. See also, Shantha Sinha and M. Nagarjuna (2004) "The Poverty Argument: In the context of Total Elimination of Child Labour", Azad Reading Room, Hyderabad; Sucheta Mahajan (2003), "MVF India:Education as Empowerment", *Mainstream*, 16 August.
2. Davuluri Venkateswarulu and Lucia Da Corta (2001), "Female Child Bonded Labour in Hybrid Cottonseed Production". Paper presented at the National Consultation on *Fifteen Years of Interventions Against Child Labour. A Collaborative Social Audit*, Indian Habitat Centre (IHC), New Delhi, 27-29 November, p. 1.
3. Ibid.
4. Ibid. p. 2.
5. Neera Burra (2001), "Cultural stereotypes and Household Behaviour. Girl Child Labour in India," *Economic and Political Weekly*, Vol. XXVI, Nos. 5 & 6.
6. Khandelwal, Ashok, Sudhir Katiyar and Madan Vaishnav (2007), "Child Labour in Hybrid Cottonseed production in Gujarat. Tracing linkages between Companies and Inter-State Migrant tribal Child Labour", Draft report, November, Dakshini Rajasthan Majdoor Union, p. 7. The report provides a detailed account of the prevalence of child labour, the conditions of work and the method of recruitment of children.
7. Ibid.
8. Ibid.
9. Ibid., p. 8.
10. Roy, Arindam (2000), "Breaking the Shackles. Kol Tribal Labourers", *Economic and Political Weekly*, February 5-11, Vol. XXXV, No. 6, pp. 425-426.

11. See *Indian Express* (2007), "GALU gears up to stop child labour on BT cotton farms in North Gujarat," 21 June and *Indian Express* (2007), "Activists, officials discuss ways to curb child labour", 8 September.
12. Jayachandran, (2001) Taking Schools, *op cit*, p. 3350.
13. Ibid, p. 3350.
14. "Declaration on child labour mandatory," Special Correspondent, *The Hindu*, 14 September, 2007.
15. Nira Ramachandran (2002), "Introducing the Concept" in Nira Ramachandran and Lionel Massun (eds.) *Coming to Grips with Rural Child Work*, *op cit*, p. 7.

PART III

Public Policy and Inclusive Growth

8

Moving Beyond Reservations in an Era of Globalisation: The Debate on Affirmative Action

Sudha Pai

With globalisation questions have been raised about the continued usefulness of the policy of Protective Discrimination or reservations for dalits. There is a growing feeling that in the changed context it does not contribute to the agenda of Social Justice. Two developments have contributed. With the shrinking of the State and use of new forms of governance, employment opportunities in the public sector have gradually declined. Second, the emergence of a small, but influential generation of young, educated, and politically conscious, middle class of dalits who strongly feel they should receive a 'fair share' in the fruits of globalisation which has resulted in higher growth rates, a strong private sector, high-paid professional occupations and business opportunities. A significant fallout has been the rise of a contentious debate—among both dalit and non-dalit scholars/activists—on the working of the policies of reservation in the post-independence period, the benefits that have accrued to them, and the new types of preferential policies that are required so that dalits can also reap the benefits of globalisation.

This paper analyzes this debate. While the demand for extension of job reservations to the private sector is well known. The focus here is on policies based on affirmative action such as 'Supplier Diversity' (SD)—first discussed at the Bhopal Conference 2002—that could lead to 'democratisation of capital' which its supporters argue would enable them to participate in the new market economy, removing in the long run the need for reservations. To understand the rationale underlying these policies, the paper briefly draws upon two SD programmes implemented by the Madhya Pradesh government following the Bhopal Conference. Analyzing the debate, the paper argues that in a globalizing economy, such policies hold considerable latent possibilities to create over time, an entrepreneurial business/industrial dalit class, so far lacking. In recent years dalits have obtained political empowerment i.e. entered the political arena, formed political parties and governments, but remain conspicuously absent in the business/industrial sector. Such policies would provide economic empowerment and end the marginalisation that this disadvantaged group faces in this sector.

In recent years with globalisation of the economy, questions have been raised about the continued usefulness of the policy of Protective Discrimination or reservations. There is a growing feeling that in the changed context it does not contribute to the agenda of Social Justice which has come to occupy centre stage. Two developments have contributed. With globalisation and the shrinking of the State and use of new forms of governance, employment opportunities in the public sector have gradually declined. Second, is the emergence of a small, but influential generation of young, educated, upwardly mobile and politically conscious, middle class of dalits who strongly feel they should receive a 'fair share' in the fruits of globalisation which has resulted in higher growth rates, a strong private sector, high-paid professional occupations and business opportunities. Equally important, this new dalit class reached a "critical mass" during the 1990s, precisely when the Indian polity underwent globalisation moving towards a market-oriented economy. It represents a different strand in the dalit movement as it has evolved in the last two decades. While dalit movements/ parties such as the BSP have mobilized on issues of *political empowerment* such as dignity and self-respect. Middle class dalit intellectuals have emphasized on the need for *economic empowerment* through a variety of alternative means through policies based on affirmative action.

In this context an attempt is made to analyze this debate among intellectuals/activists on the future direction that reservation policy should take for disadvantaged sections. Much of the academic debate on the subject has centred on issues such as the demand by OBCs for 27 per cent reservation in higher education; removal of the 'creamy layer' among SCs, or the need to extend reservations to the private sector (Mohanty 2006; Yadav and Deshpande 2007; Thorat, Aryama and Negi 2005; Thorat and Kumar 2008). Our focus more specifically, is to discuss the policies based on affirmative action put forward in this debate that would enable dalits enter into the private sector.

The term affirmative action—widely employed in this debate—was first employed in the US in 1961 by President John F. Kennedy to introduce policies in the public and private sphere that would provide equality of opportunity to all citizens and end discrimination against African Americans. (Weisskopf 2004; Sowell 2006) In contrast to the traditional policy of reservation as practiced in India the state does not fix quotas, these policies are voluntary by nature, and encourage institutions to show *a degree of preference* to select persons from groups that have faced discrimination. In the US they have not been made into laws though in the 1970s the federal government set targets and courts have taken cognizance of their existence and pronounced on their implementation (Glazer 1975:44-48). Diversity is one aspect of affirmative action policies based on the principle of *preference for weaker sections within the existing system* in a number of areas, most often education, employment and business/industry that create 'diversity' i.e. provide opportunities to disadvantaged sections leading to a more egalitarian society (Weiner 1984; Wasby 1986; Katz 1977). Thus, introduction of policies based on diversity in India would mean extending the existing PD policies to the private sector and/or designing new policies based on a *greater element of voluntariness* rather than fixed quotas.

In the contemporary debate while the term affirmative action is used and the American model invoked the kind of policies to be used remain controversial. Broadly two positions are visible: reservation in the private sector and second, policies of diversity to be adopted by the state and the private sector to bring dalits into the field of business and industry. The former has been extensively articulated by scholars and activists (Thorat) who are demanding "equal opportunity" or extension of job reservations to the private sector, but sanctioned by legal means to overcome discrimination in employment practices. In fact, they use the terms reservation and affirmative action interchangeably as they visualize the policy as state-supported.

It is the latter policy, put forward mainly by the authors of the Bhopal Document (BD) 2002, and which is not as well known, that is the focus of this paper. Critical of the demand for extension of reservation of jobs to the private sector—that would help only a small number—the BD argues for "democratisation" of control over "capital that could provide "economic empowerment" to the increasing number of educated, unemployed dalit youth creating an entrepreneurial and business class at present lacking. Its supporters point out that due to the caste system, historically dalits have been kept out of business and industry which has been the preserve of the trading and the upper castes. Consequently they have not been able to enter into areas which are becoming important in India's globalized economy, remaining on the fringes of the expanding professional and business market. Through dealer and supplier contracts provided by the government, dalits can overcome these obstacles, enter into "the supply chain" and eventually into manufacturing. They also hold that such a policy would be able to economically empower a large number of dalits doing away in the long run with the need for reservations. These arguments are also based upon a growing recognition that while many forms of exclusion have been studied, there has been little effort to understand various forms of caste-based discrimination in the market against dalits.

Based on analysis of this debate, this paper argues that in a globalizing economy with fewer jobs available in the government sector, policies of SD hold considerable latent possibilities to create over time, a business/industrial dalit class. In recent years dalits have entered the political arena in large numbers, formed political parties and governments, but remain conspicuously absent in the business/industrial sector. It would end the marginalisation that these disadvantaged sectors face in the economic arena which, as the paper shows, has relegated them to the unorganized sectors of the business/ industrial sectors. The paper is divided into in two parts: the first traces the contours of the debate, the second deals with policies such as supplier diversity that aim to create dalit entrepreneurs.

I. FROM PD TO AFFIRMATIVE ACTION: THE CONTEMPORARY DEBATE

Till the late 1980s scholarly attention was centred on the effectiveness of the policy of PD, more specifically reservations. Beginning with the discussion in the constituent assembly these policies have encountered much controversy in post-independence India (Dharmpal 2000; Mcmillan 2005). Criticism of the policy has ranged from poor implementation, jobs being only in the lower rungs of the bureaucracy, the policy not having the desired impact, only better-off urban-based groups benefiting, encouragement to sub-caste divisions, to more fundamental issues of individual rights, justice, merit and efficiency (Ramaswamy 1974; Sowell, 2004; Velaskar 1998; Weisskopf 2006). Quite early some of these problems were also pointed out by government reports (Elayaperumal Committee 1969; Report of the Commission for SC and ST, First Report July 1978-March 1979). But not all scholars are convinced. Some argue that reservations are the "most workable method" to help remove long-standing discrimination (Ghosh 2007); others that reservations follow the democratic and rational path of change chartered by Ambedkar (Iliaih 2006). A study examining the working of PD policies in India and the US held that the case for such policies remains strong if "the policies are carefully designed to maximize the benefits and minimize the costs" which it admits is not the case most of the time (Weisskopf 2006).

Until recently, this discussion remained largely confined to problems of implementation and did not question the viability of the policy or need to replace/supplement it. It is with the adoption of policies of globalisation of the economy in the 1990s that the continued usefulness of this policy for dalits in the changed economic context, has come to be contested. Another reason for the stridency, which the demand for affirmative action has acquired, has been the internationalisation of the debate. A strong contingent of human right activists raised the issue at the World Conference Against Racism held in Durban in 2001 despite the position taken by the Indian government and some scholars that race is not caste (Thorat and Umakant 2004). A range of PD instruments have also been evolved to do away with discriminatory practices such as the International Convention on the Elimination of All Forms of Racial Discrimination that has a number of Articles that call for measures to remove all forms of racial ethnicity-based discrimination. Due to these influences in recent years many scholars have put forward the American, Malaysian and South African model as worth emulating. In this changed situation questions have been raised whether affirmative action can be a useful method to reduce the social and economic marginalisation of these communities.

Contrasting Positions and Supplier Diversity

While there is growing recognition of the need to move beyond state-led reservation policies and devise new and innovative affirmative action policies to help dalits. Scholars/activists are divided over the *type of strategies* to be used. One set of scholars believe extension of reservations to the private sector is needed, as this is the fastest growing sector in the country today. It also argues that legal sanctions are required without which the policy unlike in the US, will not be successful. The private sector it is alleged practices caste-based discrimination and human capital differentials such as education, skills, and training alone cannot explain the lack of advancement of disadvantaged groups. This has been true historically in India and has continued through the colonial period to the present (Papola 2005; Thorat and Newman 2007). Neither greater investment in education or globalisation and the emergence of a more open, competitive market and a strong private sector with more jobs, can correct this "inefficiency in labour allocation" based on serious discrimination. They therefore point to the urgent need for state regulation and sanction (Thorat and Newman 2007).

The second position in keeping with liberalisation, lays greater emphasis on the market mechanism and demands that both the state and the private sector practice diversity policies such as giving dealerships and contracts to dalits together with other supportive measures such as provision of credit to bring them into the field of business/industry (Bhopal Document 2002). It is based on this position, discussed in detail below, put forward in the Bhopal Conference that the policy of "Supplier Diversity" (SD) was formulated and implemented in MP in 2002 by the Digvijay Singh-led Congress government.

The advocates of the second position do not recommend doing away with reservations; they expect the government to implement the policy better and fill the entire backlog. But they are critical of both the excessive reliance on reservations and various forms of state welfarism by dalits as the "most decisive tool of progress" and the demand for extension of reservation to the private sector. They point to the limits of the "emancipatory role" (Prasad 2005: 167) as well as many problems of the state-led reservation model such as poor implementation, slow progress seen in the fact that even after 60 years of independence the number of class I officers remained few and posts were difficult to fill. Chandrabhan Prasad one of the authors of the BD argues that mere extension of this model i.e. of reservations into the private sector being demanded by many scholars/activists would not be of much use as it would still leave a large number of SC/ST without employment. According to the Annual Report of the Union Ministry of Labour 2000-2001, the total number of jobs under the State (Union government, PSU, state governments, local bodies) are 1.94 crore. This means that if the SC/STs total existing quota of

22.50 percent is given to them, the total number of their employees cannot go beyond 45 lakh, which if multiplied by 5 (assuming that every SC/ST employed under the state caters to a family of five) the benefits cannot reach beyond a population of 2.25 crore. This still leaves as many as 18 crores of dalits seeking employment. [1]

Extension of this model i.e. of reservations into the private sector being demanded by many scholars/activists Prasad argues would not be of much use. At a conservative estimate, low skilled, semi-skilled and unskilled workers add to more than three-fourths of the workforce. In the private sector the total employment available according to the Annual Report is about 86.98 lakhs. If the private sector were to religiously implement reservations it would lead to an additional 19.57 lakh jobs, which if again multiplied by five would benefit another 97.85 lakh SC/STs. Even then about 17 crore would be left which exemplifies the limits of reservations.[2] Moreover, Prasad argues that reservation of jobs in the private sector if introduced, must be voluntary and part of the diversity policies adopted by both the government and private sector, as in the case of the United States described below. Also it remains to be seen if the private sector will calculate the backlog in these jobs—which are currently held by non-dalits—and fill the vacancies. Even the government has not been able to do so till date.

The Bhopal Document: A New Dalit Agenda

The main source of the debate on the need for policies such as SD is the Dalit Agenda contained in the Bhopal Document (BD).[3] The BD can be described as a middle class Document i.e. it is the product of the new educated dalit class keen to put forward new policies in sync with the changing economic context in the country. The Document had its origins in the late 1990s in the attempt by a group of dalit intellectuals and activists to present to the Congress leadership a report containing alternative proposals beyond the conventional state policies for their community. Though supportive of the innovative document, as the Congress was not in power at the centre, the report was sent to MP the only state in north India where the party was in office and based on it the Bhopal Conference was held on January 12-13, 2002 with the full support of the chief minister, Digvijay Singh. Its immediate intellectual origin was the *Dalit Millennium* published by *The Pioneer* on 30th January 2000—one of a number of *Millennium Supplements*—issued to mark the dawn of the millennium. Consisting of about 8 pages it was put together by a number of dalit intellectuals drawn from writers, academics and journalists.[4] It dealt with a wide range of issues of significance for dalits some of which, found an echo in the BD later: problems with reservation policy, the controversial issue of merit, representation of dalits in state institutions such as the judiciary, need for better educational attainments, leadership, caste atrocities, the plight of dalit women etc. Some articles pointed out that "diversification of dalits from government service to other fields" should become the major trends in the years to come and the need for a new "Dalit Bourgeoisie" in the field of business and industry.

The authors of the BD demand that both the state and the private sector practice diversity policies based on affirmative action such as SD to enable dalits to enter the business/industry sector (Bhopal Document, 2002). A major reason for the need for some form of affirmative action is as Chandrabhan Prasad says "Trade and enterprise have never been part of our tradition."[5] He holds that rather than reservation in the private sector, it is the business sector, which has not been explored yet, and which holds the greatest promise. in the years to come with large number of educated unemployed moving out of universities and colleges. Pointing to the need to "democratize the ownership of capital" the BD holds that voluntary policies based on the American model, making use of the market, competition, technology and skill development, rather than state-led policies of reservation based on caste-quotas—can play a determining role in ending the marginalisation of dalits from participation and decision-making in the field of business/industry. This is particularly true with globalisation/liberalisation of the economy and emergence of a strong private sector. The SD policy has features that borrow from both the PD policies of the past and from affirmative action. On the one hand it is a state-supported policy implemented by the bureaucracy. On the other, it is also a market-based, voluntary policy, whose success depends upon the entrepreneurial skills and ability to supply goods and services in a time-bound manner in keeping with laid down standards and face caste-bias, competition and even monopoly from the traditional suppliers to the government belonging largely to the upper/middle castes.

Many of these arguments are based on a realisation that various forms of discrimination in the market creates obstacles which effectively keeps disadvantaged sections from entering into the field of business or industry. Some elaboration of the concept of discrimination has come from mainstream economics in the context of race and gender (Dalton 1999). Amartya Sen (2000: 10-13) has also argued that social exclusion results in 'capability deprivation' due to exclusion from social relations which can lead to other relational deprivations such as lack of education, employment, and exclusion from markets leading to economic impoverishment, which limits opportunities. A recent study attempts to develop a concept of caste-based economic discrimination, and market discrimination in particular, and relevant indicators for its measurement by carving them out of the larger concept of social exclusion which is multi-dimensional as it encompasses deprivation through exclusion in multiple spheres (Thorat 2009a). Another using a three-fold criteria to measure the incidence of market discrimination argues that market relationships are determined by structural, resource and normative logic of the dominant agents in the market who belong to the dominant upper castes, leading to high losses in terms of opportunities, income and confinement to low income sectors for dalits (Thorat 2009b: 138-144). However, much of the data is on labour discrimination experienced by landless labour in rural areas, in irrigation and land markets and access to common property resources (CPRs). Clearly, there is need to develop frameworks for understanding the manner in which market discrimination works to keep dalits and tribals from participating in business and industrial sectors of the economy.

Apart from the BD a growing number of studies point out that official data shows that few dalits have been able to enter into the field of business/ industry. The latest Economic Census 2005 shows that over half the business establishments i.e. 51 per cent are owned by socially disadvantaged groups mostly OBCs with a slim contribution from the SC and STs (Nagrajan 2008(a)). This is a rise from 45 per cent at the time of the last Economic Census in 1998, with OBCs registering the largest chunk of this growth. However, a closer look at the data shows that over three quarters of businesses owned by SCs and STs are family-owned establishments i.e. OAE (own account establishments) without any hired labour and possibly mainly efforts at self employment (Ibid.). The proportion of such establishments owned by OBCs is 71 per cent and by the general category 56 per cent.

A study provides data on the ownership patterns of business among the weaker sections. It shows that business ownership by the SCs is very low compared to the OBCs and general category, and is limited to a few states such as Punjab, HP, West Bengal, MP and Haryana which have a considerable SC population. Among STs it is high only in states in the north east where they form a substantial chunk of the population (Nagrajan 2008(b). Another study that examines the present day pattern of ownership of private enterprises in India also shows that they are not equally distributed across social groups (Kundu and Thorat 2007). Of the 98 per cent of enterprises that were owned by the private sector in 1998, SC and ST showed low ownership of private enterprises: the SCS owned 10.2 per cent and STS 5.84 per cent of private enterprises in rural India, while OBCs owned 40 per cent and others 43.2 per cent. In urban areas the disparity is even more: SC owned only 6.1 per cent and ST 2.4 per cent in comparison with OBCs 30.5 per cent and others a high of 61 per cent. More important, the study also underlines that SC/ST owned largely small self-owned household enterprises—mostly agricultural-based—either using household labour or very little outside labour (Ibid.). The Bhopal Document also provides figures that show that both in the ownership and worker category in large-scale private industry, SC/ST remain peripheral. Both these categories have a very low presence in trade and commerce being largely confined to low value businesses/occupations. For example they are mainly workers in transport and storage industries while the non-SC/ST own the trucks, buses and godowns etc. It is only in government employment where there is reservation that SCs/STs are not as badly under-represented (Bhopal Document 2002). The situation described above is a reflection of the historical exclusion from assets such as land and capital and from business and industry of dalits the policy of affirmative action hopes to address.

One of the important reasons for the low presence of dalits in business/

industry is that their access to credit has a very poor record. The government of India has established agencies such as the National Scheduled Castes Financial Development Corporation (NSCFDC), Scheduled Castes Development Corporation (SCDC) and the National Backward Classes Financial Development Corporation (NBCFDC) to provide loans to SC/ST and train them for income-generating activities. But there is little evidence whether such loans have had a significant impact and are cost effective. A review of the NSCFDC state corporations by the National Institute of Financial Management in 2006 paints a poor picture (Varma 2007). Most of these agencies have put their funds in fixed deposits instead of giving loans to needy dalits—on an average their equity-debt ratio was 65:35. The report says that there is widespread irregularity in selection of beneficiaries—cases of submitted lists not matching actual recipients have been recorded. Most state corporations have not prepared accounts for anything between 6 to 16 years. Loan recoveries are about 45 per cent with some states like Assam having as low a rate as 14 per cent (Ibid).

A parliamentary committee looking into the working of NSCFDC found that between 2001 and 2004, only 281 dalit artisans had been provided loans, in the entire country. The number of dalits provided job-oriented training was low ranging between fourteen hundred to a little over two thousand. Nor are dalits receiving bank credit to run their own businesses if they cannot get funds from the government. Data from the Reserve Bank of India shows that the amount of credit per capita declined from Rs. 495 in 1993 to Rs 285 in 2001 and further to Rs 225 in 2004 while that for non-dalits per capita rose to 708, 756 and 936 for the same years respectively. In fact, the number of small borrowal accounts of dalits declined from 77 to 23 per thousand. With liberalisation of the economy public sector banks are no longer as willing as in the past to provide loans to disadvantaged sections (Ibid). This makes the policy of SD more necessary.

II. Creating a Class of Dalit Entrepreneurs

Based these arguments the authors of the BD argue that dalit entrepreneurs can be "created" with state support. They point out that most big business houses including Reliance, have emerged due to state support and patronage in the form of tax benefits, credit policies, dealerships of all kinds etc. Until the 1990s they were also provided protection against competition from the world economy. Even in the contemporary period of liberalisation the state has provided them "concessions" and "incentives" of various kinds. Moreover the caste system has provided upper castes privileges such as better education, family background and support from the ruling political class. Dalits being a disadvantaged section require greater amount of help as historically they have not participated in the business/industry sector. Rather years of PD have only prepared them to exploit opportunities in government services.

The rationale underlying the policy of SD is that it will provide a livelihood to educated, unemployed dalit youth—those who have passed high school or who havea graduate degree—and create an economically independent, entrepreneurial class among them. State supported attempts can begin with SD policies for dalits in areas where little formal education and no complex skills are required (BD). Here the two policies of SD implemented by the Madhya Pradesh (MP) government based on the BD are instructive in understanding the arguments proffered: the thirty percent scheme and the Margin Money scheme.[6] These have been continued by the successor BJP government and become part of the affirmative action policies for dalits and tribals in the state. In the case of the former, government departments buy a number of ordinary items such as stationery, furniture, office lunches, plants, uniforms, furniture, office equipment, electrical gadgets etc. from suppliers in the market in great bulk and give dealerships for petrol, diesel and kerosene and LPG etc. In MP the government reserved thirty percent of these goods or supply contracts for dalits. It was felt that dalit businesses could be stimulated if government departments reserve even small government contracts that run into a few lakh each for them. Over time such entrepreneurs could graduate to becoming manufacturers. The Margin Money scheme was designed to provide the margin or 'initial' amount required to enable dalits to obtain a loan from banks, which are reluctant to lend to persons with few assets. This would remove a formidable barrier for entry of dalits into the business/industrial sector.

The most important feature of these policies according their supporters is that they address a major obstacle that dalits face in setting up a business or industry. This is not so much obtaining the initial capital or even knowledge. *The greatest difficulty lies in getting a steady and assured stream of orders for the goods to be marketed in the beginning without which achieving financial stability and independence is impossible.* For new entrepreneurs finding a buyer takes time and is fraught with uncertainties, which is critical for a new industry to survive. Without this many businesses fail as achieving financial stability and repaying loans is very difficult. In the case of dalits, the difficulty is much greater as they face caste bias or lack of information and contacts and breaking the 'monopoly' often held by established manufacturers or traders is difficult as they are new entrants into the industrial/trade sector. In this situation, if government were to provide a share in government contracts/supplies and orders to dalits it would enable them to repay loans and establish themselves. It would be a case of "protection" to struggling infant businesses in their initial critical years. Once established with initial support from the government as a supplier, a dalit might gravitate to supplying more complex items eventually becoming an industrial entrepreneur selling in the open market as well.

Supporters of the policy in MP agreed when the policy was initiated that there would be "teething problems" such as corruption in government departments, lack of credit, opposition, discrimination and monopoly in the market, etc. Use of middlemen or 'proxy' they pointed out was seen in other policies for disadvantaged sections initially. For this correctives on the part of the state government would be required. But the policy they believed, with government support would give dalits a "toehold" into the market and once a sizeable number got in, the rest would follow. Such policies would also prepare dalits to operate within the new market economy in which the presence of the government is much less and where private capital would play a bigger role. At the same time they agreed that in the short term certain conditions were necessary without which the scheme cannot be successful: training, credit, tax incentives but also a "sympathetic government" that would provide a "friendly environment" for the policy to function properly.

Regarding the private sector, Prasad argues that if it has a problem with job reservations, they should start by making dalits partners in the business by keeping aside 5 or 10 per cent outsourced services for them. As these groups are not in the social loop, industry has to make a conscious effort of "integrating them in the supply chain".[7] It would he argues, lead to much lower displacement than job reservations in the private sector, would not become an emotive issue and there would be less social polarisation. Moreover, it is not necessary to replace existing dealers, but when new dealerships are given out, some could be reserved for these groups. He provides two examples where both these groups and the industry concerned could gain. The first example is Hindustan Lever, which has 43,000 employees and two lakh dealers. As the latter is a larger pool, giving a share to dalits would not displace many. Assuming a Hindustan Lever dealer gets a 1 per cent commission, he can earn a minimum of over Rs 60 lakh a year. A dalit could take up this dealership, taking less commission than others. A second example is of a small factory making gear stick covers for Eicher tractors which is sold to a wholesale dealer for Rs 5 a piece, who in turn sells it to Eicher for Rs 10. If Eicher bought the same item directly from a dalit/tribal manufacturer, without compromising on quality, it would cost Rs. 7.50 in which case both gain financially. Starting with these small ventures, these groups can earn enough to educate their children who will then not need reservations.[8]

Underlining that coming together of the upper and lower castes through business is much better than passing social reform laws that create divides. Prasad points out that the Congress party throughout its four-decade rule in the country has not been able to create a dalit or tribal entrepreneurial class. At present the party is selling the "private sector job quota dream" which is a repeat experience of the reservation policy when these groups competed for government jobs and provided the electoral support base of the party. An economically strong dalit community could be "a headache for the mainstream polity" and they are not keen to create it (BD 2002: 169).

Prasad feels that well educated and better off dalits should enter into the business arena. This will end the marginalisation and exclusion these of disadvantaged groups in the economy. The emergence of a creamy layer will take time and only later there should be any restriction. The emergence of an entrepreneurial class will also take the pressure off demand for higher education. He also feels that it is less contentious than giving land to dalits which produces conflict. The rise of a dalit bourgeoisie would help eliminate social tensions and if the big industrialists understand this reality, it would further good relations and remove social bias. But he agrees that until they agree to some form of affirmative action either due to fear of government legislation and quotas, or a realisation that it was of benefit to them and society as a whole, there was little sense in adopting them.

Invoking the American Experience

The authors of the BD draw on the US experience because they point out that the American State has adopted a number of measures to bring minorities into the area of business and industry that are of considerable relevance in any attempt to design policies based on affirmative action in India. Since the 1970s the federal government has particularly made serious attempts at "Democratizing Capital" in the domestic market. Conceding that empirical evidence demonstrates that there is a disparity in credit accessibility among certain demographic groups and that the future of the nation's economic growth depends on the inclusion of minority-owned businesses, the following steps were taken:

(1) All purchases by the government have to have at least 5 per cent set aside to purchase from minority suppliers. The total expenditure on this count came to US$ 195 billion in 1998 of which US$ 11.3 billion were from black/other ethnic groups. This means that large number of minority suppliers/business houses benefited from this policy and in fact some turned into millionaires (Bhopal Document 2002: 84).

(2) All government contractors are bound to have a certain percentage of their contract work sub-contracted to minority sub-contractors, obligatory by law

(3) Obligatory non-discrimination by law in any constructions contract where federal funds (grants or loans) or assistance (insurance, guarantee, contract) are involved such as buildings, bridges or involving real estate.

(4) Non-discrimination obligations from all government contractors that they will not discriminate in their employment practices. While there is no constitutional sanction behind this policy the Equal Employment Opportunities Commission, oversees government and private sector practices and can sue for damages if either is found practicing discrimination.

In 1977 the US government also enacted a legislation titled "Community Reinvestment Act" (CRA) making it mandatory for banks and other financial institutions to cater to credit requirements of "underserved" groups including elderly and small businesses. The BD claims that so far US $ One Trillion has been invested/lent out by the CRA reporting institutions to "underserved communities". Consequently, black/ethnic minority owned businesses registered a growth rate of 17 per cent during 1987-97 six times higher than the overall business in America. Further, sales across all firms rose by 13 per cent annually and for blacks/ethnic minority owned firms sales rose by 34 per cent, more than twice the national average. Drawing an analogy with statements heard in India, the authors of the BD point out that till about two decades ago minorities particularly blacks were considered "incompetent" in running business but are now surpassing white business (Ibid.).

Not only the government but private industrial giants in the US are also practicing diversity by both employing and providing entrepreneurial opportunities to the minorities. Some of the examples given are Exxon Mobile, IBM, Microsoft, Wal-Mart Stores, Harvard University and General and Ford Motors. Diversity Statements such as "Respect, Equality, Opportunity and Growth" adopted by Wal-Mart Stores, give diversity figures in their yearly statements and also distribute a chunk of their profits to organisations involved in civic services.[9] Companies such as Microsoft and Harvard University also offer scholarships to minorities, expand minority recruitment and retention schemes, organize professional training, and take up community programmes. The authors of the BD argue that these companies could not have risen to the top of the ladder in their respective fields if they had compromised on "merit" and "competitiveness" an argument commonly put forward by companies in India when they are expected to follow similar policies. It points to IBM a top company in the IT sector internationally, which upholds "A legacy of inclusion" on its web page on diversity (Ibid: 81). In the field of creative arts, the Writers' Guild of America commissions regular studies to "track employment trends of writers of colour, women and older writers in American motion pictures and TV networks" (Ibid: 78).

Moreover, diversity in the workplace and in business goes hand in hand, which Chandrabhan Prasad argues provides a good model for India (Prasad 2005: 170). It provides both jobs as well as a share in capital. General Motors (GM) he points out has a department of diversity which reveals details of racial/ethnic workforce composition. By 2000 the minorities composed 23 per cent of the workforce with almost 20 per cent in the managerial category. More important, in 2003 the company purchased goods and services worth US $7.2 billion from minority suppliers—$1billion more than the previous year. GM has made it mandatory that the bigger suppliers to the company—often white—purchase some of their supplies from smaller minority suppliers. For instance, Johnson Controls Inc., a major auto parts supplier to GM purchased goods and services from minority suppliers worth $1 billion during 2003-04. Under its Dealership diversity by 1999, GM had 320 minority suppliers, with sales of $9.5 billion per year. GM also has welfare programmes: it has tied up with many minority businesses who recommend candidates for jobs; supply many goods and services and its diversity department holds job fairs in minority-run institutions and 'on the spot recuitments' as part of the diversity drive. Prasad therefore holds that Indian industry should free itself from its "caste interests" and democratize its workforce and capital, which would be in its interest (Ibid.).

Further, the authors of the BD claim that analysis of the American experience of Diversity reveals that since the late 1960s, American society has "undergone a sea change in its attitude". The whites have, even if reluctantly, decided to share assets, institutions and knowledge industry with the deprived/ethnic groups: African-Americans, Native Americans, Asians and Hispanics who constitute 12.7 per cent, 0.9 per cent, 3.8 per cent and 10.9 per cent respectively i.e. together roughly a quarter of the population (BD, 2002: 67). Based on data from the US Equal Employment Opportunity Commission the BD concedes that the white majority owns most of the assets in the American economy, but holds that there is "realisation" that assets, institutions and knowledge must be shared with the disadvantaged groups if the country has to evolve into "one nation and a healthy democracy" (Ibid: 70).

Scholars also hold that today in the US it is assumed that there is an equal distribution of capacity among all social groups, that apparent differences are social and not biological and that the very existence of diverse social groups means that businesses must have representation (Omvedt 2005: 203). Referring to a recent judgment of the US Supreme Court that upheld the use of affirmative action in two cases[10] Omvedt points out that it was supported by at least 65 major US corporations including GM and Microsoft (Ibid). In fact the court in its decision argued in support of its decision that "Major American businesses have made it clear that the skills needed in today's increasingly global market place can only be developed through exposure to widely diverse people, cultures, ideas and viewpoints" (Ibid.). Consequently, today industry supports affirmative action policies on grounds of "social utility" and efficiency, as it creates a diverse environment conducive for broader societal and institutional goals like breaking down racial stereotypes, and developing a diverse business community (Puri 2005:350). Thus, they have supported affirmative action not because of altruism or recompense for past oppression but out of a realisation that it is in their own self-interest (Ibid.).

However, the authors of the BD do not take cognizance of the literature that critically assesses the American experience.[11] In fact, a scholar associated with the BD argues that the purpose of invoking the American example in the Document was to highlight the voluntary commitment of companies and community leaders to make their workforce and industry more diverse reflecting societal diversity and not so much the similarities between the actual US and Indian experiences. While Prasad concludes with an appeal to adopt the US model of Diversity in India, he is careful in maintaining that Diversity ought not to be mistaken as a 'quota' system. It is "opportunities not quotas" that is the central message of the Bhopal Conference (Babu 2003: 15).

Growing Support for SD

While the concept of democratizing capital was advocated by the BD, it has begun to find support among a range of scholars who agree that so far capital has remained the monopoly of a small and select group of individuals/families belonging mainly to the trading community. A recent study by Harish Damodaran investigating the caste origins of many of India's industrialists identifies three main historical trends (Damodaran 2008: 315-16). First, which he calls a "bazaar to factory" route, is the passage of hereditary traders into industry. However, in the specific case of northern India, he argues some castes' monopolies have discouraged them from leaving their traditionally prescribed employment. So members of north India's farming castes—for example, Jats and Yadavs—rarely own a sugar or flourmill (Ibid). Second, a route from "office to factory", that describes a recent movement of well-educated high-caste Hindus, including Brahmins, into business. Lacking capital, these sophisticates tended to enter the service sector, where start-up costs are relatively low. India's world-class computer-services industry, including companies like Infosys, is the result. The third trajectory, from "field to factory", is the transition into the business world of members of India's middle and lower-peasant castes. This must be the path of India's dalits too. But they have not trodden it yet: across India, Damodaran could not find a significant dalit industrialist, not even in the south (Ibid: 315). While a number of social groups have broken into the monopoly of the business/trading banya community, the major exception is the dalit community. With the rise of the BSP some business groups have emerged in UP but they are still small and cannot compare with big or even medium business houses in the country. It is this third group that the supporters of the policy of supplier diversity wish to create.

Commenting on policies such as SD, Vaidyanathan points out that rather than reservation of jobs in the private sector, it is more pertinent to demand a share in the ownership of private capital. The government and private capital have only a small share in the total workforce of the country most of which is in the unorganized sector. Even if all the jobs in the private sector were opened up for dalits the gains would be meager (Vaidyanathan 2005: 358). Rather what is needed is increased access of SC/ST to capital and support in becoming entrepreneurs. He points out that the Economic Survey reveals that the overall growth of enterprises belonging to persons belonging to SC has declined from 3.42 per cent in 1980-90 to 0.40 per cent in 1990-98, the decline being observed in both rural and areas (Ibid). While the reasons need to be examined, Vaidyanathan argues that if it is due to the process of liberalisation, there is need to help dalits in the new market economy.

Similarly, Rajindar Sachar holds that the need to enforce the principle of affirmative action in the private sector has become "a compulsion" because the public sector is being rapidly dismantled (Sachar 2005: 157). Following the 44th amendment to the constitution, the right to property is no longer a fundamental right, nor does Article 19 confer any inviolable right on a company or individual to carry on business with the government. Therefore, any obligation on the private sector to share proportionately its gains with dalits cannot be legally faulted particularly in funds or contracts given by the government, because this action only sub serves the constitutional directives.

However, Sachar also strongly urges that it is not jobs but "business opportunities" that need to be opened to dalits. He points out that central and state governments award thousand of crores worth of public works and contracts to the private sector. Even without legislation, a direction can be given by the government that funds spent by the private sector in connection with public works like roads etc, will carry an inbuilt clause that to start with 15 per cent would be used to procure services or supplies from businesses. Government can direct by executive orders that a certain portion of this money available will be utilized either for providing employment or for sub-contracts to dalits ("Towards Dalit Capitalism" Rajindar Sachar, *The Times of India*, New Delhi, July 12, 2006).

Taking the US example Sachar points out that the Public Works Employment Act 1997 in the US has a minority clause in it which provides that 10 per cent of the federal funds granted for local public works must be used by state and local grantees to procure services or supplies from businesses owned or controlled by minorities group members. Though challenged as running counter to the equal protection clause provided under the 14th amendment of the US constitution it was upheld by the US Supreme Court. The US court upheld the validity of the legislation because it contained provisions designed to uplift socially and economically disadvantaged persons to a level where they could participate in the US economy. Sachar points out that Article 14 of the Indian Constitution is largely adopted from this amendment. The Indian Supreme Court he argues is now "more poor-oriented" than the US Supreme Court. There is no reason for it to reject a challenge similar to that posed by the 1997 US legislation. The overriding question is whether there is political will and determination at the Centre and in the states to take up the combined forces of big business (Ibid.).

In a similar vein Pratap Bhanu Mehta points out that rather than extending reservation in the private sector to dalits, a better method is awarding of government licenses. Government disburses thousands of liquor licenses, numerous broadcasting licenses and so forth that could be used to give dalits access to the private sector. He argues that this would benefit society as a whole. The structures of entrepreneurship in a society are a creation of the ways in which governments disburse monopoly powers (Mehta 2004: 216). Every society which has a system of private industry and the market as a system of allocation, needs *social legitimation*, a part of which at least, comes from values that the society collectively decides are important. In the Indian context, the architecture of the Indian economy cannot be called socially legitimate if dalits and other marginalized communities do not have a share in the private sector profits. Secondly, it is necessary to take into consideration that a large section of dalits feel that they stand to lose from liberalisation of the economy and therefore new policies are required, a feeling that needs to be addressed (Ibid.).

A recent study also argues that policies in which resources are redistributed to members of the disadvantaged community are better than preferential selection for educational institutions or jobs (Weisskopf 2006: 718). Such resource transfers could be directed to members of those communities in such a way as to enable them to develop the skills needed to qualify for better jobs or to acquire the capital needed to launch business enterprises, thus contributing directly to economic development as well as social uplift. Preferential selection policies also concentrate losses on those applicants displaced by the admission of the beneficiaries; and this leads not only the applicants thus displaced but many other rejected applicants to attribute their rejection to the unfairness of preferential policies. A programme of developmental aid on the other hand, involves costs spread much more broadly among the general public and the burden falls largely on those who can afford to pay. This makes such policies easier to support for political leaders (Ibid.).

CONCLUSION

This paper has tried to understand the contours of the debate on the need to move from earlier policies of PD to new ones based on preferential policies of affirmative action. This debate is the result of changes in the Indian economy and polity due to globalisation and particularly the emergence of a strong private sector and new opportunities in business and industry. It also signals considerable change in ideas and rise of new aspirations and self-confidence within the younger, educated, politically conscious sections of the dalit community over the last two decades. While in the constituent assembly policies for dalits were decided by the nationalist leadership and a few dalit leaders, today these are being discussed and debated by an educated middle class within the community.

For these reasons the Bhopal Conference 2002, was an important event. It represents the first attempt by dalit and non-dalit intellectuals/activists in the post-independence period to collectively discuss the problems facing the community and draw up alternative policies, which it was felt were more suitable in the new economic and political context. The Conference threw up a number of complex issues that will be useful for scholars involved in the effort to devise new programmes for disadvantaged sections. The conference drew attention to the lack of a middle class in academia, arts, media and most particularly the sphere of business and industry which had marginalized dalits from both economic decision-making and a share in the benefits of development particularly rapid growth in recent years. Discussion on policies that would enable dalits to enter the arena of business/industry showed that while much scholarly attention has been paid to various forms of social discrimination. There is need for theoretical tools that explain the kinds of market discrimination that make entry and participation difficult for groups so far excluded and to devise policies that overcome these obstacles and greater inclusiveness.

Another fundamental issue is the boundary between the public and the private sphere and the role each is expected to play in the emerging market-oriented economy. While earlier PD policies were firmly within the public sector. With globalisation providing more space for the private sector, the role of the State in policies for dalits is being redefined though no new consensus is as yet in sight. This explains the considerable difference of opinion among scholars and activists on the kind of policies suited to the specific Indian context. Some scholars pointing to the existence of caste bias in the private sector—as more important in determining employment than differences in education and skills—advocate the extension of the existing reservation policy into the private sector with legal guarantees. They point to the reluctance of the private sector to fulfill their corporate social responsibility by providing employment to the underprivileged.

Others hold that while maintaining and improving the existing system of reservations, bringing in the private sector through affirmative action policies based upon a voluntary system would be more suitable to a globalizing and increasingly competitive economy linked to the world market. More specifically, the authors of the BD pointing to the problems encountered in traditional reservation policy such as poor implementation and slow progress, feel that rather than reserving jobs in the private sector, enabling dalits to enter into the sphere of business and industry an area traditionally denied to them, would be much better. Not only are the number of jobs few in the private sector and would therefore not yield much benefit. They argue that creating a dalit/tribal entrepreneurial class is urgently required to end the marginalisation and exclusion that these groups have suffered in the economic sphere. It would provide greater legitimacy to the Indian polity and provide all sections a stake in the economy. Such a move would displace fewer people, be less contentious, create greater social harmony and would also take the pressure off higher education. As a middle class emerges among these communities, the need for reservations in the long run would no longer be required. The supporters of this position draw upon the American experience in creating an entrepreneurial class among the Blacks and minorities, though there is recognition of the need to fashion specific policies that will work effectively for dalits.

Based on these arguments the advocates of the policy of SD argue that the State—which has helped in the rise of the industrial capitalist class in India—must now play a positive role in the "creation" of a class of dalit entrepreneurs. They provide a blueprint of the process by which this can be undertaken: government contracts through supplierships and dealerships for goods required from entrepreneurs belonging to these communities giving them an opportunity to engage in business. It is in this context that the MP experiment provides a starting point. At the same time they are keen that the SD policy must eventually be adopted by both the public and the private sector.

All this suggests that the debate on the needs of dalits in the new globalizing polity and economy has barely started, though a growing number of scholars have begun to express their opinions. For our purposes the value of the debate lies in drawing attention to the need for new policies to help dalits to enter into the areas of business and industry from which they have been traditionally kept out.

ENDNOTES AND REFERENCES

1. The Bhopal Document 2002.
2. Ibid.
3. The Bhopal Document The Dalit Agenda Charting a New Course For Dalits For the 21st Century Government of MP, Bhopal, January 2002.
4. Among those who wrote in the issue were Chandrabhan Prasad, Gail Omvedt, Tulsi Ram, Vimal Thorat, Sheoraj Bechain and journalists such as B.N. Uniyal. It also had excellent reproductions of paintings by the artist Savi Savarkar. Among them Prasad has written extensively on the SD programme.
5. Interview of Chandrabhan Prasad on *DNAINDIA.com* visited on July 15, 2007.
6. For details about these schemes see Sudha Pai, *Developmental State and the Dalit Question in Madhya Pradesh: Congress Response*, Routledge, New Delhi, 2010.
7. Ibid.
8. Ibid.
9. For details see Bhopal Document, 2002: 70-83.
10. The two cases were *Grutter vs Bollinger* and *Gratz vs Bollinger*. Although the judgments differed, in both cases they upheld the principles underlying affirmative action policies in the US and specifically in the university of Michigan.
11. It is not possible here to review the substantial and controversial literature on the US experience with affirmative action. It is worth noting that much of this literature on affirmative action is largely on the impact of policies in the field of education and employment. See, Sowell 2004, Gibson and Ogbu 1991, Killian 1990, Herman 1988, Aklimat 1988, and Holzer and Neumark 2000, Weisskopf 2004. The US experience with supplierships and dealerships by the Federal government or through private contracts has been much less researched.

9

Social Justice: Policy Initiatives and Implementation

Kamlesh Gupta

This paper addresses the question, why policy initiatives and implementation are important for ensuring social justice. The author advocates that policy initiatives by the government and their proper implementation are the chief solutions to the problem of social justice in the present perspective. The author focuses on policy initiatives for social justice after independence and compares them with the present situation and also analyses the present status of social justice. The paper is divided into the following parts: Introduction, Concept of Social Justice, Review of Literature and Methodology, Constitutional Status, Contemporary Perspective, Challenges of Policy Concern and Implementation, and Suggestions for Policy Concern and Implementation.

Democracy is considered as the best form of government, and as far as right of the people is concerned, social justice is an important concept for any democratic system. The state on its part also provided certain safeguards to disadvantaged section of the society through what is known as affirmative actions. "Through affirmative actions the state grants certain privileges to under-privileged section of society, which include various reforms, redistribution of societies, resources, and reservation etc., also known as protective discrimination. This is in consonance with the very aim of social justice (along with economic and political) enshrined in the very preamble of our constitution thereby granting special safeguard in Article 15 and 16 of our constitution. Further, these special privileges represented various groups that were historically disprivileged and who required a level playing field to exercise their right to equal opportunity. This included SCs, and STs, OBCs, women, minorities, physically handicapped."[1] Welfare of the people is the foremost and most important task of the state. Since the government has to deal with the various issues and aspects of social welfare, thereon the concept of social justice has a special importance for the existence of the democracy and social welfare as well. India is the largest democracy in the world and it has adopted the goal of socialistic pattern of society, for which it endeavours to fulfill the objective of social welfare maximisation. However, India has a wide variety and differentiation based on socio-political criteria, gender, caste, language, region, and in these circumstances social justice has a special importance. "Social justice in the present context has therefore, been reduced to reservation which is regarded as the only criteria for social equality. However what has been missed here is that without though measure at the basic level, (for example education, reforms, etc.), this soft option of reservation bill will pass void. Long-term measures are therefore found waiting in the present time."[2] The present paper attempts to examine the issue of social justice, the policy initiatives taken by the government, and status of the policy implementation against this overall backdrop. In this paper the following aspects have been analysed.

- Theoretical concept of social justice.
- Examination of the present status of social justice in India.
- Analysis of policy initiatives and status of policy implementation

Policy implementation is an important aspect for social justice because the success of governmental policy for development of SCs/STs and weaker sections can be measured only in relation to the implementation of the policies related to their welfare. Policy concerns and their implementation processes can be seen by diagram 1.

REVIEW OF LITERATURE AND METHODOLOGY

Several scholars have worked on areas related to this issue. Some of these works are: O.P. Gauba, *Dimensions of Social Justice* (New Delhi, 1983); Krishna Gupta, *Social Equality and the Indian Constitution* (New Delhi: S. Chand and Company, 1996); A.N. Bhardwaj *The Problems of Scheduled Caste and Scheduled Tribes in India* (New Delhi, 1979); Gupta S. Dutta, *Justice and Political Order in India* (Calcutta, 1978); Ishwari Prasad, *Reservation, Action for Equality* (New Delhi, 1986); D.N. Sandanshiv, Land and Social Justice (Bombay, 1978); Gokhlesh Sharma, *Human Rights and Social Justice* (New Delhi, 2007); Manoj Bhatt, *Social Demography in India* (New Delhi, 2004); S.M. Michael *Dalits in Modern India: Vision and Values* (New Delhi, 2007) K.S. Chalam, *Caste based Reservations and Human Development in India* (New Delhi, 2007); and *Dalit Development and Democracy* (New Delhi, 1999). Most of these studies are however outdated and moreover do not focus on the policy initiatives taken by the government and their implementation for ensuring social justice. The present paper tries to fulfill the gap in the past studies and tries to explore some new dimensions for this problem. In other words it intends to unearth the untouched aspects of social justice, policy concern and implementation for filling the gap in the previous research.

The present paper is based upon secondary data sources and the necessary data was collected from various publications of the government

Diagram 1

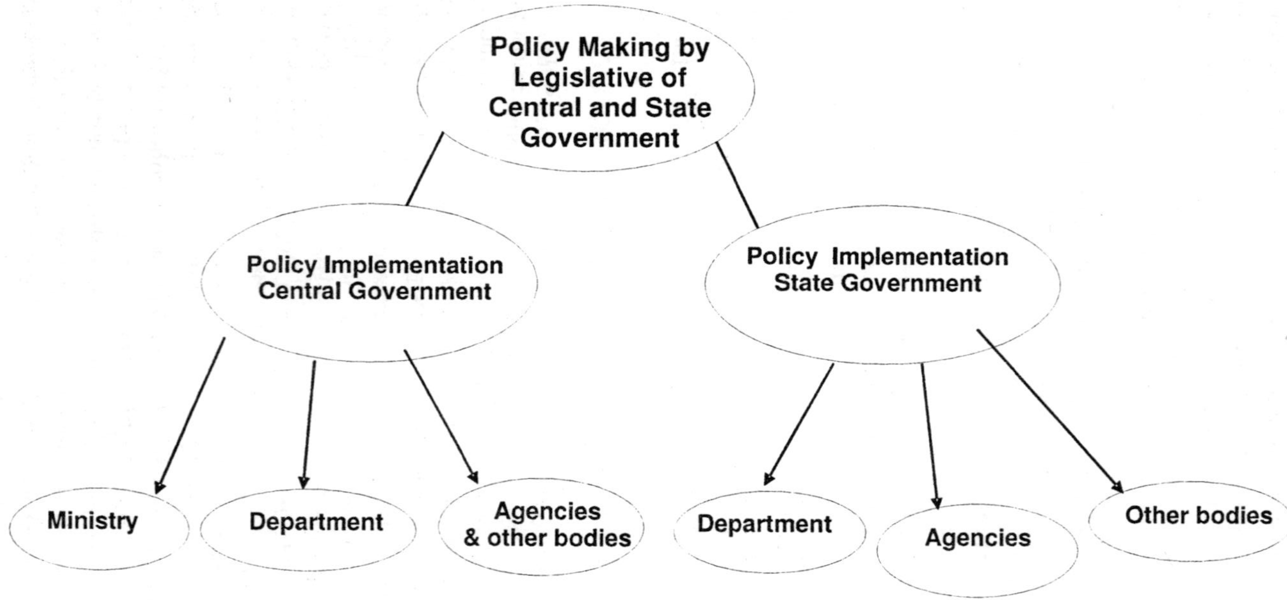

- Policy formulated by central government and implemented by central and state government Directorate and other Agencies.
- Policy formulated by state governments and implemented by state Directorate and other Agencies.

of India and as well as from other sources. These sources are: publications such as Report of the Ministry of Social Justice and Empowerment (2009-10), Report of the Ministry of Human Resource Development, data of Census 2001, Report of United Nations (2008), Report of Planning Commission (2009-10), Employment Review (2009-10), Economic Survey (2009-10) and other data published by different magazines. The data was processed by employing simple statistical tools like simple ratio analysis, average, mean etc.

CONCEPT OF SOCIAL JUSTICE

"Social justice, invokes a substantive concept of justice and unlike procedural justice,"[3] "it also deals with background fairness to elaborate this, we can say that all modern states are based on the belief in some sort of equality and claimed to treat their citizens equally. Minimally, it implies political and civil liberties, equal rights before the law, equal protection against arbitrary arrest, and so forth. These thing provide a base of a society of equal citizens".[4] The concept of justice has occupied a high place in philosophical discussions in India since the beginning of Indian philosophy. The *Gita*, which contains the substance of the Vedas and the Upanishads, for instance, proclaims, "Only those who perceive all living creatures of the world irrespective of their caste, creed, etc., as manifestations of the God, are real scholars." In fact, the *Gita* clearly mentions that the four *Varna* were created on the basis of the inherent nature of a person rather then on the ground of birth. Western philosophers have also contributed immensely towards evolving the concept of social justice and in the process have attributed different connotations to the concept. Viewing social justice in contemporary context, Rawls played a major role in reviving an interest in the substantive questions of political philosophy like 'What makes a society just? How is social justice connected to an individual's pursuit of the good life?' In *A Theory of Justice*, Rawls attempts to reconcile liberty and equality in a principled way, offering an account of "justice as fairness." Central to this effort is his famous approach to the seemingly intractable problem of *distributive justice*. The work of Nozick and Hayek too needs a mention here whose contributions added new dimensions to the then existing notions of social justice. On the other hand the recent work of Amartya Sen in his 'Idea of Justice' opens up a whole new spectrum of looking at the concept of justice.

However, in terms of democracy and popular politics, its exact meaning and implications have been hazy, one of the reasons being the fact that justice in reality is a meeting ground of many ideas, situations, concepts, expectations, mechanisms, and practices. "There are many things that intersect to form the context of social justice—ethical ideas of the people, laws, the evolving nature of claims, and the pattern of collective claim making politics, institutional issues relating to the delivery mechanisms of justice, ideas about rights and entitlements, ideas among the citizens about responsibility of the rulers towards them, plus many situations generating many conditions of justice."[5] Thus we can witness various forms of social justice in reality—social claim as justice, attainment and restoration of dignity as justice, end to discrimination as justice, retribution as justice, conciliation of claims as justice, social idea of minimal justice, positive discrimination as justice, protection of the vulnerable sections of society as justice, and finally autonomy as justice. One also finds social justice as having strong gender implications. However, a process of rethinking on the concept of social justice and its emerging contemporary issues in the changing scenario would definitely prove futile in probing its different contours for a deeper and in-depth analysis, more so when the Indian society is passing through a crucial and transformative stage. As is evident from the ever growing presence and global impact of Indian brains and work force, the country has made remarkable progress in all spheres. However, there are still certain areas where we have failed to match the aspirations of the founding fathers of our nation. Though "our country is the largest democracy in the world, but social exclusion has remained a profound problem for us. We have set landmarks in world trade but the gap between rich and poor and gender inequality has widened to magnitudes never seen before."[6] Admist such trends, Hasan obserbs: "despite the steady increases in participation in elections from the lower social order, still there remains a central contradiction at the heart of Indian democracy : an inclusive polity so far not made for a just and equal society."[7] Though we are a secular nation but incidences of religious intolerance disturb the normal life of our citizens.

According to Wikipaedia, "Social justice refers to the concept of a society in which justice is achieved in every aspect of society, rather than merely the administration of law. As there is no objective, known standard of what is just the term can be amorphous and refer to sometimes self-contradictory values of justice. It is generally thought of as a society which efforts individuals and groups fair treatment and a just share of the benefits of society. It can also refer to the distribution of advantages and disadvantages within a society."[8] The objective of social justice has articulated the broad programme for the progressive reduction in inequalities and better life for under privileged section of society through welfare activities.[9]

"The school of social justice argues that structures should be adopted and influenced in ways that can give more people a better chance in the first place. That is why opportunities and breaking down barriers are so important."[10] "Inequalities that are permissible in social justice through, say, affirmative actions and positive discrimination are acceptable. This aim becomes all the more with regard to the vast inequalities (both horizontal and vertical) that exist in the country."[11] Nehru believed that "the aim of protective discrimination was to eliminate inequalities based on past prejudices associated with the discriminatory social structure of society."[12] "Social justice, therefore, tries to go behind the structure of rules to determine who is in need, say of healthcare, educational opportunities, housing and so on. However, sum economic and social theorists suggest that these problems might be overcome by a welfare policy, which guarantees the payment of 'negative income' tax to those where earning falls below a certain level."[13]

POLICY INITIATIVES AFTER INDEPENDENCE

Unfortunately in India, with the passage of time, the *Varna* system became very rigid and degenerated into a caste system that includes the practice of untouchability. Hence social reformers and leaders of the Indian freedom struggle launched a powerful struggle against this social evil. Once India got independence the founding fathers of the Indian Constitution inscribed the ideal of social justice into the Constitution in the forms of the Preamble, Fundamental Rights, Directive Principal of State Policy, etc. Achieving social justice thus is one of the basic objectives of the Constitution of India. The Preamble of the Constitution proclaims that its aim is to secure justice—social, economic and political and equality of status and opportunity.

The development of the weaker section of the society, particularly of the Scheduled Castes and Scheduled Tribes (SCs/STs) has been on the agenda of the government since the starting of planning and development processes in our country. The overall lower socio-economic position of the SCs/STs made the framers of the constitutions realize that special attention is urgently required for their development. They believed that socially, economically and educationally backward castes cannot compete with others without the initials support given by the state and accordingly some special provisions, besides the fundamental rights were incorporated in the constitution to provide equal opportunity and justice for these sections. As a result some specific provisions were incorporated in the constitution to provide social justice to the member of these sections through the policy of 'protective discrimination'. The basic purpose of incorporating these provisions was to change the traditional social structure of our society, which is based on socio-economic and political inequalities. "These special provisions have played an important role in improving the socio-economic, other conditions and achieving a better position to the people of Schedule Caste and Schedule Tribe. Development with social justice has been the major objective of our planning process and welfare programmes in India."[14] The government not only took into account development goals, but also considered social aspects like providing access to the deprived section to participate in the development of process. Article 46 of the constitution imposes the obligation on the government to promote socio-economic interests of the Schedule Castes and Schedule Tribes.

CONSTITUTIONAL STATUS

The constitution of India established the country as a welfare state and chalked out a very detailed agenda for the promotion of social justice. "The concept of social justice for the achievement of welfare state is more realistic. Thus the directive principles are the life giving principles of the constitution.

These provisions constitute a social and economic philosophy and the substance of the constitution."[15] "The Constitution of India guarantees protection from social injustice and all forms of exploitation (Art. 46). It guarantees equality before law (Art. 14), and enjoins upon the State not to discriminate against any citizen on grounds of caste (Art. 15(1)). Untouchability is abolished and its practice in any form is forbidden (Art. 17)."[16] The constitution mandates that no citizen shall, on grounds only of caste or race, be subjected to any disability and restriction (Art. 15(2)). It empowers the State to make provisions for reservation in educational institutions (Art. 15(4) and (5)), and in appointments for posts in favour of SCs (Art. 16(4), 16(4A), 16(4B) and Art. 335). Reservation of seats for SCs in the Lok Sabha is provided under Article 330, in the State Assemblies under Article 332 and in the Local Self-Governments bodies under Articles 243D and 340T. In addition to the above, the Parliament has enacted the Untouchability (Offences) Act, 1955, renamed as Protection of Civil Rights Act, in 1976. To check and deter atrocities against SCs, the Scheduled Castes and the Scheduled Tribes (Prevention of Atrocities) Act, 1989 has also been enacted.[17]

The constitution of India has made several provisions to safeguard the interests of the STs in Articles 15(4), 16(4), 46, 243M, 243 ZC, 244, the first and second provisos to 275(1), Articles 334, 335, 338A, 339(1), and the Fifth and the Sixth Schedules.[18] Besides these, several laws have been enacted by the Central Government like the Protection of Civil Rights Act, 1955; the Scheduled Castes and Scheduled Tribes (Prevention of Atrocities) Act, 1989; the Provisions of the Panchayats (Extension to Scheduled Areas) Act, 1996; the Scheduled Tribes and Other Traditional Forest Dwellers (Recognition of Forest Rights) Act, 2006 as well as by the State Governments (relating to the prevention of alienation and restoration of tribal land, money-lending, reservations, and so on). The Center has been given the authority of giving directions to the State Governments (cf. Article 339(2), Para 3 of the Fifth Schedule) in the interest of tribal people. Further, a National Tribal Policy is on the Central anvil.

Though the Constitution does not make specific provisions for OBCs, it empowers the State to make provisions for reservation in appointments or posts in favour of any backward class of citizens which, in the opinion of the State, is not adequately represented in the Services under the State [Article 16(4)]. It also empowers the State to appoint a commission to investigate into the conditions of socially and educationally backward classes (Article 340). In pursuance of the Supreme Court judgment, *Indira Sawhney and Others* vs *Union of India* (1992), the National Commission for Backward Classes was set up on 14 August 1993 under the National Commission for Backward Classes Act, 1993. Thus, after 46 years of independence of the country, the backward classes or OBCs got recognition as a separate group of people for the purpose of 27 per cent reservation in services in the GoI and public sector undertakings. The States/UTs were free to decide the quantum of reservation based on the OBC population in their State/UT. All State Governments were also directed by the Supreme Court of India in the same case to set up a permanent body and to draw up their own list and decide the quantum of reservation as per their demography."[19]

The constitution of India has also made several provisions to safeguard the interests of the minorities in Article 15 namely Prohibition of discrimination on grounds of religion, Article 16 namely Equality of opportunity in matters of public employment, Article 25 namely Freedom of conscience and free profession, practice and propagation of religion, Article 26 namely Freedom to manage religious affairs, Articles 29 namely Right to conserve language, script, and culture, Article 30 namely Right to establish and administer educational institutions, Article 347 namely Recognition of language, Article 350 namely Redressal of grievances to any authority in the government in any of the languages used in the States, Article 350(A) namely Instruction through mother tongue at the primary stage of education, Article 350(B) namely Investigate all matters relating to linguistic minorities.

CONTEMPORARY PERSPECTIVE

The present demographic profile of socially deprived groups of India which include the SCs, STs, OBCs and minorities is that the SCs number 16,66,35,700, i.e., 16.2 per cent of total population, STs number 8,43,26,240, i.e., 8.20 per cent and minorities around 18,94,00,000, i.e., 18.42 per cent of the total population[20] according to the 2001 census. The OBCs, as per a Government of India notification of 8 September 1993, include castes and communities which are named in both the lists contained in the Report of the Backward Classes Commission and in the list of individual state governments.[21] Basing its calculation on the Census of 1931, the Backward Classes Commission headed by B.P. Mandal (1980), estimated that OBCs constitute 52 per cent of the population. Recently, the NSSO 61st Round (July 2004 to June 2005) report on 'Employment and Unemployment Situation among Social Groups in India' estimated that OBCs constitute 41 per cent of the population. State-wise, OBC-wise data on population as well as vital and demographic variables are not available, which is the main hurdle in the formulation of policies and programmes for the development of the Other Backward Classes. (Table 1)

Along with the social justice of socially downtrodden groups it is also necessary to think of social justice of minorities, women, social deviants, persons with disability and other disadvantaged groups. According to the Census of 2001, 18.4 per cent of our population belongs to minority communities. Of this, Muslims constitute 13.4 per cent, Christians 2.3 per cent, Sikhs 1.9 per cent, Buddhists 0.8 per cent and Parsis 0.07 per cent of the country's total population. In absolute numbers, Muslims (nearly 140 million) account for 72.8 per cent of the total minority population of 189.5 million. The Census 2001 and NSSO 2002 figures for persons with disabilities are 2.13 and 1.8 per cent, respectively but these figures could be an underestimation. According to the United Nations, the proportion of disabled people and the

Table 1: Population of SCs, ST, OBC, Minority and Disability People

	Male Population	Female Population	Total Population
Schedule Caste	8,60,88,760	8,05,46,940	16,66,35,700
Schedule Tribe	4,26,40,829	4,16,85,411	8,43,26,240
OBC	—	—	In 2004-05 estimated 41 per cent of total population
Minority	—	—	18,94,00,000
Person with disabilities	—	—	2,19,00,000

Source: Census 2001, Government of India.

percentage of disabled people among the total population of any country would depend on the definition of 'disability' in that particular country as well as the enumeration methodology and its accuracy. In India, the definition of disability used in the Census is very different from that in the Persons with Disabilities Act, 1995. There is an urgent need for both a credible definition and a system of data collection relating to persons with disabilities. It can be reasonably assumed that persons with disabilities constitute anywhere between 5 to 6 per cent of our total population.

GOVERNMENTAL INITIATIVES

The Government of India has taken various policy initiatives to provide social justice for deprived section with following objectives:

- Ensuring removal of disparities and providing protection to the marginalised section through various development schemes.
- Ensuring that developmental benefits reach the unreached through equitable distribution.
- Ensuring the involvement of the socially deprived section in the process of planning and participation in the formulation of need based programmes, supervision and monitoring.
- Improving the social-economic status of the deprived section through effective implementation of various policies and programmes.
- Ensuring social empowerment through educational development.
- Ensuring political empowerment, through reservation of seats in different democratic bodies.
- Ensuring social justice, through implementation of the existing legislations, decisions and other measures for preventing and protecting the disadvantaged groups from atrocities, exploitation, discrimination and social disabilities.

Earlier in the Tenth Five Year Plan (2002-07), government had adopted a multipronged approach for the socio-economic development of the SCs; social empowerment through educational development; economic empowerment through income and employment enhancing avenues; protection through implementation of protective legislations and eradication of occupations such as manual scavenging; and holistic development through earmarking of funds proportionate to the population [Scheduled Caste Sub-Plan (SCSP) and Tribal Sub-Plan (TSP)].[22]

In view of the persistent and wide-spread socioeconomic backwardness of SCs and STs, a distinct need was felt for innovative policy intervention to enable these groups to share the benefits of growth in a more equitable manner. The government prepared a separate Development Plan called Tribal Sub Plan (TSP) for STs in 1976. It was followed by the Special Component Plan for the SCs in 1978 (recently renamed the Scheduled Caste Sub Plan [SCSP]). The SCSP and TSP aim at facilitating convergence and pooling of resources from all the other development sectors in proportion to the population of SCs and STs, respectively for their overall development. With respect to the educational development of SCs, the Central Government has introduced several scholarship programmes. The other important schemes for the educational development of SCs are:[23]

- Providing coaching facilities to students to prepare them for various competitive examinations being conducted by Union Public Service Commission (UPSC), State Public Service Commissions, banks, and so on;
- Hostel facilities to both boys and girls for pursuing education from middle level onwards. With respect to the educational development of SCs, the Central Government has introduced major scholarship programmes';
- Implementation of the Scheduled Caste Sub-Plan (SCSP) and Tribal Sub-Plan (TSP).

For the welfare of the minorities, the Prime Minister's new 15-Point Programme was launched in 2006 which aimed at ensuring their well being, protection and development. While the 15-Point Programme of 1983 centred on communal riots, representation of minorities in services and ensuring flow of benefits to individual beneficiaries, the focus of the new Programme is to make certain that benefits of various schemes/programmes flow equitably to the minorities. For this, it quantifies a certain portion of development projects to be established in areas with a concentration of minorities. It stipulates that wherever possible, 15 per cent of targets and outlays under various schemes will be earmarked for the minorities.

The National Policy for Persons with Disabilities was adopted in 2006. It recognizes that disabled people are valuable human resources for the country. The policy focuses primarily on prevention of disability, early detection and appropriate interventions, physical and economic rehabilitation measures, inclusive education, employment in the public as well as private sector and self employment, creation of a barrier-free environment and development of rehabilitation professionals.

India has the second largest population of older (60+) persons in the world. The number of older persons in the population is expected to increase from 71 million in 2001 to 173 million in 2026. A majority (80 per cent) of the elderly population in India is in the rural areas, thus making service delivery to them a challenge, and there is a large number of 80+ persons in the country.

The Ministry of Social Justice and Empowerment is responsible for the implementation of the following Acts for the welfare of deprived sections.[24]

- The Protection of Civil Rights Act, 1955.
- The Scheduled Castes and the Scheduled Tribes (Prevention of Atrocities) Act, 1989.
- The Rehabilitation Council of India Act, 1992 (34 of 1992).
- National Commission for Backward Classes Act, 1993.
- The Persons with Disabilities (Equal Opportunities, Protection of Rights and Full Participation) Act, 1995 (01 of 1996).
- The National Trust for Welfare of Persons with Autism, Cerebral Palsy, Mental Retardation and Multiple Disabilities Act, 1999 (44 of 1999).
- The Maintenance and Welfare of Parents and Senior Citizens Act, 2007. The following Table 2 shows the expenditure of the Government of India on social justice.

Table 2: Government of India Expenditure on Social Justice[25]

(Amount in crores)

Contents/year	2001-02	2002-03	2003-04	2004-05	2005-06	2006-07	2007-08	2008-09	2009-10 on 31.3.2010
1. Social Justice	2321	2302	2224	2497	3009	3485	4065	4736	6187
2. Welfare of SC	729	742	767	803	952	1071	1707	1815	1921
3. Welfare of ST	967	1018	872	1082	1409	1648	1524	1805	3205
4. Welfare of OBC	...	...	...	...	...	...	200.5	248	289
5. Social Security	333	296	298	298	321	350	417	434	386
i. Welfare of Handicaped	248	203	208	203	221	232	266	254	232
ii. Child Welfare	24	23	21	23	20	23	82	99	70
iii. Social Welfare	61	70	69	72	75	94	69	81	84

Source: Eleventh Five Year Plan, 2007-12, Planning Commission, Vol. I.

It is revealed from the above table 2 that the Government of India has paid considerable attention towards social justice in India as indicated by the simple growth rate. It is also welcome that the government has paid increased attention towards social justice of STs. But if population is taken into account

SCs have got comparatively small share of the expenditure. The government has also tried to provide social security services, but their growth is very slow.

CHALLENGES OF POLICY CONCERN AND IMPLEMENTATION

Many policy analyst believed that production for policy process is really a cyclical process starting from "realization of problems" and moving to "finding a solution", "implementing the solution."[26] However, in reality it is not so. "Social scientists and policy analysts have identified various factors that can influence the policy process and make it unpredictable."[27] "In other words it is now realized that all problems related to social justice issues do not produce policies, all policies do not invite implementation, and similarly all implementation do not affect the society in the manner intended. And there can be a wide gap in policy formulation and policy implementation. It may also be noted that the assumption once say policy has been formulated, it will be implemented, is not true in developing countries."[28]

"Governments in these nations tend to formulate broad sweeping policies and the bureaucratic organization often lack the capacity for implementation. Lack of qualified personnel, in sufficient opposition to policy, rampant, corruption, etc. while in the western nations, policies tend to be incremental in nature in the developing countries; they are ambitious, sweeping, design to bring about development and social reform creating new pattern of actions and institutions and in the process generating tension both within and between the component categories of idolized policies."[29]

"Public Policy Implementation in Modern times has often been characterized by a skepticism about the capacity of Governments to meet their goals and objectives."[30] Promoting social justice is the main responsibility of the government and its significance increases since India is a democratic system and a welfare state. In the previous sections author saw that the government has focused on the welfare of SCs/STs and other weaker section in recent years through welfare scheme and other developing programmes and policies. However the uplift of these sections needs proper implementation of policies. After in-depth analysis of the issues involved author found some major challenges in policy concerns and implementation.

Lack of Coordination between Central and State

The balance which is expected between the State and the Central in the context of policy implementation is not present in India. In addition corruption has also struck deep roots in the proper policy and programme implementation and benefits. There is a clear problem of coordination between Central and State governments.

Status of Policy Implementation

The implementation of the policies has been stalled at present because most governmental development programmes are not running in the proper way even though they were set up a long time back. In the same manner the implementation of other decisions has also not been done and the situation is that the policies are formed but are not implemented properly. The efforts of the Central Government should be to revamp the condition of policy implementation concern in India for better result about social justice policy concern.

Research and Monitoring

Developmental programmes for the welfare of socially disadvantaged groups and marginalized sections of society have been in operation from the First Five Year Plan onwards. Whether the benefits of these programmes reach the targeted persons needs to be monitored on a periodical basis at the district, state and national levels. Continuous monitoring and evaluation would justify the continuation of programmes. The Ministries of Social Justice and Empowerment, and Tribal Affairs and Minorities have developed mechanisms for monitoring and evaluating their programmes. These ministries also sponsor research studies by independent agencies such as university departments/reputed research bodies. Based on the findings of such studies, efforts are made to improve upon the strategy for implementation of schemes. However the results are not coming better because the policy of monitoring and evaluation is not perfect. The government is trying to make proper efforts and during the Eleventh Five Year Plan particular stress will be laid on ensuring that such evaluation does not become routine but results in actual improvement in the schemes.

Evaluation and Control

Evaluation and control of the existing programmes is a difficult exercise since it involves specifying the goals of the programmes. The evaluation and control of the programme is confounded by many factors. "The final stage of the policy process is the assessment of what has happen regarding the implementation of the policy.[31] Evaluating a public policy involves the listing of the goals of the policy and measuring a degree to which these goal have been achieved.

Status of Database

The Census of India and NSSO are the two agencies which make available data on various aspects of social groups. Data on SCs, STs, Minorities and Persons with Disabilities have been made available by these agencies. Census data are not available for OBCs and persons who are victims of drug addiction and alcoholism. The Eleventh Plan will address the need for survey of such category of persons for proper formulation of policies and programmes towards their welfare and rehabilitation.

Affirmative Legislation Action

The prevailing gaps in socio-economic status between SCs, STs and other disadvantaged groups vis-à-vis the rest of the population need to be speedily bridged by taking innovative measures. As a first step, there is a need to assess the gaps between SCs and other social groups with respect to various parameters of growth and development and construct an index of development/vulnerability/deprivation on the basis of which policy and programme interventions can be formulated and administered. State governments, Central ministries/departments and public authorities should be made accountable for purposeful and affirmative action within their jurisdiction to bring about overall development of the people belonging to SCs/STs and to bridge the gaps between their and other social groups.

POLICY RECOMMENDATIONS AND SUGGESTIONS FOR THEIR IMPLEMENTATION

In a welfare state, services like education, health and justice should be provided either free or at subsidized rates to the citizens of the country and the government should take appropriate steps in this direction. If Indian Government is seriously interested in establishing itself strongly among the other developed countries then it has to empower itself in the field of policy concern & implementation of social justice. For this purpose the reforms should be implemented within a stipulated period of time. The government should also try to develop and maintain a creative balance between the private and government sector under government control for the implementation of these programmes. Proper implementation of the governmental policies made for reforming the state of social justice of the country are not being done, which should be done as soon as possible. For this purpose it is necessary that the policies formed by the government should be properly implemented and alongside there should be an effective system for controlling these institutions at both the national and the state level. After discussing the challenges, author offer a few suggestions for policy concern and their implementation.

Promote Social Justice and Empowerment through Policy Initiatives

The government of India promotes social justice and empowerment as well as social development through policy initiatives, social welfare schemes and programme, but the lack of literacy and awareness of SCs, STs and marginalised sections is a big barrier in the government's efforts. "Perhaps the most important intervening variable between development plans and their implementations is the bureaucratic machinery, whose function is to translate planed goal into action. It has been argued that despite the relative effectiveness of bureaucracy in India in the area of policy exclusion and implementation. The traditional bureaucratic structure and process are incompatible with the implementation of the development task."[32]

Effective Implementation

As per government data, the government has taken several policy initiatives after independence but there has been little progress in the sector of social justice. There is urgent need to develop an effective implementation of the various schemes and programmes for the social justice. For this purpose we need a unitary programme implementation administrative system. "Important to this has been emergence of the New Public Management (NPM). NPM allows private bodies to take greater responsibility for the delivery of services through privatization, contracting out and market testing. These ideas have been taken out most enthusiastically in New Zealand, UK, USA, and Scandinavia."[33]

Role of the State

Role of the state is very important in promoting social justice since the state is also responsible for implementation of social justice policies and programmes. State is basically policy iniciative and implementation agency, but there is lake of concerted coordination in the implementation of social justice policy/programmes.

Coordination between Central and State Governments

Coordination between Central and State government is also an important factor because social welfare policy is the subject of state directive policy and in India state governments are the implementation bodies.

Need of Unified Programme Implementation Agency

In present perspective, for better implementation of social justice programmes, we need a Unified Programmes Implementation Agency (UPIA) in block level. UPIA work with coordination of Programme/policy concern department and implement various programmes of social justice.

Need of Evaluation and Control Board

In any decision-making process and policy-formulation, there is always need for a detailed working out of strategic programs and suitable administrative organizations and operational steps. "Administrative planning begins where economic planning ends. It is conveyor system without a dichotomy between planning and implementation, but there is always feedback from implementation to make planning much more purposeful. From time to time bureaucracy had indeed risen to deliver the goals in time of crises. It is, thus responsibility of the bureaucracy to ensure that the policies are conceived so as to we relevant to prevailing conditions and implemented with patience and conviction."[34] In the present perspective there is an urgent need to develop proper controlling and evaluation system for better and proper implementation of social justice policies and programmes. Along with policy implementation for reforming social justice, it is necessary to develop an

Diagram 2: Central Evaluation and Controlling Board (CECB)

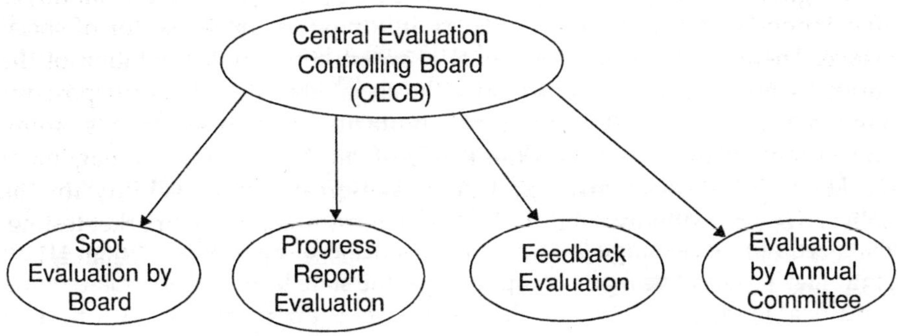

- **Spot evaluation by evaluation board and prepared a report on the basis of evaluation.**
- **Sending annual progress report by implementers agency should be compulsory before the beginning of financial year.**
- **Feedback evaluation of the Policy/Programmes/schemes by board/ committee.**
- **Annual evaluation committee should prepare report every year for grading system.**

Diagram 3: State Evaluation and Controlling Board (SECB)

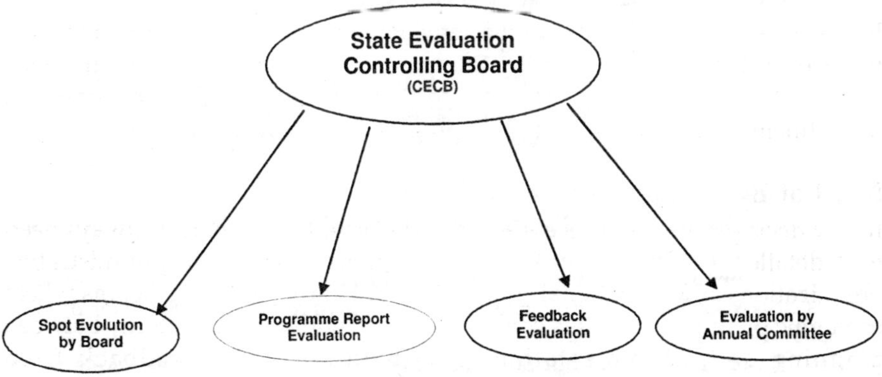

- **Spot evaluation by evaluation board and prepared a report on the basis of evaluation.**
- **Sending annual progress report by implementers agency should be compulsory before the beginning of financial year.**
- **Feedback evaluation of the Policy/Programmes/schemes by board/ committee.**
- **Annual evaluation committee should prepare report every year for grading system.**

evaluation system which can be done at the Central and State level by a central evaluation and control board and a state evaluation control board. The organization of these boards are shown in the following diagrams 2 and 3. Through these controlling and evaluation boards it will also be possible to determine the state of policy implementation. These kinds of boards are very important for raising the overall policy implementation in India, which will also supervise the overall policy implementation.

The effort of the central government to revamp the condition of social justice in India is commendable but the policy implementation system in India also needs to be revamped. The implementation of the policies taken at the central level should be made compulsory at the state level and adequate funds should also be provided to the states for their implementation. The implementation of the above suggestions should not be confined to the central level but they should be implemented in all the states with effective control and evaluation system. It is also to think of social justice for women, social deviant person with disability and other disadvantage group. For this purpose there is urgent need of a data collection system for minorities and disabilities.

Endnotes and References

1. Neera Chandok and Praveen Priyadarsi, Contemporary India: Economy Society and Politics, Pearson Education, 2009, pp. 206-09.
2. Ibid, pp. 208-09.
3. Procedural justice associated with various rights of individuals and in narrowed sense used to morally evaluate the action of in individuals the term of fairness.
4. Neera Chandok and Praveen Priyadarsai, Contemporary India: Economy Society and Politics, Pearson Education, 2009 pp. 206-09.
5. http://www.mcrg.ac.in/justice.htm
6. http://www.baniss.org/circular.doc
7. Weiner, The Struggle for Equality: Caste in Indian Politics in Atul Kohali (eds.), The success of Indian Democracy, Foundation Books, New Delhi ,2002, p. 20. See Constituent Assembly Debate, Vol. 8, 16th May to 16th June 1949, Lok Sabha Secretariat, New Delhi, 2001, p. 311.
8. Wikipedia (Encyclopedia).
9. Gokulesh Sharma, Human Right and Social Justice, Deep and Deep Publication, New Delhi, 2007, p. 466.
10. Commission on Social Justice, What is Social Justice? in Cristopher Pierson and F G Casteles (eds.), The Welfare of State: A Reader, Polity Press, Blackwell (Oxford), 2000, pp. 55-56.
11. Zoya hasan, more Equal but Still not Equal? State and Inter-Group Equality in Contemporary India, in Imtiaz Ahmed, Partha S Ghosh and Helmut Refield (eds.)Pluralism and Equality: Value in Indian Society and politics, Sage Publications, New Delhi, 2000,pp.80-100.
12. P. Singh, Equality, Reservation and Discrimination in India: A Constitutional Study of Scheduled Caste, Schedule Tribe and Other Backward Classes, Deep & Deep Publication, New Delhi, 1982, p. 99.
13. Milton Fisk, The state and Justice: An Essay in Political Theory, Cambridge University Press, Cambridge (UK), 1989,pp185-86.
14. http://www.nird.org.in/OctLevel%209.pdf

15. Gokulesh Sharma, human Right and Social Justice, Deep & Deep Publications Pvt. Ltd., New Delhi, 2007, p. 466.
16. http://planningcommission.nic.in/plans/planrel/fiveyr/11th/11_v1/11v1_ch6.pdf
17. Eleventh five year plan (2007-12), Planning Commission, vol. I, pp. 102-05.
18. Provisions are defined in Constitution of India, Government of India.
19. Eleventh five year plan (2007-12), Planning Commission, vol. I, pp.102-05.
20. Census 2001, Government of India.
21. Annual Report (2005), ministry of social justice and empowerment, Government of India, New Delhi, part II chapter 3, p. 159.
22. Eleventh five year plan (2007-12), Planning Commission, vol. I, p. 102.
23. Eleventh five year plan (2007-12), Planning Commission, vol. I, p. 103.
24. Annual report(2008), ministry of social justice and empowerment, Government of India, New Delhi, chapter 1, p
25. Reports of ministry of social justice and empowerment, Government of India(2001-10), New Delhi; Reports ministry of tribal affairs Government of India (2001-10), New Delhi; Reports of Ministry of Women and Child Development Government of India(2001-2010), New Delhi .
26. Renu Khator, Bureaucratic Expansion and Policy Performance: A Quantitative Study of Indian States, a paper presented at the 1986, Mid-West Political Science Association Meeting, Chicago, (III) , March 10-12, 1986 and W N Dunn, Public Policy Analysis, Englewood Cliffs (N J), Prentice Hall, 1980.
27. R W Cabb and C D Elder, Participation in American Politics: The Dynamics of Agenda Building, Baltimore (MD), John Hopkins University Press, 1972 and Anthony Downs, Up and Down with Ecology—The Issue Attention Cycle, Public Interest, Vol. 28, pp.28-50.
28. R B Jain, Managing Public Policy in India: The Implementation Gap, Indian Journal of Public Administration, vol. 42, no. 3 July-September1996, IIPA, New Delhi, pp. 345-361.
29. Q U Khan, A Model of Pubic Policy Implementation Process, *Indian Journal of Public Administration*, Vol. 33, January–April 1987, IIPA, New Delhi, p. 37.
30. R B Jain, The Role of Bureaucracy in Policy Development and Implementation in India, International Social Science Journal, 123, February 1990, p 31-45.
31. R K Sapru, *Public Policy*, Sterling Publishers Pvt. Ltd., New Delhi, 1998, pp.124-125.
32. Kamla Chaudhary, Bureaucracy and Development Tasks in SC Dubey (ed.), Public Service and Social Responsibility, New Delhi, Vikas Publication, pp.111-121.
33. Andrew Heywood, Politics, Palgrave Mac Millan, New York, 2010, p434.
34. R N Haldipur, Bureaucracy's Response to New Challenges, in SC Dubey (ed.), Public Service and Social Responsibility, New Delhi, Vikas Publication, p. 216.

10

Extent of Inclusiveness during the Post-reform Period

Rakesh Kumar

The year 1991-92 marked a significant shift in the history of India's economic policy as it shifted from the traditional state-regulated approach to a new neo-liberal approach. This new approach believed in lesser government intervention in economic affairs and relied more on market forces. This approach started with deregulating the economy with the purpose of achieving high rate of economic growth and breaking the jinx of what Prof Raj Krishna called the Hindu rate of growth. The new approach believes that it would generate high rate of economic growth that would benefit all sector of the economy as also all sections of the society by trickling down to the lowest order. During the post-reform period three PMs i.e. Narashimha Rao, Vajpayee and now Manmohan Singh adopted more or less the same approach. Actually, the new policy is part of the process of globalization whereby the national economy is being integrated with the global economy through many channels. This process has multi-dimensional implications, which establishes new linkages—global to local and local to local—across international boundaries. Babu (2005) prefers to call it 'Glocalisation'.

The term "inclusive growth" is not a new idea although it was not used until the arrival of the UPA government which adopted these words to make itself distinct from the NDA and its "India Shining" perspective. The concept of inclusive growth is based on a long term perspective and believes in sustained and broad-based growth for poverty eradication. The 11th Plan defined inclusive growth as "growth process which yield broad-based benefits and ensures equality of opportunity for all"; it stands for "equitable development" or "growth with social justice".

Inclusive growth is typically fueled by market-driven sources of growth with the government playing a facilitating role. It is not defined in terms of specific targets such as employment generation or income distribution. These are potential outcomes, not specific goals. In a way we can say that high rate of growth fuelled by market forces with little state intervention that benefit every sector of the economy and the fruits of which reach to the lowest strata of the society is what inclusive growth is all about.

Now, there has been much debate in India about whether the country's economic reforms fulfilled the objective of inclusive growth and whether it helped India's poor through the so-called trickle down mechanism. Earlier, supporters argued that the reforms would help India to exploit better its comparative advantage in the production of labour-intensive goods and services, and that this would directly benefit the poor (Joshi and Little 1996). By this view, the reforms would help in the fight against poverty through trickle down effect and would help to break the jinx of Hindu rate of growth.

If we talk about the growth rate of the economy during the post-reform period, India has, of course, achieved a growth, which has termed India as one of the fastest growing economy of the world. Liberalization in both domestic as well as external sector has been accompanied by sufficient productivity growth in the domestic economy to assure a higher growth rate of national output. During the 10th plan, the growth rate of 7.7 per cent was highest during any plan period. Now the 11th plan is also likely to achieve a growth rate of over 8 per cent. The percentage of the population below the official poverty line has come down from 36 per cent in 1993–94 to 28 per cent in 2004-05.

While this high growth phase is indeed commendable and that, it is necessary though not a sufficient condition for achieving inclusive growth, but the pattern of post-reform growth has been a concern. There arose serious concerns about a number of imbalances in the growth scenario—inter-sectoral, inter-regional, and inter-class. Gender inequality also remains a pervasive problem and some of the structural changes taking place have an adverse effect on women. Besides, the pattern of growth has compromised with the environmental concerns. The lack of inclusiveness is borne out by data on several dimensions of performance.

Firstly, the rate of decline in poverty has not accelerated along with the growth in GDP, and the incidence of poverty among certain marginalized groups, for example the STs, has hardly declined. Because population has also grown, the absolute number of poor people has declined only marginally from 320 million in 1993–94 to 302 million in 2004-05. This performance is all the more disappointing since the poverty line on which the estimate of the poor is based is the same as it was in 1973–74 when per capita incomes were much lower. Other indicators of deprivation suggest that the proportion of the population deprived of a minimum level of living is much higher. For example, National Family Health Survey-3 (NFHS-3) shows that almost 46 per cent of the children in the 0 to 3 years' age group suffered from malnutrition in 2005–06, and what is even more disturbing is that the estimate shows almost no decline from the level of 47 per cent reported in 1998 by NFHS-2. It may be due to the fact that there is a difference between market production, represented by GDP, economic well-being, quality of life and sustainability. GDP does not measure economic well-being; economic well-being does not ensure equal quality of life, which in turn, does not ensure sustainability (Stiglitz-Sen-Fitoussi Report, 2009).

Secondly, income inequality has increased along with acceleration in the growth rate during the post-reform period. This income inequality has been higher during the post-reform period, after a period of negligible rise in inequality in the decade before that. The post-reform growth process has widened urban-rural disparity. According to Dutt and Ravallion (2002), the post-reform process of economic growth does not appear to have favoured the rural sector and there are signs of geographic and sectoral divergence in India's growth process. Most worrying of all, there are reasonably clear signs of rising inequality, with the relative (and absolute) consumption gaps between rich and poor widening in the post-reform period. Evidence of rising inequality in India since 1991 is reported in Deaton and Dreze (2002), and Sen and Himanshu (2004). So there has been a higher growth, with the higher inequality. The 11th plan also admitted this. "These positive factors notwithstanding, a major weakness in the economy is that the growth is not perceived as being sufficiently inclusive for many groups, especially SCs, STs and minorities."

However, the sharp rise in inequalities in the post-reform period cannot be attributed entirely to economic reforms as such. Rather, they can be traced to the initial conditions obtaining in the pre-reform period itself (Rao, 2009). Economic reforms introduced in the country in the early 1990s released the initiatives and enterprise to those adequately endowed with infrastructure, resources, skills, power and influence. States which were well advanced took the lead. Similarly, people who were well-endowed and influential were the first to take advantage of the opportunities, whatsoever, provided by the new economic policy. This is also one of the major reasons behind the imbalances created during the post-reform period.

Thirdly, during the post-reform period, growth in different sector has not been balanced. Industry and services have recorded high growth rate but agriculture has lagged behind and as a result urban-rural disparity has widened further. Within industry, growth has not been balanced. Production of consumer durables like automobiles has increased sharply whereas consumer non-durables have lagged behind. As we know nearly 70 per cent of India's population live in rural area and 55 per cent of the population depend on agriculture for their livelihood. Without a dynamic agriculture, inclusive growth becomes a mirage. The long standing goal of achieving at least 4 per cent growth in agriculture remains elusive. Even within agriculture, the persistent stagnation in pulses output, with adverse consequences for the nutritional intake of poor households, is a deep-seated issue of imbalance in food security. Due to the much talked on Green Revolution, India is said to have achieved self-reliance in food production. But now it is being realized that the strategy of intensive farming did not prove sustainable both economically and environmentally, and that optimum productivity level in areas where Green Revolution took place has been achieved and their potential in meeting the future food demand is limited. Besides, in rain-fed areas problem of land degradation has reached irreversible level. According to Reddy (2000), the rate of degradation for land in dryland areas in the 1990s (post-reform period) nearly doubled as compared to the rate observed in the 1980s basically on account of soil erosion from surface run-off. Although the government launched the watershed programme during the post-reform period to restore the productivity of land in rain-fed areas but due to poor implementation, it could not produce the desirable results.

As pointed out earlier, employment generation is said to be the potential outcome of inclusive growth. But the high growth rate during the post-reform period failed to create enough jobs. The latest NSS report on the 64th round suggests that the high GDP growth during the 2004-07 periods failed to create enough jobs. The Report shows that the total employment created, according to the usual status, between 2005 and 2008 was only 2.4 million, which was just 0.8 million per year(a growth rate of 0.17 per cent per year) or a mere fraction of the 12 million created per year (a growth rate of 2.85 per cent per year) between 1999-2000 and 2004-05. This is the lowest rate of employment generation in the last three decades, even lower than the previous spell of jobless growth of 1993-2000 when employment increased by less than 1 per cent per year (EPW, 2010).

The unorganized sector, where maximum employment generates, could not perform well. The National Commission for Enterprises in the Unorganised Sector (NCEUS), set up in September 2004, has labeled 'unemployment' as the most important problem in the time to come (GoI, Report 2009). According to Breman (2010) between 1993-94 and 2004-05, that is in the decade when the neo-liberal reforms of the early 1990s started to take off, "the rate of employment growth declined significantly to 1.85 per cent from the previous 10 years when it went up a little over 2 per cent on average. Thus, these years of high economic growth were not accompanied by a spurt in employment generation and a rise in average earnings of the workforce."

Gender inequality also remains a pervasive problem and some of the structural changes taking place have an adverse effect on women. Often, in our haste to deliver, we overlook the long-term impact of development projects on women—be they industry/agriculture or infrastructure related, or the expansion of the frontiers of cities. Women have been more vulnerable to such changes as compared to their men counterparts. The centralized policy formulation based on cost-benefit assessment completely bypasses the assessment of the intangibles such as displacement of women and their homes. Therefore, it in high time to look into this matter. The 11th Five Year Plan has acknowledged this and has decided to move beyond empowerment of women and recognize them as agents of sustained socio-economic growth and change.

Besides, the post-reform growth pattern has also created environmental problem which has long term implications. It has also created problem of displacement. Land alienation continues to be a serious problem in tribal areas. According to Nathan (2009), "the inevitable displacement of indigenous people due to transformation of their habitats for use in industrial projects is one of the consequences of the Indian economic growth." He raises many issues such as compensation, provision of social security, and reconstruction of the livelihood for those who are displaced. The usual approach to involuntary displacement has been to offer compensation to the displaced. But the usual calculations of compensation of the basis of the price of land are quite insufficient for any meaningful resettlement of land. Land in this case represents to the unwilling seller not its price as land, but a source of livelihood. According to Cernea (2003), the consequence of the insufficient and poorly conceived compensation and resultant failure to recreate livelihoods is impoverishment. A study of displaced households from a coal mining project in Jharkhand, (Herbert and Lahiri-Dutta 2004) showed that they are subjected to (i) settling on relatives' land on other places; (ii) head-loading in the adjacent local sale coal dump; and (iii) running pilfered coal on cycles to local markets—an illegal activity. Similar impoverishments are reported in other studies such as Walter Fernandes (1997); Alex Ekka and Mohammad Asif (2000).

Last but not the least, post-reform period has generated a passion for earning money by any means and has increased corruption at high places. The adverse impact of such things falls disproportionately on poor. Madhu Koda and his unholy nexus with the mining tycoon which surfaced recently in Jharkhand is a glaring example of this phenomenon.

However, it would not be fare to blame the new economic policy for all of these evils. State like Bihar known for its backwardness, under the leadership of Nitish Kumar, has been one of the best performing states. Much depends on the commitment of the government.

Now that the process of globalization, to which the neo-liberal economic policy is a part, is irreversible, we must think over the way to mitigate the adverse consequences of the policies during the post-reform period. Of late the government has come to realise this. The government launched NREGA and several other schemes, which targeted those who were left behind. Due to increase in the growth rate, especially after 2004-05, the government revenue has increased substantially. It is high time this money be used to compensate those who have been hit hard by these policies. A C Pigou in his famous book "The Economics of Welfare" emphasized on the "external effects" of market transactions and suggested that social services could reduce these effects. He contended that external diseconomies exist when the value of the marginal social product is less than the value of marginal private product. He suggested that for a competitive system to be in equilibrium the value of both must be equal. Sen (2009) in his paper has quoted Pigou as one of those whose suggestions are relevant for responding positively to the sufferers of the recent economic policies.

ENDNOTES AND REFERENCES

Babu, B. Ramesh (2005): "Glocalisation and the Indian Nation-State: A Millennial Challenge" in Rajen Harshe (ed.) *"Interpreting Globalisation: Perspectives in International Relations"* ICSSR, New Delhi, Rawat Publication, Jaipur.

Breman, Jan (2010):" India's Social Question in a State of Denial" *Economic and Political Weekly*, June, 5.

Cernea, Michael (2003): "For a New Economics of Resettlement: A Sociological Critique of the Compensation Principle" *in International Social Science Journal*, March, No 175, Basil Blackwell.

Deaton, Angus and Jean Dreze (2002): Poverty and Inequality in India: A Re-examination", *Economic and Political Weekly*, September 7.

Dutt, Gaurav and Martin Ravallion (2002): "Has India's Post-Reform Economic Growth Left the Poor Behind", *Journal of Economic Perspective*, 16(3): 89-108.

Ekka, Alex and Mohammed Asif (2000): Development Induced Displacement and Rehabilitiaon in Jharkhand, 1951 to 1995: A Database on its Extent and Nature (New Delhi: Indian Social Institute).

EPW (2010): Jobless Growth, September 25.

Fernandes, Walter (1997): "Hundred Years of Displacemnt in India: Is the Rehabilitaion Policy an Adequate Response?" In Walter Fernandes and Vijay Paranjapaye (ed.), *Rehabilitation Policy and Low in India: A Right to Livelihood* (New Delhi: Indian Social Institute)

Herbert, Tony and Kuntala Lahiri-Dixit (2004): "Coal Sector Loans and Displacement of Indigenous Populations: Lessons from Jharkhand" *Economic and Political Weekly*, June 5.

Joshi, Vijay and Ian Little (1996): *India's Economic Reforms 1991-2001* (Oxford: Clarendon Press).

Nathan, Dev (2009): "Social Security, Compensation and Reconstruction of Livelihoods", *Economic and Political Weekly*, July, 25.

Rao, C H Hanumantha (2009): "Inclusive Growth: Recent Experience and Challenges Ahead" *Economic and Political Weekly*, March 28.

Report (GoI, 2009):Volume I Main Report and Volume II Annexures. Report of the National Commission for Enterprises in the Unorganised Sector, Govt. of India, Academic Foundation, New Delhi.

Sen, Abhijit and Himanshu (2004): Povery and Inequality in India-II: Widening Disparities during the 1990s, *Economic and Political Weekly*, September 25.

Sen, Amartya (2009): "Capitalism Beyond the Crisis", *The New York Review of Books*, Vol. 56, No. 5, March 26.

Stiglitz-Sen-Fitoussi Report (2009): Report by the Commission on the Measurement of Economic Performance and Social Progress set up by Govt. of France (Joseph E. Stiglitz, Amartya Sen and Jean-Paul Fitoussi), *source: www.stiglitz-sen-fitoussi.fr*, accessed on 15.11.2010.

11

Caste-based Reservation in Private Sector: Contentions and Affirmations

Pragyanshu Amaoni

Since the independence of India, there has been a continued debate on the affirmative action to ensure equality and social justice for the disadvantaged section of society. The Indian Constitution provides measure for upliftment for the weaker section in the forms for 'positive discrimination', and to a certain extent, it has succeeded as well. But there is neither any 'trickle down' effect of the fruits of development nor any upward mobility in the social hierarchy. The onslaught of Liberalisation, Privatisation and Globlisation (LPG), the fast-changing economy poses challenges and demands a review in the existing policies of the government. The retreat of the state and the advancement of the market have changed the context for affirmative action and its demand in the private sector is a critical component not only in the academic discourses but also for the agitation for a just society. This paper will attempt to explore the theoretical understanding of the affirmative action with respect to such policies of other countries. The pre-constitutional and post-constitutional provision alongwith the debates from the perspectives of proponents as well as opponents will be analysed. This paper argues for better policy designs in affirmative actions in the rapid-changing environment. It also argues that caste-based reservation is not about 'appeasement' but eliminating the historical disadvantages in an unequal and unjust society. The extension of reservation to the private sector should alter the socio-economic profile of job-holders in the neo-liberal capitalist economy in India. The utmost requirement of developing India is the 'nation-building' which should be based on an egalitarian society so that it can provide a leadership at the global level.

The Constituent Assembly of India has extensively debated on the provision of reservation in educational institutions, employment and political officers to certain social groups. Since then, the issue of reservation is a highly emotional subject and has been evoking considerable amount of controversy and more so in recent times. The nature and content of such debates have grown in complexity and intensity considering the level of development or underdevelopment through various indicators and ignited many agitations and even violence in some parts of the country.

Discrimination exists in many nations under various social, economic and political systems. In order to correct the inequality, many countries have adopted reservation system, affirmative action, and positive action or equal opportunity polices for weaker groups. These countries include United States, United Kingdom, Northern Ireland, Yugosolavia, Brazil, Bolivia, Peru, Nigeria, South Africa, Malaysia, Pakistan, China, Japan and India.

Various provisions in the Indian Constitution have a three-fold purpose namely, remedial, preventive and protective. It has used two types of strategies for development and upliftment of deprived castes and marginalised section of the society: *first*, legal safeguards against discrimination and exploitation, and *second*, pro-active measures in the form of reservation policy in public sectors and state supported sectors.

ARGUMENTS FOR 'MERIT' AND EFFICIENCY

The central argument of meritarian principle conveys that all the social goods and benefits should be allotted on the basis of one's merit on ability, whether natural or acquired and the candidates are to be selected on the basis of their individual merit. Further, there are claims that 'merit' assures that selection of the best and suitable individuals amongst a large number of opportunity seekers for the limited goods or opportunities available for distribution. It also assures a strong society and its overall progress. Thus, Beteille (1992) argues that 'merit' is important for institutional well-being. Anti-reservationists argue that individual merit is ignored in the name of social justice, which results in injustice to meritorious. This leads to frustration among them and hence affects the efficiency of the society as a whole. So, they argue that affirmative action policy in general, and, reservation policy in particular, reduces competitiveness and efficiency.

ARGUMENTS FOR SOCIAL JUSTICE

But, Ghosh (2006:2429-30) maintains that the contradiction between reservations on the one hand, and merit and efficiency on the other, is a false one. Thus, there is a belief that the entire system should be based on merit in the competitive examinations. The opponents of reservations do not consider the fact that the children from the reserved category, in general, do not have the similar facilities, such as books, schooling, private tuitions, convent schooling, educated parents at home and tradition of education within the family and in their kinship network. So, it a distortion of facts to assume that reservations provided to the underprivileged and to the lower rungs of society violates the principle of merit.

Much of the heat is generated in the name of merit as measured by marks in the examination but the marks are determined by several factors such as schooling, accessibility to the economic resources, environmental factors etc. Most of these factors are loaded heavily in favour of upper castes. The so called 'merit' traces its roots through a process of socialization. The processes of caste discrimination begin from birth, through poverty, lack of opportunity and the real prejudice faced by these sections.

Caste based reservations are questioned on the issues of efficiency. In simple terms, efficiency is the relationship between inputs and the outputs, and in other words, the extent to which maximum output is achieved from a given input, or vice versa. For instance in case of education, the inputs of the students may be the home background, kind of school attended, familial education etc. and the output will be the achievement in the examinations or the student's intelligence quotient. Obviously, the inputs of the weakers sections in general, are low as compared to the students of the privileged section and the output of any score in this case will be higher than their efficiency in the system. Social efficiency is affected by capitation colleges for the children of the rich with money and power manipulating academic merit (Chalam 2007: 110-111). He further argues that the question of efficiency in traditionally refined jobs of the elite class cannot be taken as the criterion to judge social efficiency and cites and example:

> If a Brahmin is asked to work as a sweeper and the scavenger as a clerk, it would be clear soon that is change in traditional roles would affect their efficiency. This is not correct measure of efficiency. (Chalam 2007:112)

ISSUES OF EXTENSION OF THE RESERVATION POLICY TO THE PRIVATE SECTOR

The contention and affirmation regarding the extension of reservations to the private sector revolves around some central questions. Firstly, why there is no provision of reservation in the private sector; secondly, if it is not provided in the private sector from the very beginning, then why the same is demanded now?

The caste system in India regulates the social and economic life and had the characteristics, of fixed civil, cultural, religious, and economic rights for each caste by birth with no mobility. Exclusion in economic sphares such as occupation, education and labour employment in internal and inherent in the caste system. In the market economy framework, the cast-based relation in occupational immobility operates through restrictions in various markets such as land, labour, credit, inputs and services necessary for any economic activity in the society. Thus, the caste system having the characteristic of ascribed and compulsory occupations implies exclusion of one caste from undertaking the occupation of the other castes in practice.

Caste can be seen as an economic asset of a group of individuals in proportion to the ritual status in the social order of the Hindu society. W.H. Wiser has tried to measure the economic relations between different castes considering the *jajmani* relations.

Viewing the relation of caste and economic inequalities it has been found that it is the power which takes into account of the social relationship between two individuals or more. Power acts through domination and subordination. It depends upon the historical settings, social structure, and nature of the state and economy. Alternatively, caste has been used as a source of social and economic power since its earliest stages.

At the time of independence, most of the leaders were against the reservation and what was included in the Constitution, was done so only through the pressure of anti-caste movements. The movement however, was not strong enough to push further. Thus the question of 'other backward castes' was left *hanging*, and only the government sector was seen as an appropriate place to insure opportunities for employment (Omvedt, 2001).[1] Also at that time, private firms were not there in large numbers and there was belief that the reservation in the private sector would have negative impact on competitiveness and productive efficiency in those sectors.

Liberalisation, Privatisation and Globalisation are ushering in the power of markets and has brought down public sectors significantly in the form of disinvestment (Louis, 2004:3691-92). This led to the serious concern about the fate of the present public sector reservation policy and hence, the idea of the reservation in the private sector has been brought forward. Since reservation policy is applicable to the public sector only, it is therefore necessary to demand for some sort of affirmative action policy for the private sectors also (Thorat, 2005).[2]

ARGUMENTS AGAINST EXTENSION OF THE RESERVATION POLICY TO THE PRIVATE SECTOR

The opposition is mainly posed from the privileged class i.e. the upper castes and classes in particular, and the corporate sector in general. There is complete consensus in the corporate sector to not implement reservations. The most common arguments for the opposition to the reservation policy may be cites as; firstly, reservation interferes in the free 'invisible hand' of market; that employment of persons from discriminated groups presumably with lower qualification hampers productivity and efficiency because corporate sector is ruled by meritocracy; secondly, the reservation policy for the private sector will not help the poor; and, thirdly, alternative remedies related to education, skill development and entrepreneurship development are better alternatives than providing reservation in the private sectors.

So, it is precisely absent in the labour markets and in private and corporate sectors. Indian private industry are characterised by exclusionary and discriminatory because of never being freely competitive, highly segmented by institutions and practices created by the employers, hiring persons on bases other than merit such as caste, community, language and regional affiliation and above all, all these practices have been justified on the basis of 'efficiency' (Papola, 2005: 102-103). There exists a type of nepotism (i.e. *bhai-bhatijavad*) in hiring the employees. Thus, the recruitment of new ones in the Indian private industries has been found to be highly personalise and formal and the channels of information and routes of recruitment were available only to a few persons. Here, the network and interpersonal connection are important.

It is often seen that fairly young members of the corporate families are pushed to the top whereas those who have worked for a company and proved their talents over a long time never get the top positions. It is considered that if reservations are based on families it is fine, but the moment caste forms the basis for reservations, there are oppositions.

The opponents of the reservation on the base of social and individual justice argue that how a political system that protects private property and the freedom of enterprise can dictate a private company about the social composition of its employees. They should be left free to make their own contribution by creating facilities for the education and training of talented individuals from socially disadvantaged communities of the society (Beteille, 2005:225).

The opposition of caste-based reservation has been resurgent after there are proposals for implementation in the private sectors. The private and corporate sector heavily emphasised on the need of philanthropic activities and affirmative action to empower the discriminated groups, but not the caste-based reservations. The institutions like Federation of Indian Chamber of Commerce and Industry (FICCI) and Confederation of Indian Industries (CII) suggests for educational development by member-companies through scholarships, collaboration of various institutions and developing entrepreneurship skills and helping artisans to strengthen macro-enterprises and self-help groups (SHGs), generating resources for them helping them in the setting up enterprises (Thorat et.al. 2005: 38-39).

So, it can be assumed that the private and corporate sectors somewhere feel the need to improve the status of discriminated groups, but focus only on economically backward section, irrespective of caste, creed and religion. These sectors, however, stick to the contentious issues of 'merit' and strictly on a voluntary basis.

ARGUMENTS IN FAVOUR OF RESERVATION IN PRIVATE SECTOR

The caste system's fundamental characteristic such as fixed civil, cultural and economic rights for each caste, which implies 'forced exclusion' of one caste from the rights of the other castes.

This in turn, in the case of the lower castes, leads to deprivation and poverty as well as worst living conditions (denial of human rights) along with forced services to the upper castes or the privileged ones. Dr. Ambedkar, suggested some measures as: the provision of equal rights to all; legal safeguards against violation of rights in terms of punitive measures; measures to ensure equal access and participation (through a reservation policy) in civil, political and economic spheres; and in addition, a definite strategy of the state aimed at the development and empowerment of untouchables to compensate for denial of equal opportunities in the past. Dr. Ambedkar also suggested legal safeguards against the practice of caste discrimination both for the private and the public sectors (Thorat, 2007:293).

On the need of compensatory discrimination programmes in the private sector, there is an incident quoted by Gail Omvedt (2001):

> There is a story about Shahu Maharaj, the low-caste non-Brahman ruler of the state of Kolhapur in the early decades of the 20th century. The Maharajah helped Gangaram Kamble, a Mahar, to set up a teashop, and then after returning from hunting with his sardars, he began the habit of stopping at the shop, and taking tea from the hands of a Dalit! The Maharaja's actions symbolize the various types of programmes of "social Justice" needed to overcome the heritage of the caste system. For it necessary, metaphorically, for Dalits not only to have the right to drink tea wherever they want, but also to have employment in the tea shops, and even more important, to have the capacity to own them and freely do business with them! And for this, state intervention is necessary.[3]

It has been argued that in identifying the beneficiaries, the sole criteria should be economy i.e. economic deprivation, income and not caste. There are arguments for economic and class based alternatives to the current parameters of reservation, while others resist such considerations by denying the existence of any "creamy layer", or economically advanced individuals among the backward classes. However, these criteria seem to be problematic and it is argued that reservation should never be based on economic status for various reasons as follows:

1. Caste is the major form of social exclusion and not poverty.
2. An individual's economic status can change but caste cannot.
3. There are various difficulties in improving economic status of an individual, so the weak and needy may suffer.
4. In a country like India, which is infested with rampant corruption, it is certainly more difficult to buy a 'false' caste certificate than a 'false' income certificate.

Chalam (2007: 170-72) emphasizes that caste is omnipresent at our conscious and subconscious level and thus, it needs to change the consciousness of the society.

Reservation were confined to the public sector. The total employment was steadily declining in public sector since 1990. There is very strong correlation between the economic status and education to the very small number of jobs which is likely to be grabbed by the privileged. It is well known that the income can be easily underreported. Kashi Ram was walking in the footsteps of Ambedkar, who also considered that capturing power had to be a priority (Jaffrelot 2007:261-69). In the late 1980's and the early 1990's, there was political slogan raised by the BSP, somewhat on the issues of reservations, which reads as: *jiski jitni sankhya bhari, uski utni hissedari* (i.e. proportional representation). The proposed model as an alternative argues for the representation according to the various spheres of social life.

Mohanty (2007)[4] attempts to construct a new perspective that is more in sync with recent ethical theories, cross-time values, narrative perspective, historical context and organic unity. The two prevalent perspectives are (i) forward-looking perspective, and (ii) backward-looking perspective. The former focuses on the letter focuses on making reparations for the injustices heaped on the marginalised sections of the society. Mohanty (2007) explores a synthesis in the context of social transformation envisaged in the post independence era and the need for justice and equity to the marginalised sections of the society without hampering overall social harmony.

THE WAY FORWARD

Today, when India is 'going global', it is important to realise that a truely modern society requires the conscious creation of opportunities for all of its citizen, and a truly competitive society cannot afford to waste any talent. This means that social justice programmes are not only in the interest of Dalits and Adivasis, but in the interests of the nation as a whole- and they require policies that take account of every sectors in a modern and growing economy. In the words of Omvedt (2005:136), if liberalization wants to be successful, the private corporate sector cannot remain an island of "upper" caste privilege.

The caste-based reservation system, despite its flaws, has undoubtedly made a vital contribution to Dalit opportunity and upliftment. It is a remarkable and commendable system that exceeds any others affirmative action programme in the world, in terms of scale and ambition. It plays a vital role in providing representation, and improved education and employment prospects for the backward marginalized castes of the Indian society.

This policy of reservation is not the only or the best option for development in the context of a hierarchically ordered society like India. Other option include provision of free or cheap good quality education in schools which are accessible to everyone, land reforms by giving land to the actual cultivator, strict implementation of minimum wages, and a complete stoppage of all forms of discriminatory behaviour whether in the villages or in the corporate sectors. If all these were successfully implemented, there will be no need for reservation for any section of the population now.

ENDNOTES AND REFERENCES

1. Omvedt, Gail (2001), "Reservation in the Corporate Sectors", the Hindu, Thursday, 31 May, 2001, assessed on 30 January, 2011, http://www.hindu.com/thehindu/2001/05/31/stories/05312524.htm
2. Thorat, Sukhdeo (2005), "why Reservation is Necessary", Seminar, Vol.549
3. Omvedt, Gail (2001), "Reservation in the Corporate Sector", The Hindu. Thursday, May 31, 2001
4. Mohanty, Amarnath (2000), "Affirmative Action in India: An Alternative Perspective", *Economic and Political Weekly*, July 28,2007.

Beteille, Andre (2005), "Quotas for Companies", in Thorat, S. et. al. (ed.). *Reservation and Private Sector: Quest for Equal Opportunity and Growth, Published in* association of IIDS, New Delhi and Rawat Publications, Jaipur.

Chalam, K.S. (2007), Caste-Based Reservation and Human Development in India, New Delhi: Sage Publication.

Galanter, Marc (1992), *Law and Society in Modern India*, New Delhi: Oxford University Press.

Galanter, Marc (1984), *Competing Equalities*: Law and the Backward Classes in India, Berkeley: University of California Press.

Ghosh, Jayati (2005), "On Reservation in the Private Sector", *Frontling*, Issue 22 Oct–22 Nov 04 2005, *http://www.flonnet.com/fl2222/stories/20051104004110800.htm*

Ilaiah, Kancha (2006), "Merit of Reservations", Economic and Political Weekly, June 17, 2006. pp. 2447-2449

Jaffrelot, Christophe (2007), "B.S.P. in Uttar Pradesh", in Machael, S.M. (eds.) Dalits in Modern India: Vision and Values, New Delhi: Sage Publications.

Keane, David (2007), *Caste-based Discrimination in International, Human Rights Law*, Hampshire: Ashgate Publishing.

Kumar, Vivek (2005), "Understanding the Politics of Reservation: A Perspective From Below", *Economic and Political Weekly*, February 26, 2005. Pp. 803-806.

Louis, Prakash (2004), "Affirmative Action in Private Sector", *Economic and Political Weekly*, 39 (33) : 3691-3692.

Omvedt, Gail (2005), "Mythologies of Merit", in Thorat et. al. (eds.), *Reservation and Private Sector: Quest for Equal Opportunity and Growth*, Published in association of IIDS, New Delhi and Jaipur: Rawat Publications.

Papola, T.S. (2005), "Social Exclusion and Discrimination in Hiring Practices: The Case of Indian Private Industry", in Thorat, S. et. al. (eds.), *Reservation and Private Sector: Quest for Equal Opportunity and Growth*, Published in association of IIDS, New Delhi and Jaipur: Rawat Publications.

Radhakrishanan, P. (2004), "Job Quotas in the Private Sectors", *Economic and Political Weekly*, 39 (40):4403-4404.

Shah, Ghanshyam (1993), "*Of Reservation, Merit and Distributive Justice*", *Economic and Political Weekly*, 28 (15): 633-635.

Thorat, Sukhdeo (2009), *Dalits in India: Search for a Common Destiny*, New Delhi: Sage Publications.

Thorat, Sukhdeo (2005), "Reservation and Efficiency: Myth and Reality", *Economic and Political Weekly*, February 26, pp 808-810.

Thorat, Sukhdeo (2004), "On Reservation Policy for Private Sector", *Economic and Political Weekly*, 39 (25): 2560-2563.

12

Child Labour in India: Present Status and Policy Analysis

Lalima Singh

INTRODUCTION

"India is a developing nation". It may be true in certain areas or issues. But, when it comes to literacy, per capita income, social justice, child labour, infrastructure facilities, social awareness, India cannot project itself as a developing country, but she has to call herself an underdeveloped country. Among the above mentioned problems, child labour is continued to be a more serious problem which hampers the health and growth of the child i.e. the growth of future India. Moreover, the mindset of the Indians, who worry only about themselves and not about the society in which they live, is a major cause for the social evils like child labour to prevail continuously. Children are considered as an asset of society and children are the one who take the nation forward in a due course. But unfortunately social problems such as unemployment, poverty, ignorance and illiteracy of parents force them to work. Child labour implies that children who are in the age group below 14 years and who work for themselves or for their family for an income and who contribute a significant share to the labour force of India.

Among the total child labour force, a significant portion of them work in organized sector which is governed by all social security legislations and government appointed inspectors like Inspector of Factories, PF Inspector, ESI Inspector, and their higher ups. If this is the fate in the organized sector, it is not necessary for us to think about the children working in their own families or in an unorganized sector.

OBJECTIVES OF THE STUDY

Understanding the history of child labor in India and also discovering the current state of child labour on a global scale.

- What is meant by child labour?
- What are the causes of child labour in India?
- The effects of child labour.
- How do governmental policies affect it?
- What role does education play in regard to child labour in India?
- Why do companies employ children?
- The ways of stopping child labour.

WHAT IS CHILD LABOUR?

Child labour is done by any working child who is under the age specified by law. The word, "work" means full time commercial work to sustain self or add to the family income. Child labour is a hazard to a Child's mental, physical, social, educational, emotional and spiritual development. Broadly any child who is employed in activities to feed self and family is being subjected to 'child labour'. Technically the term 'child labour' is used for children occupied in profitable activities, whether industrial or non industrial. It is especially applicable for activities which are detrimental to their physical, psychological, emotional, social and moral development needs. It has been researched and proved that the brain of a child develops till the age of ten, muscles till the age of seventeen and his lungs till the age of fourteen. To be more specific, any activity which acts as a hazard for the natural growth and enhancement of these vital organs can be considered harmful for natural human growth and development and termed—'Child Labour'.

CAUSES OF CHILD LABOUR

According to UNICEF, children are employed because they are easier to exploit. Poverty is generally the first answer for why children work at inappropriate jobs for their ages. But there are other reasons as well such as population explosion, cheap labour, non-implementation of available laws, parents unwilling to send their children to schools (they would rather send them to work, so that the family income goes up) and abject poverty in rural areas. And what can one do when child labour is the only means of a family's survival? Main causes are as follows:

- Children come to work or parents send them to work due to poverty.
- Due to lack of education, lack of knowledge and lack of awareness about the side effects of child labour.
- Because of over population.
- Due to government authority's carelessness.
- Government's unfair attitude towards poor and backward classes.
- Profit earning mentality of the corporate and organized sector people.
- Dominance of the powerful people, and higher authorities over the poor people, forcing them to send their children to work.
- Illegal profit earning behaviour of the localities and other people.

- Poor families often rely on the labours of their children in order to survive. Sometimes it is their only income.
- Inefficient government machinery and its legislations.
- The governmental personnel who are responsible for administering the provisions of the legislations have a neglecting attitude as they are not given adequate protection when they discharge their duties.

The major determinant of child labour is poverty. Even though children are paid less than adults, whatever income they earn is of benefit to poor families. In addition to poverty, the lack of adequate and accessible sources of credit forces poor parents to engage their children in the harsher form of child labour—bonded child labour. Some parents also feel that a formal education is not beneficial, and that children learn work skills through labour at a young age. These views are narrow and do not take the long term developmental benefits of education into account. Another determinant is access to education. In some areas, education is not affordable, or is found to be inadequate. With no other alternatives, children spend their time working. Parents of the children who send them to work may be illiterates who are not much aware of the consequences of child labour to the child, to their family and in total to the society.

Recently, Child Rights and You (CRY) also expressed its concern over the problem of child labour in India. According to CRY, child labour is not being addressed properly and the conviction rate is also low. It's not that only the hospitality sector is employing children as workers, but household manufacturing sector and many other sectors are doing the same.

SOME INDUSTRIES THAT EXTRACT CHILD LABOUR

Table 1: Industries that extract Child Labour

Industry	Locations
Carpets Making	Bhadhi, Varanasi , Mirzapur , J&K
Diamond Industry	Surat
Glass and Bangles	Ferozabad
Footwear & Leather Units	Agra , Kanpur , Durg, Rajasthan
Beedi Making	Nizamabad, North Arcot District
Matches, Fireworks and Explosives	Sivakasi
Lock-making	Aligarh
Brassware	Moradabad
Export Oriented Garment Industry	Tiruppur
Gem Polishing Export Industry	Jaipur, Rajasthan
Slate Mines and Manufacturing Units	Markkapur

Carpets

Between 300,000 and 400,000 Indian children work in the manufacture of hand-knotted carpets, the most coveted carpet in the market in today. These children work in a region concentrated around Bhadohi, Mirzapur and

Varanasi in Uttar Pradesh (UP). They suffer from endemic tuberculosis and other respiratory diseases, skin trouble and eye strain and worn out limbs (a National Council of Applied Economic Research study found that "the children surveyed appeared to be famished and had a stunted growth"). In 1993, India exported more than $170 million worth of carpets to the US. In Pakistan, about a million children work in the carpet industry.

Diamond Industry

Between 6,000 and 100,000 Indian children work in the diamond industry, where they cut and polish diamond chips for export to the US and Europe. In 1993, India exported more than $1 billion worth of gem-stones; in that year, the largest export by value from India to the US was in gem-stones. The Operations Research Group singled out the conditions in the diamond plants in Surat, Gujarat (site of a recent plague and of the riots of 1993): "It found children, mostly boys between 12 and 13 years old, polishing diamonds for an average of seven to nine hours a day in unhygienic conditions." The children suffered from eye strain, headaches, leg and shoulder pain, malaria, discoloration of hair, rotten teeth and dysentery.

Glass and Glassware

Between 8,000 and 50,000 Indian children work in the glass and glassware industry. In 1992, India exported more than $2 million worth of these products to the US. In a report in May 1994, the International Labor Rights Education and Research Fund described the glass factories in India as "'Dante's Inferno' due to the intense heat of the furnace, lack of ventilation, broken glass everywhere, dangling electric wires, and workers with no protective equipment." The children in Firozabad, Agra District, UP, who work in local glassware factories suffer from tuberculosis, mental retardation, asthma, bronchitis, liver ailments, chronic anemia, severe burns (which are not treated) as well as fundamental damage to their genetic matter.

Footwear

About 25,000 Indian children work in footwear industry. In 1993, the US imported more than $107 million worth of footwear from India. The children, who work in footwear factories, the US Department of Labor says, are "cramped in poorly lit rooms, suffer from continuous skin contact with industrial adhesives and breathe vapors from glues."

PRESENT SCENARIO

A recent incident shows the actual picture of child labour in India. An investigation conducted by a newspaper revealed that children in the Shahpur Jat area of New Delhi had been sold for £10 (1,000 rupees) into bonded labour. It is common for children to work 16 hours a day. According to the Indian census of 1991, there were 11.28 million working children under the age of fourteen years in India. Over 85 per cent of this child labour is in the country's rural areas, working in agricultural activities such as fanning, livestock rearing, forestry and fisheries. The world's highest number of working children is in India. Nothing has changed since Oct 10, 2011. Child labour is still a major problem in India. The Hindi belt, including Bihar, Madhya Pradesh, Rajasthan and Uttar Pradesh, account for 1.27 crore working children in the country, engaged in both hazardous and non-hazardous occupations and processes. Over 19 lakh child labourers in the 5-14 age group are in Uttar Pradesh. Rajasthan accounts for over 12.6 lakh workers followed by Bihar with over 11 lakh and Madhya Pradesh with 10.6 lakh. However, according to the 2001 census, in state-wise distribution of working children in the 5-14 age group, Andhra Pradesh with 13.6 lakh child labour stands second in the national list after U.P.

Table 2: Variation in Population and Child Labour since 1961

Year	Total Population (in millions)	Total Child Labour Population (in millions)
1961	439.2	14.5
1971	548.2	10.8
1981	683.3	13.6
1991	846.3	11.3
2001	1028.7	12.7

SOME STATISTICAL FACTS

Child labour is growing at a very fast rate. How big is really this problem? The question is very vague and somewhat difficult to answer. However,

Fig. 1: Variation in Population and Child Labour since 1961

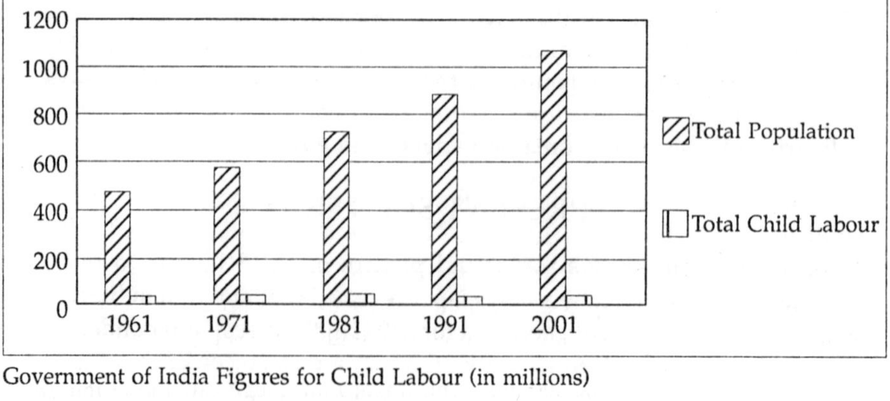

Government of India Figures for Child Labour (in millions)

according to certain statistics an estimate can be drawn out to introduce ourselves to the size of the problem. Certain statistics concerning the number of child labour are given below:

1. Survey by National Sample Survey Organisation in the year 1977-78 estimated the percentage of labour force was around 11 per cent whereas in 1993-94 the percentage came down to 6.2 per cent.
2. The 1981 Indian census reports that there were 13.6 million child labourers in India (Census of India 1981 cited in Weiner 1991, 20).
3. In 1991 census of India, the numbers indicated 11.28 million child labourers.
4. Survey by National Sample Survey Organisation 1993-94 estimated 13.3 million out of which 10.1 million to be employed full time.
5. Although the figure for the number of child labourers varies, they are all significantly high when considering that the Child Economic Activity rate for 1980-1991 was 13.5 per cent for males and 10.3 per cent for females (International Labour Organization, 1995, 113).
6. In comparison, other developing countries such as Sri Lanka and Malaysia (where data is available), have lower activity rates: 5.3 per cent for males and 4.6 per cent for females in Sri Lanka, and 8.8 per cent for males and 6.5 per cent for females in Malaysia (International Labour Organization, 1995, 113).
7. 8.4 million children are in slavery, trafficking, debt bondage and other forms of forced labour, forced recruitment for armed conflict, prostitution, pornography and other illicit activities (2002)
8. Girls are particularly in demand for domestic work
9. Around 70 per cent of child workers carry out unpaid work for their families.
10. According to the Government, the number of working children, estimated at 17.58 million in the 43rd round of child labour estimates, rose to 18.17 million in 1990 and was estimated to be 20.15 million in the year 2000.
11. The estimate of Operations Research Group in a study sponsored by the Labour Ministry reveal that about 44 million children in the 5-14 age group are in the labour force. A subsequent assessment has placed the figure of working children even higher at 114 million.

EFFECT OF CHILD LABOUR

Health: Child slaves are easily replaced; it is more expensive to nurse a sick child to health than to buy a new slave. Consequently, children rarely get medical or psychological attention if needed.

Education: Child slaves are often denied access to education. Thus, even if they escape slavery, they do not have the skills necessary for higher-paying jobs.

Table 3: State-wise Distribution of Working Children according to 1971, 1981, 1991 and 2001 Census in the Age Group 5-14 Years

S. No.	Name of the State/UT	1971	1981	1991	2001****
1	Andhra Pradesh	1627492	1951312	1661940	1363339
2	Assam *	239349	**	327598	351416
3	Bihar	1059359	1101764	942245	1117500
4	Gujarat	518061	616913	523585	485530
5	Haryana	137826	194189	109691	253491
6	Himachal Pradesh	71384	99624	56438	107774
7	Jammu & Kashmir	70489	258437	**	175630
8	Karnataka	808719	1131530	976247	822615
9	Kerala	111801	92854	34800	26156
10	Madhya Pradesh	1112319	1698597	1352563	1065259
11	Maharashtra	988357	1557756	1068427	764075
12	Chhattisgarh				364572
13	Manipur	16380	20217	16493	28836
14	Meghalaya	30440	44916	34633	53940
15	Jharkhand				407200
16	Uttaranchal				70183
17	Nagaland	13726	16235	16467	45874
18	Orissa	492477	702293	452394	377594
19	Punjab	232774	216939	142868	177268
20	Rajasthan	587389	819605	774199	1262570
21	Sikkim	15661	8561	5598	16457
22	Tamil Nadu	713305	975055	578889	418801
23	Tripura	17490	24204	16478	21756
24	Uttar Pradesh	1326726	1434675	1410086	1927997
25	West Bengal	511443	605263	711691	857087
26	Andaman & Nicobar	572	1309	1265	1960
27	Arunachal Pradesh	17925	17950	12395	18482
28	Chandigarh	1086	1986	1870	3779
29	Dadra & Nagar Haveli	3102	3615	4416	4274
30	Delhi	17120	25717	27351	41899
31	Daman and Diu	7391	9378	941	729
32	Goa			4656	4138
33	Lakshadweep	97	56	34	27
34	Mizoram ***		6314	16411	26265
35	Pondicherry	3725	3606	2680	1904
	Total	**10753985**	**13640870**	**11285349**	**12666377**

Note: * 1971 Census figures of Assam includes figures of Mozoram.
** Census could not be conducted.
*** Census figures 1971 in respect of Mozoram included under Assam.
**** includes marginal workers also.

Family Ties: child slaves are often separated from their families. Even if these children escape from slavery, their families still may not welcome them home.

Cheap and Replaceable: The average slave today costs less than $100.

Overpopulation in some regions mean there is an abundant supply of children who are available as slaves.

Child Abuse: A recent study on Child Abuse: India 2007, conducted by Ministry of Women and Child development (GOI) revealed that across different kinds of abuse, it is young children, in the 5-12 age group, who are most at risk of abuse and exploitation. The abuse involves physical, sexual as well as emotional abuse. The study throws light on the following facts:

Physical Abuse: Two out of every three children were physically abused. Out of 69 per cent children physically abused 54.68 per cent were boys and Over 50 per cent children were being subjected to one or the other form of physical abuse. Out of those children who are physically abused in family situations, 88.6 per cent were physically abused by parents. 50.2 per cent children worked seven days a week.

Sexual Abuse: 53.22 per cent children reported having faced one or more forms of sexual abuse. 21.90 per cent child respondents reported facing severe forms of sexual abuse and 50.76 per cent other forms of sexual abuse. Children in Assam, Andhra Pradesh, Bihar and Delhi reported the highest incidences of sexual assault. 50 per cent abuses are persons known to the child or in a position of trust and responsibility.

Emotional Abuse and Girl Child Neglect: Every second child reported facing emotional abuse. Equal percentage of both girls and boys reported facing emotional abuse. In 83 per cent of the cases parents were the abusers and 48.4 per cent of girls wished they were boys.

REMEDIAL MEASURES

Strategies to be Adopted

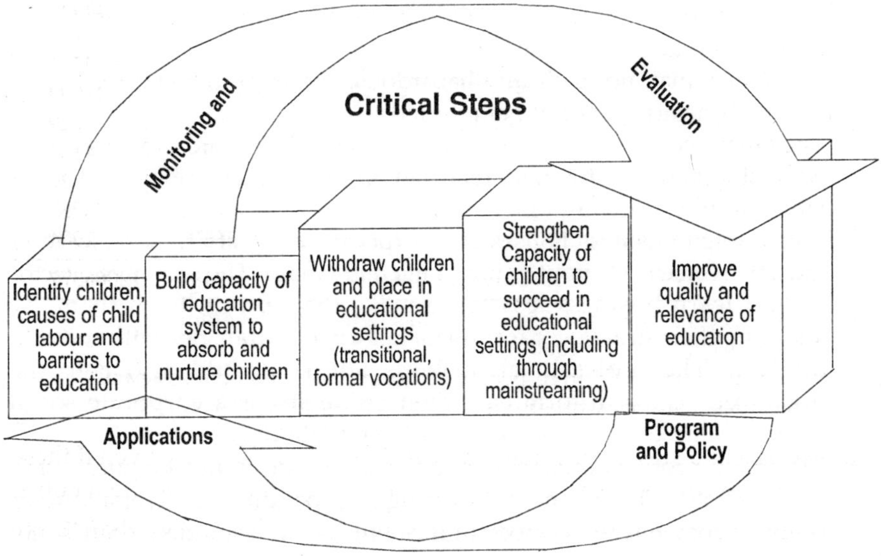

The following strategies may be adopted to curtail this injustice made to children—

- Child labour laws to be implemented strictly in all civilized countries to control child labour .
- The children act 1938, 1960, 1978, and 1986 prohibits the employment of child workers who have not completed 14 years.
- All Medias like televisions, radios, hoardings, slide shows, documentary films should be utilized to create awareness among the general public and the parents about the evils of child labour.
- People from the organized sector should not entertain child labour at the first instance and make it as their policy, so that generations together may not follow it.
- Prohibit their employment at night in one or more kinds of work and without medical certificates of age and fitness.
- Prohibition of employment of young children (sec 67). Non-adult workers to carry tokens stating fitness, certified by doctors.
- Rules regarding child labour as covered in Factories act and Mines act etc.
- There are also two general acts on the subject.the children (pledging of labour) act (act 11 of 1933) prohibits the making of agreement to pledge the labour of children and employment of children whose labour has been pledged.
- The government and the NGOs should take the responsibility of appointing/utilizing professionally trained social workers to create awareness/through social casework and social group work.
- Movies, which are a tool of mass media communication, should be utilized efficiently; this can be done by compulsorily screening the documentary films before the screening of main movie.
- If they are forced to employ children, due to competition, or any other business situation, they should take care of the children by offering them jobs which may not be health hazardous, and easy to be performed so that their health does not get affected.
- They may reduce the working hours of the children and offer them free education and free food, so that they grow parallely along with their job, both physically and mentally.
- Professional business houses and corporate, diversify they make their growth overseas without employing child labour. The organized sector should learn business lessons to make their profit, from them, by adopting their strategy or formulate tailormade strategies with the help of them. The professional business houses should also help the organized sector to formulate their strategies as a corporate social responsibility towards prevention of child labour.
- "To make profit is business, to do profiteering is not business. It is exploitation." There is nothing wrong in expanding or diversifying or utilizing new business opportunities but the job providers should not

think of creating assets for generations together as this may force them to indulge in all unethical practices including child labour.

- When employers pay their employees, they should have at least a minimum consideration on The Payment of Wages Act, The Minimum Wages Act, The Equal Remuneration Act, because if they are paid with a minimum salary they may not be in a position to send their children for work, by which, they may play a vital role in the eradication of child labour.

DISCUSSION

The analysis above leads to certain implications for the international community:

- Collect/study child labour data and devise interventions that allow for the possibility of children being in school and working;
- Improve the quality of schooling by investing in education so as to increase its value to children and parents;
- Provide subsidies to poor families prone to having working children so they can afford their children's schooling (income subsidies, nutritional supplements); and
- Establish partnerships of international organizations dedicated to improving children's lives.

Some recent efforts to protect jobs in developed countries are misguided. Competition from developing countries is probably not the cause of unemployment in developed countries. Under the guise of protecting workers' rights, some developed countries propose that minimum global labour standards be adopted by the GATT successor, the World Trade Organization. Among the issues proposed is the prohibition of child labour. Developing countries argue that such measures would rob them of their comparative advantage: lower labor costs. Many see the issue as just that: rich nations attempting to wipe away developing countries' comparative advantage by arguing for human rights. Genuine human rights concerns are important, but protectionism is not the answer. High levels of unemployment have many causes other than trade, so labour standards in one country may not affect levels of employment in another.

CONCLUSION

Thus child labour is still a burning problem in India and we must be ready and, more importantly, willing to combat this evil which is spreading its wings larger day by day. However, the government is trying but without the concern of the people, this problem cannot be eradicated. The recently conducted surveys are telling that laws enforcements leaves lot to be desired. On the other hand if a child or his/her parents are unaware of the rights they are privileged with, it makes the task harder. If the family is poor and illiteracy resides in the houses, it becomes a very difficult matter, if not impossible, to eradicate this problem solely by the government itself. Therefore, if the society and the government work together hand in hand, it would be an able effort to regulate and eradicate this problem from our country and make it a better country of our dream. Child labour is a threat to society and well being of the children. Child labour adversely affects the growth of the healthy society. Child labour is an evil to the society and it should be curved down. Government has taken various remedial measures to eradicate child labour from the society and also the NGOs are working upon the eradication of the same. Proper education to the people and parents would definitely reduce these bad practices. The Latin Maxim 'boni judicis est ampliare juridictionem'(meaning law must keep pace with the society to retain its relevance, for if the society moves but law remains static, it shall be hard for both.) must be followed practically. "Children are our assets." The common people should consider this quote and the children must utilize their potential for the welfare of the nation and to make our "DREAM NATION" the "TRUE NATION".

> *"If we are to reach real peace in this world, and if we are to carry on a real war against war, we shall have to begin with children"*
>
> — ***Mahatma Gandhi***

ENDNOTES AND REFERENCES

1. S. Vijayagopalan, *Child Labour in the Carpet Industry* (New Delhi: National Council of Applied Economic Research, 1993), 56.
2. UNICEF, Child Labor in the Carpet Weaving Industry in Punjab (Lahore: UNICEF, 1992), 7 and B.N. Juyal, Child Labour and Exploitation in the Carpet Industry (New Delhi: Indian Social Institute, 1987).
3. Operation Research Group (Madras) study cited in BSTC, 78.
4. Cited in Sukumar Singh, *Exploited Children in India* (Calcutta: Shila Singh, 1989), 115.
5. M.C. Shukla, (2004), *Mercantile Law*, Mumbai.
6. P. Saravanavel and S. Sumathi, (2007), *Business Law for Managers*, Himalaya Publications, Mumbai
7. Swaminathan, M, (1998), "Economic growth and the persistence of child labor: Evidence from an Indian city". World Development 26: 1513.
8. Tanna, Ketan (February 14, 2005). "Child Labor Practice Drops in India".
9. "National Legislation and Policies Against Child Labour in India". International Labour Organization. *http://www.ilo.org/public/english/region/asro/newdelhi/ipec/responses/india/national.htm.*
10. The Child Labour Prohibition and Regulation Act (1986)". National Resource Centre for Woman. http://nrcw.nic.in/shared/sublinkimages/28.htm. Retrieved 2009-10-20.
11. Other Initiatives Against Child Labour in India". International Labour Organization. http://www.ilo.org/public/english/region/asro/newdelhi/ipec/responses/india/other.htm. Retrieved 2009-10-21.
12. "485 child laborers rescued," *The Hindu*, Nov 22, 2005.
13. Child labour act, http://www.betterworld.net/quotes/children-quotes.htm
14. Child labour photos, http://www.childlaborphotoproject.org/childlabor.html
15. S. Prabakar, *Issues relating to Child Labour.*
16. http://www.unicef.org/protection/index_childlabour.html
17. www.google.com
18. www.msn.com

13

Theory of Social Justice as the Rational Basis of the Affirmative Action Policies: The Indian Context

S.V. Pande, Archana Srivastava and Sushil Pande

The origin of the contemporary socio-political discourse on social justice lies in the Aristotlian formulation of refraining from *pleanexia*, that is, refraining form "gaining advantage for oneself by seizing what belongs to another or by denying a person that which is due to him, and so on" (Rawls:1973). The Western democratic intellectual tradition envisages that inequalities of wealth, authority and other institutions legitimizing social opportunities for determination of status of members of whatever groups are just only if they result in compensating benefits for all of them, and in particular for the least-advantaged members of society. Clearly the equalitarian basis as the central point of the concept of social justice is all too evident. John Rawls, who is regarded as the pioneer theorist of social justice, put special emphasis to prove that the principle of justice as fairness is primarily based on public interest which can be discerned in most situations by applying two principles of justice: (1) that each person is to have an equal right to the extensive basic liberty compatible with similar liberty for other, and (2) that social and economic inequalities are to be arranged so that they are both (a) reasonably expected to be to everyone's advantage, and (b) attached to positions and offices open to all, leading ultimately to the dignity of man as the paramount goal. It may sometimes be found to be expedient but not just that some should have less in order that others may prosper.

THE CONCEPT OF SOCIAL JUSTICE

Formulations such as these inspired some western thinkers in the fields of political science, sociology and economics to question the validity of classical theories. In an effort to conceptualize the usefulness of Rawls' theory of justice as fairness, attempts were made by contrasting it to other philosophies like intuitionism, perfectionism and utilitarianism, for example, those of Bentham, Mill and Adam Smith. Without going into the technical details of their theories, let it be clarified at the outset that the traditional idea of 'justice' and the modern idea of 'social justice' must be distinguished from each other, for such a distinction would be based not only on the change of scope but on the shift of focus itself. In that sense, the idea of social justice would appear to be relatively of recent origin, largely a product of modern social and economic developments.

It would become further evident that whereas the traditional idea of justice focused on the individual qualities of being just (or virtuous) man, the modern concept of social justice postulates a 'just society'. The former was aimed to enhance an individual's moral worth determined by the prevalent notions of morality, law, social customs and mode of thought, the latter is concerned with evolving a social order which could secure suitable rights and advantages for the different sections of society, particularly for the vulnerable and underprivileged population.

Although the conceptualization of the utopia of a just society was present in the traditional thought of almost all great civilizations (including India), yet the contemporary formulation of the idea by western thinkers regards it to have originated from the judaeo-Christian doctrine of common brotherhood of all the sons of God. To quote Friendrich: "The idea of social justice has its roots in the Old and New Testament. In ancient Israel, there was a provision for a kind of redistribution of wealth. Every so often, all debts were abolished. The pursuit of social justice thus became an important element in the judaeo-Christian tradition and persisted into the Middle Ages"(1967:30-31).

More directly, the modern concept of social justice embodies a novel idea which originated in the conditions created by the modern times. Two factors crucial in the process, namely, the Industrial Revolution and the French Revolution: they facilitated the necessary conditions required to actualize it in practical socio-political and economic life of people in societies all over the world. While the ancient and medieval thinkers took social inequalities for granted and tended to justify or rationalize them, the modern thinkers tended to analyze them from a critical and scientific viewpoint. The modern writers proved how the previous social arrangements/structures arose or intended only to sustain particular forms of social order which served the interests of dominant classes under the prevailing social-economic settings.

Monarchy, feudalism, dictatorships, capitalism, aristocracies, caste-based social structures—all come to be viewed under the lens of critical perspective.

Without going into detailed elaboration of this aspect, we simply limit ourselves to say here that the guiding ideology of the French Revolutions i.e. the trinity of the principles of liberty, equality and fraternity led to establishment of modern democratic social orders, and it was soon realized that the kernel of real equality lay in social equality without which political equality would largely remain an illusion (Benn and Peter: 1975). Clearly, the condition of social equality is the bedrock of social justice, or, in fact, it inheres the spirit of democracy itself. But the question of justice postulates value-judgment, and it does not follow that the goal of social justice has been achieved by establishing a political democracy only. The search is still on; the idea is still taking practical shape as the complexities of modern social conditions are being progressively revealed. In fact, it is not possible to evolve a final formula of social justice which could be mechanically applied to all situations.

Some broad requirements for it can, however, be suggested for its universal application by which the proposed or actual policy measures could be tested. Articulation of the voice of the oppressed or weaker sections of society, precedence of human element over material elements, emphasis on abolition of unjust social and political institutions and therefore on structural changes—all of which to pave the way for social justice as the basis of the concept of social development—are such test points of the said policy. As development of social consciousness on the one hand and of science and technology on the other is a common feature of all present-day societies, the demand for social justice continues to be articulated in newer and newer forms.

Some authors regard social justice purely as a problem of distribution of wealth, offices, opportunities, and other resources available in society, thus equating it with distributive justice. Miller (1976) identifies various models of social justice according to the different views regarding such distribution eg. according to rights and needs. When we speak of 'economic growth with social justice', we mean it in the sense of distributive justice, implying thereby that the benefits of economic growth are justly distributed among various sections of society, particularly so that they percolate to the lower strata of society. In fact the process of securing social justice cannot be divorced from the process of securing social development.

THE INDIAN CONTEST

In the contemporary Indian society, Ambedkar was undoubtedly the most outstanding champion of social justice. According to him, for securing an effective change in the direction of social justice, two conditions must be fulfilled: (a) there should be a general awareness of the goal, i.e. there has to be a mass support for the proposed change; and (b) there should be an enlightened and energetic group with a firm determination to achieve this goal. And Ambedkar (1936) would have us believe, particularly in the Indian context, that social democracy must precede political democracy in order to achieve real social development.

In the Indian context, it precisely means treatment to be meted out to the dalits, tribals, women, minorities, and various other weaker sections of society. The policy of social justice adopted by the Union Government and its states is declaredly based on the ideology of protection of human dignity. It has been unambiguously asserted that liberty, equality and fraternity are those primordial values on which the notion of social justice rests, and the Constitution of India guarantees all of them as the fundamental human rights for all the citizens of India. Abolition of social disabilities like untouchability and exploitation in all its forms provide further testimony to this policy. These fundamental rights and their explanations are spread through articles 13 to 23 of the Constitution and in order to protect them, the judiciary has been kept independent of state control. Thus all forms of social, economic, political and cultural disabilities from which the former *shudras* suffered have been meticulously sought to be abolished by the state.

The practical implications of the policy of social justice in India operate through Articles 330 to 335 of the Constitution, which guarantee reservation of seats to the members of scheduled castes/tribes in the Lok Sabha and the state legislatures, and also ensure reservation to them for appointments in government jobs of various kinds. All these provisions are besides the one for ensuring their quota in the medical, engineering and other academic institutions in respect of seats for their admission, and also for their proportional representation in teaching and the related jobs. Now this policy has to a large extent been extended to the members of 'other backward castes' after the government's acceptance of the Mandal Commission's Report (1990).

However, the real success of the policy of social justice as the crucial indicator or requirement of social development depends more on the attitudinal changes marked by a sense of fraternity between and among various castes when exhibited spontaneously in the behavioral patterns of both the upper and the lower castes, that is when the upper castes start treating the lower as their natural equals and the letter start treating the former with brotherly trust. There is evidence to show that the caste system does not inherently lack in the required resilience and the desired adaptability. Mutual tolerance and intercaste marriages are likely to increase in conjunction with the other forces of modernization like education, science, technology, mass media and democratization of the public mind through various means and measures.

The observation can be further elaborated by pointing at the fact that in India, the planned economic development blended with the spirit of social justice has led to various social-structural changes. A few examples as following ones would suffice to bring out the present-day chanting reality in so far as the landed aristocracy abolished as a class; the power structure in the villages has passed almost completely from the traditional rural elites to a new rural middle-class. A new class structure has emerged in the villages and a middle-class, which is aggressively entrepreneurial, has quickly adopted scientific methods and techniques of agriculture. The monopoly in higher education, previously a privilege of upper castes and classes, has now slowly started percolating to the middle and lower classes and castes in the villages.

These changes, according to Singh (1993), are a result of legislation and other reform measures. The reservations which the Constitution accorded in the legislatures, government services, and schools for the underprivileged have now successfully spawned a new generation of educated youth. All of them have together contributed to the increasing mobilization in the social structure. To quote him (1993; 120): "India has deliberately chosen a path of development and social change which promotes social mobility, opportunity, and well being of the deprived sections of society in a nation which is no doubt dominated by the rich and the elite. It does, however, employ a method of legal consensus which is based on a reconciliation model. In such a model, the responsibility of the dominant classes becomes acute because reconciliation implies, almost in a Gandhian Style, the voluntary accommodation of the demands of the poor, the weak and the deprived, and the underprivileged. Its logical compulsion is more pragmatic than ethical; the privileged should know that such accommodation is also in their self interest. In Marxist terminology, it is the tactics of the intelligent national bourgeoisie who, forewarned of revolutionary potential, attempts to contain it. On the contrary, the specificities of the Indian social structure and its historicity would show imperfections both logical and historical in the nature of alternative paths of development and modernization."

However, the state policy of caste-based quotas or reservations in government services, legislatures, educational institutions and elsewhere (mistaking it as the panacea of social justice and development) has been decried by eminent social scientists since long (Kothari: 1970; Srinivas: 1959, 1962, Mayer: 1967; Beteille: 1965; Rudolf: 1962; Rao: 1968) mainly due to the fact of its politicization and creation of vote-bank politics by unscrupulous political forces. An example reflecting the views of Prof. Andre Beteille (2009) would be apt in the present context: "Recourse to quotas for addressing every perceived social imbalance has become a habit of mind among leaders of every political party. The habit has become so deeply ingrained in our political culture that even to raise a question in public abut its wisdom is to risk causing a scandal in the political establishment. It is in this environment remarkable for any single political leader, no matter how high his standing in his party, to question the advisability of quotas for his own community ... if serious thinking has begun in political circles about the limits of numerical quotas and the need for affirmative action in the case of Muslims, should there not be the same kind of thought given to policies relating to women?"

So it seems apropos here to emphasize that the equal-opportunity principle must be allowed to work through creation of abilities and personality development of the historically deprived populations, not only by the negatively-oriented legal removal of the disabilities. Social justice being the mainstay of the culture of democracy is the surest index of all social development.

CONCLUSION

In the foregoing analysis, an attempt has been made to formulate a more adequate construct of social development by including in it the normative dimension of social justice as its supreme indictor: the more we achieve it, the higher the level of social development achieved in any specific society. The normative upgrading of this non-material aspect of social life is more crucial to social development than improvement on material conditions insofar as it directly ensure a better quality of life which is a function not only of the objective characteristics of anyone's situation but also of his (subjective) expectations and aspirations aimed to lead a dignified life. It is because of this assumption that measures of material welfare are deemed inadequate unless supplemented by this measure of life quality, for one's life satisfaction might be found to decrease even as per capita income/GDP might be rising.

So, what is needed is the internalization of the norm of social justice, that is, 'others before self' in the personality integration of the members of society. It is this sentiment that leads us to the importance of normative upgrading of society (as a measure of its development). From (limiting one self to self seeking) to intense humanitarian concern for other is a sure index of the operation of the principle of spontaneous social justice, and therefore a clean index of normative upgrading/social development. Needless to assert that it is all the more required in modern times in view of its preference for an unbridle indulgence in material pleasures and consumerism, having lost in large measure its sensibilities towards others' sufferings. Surely, a society devoid of its concerns for social justice cannot be regarded as a developed society.

It is thus concluded that the process of social development consists in the rise or evolution of a society from less just to more just or less human to more human stage. That is where truly the crux of the social dimension of social development lies.

ENDNOTES AND REFERENCES

Ambedkar, B.R. (1936), Annihilation of Caste, Bombay: Bharat Bhusan Press.

Beteille, A. 'Break the Quota Routine: Push Social Uplift Through Affirmative Action' New Delhi: the Times of India, p-12.

Ibid. (1965), Caste, Class and Power, Berkeley: University of California Press.

Benn, S.I. and Peters, R.S. (1975), Social Principles and the Democratic State, Landon: George Allen & Unwin.

Blumer, H. (1966), 'The Idea of Social Development' Studies in Comparative International Development, Vol.2, pp. 3-11.

Drewnowski, J. (1967), 'Indicators of Social Development', Social Change and Economic Growth, Paris: Development Centre.

Eisenstadt, S.N. (1966), Modernization: Protest and Change, New Jersy: Prentice Hall.

Ibid.(1961), Essays on Sociological Aspects of Political and Economic Development, The Hague: Moutan.

Friedrich, C.J. (1967), An Introduction to political Theory, New York: Harper and Row.

Kothari, R. (1970), Caste in Indian Politics, Delhi: Orient Longman's Harper and Row.

Mayer, A.C. (1967), 'Caste and Local Politics in India' in Philip Mason(ed.), India and Ceylone: Unity and Diversity, New York: Oxford University Press.

Miller, D. (1976), Social Justice, Oxford: Clarendon Press.

Mukerjee, Ramkrishna (1975), Social Indicators, Delhi: Macmillan.

Rao, M.S.A. (1968), 'Political Elite and Caste Associations', *Economic and Political Weekly*, May 18.

Rawls, J. (1973), A Theory of Justice, Landon: Oxford University Press.

Sharma, S.L. (1980), 'Criteria of Social Development', *Social Action*, Vol. 30, Jan-March, 1980.

Singh, Y. (1993), Social Change in India, Delhi: Har-Anand Publications, p. 120.

Srinivas, M.N. (1959), 'The Dominant Caste in Rampura', *The American Anthropologist*, Vol. 61, No.1.

Ibid. (1962), Caste in Modern India and other Essays, Bombay: Asia Publication House

PART IV

JUSTICE, GENDER AND DEMOCRACY

14

Gender and Social Justice

Sumita Parmar

India is often feted because of its cultural wealth and diversity, its multiplicity of language and religion. This multiplicity, in earlier times, was held together in a fairly harmonious manner, with different communities interdependent on each other and complementing each other's life support systems by way of commerce and cultural practices. However, this harmony has progressively become fragile and tenuous. One would have expected that these divisions might have lessened after more than six decades of independence. But our mutual distrust and differences have continued and indeed, some would claim, have become even more defined and active in contemporary times. Ours is an old and traditional society. It is clearly caste based and deeply fissured. With the onset of modernization and in more recent times, liberalization, no doubt there have been some changes in our life styles and patterns. Perhaps it can be contended that urbanization and liberalization together have been responsible for the onslaught on the caste system which appears to be giving way at least in the big cities where one can find a reversals in the hierarchy of positions of work e.g. dalit corporate mangers and so-called high caste boys and girls working in the malls in menial positions. But most of these changes are cosmetic. The attitudes and the approaches of people have remained fundamentally the same, systemic changes have been small and at the deeper levels we still continue to function with our old prejudices and stereotypes.

When the founding fathers of this nation wrote the constitution of the country and in their wisdom extended civil rights and justice to all irrespective of sex, caste and religion, they were attempting to lay the foundations of a society that would be civil and fair and in the eyes of the law all citizens would be equal. Articles 14, 15 and 16 promise equality and equal protection of laws, prohibition of discrimination and equality of opportunity in the matter of public employment. "In other words, the liberal state is formally committed to the economic, political and cultural rights of individuals. But so far as women 'individuals' are concerned, the state tends to relate to them through the 'family' and 'community as evidenced in all the three cases of development, political participation and culture. This process gets further aggravated in India with its complex legacy of colonial history and embittered community relationships." (Rege, 363). Women continue to be treated as the single largest under-privileged group in India. In such a context the role of justice is specially vital and significant. This article will look at justice within the framework of the nation and its laws and its implications and ramifications vis-a-vis women.

- To the ordinary person what does the word justice denote?
- In every day life what is the role of justice?
- Is there a distinction between mere punishment and justice or are the terms synonymous?
- Or is punishment always the consequence of the enforcement of justice?

More important and significant, how does the mechanism of the implementation of civil justice function? How effective is this implementation when it comes to the weaker sections of society of which women are inevitably a part?

An elementary examination of the basic concept of justice as perceived by the average person indicates that it has several manifestations. There is the iconic figure of the blindfolded woman with a pair of weighing scales in her hands. The blindfold suggesting that there is no bias and prejudice in the dispensation of justice. In other words, that there is no injustice. In our own popular legends, there are many stories relating to Emperors and kings known for their sense of justice. Literature has its own versions. Poetic justice in literature is distinct from ordinary justice. Generally outside the purview of law, it is handed out by a divine power and manifested by *kismet* or fate to a person who has apparently escaped the consequences of his terrible actions. Revenge plays an important role in this concept wherein an earlier wrong is righted or 'proper' punishment meted out to the perpetrator of the wrong. Both Literature and films abound in this theme and the sense of satisfaction that is derived by readers/audience is testimony to the popular desire to see that the doers of wrong meet a deserved end/punishment. In literature there is also the idea that the consequences of the sins of the father are visited upon the heads of the children. This is a particularly powerful form of punishment for nothing can be more terrible than to see one's child suffer and be unable to help him/her. Sometimes, the philosophy of an eye for an eye finds acceptance in the popular imagination, which leads to vigilante justice. One also hears of cosmic justice meted out to the human species for having ravaged the planet earth to such an extent that natural disasters like the tsunami, cyclones, and earthquakes occur taking the form of punishment to man—an act of justice.

But what is of relevance here is secular justice the concept of which emerged and quickly developed in the late 20th century. Pioneered by John B. Rawls (1921-02) in his seminal book *The Theory of Justice*, it was based on the idea of human rights and equality and more important, equality of opportunity. Rawls tried to reconcile equality and freedom locating social justice within the framework of the structures in society which are responsible for good and fair governance. Within this broad framework of secular/social justice is embedded the question of gender justice although feminists questioned whether "the method of arriving at principles of justice proposed by Rawls really succeeded in dealing fairly and impartially with the interests of both men and women." (Ball, 509)

Where the question of women and justice is concerned, the issues that transpire concern certain dimensions pertaining to social and economic contexts generally otherwise sidelined. "All historical explanations of gender are agreed on one fact; masculinity and feminity are not eternal, given norms. They were elaborated, institutionalized and made to seem eternal, to justify the power and authority which men enjoyed at the expense of women. This power and authority exists at several levels: the economic, the sexual, the social and the psychic. (Geetha, 100). Indeed even a cursory look at our cultural history will affirm the secondary position that women have occupied in our social structures. Explaining how this process happened, Imhalsy Gandhy states:

> Behavioural patterns are linked to thought patterns within the mind. Deeply entrenched ways of behaviour, even in modern day society, have their supportive myths and legends that pass on the collective thought forms. If we look back at our history, we could claim that Dravidians were the founders of the earliest Indian civilization that was matrilineal and shared an attachment with the great Mother goddess. The traditional confrontation between the sexes in contemporary India has traces and mindsets that were established during the initial subjugation of the patrifocal Aryan system over the matrifocal non-Aryan one. Patriarchy was established via Brahmanization/Sanskritization, wherein most of the spiritual disciplines were ascetic and life denying. It relegated the female to the position of a devotee. It used mythological weaponry and religious license to transform culture and induce a societal and sexual shift away from the strong position that women had originally occupied. (Sita, 71)

Expanding the idea further, Sociologist Sharmila Rege notes that "Feminist critiques have underlined how the sociological explanations of the emergence, maintenance and transformation of social institutions have 'naturalized' the secondary status of women in these institutions. Feminist sociological analysis has sought to address the ways in which the social institutes are fundamental conduits for gender oppression in society. They argue that all social institutions are gendered and that gender is embedded into their structure and processes." (Rege, 127)

In this context, more than two decades ago in 1986, Lotika Sarkar, examining the backdrop of the Constitution of India, referred to "some contradictions within its provisions that proclaim equality of the sexes, but allow the reentry of discrimination through loopholes within the constitutional framework, its interpretation and the implementation of law." (Khullar, 99) Thus though the constitution grants equal rights to both men and women, the fact of the matter is that women frequently find it close to impossible to access justice. Theoretically on paper, there ought to be no problems for women to get justice, and indeed there are several laws promulgated specifically for the protection and benefit of women in the country, but the ground reality is that it is difficult for them to benefit from the laws made for their protection. "Some positive developments notwithstanding, negative aspects far outweigh the former and prevent women from securing equal status. These include high mortality rates amongst female children and young women. Low female literacy, inadequate nutrition and unsatisfactory access to gainful employment and discriminatory wages. Crime and atrocities against women have also been showing an alarming increase. Large majorities of women have not been able to get the benefits provided by various laws and socio-economic measures, and millions of women continue to be oppressed and face discrimination." (NCW Report, 66) The reason for these conditions lie deeply embedded in our social reality.

The justice system functions like any other social structure in society and those who pass judgments are as much a part of society as anybody else—vulnerable to and socially conditioned by the general prevailing social codes. Speaking at a Conference on "Gender-based Violence and Justice in South Asia", organized by UNWomen and others in October, 2011, Justice Ranjana Desai of the Supreme Court of India referred to this fact and "lamented the deep and pervasive cultural attitudes that prevailed in many societies including India and... emphasized the need to evolve methodologies for making gender-sensitive judges, inculcation of equality doctrines in the minds of judges and giving effect to principles contained in the Constitution of India...." (*The Statesman*). These men view women in stereotyped ways and are often not able to function as unbiased and fair dispensers of justice as they are expected to. This is borne out by the fact that there have been many cases where the judges concerned have given verdicts which have been reactionary and biased and in the context of law, "a miscarriage of justice will arise from the acquittal of the guilty, no less than from the conviction of the innocent." (Saxena, 42) Sometimes even the language used has been disrespectful and offensive and has evoked angry reactions from women's groups resulting in building pressure on them to apologize. But though the apologies have been rendered, their attitudes are both indicative and representative of certain ways of perceiving and comprehending and a case in example is the infamous one where a 14 years old tribal girl was raped by two police constables. To the dismay of women, the trial court decreed that sex for the girl was passé and there was no proof to indicate that the constables had forced themselves on her. "This verdict which was upheld by a higher court served as a catalyst to bring into existence a dormant feminist sensibility on the subject of sexual violence. The terms of discourse, as they were outlined by various women's groups, identified sexual violence as an expression of power. They also pointed out that in a context of power, neither a woman's prior sexual history nor the question of her consent to the vile act are relevant. Sexual violence, it was argued, could not be explained in terms of male lust or desire, either. It was the ultimate act of male terror, meant to intimidate and silence the victim." (Geetha, 95)

There is enough evidence available based on the work of NGOs to establish that it is only when social justice is denied to them that out of desperation will women knock at the doors of the legal system. However, the way to the legal system is via the police stations. Gender Justice like other instruments of law and governance is intimately connected to the police system which plays a crucial role in carrying out the instructions and orders of the Court. Thus, the police are a crucial link in this chain and the road that the victim has to travel in order to access justice inevitably passes through it. Indeed, if legal justice is properly dispensed and efficiently implemented by the police, then, a logical corollary would be an increase in the overall improvement of the texture and standards of civil society. The need for greater gender sensitization of the police arises due to the following reasons:

- The concept of gender is grossly misunderstood by a large majority of police officers.
- Lack of awareness and appreciation of the prevailing gender inequalities among police officers in the country.
- Cult of masculinity prevailing in the police organization which does not easily permit a change of attitudes and behaviour of male police officers towards women. (NCW Report, 9)

Empirical data confirms the negative attitudes with which women are confronted when they approach the police stations. Often the victims register complains against men who are their husbands or relatives. Police often side with the male members of the family.

In the light of this situation the NCW made several suggestions, some of which are:

- Personnel on duty at the police station should be trained mandatorily for gender sensitization whether it is man or a woman.
- The Government should carry out aggressive publicity for motivating women to join the police force.
- In every collectorate, there should be a vigilance for watching and reporting atrocities on women.
- All police recruits should be required to undergo gender awareness training.
- There should be a provision for severe punishment if police personnel commit a crime. (NCW Report, 25)

In those cases where the accused are powerful, especially when they happen to be politicians, the single woman simply does not stand a chance. In our country, "the legal process is long, tardy and expensive. A woman without resources cannot even dream of setting it in motion, getting justice is a far off cry." (Saxena, 42) The consequences of the fierce conflicts of the upper versus lower castes are visited upon the bodies of women. If the victims happen to belong to the so called lower castes, or are tribals and dalits, they are ill-treated in the police stations, threatened and sent away. A report of the National Commission of Women stresses this point saying "the increase in violence against women, the delays in investigation of cases, the perfunctory nature of investigation and delay in the disposal of cases, all point to the urgent need for sensitizing law enforcing officials on this issue." (NCW Report, 40)

Thus the fact is that the gap between the enacted law and its rendering at ground level is disconcertingly wide. Dowry is a clichéd but nevertheless apt example. "Dowry murder is a crime ... that takes place when faltering traditional values collide with unbridled 20th century consumerism. Most of the killings seem to involve a breakdown of the traditional moral constraints, the increasing acquisitiveness of the burgeoning middle class and the disregard for women that is rooted in certain values of conservative Hinduism."(Saxena, 157) When the anti-dowry law was initially enacted, there was great hope that this social evil would be contained. On the contrary, dowry has reached gigantic proportions in our society. Huge amounts are given and received with impunity. The law is a dead one, a paper tiger and although the punishment for demanding dowry has been made more stringent, yet perhaps more wives were burnt in the last fifteen years than in the hundred years past." (Saxena, 8) In fact, in an ironic twist, new evidence indicates that the law instead of serving the purpose for which it was enacted is being misused by unscrupulous women to harass their husband's families or to settle old personal scores. In the final count it is a question of the subordinate status of the woman versus the predominant one of the man. "Man can get away with maltreating, beating and throwing out his wife, because he knows that she is easily replaceable. There are enough desperate parents willing to marry their daughters to just about any man available, but such is not the case with a woman.... The woman controls nothing in her marital family.... She is forced to accept that it is better to suffer in silence like so many other women than to revolt." (Saxena, 45)

The reality of a society deeply segregated on gender, caste and religious lines is brought rudely home by the spate of 'honour' killings which have become an almost routine occurrence in our times. They bear testimony to the rigidity of the caste attitudes of people and accentuate the fact that the appearance of homogeneity is deceptive while the factors that divide us are indeed powerful and effective. The majority of the times women are the victims of such crimes. Purna Sen, a Programme Director of the Asia Region at Amnesty International states that:

> in order to understand and give social meaning and locus to crimes of honour, we should concentrate on six features that identify crimes of honour: (1) gender relations that problematize and control women's behaviour (specially women's sexuality); (2) the role of women in policing and monitoring women's behaviour; (3) collective decisions regarding punishment, or in upholding the actions considered appropriate for transgressions of these boundaries; (4) potential for women's participation in killings; (5) the ability to reclaim honour through enforced compliance or killings; and (6) state sanction of such killings through recognition of honour as motivation and mitigation. (Welchman, 61)

But in spite of this discouraging scenario, some progress has been made. "In society, the administration, the police, the judiciary, the NGOs the media cannot function as separate entities. They are interdependent (NCW, 18) till a few decades ago, apart from the laws which dealt specifically with issues like marriage, or the custody of children or divorce and necessarily involved women, general laws were not women sensitive. "Indeed it goes to the credit of the contemporary women's movement's continuous efforts that laws have become more gendered now. Often campaigns have been initiated around the legal frameworks of the state, either in the way of demanding more women friendly laws or for getting intervention through better implementation of the existing legal machinery." (Khullar, 98) Women's groups have pressured the government to address the loopholes in existing laws so that they cannot be used by the offenders. They have been both watchdogs and advisors to the government and have helped formulate laws that will be more effective. This gendering of laws has resulted in the increased empathy and awareness of those who address the cases of women. By taking into account the social and economic background of the supplicants, the judgments can be fairer and enable women to get the kind of justice that was not available to them before...

Running parallel to this has been a steady rise in the number of women seeking a better quality of life for themselves. One of the reasons for this has been the growing numbers of educated women more confident and less willing to bear silently the injustices meted out to them in both the sites of workplace and family. Consonant with this is the growing awareness of the laws and the confidence to use them. A larger number of support groups, places of refuge and shelter homes have also sprung up for women to access. Widespread electronic communication facilities are accessible to many and crimes are proportionately more difficult to hide.

With India being a signatory to the Millennium Development Goals of the UN and the target date steadily approaching, the efforts at ending gender-based injustices that create barriers to women's and girls' opportunities are gathering momentum. The UN recognizes that "all of the Goals—from reducing poverty and hunger, to achieving universal education and stopping the spread of HIV and AIDS—are interdependent and each one depends on making progress on gender equality and women's empowerment. Achieving these Goals is also an essential precondition for women to access justice. Without education, awareness of rights and decision-making power, women are often unable to claim their rights, obtain legal aid or go to court." If the Government displays some political will and concerted efforts in consonance with NGOs, activists, and all those who are stakeholders in the empowerment of women, increase, some impact, however small is bound to be made.

Endnotes and References

Maya Khullar, "Legal Frameworks" in *Writing the Women's Movement a Reader*, Maya Khullar, ed. New Delhi : Zubaan, 2005.

National Commission for Women, Report of the Workshop on "Gender Justice: Forging Partnership with Law Enforcement Agencies" New Delhi, 2000.

Purna Sen, "'Crimes of Honour' Value and Meaning" in *'Honour' Crimes, Paradigms, and Violence against Women*, eds. Lynn Welchma and Sara Hossain, New Delhi: Zuban, 2006.

Rashna Imhasly-Gandhy, "Matrinileal and Patrinileal" in *In Search of Sita Revisiting Mythology*, Malashri Lal & Namita Gokhale, eds. New Delhi : Penguin, 2008.

Sharmila Rege, *Sociology of Gender*, New Delhi: Sage, 2003.

Shobha Saxena, *Crimes Against Women*, New Delhi : Deep & Deep Publications, 1995.

The Statesman, Saturday, October 29, 2011.

The Cambridge History of Political Thought, eds. Terence Ball and Richard Bellamy, Cambridge: Cambridge University Press, 2003.

V. Geetha, *Patriarchy* Calcutta : Stree, 2006.

15

Constitutional Vision and Gender Justice

Sonal Shankar

It is very difficult to define the term 'Social justice'. It can be said that social justice is concerned with equal justice in all aspects of society. The issue of social justice can not be complete without giving a considerable thought to gender justice. Women rights are inalienable part of human rights. Women are placed at various disadvantageous positions due to gender differences and bias. They have been at the receiving end of violence, exploitation and subjugation by the male dominated society all over the world. "Gender inequities throughout the world are among the most pervasive forms of inequalities. Gender equality concerns each and every member of the society and hence, the issue of gender justice is of enormous magnitude and of mammoth ramification engulfing an all embracing and illimitable canvas. In the midnight of August 15, 1947 when India woke to life and freedom: most of its 170 million women scarcely knew what the 'Tryst with Destiny' was all about. Victims of poverty, ignorance and oppressive social institutions, they hardly knew their destiny and who controlled it. However, the stalwarts who led India to its independence were aware that if the new India of their dreams was to become a reality and not remain only a figment of imagination, it would need social engineering on a massive scale in respect of the backward and oppressed sections of the society and above all its women."[1]

Framers of the constitution were aware of the need for improving the position of women, hence certain sacrosanct rights were put in place to *inter alia* grant women there due place in the society. The ultimate aim of the makers of the constitution was to have a welfare state. In 1931, the Fundamental Rights Resolution passed by the Indian National Congress adopted gender equality as a guiding principle. This indicated a deep concern even during the pre-independence period with the status of women and the recognition that the forward march in the name of progress of the nation is integrally linked with the advancement of women. This premise has been at the centre of the planning after India gained freedom in 1947.

Preamble of the Constitution of India, drafted after independence, promises "to assure all its citizens, Justice - social, economic and political, Liberty of thought, expression, belief, faith and worship, Equality of—status and opportunity, and to promote among all the citizens Fraternity, assuring the dignity of the individual and Unity of the Nation."

Fundamental Rights and Directive Principles of the Indian Constitution are the tools to attain the national objectives of Justice, Liberty and Equality. These rights confer on people the freedom of speech, protection of life and personal liberty. It also prohibits discrimination or denial of equal protection. The Constitution is pledged to foster equality among men and women in the country. It guarantees equality of opportunity and status to women and men. It directs that women shall not only have equal rights and privileges, but also provides discretion to the state to make provisions for the welfare of women. In spite of the fact that women in India constitute nearly half the population, they are still subjected to various disadvantages and inequalities. It may be noted that their participation in economic development has come into focus only during recent years. Improvement in the status of women can be ensured only through full integration and participation in the task of national development. Progress of women assumes importance for sustainable human development. It is necessary for the purpose of economic and social development that female gap in human resources is filled by investing in women. New opportunities have today come up for qualified women. However all said and done, discrimination looms large in the organisational structures.

The important question that arises for deliberation is that, have the women been able to reap the benefits provided for them under the Constitution of India? The answer unfortunately, is not a very happy one. Despite the above constitutional guarantees women in India who constitute nearly half the population are still subjected to many disadvantages, disabilities and inequalities in our male dominated society. "Oppression and violence against women undoubtedly has a psychological, material sociological base. Gender violence is rife at every structure and level of an intensely feudal and patriarchal society as ours. It has reached epidemic issue being recognized in international jurisprudence as a violation of the Human Rights of women. Yet it is the most debased and ignored human rights issue."[2] There is still a long way to go to achieve the goals enshrined in the Constitution. In spite of special constitutional guarantees and other legislations, crimes against women in the form of child marriage, rape, dowry, practice of Sati, trafficking of the girl child, prostitution, domestic violence and sexual harassment at work place are on the increase. As was rightly observed by Justice K. Ramaswamy in the case of *Madhu Kiswar v. State of Bihar*.[3]—"Indian women have suffered and are suffering discrimination in silence. Self sacrifice and self-denial are their nobility and fortitude and yet they have been subjected to all inequities, indignities, inequality and discrimination."Justice Krishna Iyer has rightly pointed out that "gender justice, in the Indian context whatever the resolutions in the Constitution...has yet to arm the women with the confidence that in this country she matters as a free partner at home, in public places and offices, in opportunities of economic pursuits and social status, in family rights and participation in state processes."[4]

It is rather sad that while we celebrate women's rights in all spheres, we are hardly concerned about her dignity. Crimes against women have risen alarmingly in recent years despite the constitutional and legal safeguards provided for them. However, time and again the Indian judiciary has played a proactive role by their positive interpretation of the various Constitutional provisions for women , upholding the validity of various legislations and laying down exhaustive guidelines to realize the concept of 'gender justice' and gender equality. The Apex Court of our country has maintained that democracy, development and respect of human rights and fundamental freedoms are inter-dependent and have mutual reinforcement. The human rights of women, including the girl child are therefore, inalienable, integral and indivisible part of universal human rights. All forms of discrimination on the grounds of gender are violative of fundamental freedoms or human rights.

Our constitution firmly reflects equality of sexes. In most of the nations women are given a secondary role, which needs to be transformed to primary one so that women can share an equal platform with men. Constitution seeks to achieve such transformation.

The Preamble of the Constitution is a key to open the mind of the makers of the constitution which may show the general purpose for they made the Constitution. It declares the rights and freedoms which the people of India intended to secure to all citizens. The preamble beings with the word "We, the people of India..." which includes men and women of all castes, religious, etc. It wishes to render "Equality of status and opportunity" to every man and woman. The Preamble again assures "dignity of individuals" which includes the dignity of women. On the basis of the Preamble, several important enactments have been brought into operation, pertaining to every walk of life-family, succession, guardianship and employment—which aim at providing and protecting the status, rights and dignity of women. The Constitution of India, the first important legislation in free India is an important measure which completely prohibits discrimination on the ground of sex. The Supreme Court has upheld gender equality and right to work with human dignity in Articles 14[5], 15[6], 19(1)(g)[7] and 21[8] of the Constitution. The meaning and content of the Fundamental Rights guaranteed in the Constitution of India are of sufficient amplitude to encompass all the concepts of gender equality including preventions of sexual harassment and domestic violence.

"The Indian constitution, which is the fundamental legal document, is at the same time a social document as well. It seeks to ameliorate the suffering of the weak, the oppressed and suppressed classes or groups."[9]

While all the provisions of the Indian Constitution are applicable in equal measures to men and women and can therefore be invoked by women for the assertion of their rights, there are some provisions, which accord a special protection to women.

The constitutional provisions which have bearing on women and their rights can be divided into two groups, one conferring rights on women as provided in Part III of the constitution and the other in the nature of directions to the state to take appropriate measures for the welfare of the women as enshrined in Part IV of the Constitution. Discussed below are the constitutional provisions, which have a special significance for women.

A. Article 14[10]—Equality before Law: Article 14 guarantees to every person the right to equality before the law or the equal protection of the laws within the territory of India. The first expression 'equality before law' which is taken from the English Common law, is a declaration of equality of all persons within the territory of India, implying thereby the absence of any special privilege in favour of any individual. The second expression, the equal protection of the laws is the essence and core of the right of equality under which the State in under an obligation to take necessary steps so that every individual, man women alike, is given equal respect which he or she is entitled to as a human being.The idea is to treat equals alike and not un equals alike. Since early 1970s equality in Article 14 has acquired new and important dimensions. Until then the requirements of Article 14 were met if a law or administrative action satisfied the reasonable classification doctrine based on nexus test. Towards the end of 1973, however, Bhagwati J. speaking for himself, Chandrachud and Krishna Iyer, JJ. In a concurring opinion in *E.P. Royappa v. State of T.N.,*[11] propounded a new approach to Article 14 in the following words:

> "Equality is a dynamic concept with many aspects and dimensions and it cannot be cribbed, cabined and confined within traditional and doctrinaire limits. From a positivistic point of view, equality is antithetic to arbitrariness. In fact, equality and arbitrariness are sworn enemies; one belongs to the rule of law in a republic while the other, to the whim and caprice of an absolute monarch. Where an act is arbitrary, it is implicit in it that it is unequal both according to—political logic and constitutional law and is therefore violative of Article 14."

Article 14 indeed contains important provisions for protecting the rights of women and the interpretation of this Article by the judiciary enables the establishment of equality between the sexes

B. Article 15[12]—Prohibition of discrimination on grounds of sex: Article 14 embodies the general principle of equality before the law. A specific application of the same principle is provided in Article 15. Article 15 concretizes and enlarges the scope of Article 14.

The true intendment of Article 15 is that other qualifications being equal, sex only shall not be a ground of preference or disability. Article 15(1) prohibits the State from discrimination on the grounds of religion, race, caste, sex, place of birth or any of them. In other words, all laws are to be applied to members of both sexes equally, and there is an express prohibition of discrimination on the ground of sex. The right guaranteed in clause (1) is conferred on a citizen as an individual and is available against his being subjected to discrimination in the matter of rights, privileges and immunities pertaining to him as a citizen generally. The expression 'discriminate against' means to make an adverse distinction with regard to; to distinguish unfavorably from others. Discrimination involves an element of prejudice and it is in that sense that the expression has to be understood. If prejudice is disclosed and is based on any of the grounds mentioned in Article 15, the law will be struck down as being violative of the constitutional prohibition.

If we take an example, a law which would deprive a female proprietress to hold and enjoy her property on the ground of her sex would be violative of Article 15.

Article 15(3),[13] empowers the State to make special provisions for them. The main object of Article 15(3) is based on 'protective discrimination' keeping in view the weak physical position of women. In other words, the provision enables the State to discriminate in favour of women. The reason is that "women's physical structure and the performance of maternal functions place her at a disadvantaged position in the struggle for subsistence, and her physical well-being becomes an object of public interest and care in order to preserve the strength and vigour of the race."[14]

C. Article 16[15]—Equality of opportunity in matters of public employment: Article 16 is an instance of the application of the general rule of equality before law laid down in Article 14 and of the prohibition of discrimination in Article 15(1) with respect to the opportunity for employment or appointment to any office under the State.

Explaining the relative scope of Articles 14, 15 and 16, Das, J. said, "Article14 guarantees the general right of equality: Articles 15 and 16 are instances of the same right in favour of citizen in some special circumstances."[16]

Article 16(1) and (2) embody the general rule that the State shall provide equal opportunities for all citizens in matters relating to employment or appointment to any office under the State. There shall be no discrimination on the grounds of religion, race caste, sex, and place of birth, residence or any of them in providing employment. These provisions are an extension of the principle of equality before law and of the goal of equality of status and opportunity as set in the Preamble of the Constitution. The import of these provisions is that a woman has the same rights in matters of employment under the State as a man the State shall not discriminate against women on this count. It operates equally against any such discriminative legislation or discriminative executive action. If any law is passed or any executive action is taken to prevent the women from taking up employment under the State, such law or executive action could be challenged under Articles 16 (1) and (2). The principle of equal pay for equal work is also covered by equality of opportunity in Article 16 (1)[17]. Difference in the pay scales and promotional avenues between male and female employees is also prohibited by Article 16(2).[18]

D. Article 19(1)(g)[19]—Freedom of Trade and Occupation: Article 19(1)(g) of the Constitution guarantees that all citizens have the right to practice any profession or to carry on any occupation or trade or business. The right under Article 19(1)(g) must be exercised consistently with human dignity. Therefore, sexual harassment in the exercise of this right at the work place amounts to its violation. In the case of *Delhi Domestic Working Women's Forum v. Union of India*[20] relating to rape and violence or working women, the Court called for protection to the victims and provisions of appropriate legal representation and assistance to the complainants of sexual assault cases at the police station and in Courts. To realize the concept of 'gender equality' the Supreme Court has laid down exhaustive guidelines in the case of *Vishaka and others v. State of Rajasthan and others*[21] to prevent sexual harassment of working women at their work place. The Court in the above case held that it is the duty of the employer or other responsible person to prevent sexual harassment of working women and to ensure that there is no hostile environment towards women at their working place. These guidelines were framed to protect the rights to working women to work with dignity under Articles 14, 19 and 21 of the Constitution. Their Lordships also observed that each incident of sexual harassment is a violation of fundamental right of Gender Equality and the Right to Life and Liberty.

In the case of *Miss. C.B. Muthamma, IFS v. Union of India*[22] and others the constitutional validity of Rule 8(2) of the Indian Foreign Service (Conduct and Discipline) Rules 1961 and Rule 18(4) of the Indian Foreign Service (Recruitment, Cadre, Seniority and Promotion) Rules, 1961 was challenged before the Supreme Court. The impugned provision i.e. Rule 8 (2) required a "woman member of the service to obtain permission of the Government in writing before her marriage is solemnized and at any time after the marriage, women member of her service may be required to resign from the service, if the Government is satisfied that her family and domestic commitments are likely to come in the way of the due and efficient discharge of her duties as a member of the service." Further, Rule 18 (4) also runs in the same prejudicial strain that "no married woman shall be entitled as a right to be appointed to the service". The petitioner complained that under the guise of these rules, she had been harassed and was shown hostile discrimination by the Chairman, UPSC from the joining stage to the stage of promotion. The Hon'ble Supreme Court held that these Rules are in defiance of Articles 14, 16 and 21 and Krishna Iyer, J speaking about Rule 18(2) pronounced that

"Discrimination against woman, in traumatic transparency, is found in this rule. If a woman member shall obtain the permission of government before she marries, the same risk is run by government if a male member contracts a marriage. If the family and domestic commitments of a woman member of the Service is likely to come in the way of efficient discharge of duties, a similar situation may well arise in the case of a male member. In these days of nuclear families, inter-continental marriages and un-conventional behaviour, one fails to understand the naked bias against the gentler of the species"[23]. On rule 18(4) it was observed that "At the first blush this rule is in defiance of Art. 16. If a married man has a right, a married woman, other things being equal, stands on no worse footing. This misogynous posture is a hangover of the masculine culture of manacling the weaker sex forgetting how our struggle for national freedom was also a battle against woman's freedom. Freedom is indivisible, so is Justice"[24]. It was further observed, "That our founding faith enshrined in Arts. 14 and 16 should have been tragically ignored vis-a-vis half of India's humanity, viz., our women, is a sad reflection on the distance between Constitution in the book and Law in action and if the Executive as the surrogate of Parliament, makes rules in the teeth of Part III, especially when high political office, even diplomatic assignment has been filled by women, the inference of die-hard allergy to gender parity is inevitable."[25]

In case of *Madhu Kiswar v. State of Bihar*[26] it was rightly observed "Articles 14, 15 and 16 frowns upon discrimination on any ground and enjoin the State to make special provisions in favour of the woman to remedy past injustice and to advance their socio-economic and political status. Economic necessity is not a sanctuary to abuse woman's person." It was further observed that "The public policy and constitutional philosophy envisaged under Articles 38[27], 39[28], 46[29], and 15(1) and (3) and 14 is to accord social and economic democracy to women as assured in the preamble of the economic empowerment and social justice to women for stability of political democracy".

In other words, these provisions frown upon gender discrimination and aim at elimination of obstacles to enjoy social, economic, political and cultural rights on equal footing.

E. Article 21—Protection of life and Personal Liberty: Article 21 contains provisions for protection of life and personal liberty of persons. It states: "No person shall be deprived of his life or personal liberty except according to procedure established by law."

This short sentence in which Article 21 has been couched has made long strides due to the judicial interpretation received at the deft hands of judges of the Apex Court. Article 21, though couched in negative language, confer on every person the fundamental rights to life and personal liberty and it has been given a positive effect by judicial interpretation. It has been time and again recognized by the judiciary that "Life" in Article 21 is not merely the physical act of breathing.

The right to life which is the most fundamental of all is also the most difficult to define. Certainly it cannot be confined to a guarantee against the taking away of life; it must have a wider application. With reference to a corresponding provision in the 5th and 14th amendments of the US Constitution, which says that no person shall be deprived of his "life, liberty or property without due process of law", in *Munn v. Illinois*,[30] Field, J. spoke of the right to life in the following words "by the term life as here used something more is meant than mere animal existence. The inhibition against its deprivation extends to all those limbs and faculties by which life is enjoyed. The provision equally prohibits the mutilation of the body by the amputation of an arm or leg, or the putting out of an eye, or the destruction of any other organ of the body through which the soul communicates with the outer world."

This statement, which has been repeatedly quoted with approval by the apex court,[31] has been further expanded in *Francis Coralie v. Union Territory of Delhi*,[32] by the statement "that any act which damages or injures or interferes with the use of any limb or faculty of any person, either permanently or even temporarily, would be within the inhibition of Article 21". In the same case Bhagwati, J. held "we think that the right to life includes the right to live with human dignity and all that which goes along with it, namely, the bare necessaries of life such as adequate nutrition, clothing and shelter over the head and facilities for reading, writing and expressing oneself in diverse forms, freely moving about and mixing and commingling with fellow human beings."[33] The learned judge further conceded that, "Of course, the magnitude and content of the components of this right would depend upon the extent of the economic development of the country, but it must, in any view of the matter, include the right to the basic necessities of life and also the right to carry on such functions and activities as constitute the bare minimum expression of the human-self. Every act which offends against or impairs human dignity would constitute deprivation *pro tanto* of this right to live and it would have to be in accordance with reasonable fair and just procedure established by law which stands the test of other fundamental rights."[34]

Judiciary has used Article 21 to champion the cause of gender equality. In view of the global developments in the sphere of human rights the judicial decisions from time to time have played a vital role right to basic necessities of life under Article 21. In the case of *State of Maharashtra v. Madhukar Narayan Mandikar*[35] the Supreme Court has held that that "even a woman of easy virtue is entitled to privacy and no one can invade her privacy as and when he likes."

This article has also been invoked for the upliftment of the prostitutes. The Apex court has placed emphasis on the "need to provide to prostitutes opportunities for education and training so as to facilitate their rehabilitation."[36] Sexual harassment at workplace has been considered as a violation of Article 21 of the Constitution by the Apex Court and in the case of *Vishaka and others v. State of Rajasthan and others*,[37] it laid down detailed directions and guidelines on the subject which are to be strictly observed by all employers, public or private. Right to life is recognized as a basic human right. It has to be read in consonance with the Universal Declaration of Human Rights, 1948 the Declaration on the Elimination of all forms of violence against Women and Covenants of Economic, Social and Cultural Rights to which India is a party having ratified them. Supreme Court has held time and again that right to life enshrined in Article 21 of the Constitution includes the right to live with human dignity.[38]

A new judicial trend has emerged from the cases of *Maneka Gandhi, Sunil Batra, Vishaka,* etc. in which the Supreme Court has taken the view that provision of part III of the Constitution of India should be given widest possible interpretation. In *Maneka Gandhi's* case it was rightly said by Bhagwati, J. that "the correct way of interpreting the provisions of part III is that attempt of the courts should be to expand the reach and ambit of the fundamental rights rather than to attenuate their meaning and content."

Article 21 is worded in negative terms as it prohibits or restricts states actions, rather than require it to do something beneficial for the citizens, a positive aspect. By an activist interpretation, most of the fundamental rights, specially the right to equality i.e. Article 14, right to freedom specially freedom of speech and expression i.e. Article 19(1)(a) and freedom of profession, occupation, trade of business i.e. Article 19(1)(g) and right to life and personal liberty i.e. Article 21 have been converted into a regime of positive human rights unknown in previous constitutional diction. By an affirmative action the courts are trying to force the government to create favourable conditions for effective realisation of the new individual, collective, diffuse rights.

F. Article 23[39]—Right against exploitation and prohibition of traffic in human beings: For centuries women have been humiliated, exploited, tortured and harassed in all walks of life—Physically, mentally and sexually. To safeguard and protect women against exploitation, Article 23(1) of the Constitution of India prohibits traffic in human beings and begar and other similar forms of forced Labour. "Traffic in human beings means selling and buying human beings as slaves and also includes immoral traffic in women and children for immoral or other purposes.[40] To curb the deep rooted social evil of prostitution and to give effect to this Article, the parliament has passed The Immoral Traffic (Prevention) Act, 1956. This act protects the individuals, both men and women not only against the acts of the State but also against the acts of private individuals and imposes a positive obligation on the State to take all measures to abolish these evil practices. Another evil practice of the Devadasi system, in which women are dedicated as devadasis to the deities and temples was abolished by the State of Andhra Pradesh by enacting the Devadasis (Prohibition of Dedication) Act, 1988. The Supreme Court has also held that traffic in human beings includes deavdasis and speedy and effective legal action should be taken against brothel keepers.[41]

The Role of Directive Principles of State Policy in Protecting the Rights of Women—Part IV of the Constitution from Articles 38 to 51 contains what may be described as the active obligations of the State. The Directive Principles of State Policy are fundamental in the governance of the country and it shall be the duty of the State to apply these principles in making laws and to secure a social order in which social, economic and political justice shall inform all the institutions of national life. These Directive Principles are ideals which are based on the concept of 'Welfare State' and they fix certain goals; social and economic; for immediate attainment by the Union and State Governments while formulating a policy or enacting a law.

According to Article 39(a),[42] the State shall direct its policy towards securing that the citizens, men and women equally have the right to an adequate means of livelihood.[43] Under Article 39(d),[44] the State shall direct its policy towards securing equal pay for equal work for both men and women. This Article draws its support from Article 14 and 16 and its main objective is the building of a welfare society and an equalitarian social order in the Indian Union. To give effect to this Article, the Parliament has enacted the Equal Remuneration Act, 1976 which provides for payment of equal remuneration to men and women workers and prevents discrimination on the ground of sex. Further Article 39(e)[45] is aimed at protecting the health and strength of workers both men and women.

A very important and useful provision for women's welfare and well-being is incorporated under Article 42[46] of the Constitution. It imposes an obligation upon the State to make provisions for securing just and humane conditions of work and for maternity relief. Few of the legislations which promoted the objectives of this Article are the Workmen's Compensation Act, 1923, the Employees State Insurance Act, 1948, the Minimum Wages Act, 1948, the Maternity Benefit Act, 1961, the Payment of Bonus Act, 1965 and the like.

Fundamental Duties towards women enshrined in the Constitution: Article 51-A[47] under Part-IV-A of the constitution of India lays down certain fundamental Duties upon every citizen of India which were added by the Forty-Second Amendment of the Constitution of 1976. The later part of Clause (e) of Article 51-A which relates to women, gives a mandate and imposes a duty on Indian citizens "to renounce practices derogatory to the dignity of women. The duties under Article 51-A are obligatory on citizens, but it should be invoked by the Courts while deciding cases and also should be observed by the State while making statutes and executing laws.

Despite the salutary constitutional provisions which provide for gender equality, the gender inequities, discrimination and violence against women is prevalent. It is realized that despite the constitutional safeguards and the active judicial support towards the cause of women, changes in social attitudes and institutions cannot be brought about very rapidly. However, it is necessary to speed up this process of change by deliberate and planned efforts so that the pernicious social evil of gender inequality is buried deep in its grave. Laws written in black and white are not enough to combat the evil. The role of Courts and judges assume greater importance. A society sensitive judge is indeed a better statutory armor in cases of crimes against women than any amount of legislations on the point.

SUGGESTIONS FOR UPLIFTMENT OF THE STATUS OF WOMEN

No single section of the society can uplift the status of women. This responsibility has to be shared by the State, community organisations, legislators who frame the laws and the gender sensitive judiciary which interprets the Constitution and other laws in order to give effect to the legal reforms in the field of gender justice and to cultivate, dignity and opportunity for both the sexes equally.

A. Publicity

The Legislations and provisions pertaining to women rights e.g. Relevant constitutional provisions, Dowry Prohibition Act, 1961, Protection of Women from Domestic Violence Act, 2005, Section 498A, Section 304B, *Vishaka* guidelines need to be publicized widely not only at the time of their introduction but on periodical basis. The government should make a proper effort to make women aware of their rights through various channels like programs on television, not only on national television but also on popular cable channels (such publicity can be in form of stand alone programs, advertisements, tie up with various serial producers to give correct information about the women rights etc), various national and regional newspapers, radio, road shows, tie ups with NGO's, Sending groups of officials to make women in villages and rural areas aware about various laws etc.

B. Education

It is necessary to find long term solutions; education of women and their self dependence is very important in combating many of the offences against them. Moreover a chapter on 'dignity of women' must be introduced in schools as part of syllabus both at higher secondary and intermediate levels. This may be adopted as a long term policy in the field of education to bring about the much needed attitudinal change regarding the position of women and their rights. Its result may be perceived slowly but it will provide lasting solution towards sensitizing the society.

C. Gender Sensitisation of Law Enforcement Machinery

Even today, violence against women is treated as a secondary issue by the law-enforcement machinery in our country, whether it be the police, the prosecutors or medico-legal fraternity or many a times, even, the judiciary. It is essential to sensitize this entire machinery to the gender issues. A gender sensitisation module should be incorporated in all the training programmes for the police, the prosecutors, the magistrates, the forensic and medico-legal personnel and the judiciary.

D. Training for Judicial Personnel

The Supreme Court emphasized the importance of training of judicial personnel in *Santa Singh v. State of Punjab*[48]. Disparities in sentencing can be considerably reduced by training the judicial personnel in sentencing procedures Sentencing councils or boards to assist judicial personnel can be set up with experts trained in disciplines like social work, psychiatry and allied disciplines.

E. Setting up and Strengthening of Monitoring Bodies in every District

Monitoring body on the lines of *Mahila Suraksha Samiti*s as in Maharashtra and Gujarat ,consisting of police officers, legal aid workers, representatives of women organisations and counseling experts etc., should be put in place in all districts of each and every State immediately.

F. Support to Non-Governmental Agencies or Voluntary Organisations

Such organisations can play a valuable role in uplifting the status of women, educating them, providing them with shelter and medical help.

Fight for gender justice is not a fight against an individual. It is a fight against the whole patriarchal set up. Questions are too many but answers are not easy. Every one of us, as a right minded citizen, has to support and work for gender justice.

ENDNOTES AND REFERENCES

1. Dr. Krushna Chandra Jena "Violence Against Women: A Human Rights Violation", 90 All India Reporter (2003), p. 313.
2. Dr. A.S. Anand, "Dynamics of Gender Justice",47, No.10 Social Welfare (2001) p. 4.
3. AIR 1996 SC 1864 at 1866.
4. Dr. Manoj Kumar Sadual, "Sexual Harassment of women at work place: critique" 1 Criminal Law Journal (2006) p. 71.
5. Article 14. Equality before law. The State shall not deny to any person equality before the law or the equal protection of the laws within the territory of India.
6. Article 15. Prohibition of discrimination on grounds of religion, race, caste, sex or place of birth.
   (1) The State shall not discriminate against any citizen on grounds only of religion, race, caste, sex, place of birth or any of them.
   (2) No citizen shall, on grounds only of religion, race, caste, sex, place of birth or any of them, be subject to any disability, liability, restriction or condition with regard to—
      (a) Access to shops, public restaurants, hotels and places of public entertainment; or
      (b) The use of wells, tanks, bathing ghats, roads and places of public resort maintained wholly or partly out of State funds or dedicated to the use of the general public.

(3) Nothing in this article shall prevent the State from making any special provision for women and children.

[(4) Nothing in this article or in clause (2) of article 29 shall prevent the State from making any special provision for the advancement of any socially and educationally backward classes of citizens or for the Scheduled Castes and the Scheduled Tribes.]

7. Article 19. Protection of certain rights regarding freedom of speech, etc.
(1) All citizens shall have the right—
(g) To practice any profession, or to carry on any occupation, trade or business.
8. Article 21. Protection of Life and Personal Liberty—No person shall be deprived of his life or personal liberty except according to procedure established by law.
9. Heena Basharat, "Sexual Harassment of Women at the Workplace, A Socio-legal Study of Srinagar City With special reference to Hospitals and Educational Institutions", VIII Kashmir University Law Review (2000), p. 157.
10. *Supra* note 4.
11. (1974) 4 SCC 3.
12. Supra note 5.
13. Supra note 5.
14. F.N. Muller v. Oregon, 52 L.Ed. 551.
15. Article 16. Equality of opportunity in matters of public employment.

(1) There shall be equality of opportunity for all citizens in matters relating to employment or appointment to any office under the State.

(2) No citizen shall, on grounds only of religion, race, caste, sex, descent, place of birth, residence or any of them, be ineligible for, or discriminated against in respect of, any employment or office under the State.

(3) Nothing in this article shall prevent Parliament from making any law prescribing, in regard to a class or classes of employment or appointment to an office [under the Government of, or any local or other authority within, a State or Union territory, any requirement as to residence within that State or Union territory] prior to such employment or appointment.

(4) Nothing in this article shall prevent the State from making any provision for the reservation of appointment or posts in favour of any backward class of citizen which, in the opinion of the State, is not adequately represented in the services under the State.

[(4A) Nothing in this article shall prevent the State from making any provision for reservation [in matters of promotion to any class] or classes of posts in the services under the State in favour of the Scheduled Castes and the Scheduled Tribes which, in the opinion of the State, are not adequately represented in the services under the State.]

[(4B) Nothing in this article shall prevent the State from considering any unfilled vacancies of a year which are reserved for being filled up in that year in accordance with any provision for reservation made under clause (4) or clause (4A) as a separate class of vacancies to be filled up in any succeeding year or years and such class of vacancies shall not be considered together with the vacancies of the year in which they are being filled up for determining the ceiling of fifty per cent. reservation on total number of vacancies of that year.]

(5) Nothing in this article shall affect the operation of any law which provides that the incumbent of an office in connection with the affairs of any religious or denominational institution or any member of the governing body thereof shall be a person professing a particular religion or belonging to a particular denomination.

16. *Gazula Dasaratha Ramarao v. State of A.P.*, AIR 1961 SC 564.

17. *Randhir Singh v. Union of India*, AIR 1982 SC 879.
18. *Uttrakhand Mahila Kalyan Parishad v. State of U.P.*, AIR 1992 SC 1695.
19. Supra note 6.
20. (1995) 1 SCC 14.
21. AIR 1997 SC 3011.
22. AIR 1979 SC 1868.
23. Id at 1869.
24. Id at 1870.
25. Ibid.
26. AIR 1996 SC 1864.
27. Article 38. [(1)] The State shall strive to promote the welfare of the people by securing and protecting as effectively as it may a social order in which justice, social, economic and political, shall inform all the institutions of the national life.
    [(2) The State shall, in particular, strive to minimize the inequalities in income, and endeavour to eliminate inequalities in status, facilities and opportunities, not only amongst individuals but also amongst groups of people residing in different areas or engaged in different vocations.]
28. Article 39. The State shall, in particular, direct its policy towards securing—
    (a) that the citizens, men and women equally, have the right to an adequate means of livelihood;
    (b) that the ownership and control of the material resources of the community are so distributed as best to subserve the common good;
    (c) that the operation of the economic system does not result in the concentration of wealth and means of production to the common detriment;
    (d) that there is equal pay for equal work for both men and women;
    (e) that the health and strength of workers, men and women, and the tender age of children are not abused and that citizens are not forced by economic necessity to enter avocations unsuited to their age or strength;
    [(*f*) that children are given opportunities and facilities to develop in a healthy manner and in conditions of freedom and dignity and that childhood and youth are protected against exploitation and against moral and material abandonment.]
29. Article 46. The State shall promote with special care the educational and economic interests of the weaker sections of the people, and, in particular, of the Scheduled Castes and the Scheduled Tribes, and shall protect them from social injustice and all forms of exploitation.
30. 94 US 113.
31. *Kharak Singh v. State of U.P.*,AIR 1963 SC 1295, *Sunil Batra v. Delhi Administration*, (1978) 4 SCC 494, *Olga Tellis v. Bombay Municipal Corporation*, AIR 1986 SC 180.
32. AIR 1981 SC 746.
33. Id at 753
34. Ibid.
35. AIR 1991 SC 207.
36. *Gaurav Jain v. Union of India*, AIR 1997 SC 3021.
37. AIR 1997 SC 3011.
38. *Bodhisattwa Gautam v. Shubra Chakraborty*, AIR 1996 SC 922, *Chairman Railway Board v. Chandrima Das*, AIR 2000 SC 988.
39. 23. (1) Traffic in human beings and *begar* and other similar forms of forced labour are prohibited and any contravention of this provision shall be an offence punishable in accordance with law.
    (2) Nothing in this article shall prevent the State from imposing compulsory service for public purposes, and in imposing such service the State shall not make any discrimination on grounds only of religion, race, caste or class or any of them.

40. *Raj Bahadur Singh v. Legal Remembrancer*, AIR 1953 Cal 522.
41. *Vishal Jeet v. Union of India*, AIR 1990 SC 1412.
42. Article 39. Certain principles of policy to be followed by the State.
The State shall, in particular, direct its policy towards securing: (a) That the citizens, men and women equally, have the right to an adequate means of livelihood.
43. *Olga Tellis v. Bombay Municipal Corporation*, AIR 1986 SC 180.
44. Article 39. Certain principles of policy to be followed by the State. The State shall, in particular, direct its policy towards securing—
(d) That there is equal pay for equal work for both men and women;
45. Article 39. Certain principles of policy to be followed by the State.
The State shall, in particular, direct its policy towards securing: (e) That the health and strength of workers, men and women, and the tender age of children are not abused and that citizens are not forced by economic necessity to enter avocations unsuited to their age or strength.
46. Article 42. Provision for just and humane conditions of work and maternity relief.
The State shall make provision for securing just and humane conditions of work and for maternity relief.
47. Article 51A. Fundamental Duties.
It shall be the duty of every citizens of India—
(a) To abide by the Constitution and respect its ideals and institutions, the National Flag and the National Anthem;
(b) To cherish and follow the noble ideals which inspired our national struggle for freedom;
(c) To uphold and protect the sovereignty, unity and integrity of India;
(d) To defend the country and render national service when called upon to do so;
(e) To promote harmony and the spirit of common brotherhood amongst all the people of India transcending religious, linguistic and regional or sectional diversities; to renounce practices derogatory to the dignity of women;
(f) To value and preserve the rich heritage of our composite culture;
(g) To protect and improve the natural environment including forests, lakes, rivers and wild life, and to have compassion for living creatures;
(h) To develop the scientific temper, humanism and the spirit of inquiry and reform;
(i) To safeguard public property and to abjure violence;
(j) To strive towards excellence in all spheres of individual and collective activity so that the nation constantly rises to higher levels of endeavour and achievement.
[(k) who is a parent or guardian to provide opportunities for education to his child or, as the case may be, ward between the age of six and fourteen years]
48. 1976 (4) SCC 190.

16

In Between Tradition and Democracy: The Status of Land Ownership to Rural Women in Madhya Pradesh

S.N. Chaudhary

The paper is divided into three parts. Opening part deals with the status of land rights to women in India in the historical perspective. It also deals with efforts made by the constitution, state through policies and schemes and civil societies to extend land rights to women. Part second elaborate social science insight to map current state of land rights to women in different parts of Madhya Pradesh. Towards the end role of patriarchy have been explained as a barrier to the process of extending land entitlement to rural women.

I

Land has been a major source of social status, political power and class structure since times immemorial. It is the main asset around which power structure and social hierarchy get structured, at least in rural society. Owning a piece of land gives one a very immediate and physical sense of citizenship. In much of the world today the ownership of land carries with it ownership to government—the right to tax, the right to judge, the power to enact and enforce police regulations. The land ownership is a decisive determinant of the social structure, of the level of agricultural production, of the well-being of the mass of the population, and increasingly in this age when ideologies transcend frontiers, of the stability of the political system. (Jha, Singh, Nayak and Dayal: 2007).

Women as a social category do not own land. Historically they are perceived as a dependent population on their both natal and marital families. Many of them participate in agricultural activities as a wage labourer or unpaid worker as a daughter, wife and mother of Bhumiswami but they themselves are seldom Bhumiswamini or Pattadhari. As a result, they have been deprived of the right to sale or lease out the land in need. They are also incapable to stop the Pattadhari men to sale/mortgage the land as per their volition. Women are not in a position to take loan against the land even for the development purpose. Since they do not won land therefore, their participation in the decision making process within and outside the family is largely restricted (Chaudhary: 2011).

A report by the Rural Development Institute (http://www.rdiland.org/OURWORK/OurWork_WomenLand.html) highlighting the role and importance of land rights in the life of rural women said:

1. Assets and income in the hands of women results in higher caloric intake and better nutrition for the household than when in the hands of men.
2. Improving women's land rights makes a powerful contribution to household food security.
3. Women's property rights increase women's status and bargaining power within the household and community.
4. Secure land rights provide women with greater incentives to adopt sustainable farming practices and invest in their land. More than 80 percent of farmers in Africa are women, yet women in most African countries do not have secure rights to the land they farm.
5. Providing women with secure rights to land that they can farm has the potential to mitigate the impact of HIV/AIDS on food security and reduce high-risk behaviors.

Jha, Singh, Nayak and Dayal (2007) highlighting importance of land in the life of women said "when women have access and secure rights to land, they are better able to improve the lives of their families and themselves. Unfortunately, women in many poor countries do not have access to land or lack secure property rights to the land they do possess. This dearth makes women even more vulnerable to poverty" (p. 113).

Since women at large have been denied land right in India since long, therefore door of opportunity have remain closed for them in different walks of life. This state of affair was realized by many even during the ancient period.

Budhha was perhaps the first in favour of various rights to women. He permitted women to join the Buddhist Sangh. The women, in fact, pleaded before Ananda that Buddha should not ignore them while allowing men to join the Sangh. He should not discriminate against them. Ananda was convinced and subsequently he persuaded Buddha to consider the equal rights of men and women (Ramachandran 1985: 142-43). But on the basis of this and other rare example it cannot be said that women availed equality and high status in every walk of life. During the British Raj social reformers such as Ram Mohan Roy, K.C. Sen and several others attempted to remove some painful practices relating to women. As a result, the practice of burning of women along with her dead husband was given up. The Widow Remarriage Act was passed in 1856 and the Civil Marriage Act was passed in 1872 against the practice of child marriage. In the 20th century, Gandhi took up the cause of women and launched campaign in favour of the rights of women. In the same way quite a number of women's organizations such as the All India Women's Conference, Women's Council, Jyoti Sangh and so on were established to fight for women's rights between 1917 and 1947 (Sachchidananda and Sinha 1984:3). According to Jha (2009) Gandhi's thought, the efforts of social organizations and the rising consciousness among the political elite of the country regarding democratic principles all, perhaps, deeply influenced the minds of those who framed the constitution of India soon after independence (P.28). Formulation of 14, 15, 16(1) and 16(2) and 39(1) are few among several Articles passed by the constitution of India to gain and retain equality of man and woman especially in the field of employment and distribution of other fruits of development. Needless to mention that in the light of the above provision The Hindu Succession Act, 1956 was passed. According to section 4 of this Act,

> "... any text, rule or interpretation of Hindu Law or any custom or usage as part of that law in force immediately before the commencement of this Act, shall cease to have effect with respect to any matter for which provisions are made in this Act; any other law in force immediately before the commencement of this Act, shall cease to apply to Hindu in so far as it is inconsistent with any of the provisions contained in this Act... nothing contained in this Act shall be deemed to affect the provisions of any law ... in force providing for the prevention of fragmentation of agricultural holdings or for the fixation of ceilings or for devolution of tenancy rights in respect of such holdings. (emphasis added, Hindu Laws 2002: 28-29)

With the passing and promulgation of this Act all previous rules and laws based on different schools of Hindu laws which considered women as inferior to men, came to an end. Of course, the Act of 1956 was a radical departure from the earlier laws and schools of thought but from the point of view of women's interest it was also not completely free from mistakes and limitations. Some of the important limitations with this Act were the following:

1. The 1956 Act still recognizes Mitakshara joint family property and does not interfere with the rights of members of a mitakshara coparcenary except to the extent that it seeks to ensure to a female heir to a rightful share in the property of such coparcenary.
2. This Act does not apply to the distribution of agricultural land or to the fixation of ceiling, or to the tenancy rights.

Making comments on the limitations of the Hindu Succession Act, 1956 Justice Mulla also said:

> It was generally felt that radical reform was required in the Mitakshara law of coparcenary and that where one of the coparceners died it was necessary that not only in case of his separate property but also in respect of his undivided interest in the coparcenary property there should be equable distribution ... between his son and daughter.... But there was some strong sentiment in favour of the retention of the Mitakshara coparcenary ... and the rules laid down ... are a compromise ... (emphasis added, Desai 1982: 925-26)

In order to overcome these limitations, especially in the interest of women, the Hindu Succession Act, 1956 was revised in 2005. The amended act extends following rights to women.

(A) The daughter of a coparcener shall by birth become a coparcener in her own right in the same manner as the son;
(B) The daughter has the same rights in the coparcener property as she would have had if she had been a son;
(C) The daughter shall be subject to the same liability in the said coparcener property as that of a son;
(D) And any reference to a Hindu Mitakshara coparceners shall be deemed to include reference to a daughter of a coparcener; and
(E) The daughter is allotted the same share as is allotted to a son;

In the case of Madhya Pradesh, after independence, in continuation of the above efforts at the national level, number of land reform measures have been taken by the govt. of M.P. in order to change land relations. Important among these are: Zamindari Abolition Act, 1951, Abolition of the Jagir Act, 1951, M.P. Ceiling on Agricultural Holdings Act, 1960, M.P. Ceiling on Agricultural Holding Act, 1974 and so on. In all these Acts emphasis was on abolition of Zamindari System and putting ceiling on landholding size. No concerted effort was made by these Acts to extend land rights to women.

However, enactment of the Madhya Pradesh Land Revenue Code 1959 is a slight departure from the existing Acts from the point of view of extending land rights to women. It is said that in spite of its liberal, forward looking and modern character the land revenue code of 1959 is an extension of the repealed Central Provinces and Berar Hindu Women's Rights to Property (Extension to Agricultural Land) Act of 1942. According to the Act of 1942 women were given only a partial share in the produce of the land. Land should remain within the male lineage and giving access to women to the land owned by a family would result in the land going out of their hands. The Federal Court had held that the Hindu Women's Right to Property Act, 1937 could not be made enforceable with regard to agricultural land and that as a consequence it did not operate to regulate succession to such land but only operated in respect to other kinds of property (Kuppuswami 2000: 948). According to Lochan and Lochan (2009) in the Madhya Pradesh Land Revenue Code 1959, the presence of women was either non-existent or regarded merely as an appendage to men, even when they may be the lawful owner of land. The Madhya Pradesh Land Revenue Code, by default presumed that the "Bhumiswami", the owner of land, was male and that the entire code was designed with the basic presumption in mind that it is men who own the land. That word, Bhumiswami, referring to the owner, lord, master, keeper of land, itself is masculine; its appropriate feminine form which would have been "Bhumiswamini" was disregarded by our lawmakers" (pp. 149-50).

Critically speaking the M.P. land Revenue Code 1959 is both conservative and radical. It is conservative because women have received either no or footnote space in its agenda. On many occasions the Code has used the word Bhumiswami as well as men as landowner, lord, master, keeper of land and so on. It has never used the word Bhumiswamini. Also, on many occasions gender biased words like "he", "his" etc. have been used in the Code.

It is radical in the sense that it is opposed to absentee landlordism, in favour of land ceilings, in favour of protection of landowners from exploitation, and opposed to transfer of tribal land to the non-tribal forces.

There is a few reference of women in relation to land in the Code manual here and there. The following three examples may be cited.

1. If a Bhumiswami is failed to pay pre-fixed land revenue the land was likely to be resumed by the state (Section 139). However, the law made it clear that recovery could not be made at the cost of impoverishing the landowner to the extent that he would either lose his (not her) means of livelihood. The revenue Collectors appointed cannot attach or sell several essential items, including belongings of his wife and children, including ornaments etc.
2. According to the Code each Bhumiswami is supposed to be a self-cultivating farmer. "No Bhumiswami shall lease any land comprised in his holding for more than one year during any consecutive period of three years" (Section 168(i)). However, women including widows, spinsters, deserted wives and minors were excluded from this limitation along with other persons.
3. The Code has also devoted some space for the devolution of land after the death of Bhumiswami. It said that mother, widow, daughter and son had been listed as Class I heirs of the first degree who would inherit the land owned by the late Bhumiswami.

Beside land revenue code 1959 some more efforts have been made by both the state and civil society organizations to extend land rights to women and also to strengthen their status in different spheres. Important among these are:

M.P. Policy for Women

This policy was enacted in 1995. Its broad purpose was to improve socio-economic status of cross-section of women. Extension of land right to women and making them joint or single *pattadharini* is also one of the objectives of policy for women.

However, its specific purposes are the following:

1. Ensuring the survival and protection of female life.
2. Ensuring the fullest participation of women in civil society, and strengthen their role in decision- making.
3. Increasing self confidence and enhancing the status of women.
4. Empowerment of women to enable them to take the fullest advantage of development efforts in all fields.
5. Affirmative action to ensure women's full participation in economic activity.
6. Ensuring the visibility of women in all walks of life.
7. Bringing about sensitisation and attitudinal change in the larger society on the women question; and
8. Prevention of atrocities and acts of violence against women.

NGO Intervention

So far as the role of NGO in extending land rights to women in Madhya Pradesh is concerned, it is perhaps at the infancy stage. There are organizations dealing with land issues but most of these are for resettlement of the displaced, anti-encroachment, distribution of surplus land among landless and so on. In case there is voice in favour of land rights to women either from the natal and marital families or for community land in a sustained manner, it has positive impact. There are number of village level social organisations in different parts of the state which are engaged in the empowerment/protection of local population including women. Important among these are Kisan Mazdoor Sangathan, Samata Sangathan and Kisan Adivasi Sangathan in Hoshangabad area, Satpura Kisan Evam Mazdoor Kalyan Samiti and Adivasi Vikas Parishad in Betul and Chhindwara district, Khedut Mazdoor Chetna Sangathan in Jhabua district and so on. While these organizations are limited to specific district, the Ekta Parishad is working in several areas of Madhya Pradesh. Because of its intervention in some of the areas land *pattas* have been issued to the tillers, and in certain cases women have also been made *pattdhari*. Efforts have been made by villagers themselves, including women in different parts of M.P. to obtain and retain land either under the rehabilitation schemes or they have occupied community land for their livelihood, and NGOs like Ekta Parishad have helped them in this endeavour but here also women's right on land have largely been missed inspite of relentless participation of women in farming. Following few examples from different parts of M.P. support this argument.

According to Marathe (2004) Sanai village falls under the command area of the Bansagar dam of Satna district. The village is inhabited by Thakurs, Brahmins and Kol tribe. Upto 1998, Kol adivasis were rehabilitated and around 6 acres of land were provided to them. All the members of 28 displaced Kol worked day and night to improve land for farm work. They were also working in the local stone quarries as wage labourers. But partly because of labourers becoming surplus and partly due to modernisation in quarries work, the contractor reduced the wage rate. This problem was realized by the host adivasi workers. They jointly perceived this challenge as an opportunity for setting up an organisation.

Till 1988 these displaced adivasis had only 6 acres of land. But gradually land size increased upto 60 acres. They not only produced food grain in these acquired land but also maintained and retained standing trees. Also, during the non-agricultural season they seasonally outmigrated to urban areas for wage work. Because of all these development there was no availability of required number of labourer in the village. The local influentials who had major part of land in their possession became frustrated because their land remain underutilised. Hence, they instigated the local administration to arrest the encroachers and evict the encroached land. Action was taken and some of the encroachers were arrested. But due to series of meetings and a show of strength against the arrest, under the leadership of Ekta Parishad, the arrested persons were finally released within 15 days.

According to the researcher "the adivasi women were pivotal in bringing about the release. This process motivated the women and their cohesiveness united the others" (p. 276).

The other case study also underlines the importance of NGOs in this matter. According to Ekta Parishad (2007) :

1. Tikar is a small village of 60, mostly adivasis households, near to a large cement factory in Satna, Madhya Pradesh. The families are victim of multiple displacement due to irrigation projects. They generally work in stone quarries in the area to support themselves. Under the guidance of Ekta Parishad (NGO), some years ago, a group of women led by Radhabai decided to establish a better livelihood option. They occupied 20 acres of revenue land which they started to prepare for production. Through voluntary joint labour, they built bounds to conserve soil and water. They initiated cultivation of variety of local food crops. However, without irrigation facilities, they could grow a single crop in a year. In 2002-03, women built a huge well by dint of their own effort. They toiled for over three months and built a well that meets agriculture water needs throughout the year. After securing a source of food, these women went one step ahead. In 2003-04 they decided to start a poultry unit on a barren part of the encroached land. Each member of the group took up the responsibility of manufacturing 1,000 bricks, and together they built a double-storeyed structure to house the poultry unit. They started with 20 locally procured birds. Unfortunately, heavy rains in 2005 brought the structure down, causing monetary loss of around Rs. 30,000. The women did not lose heart. They decided to open a grocery (the nearest existing shop was 1.5 km from the village). By consensus, one member of the group runs the grocery on a profit-sharing basis

with the entire group. The business is doing well and in 2006, the group had capital reserves of Rs. 11,000. The women had opened a bank account on their own, and the group was earning Rs 400 a month through interest. It lends money at the rate of 2 per cent per month. The next step was politics. The women contested gram panchayat elections and won a few seats. From being daily wage labourers, the women of Tikar have become assertive citizens demanding and securing benefits from a host of government schemes.

2. Summa Tati, a dalit landless labourer of lamaniya village of Bhilai Panchayat of Vidisha district, MP, received a patta for 2.99 hectares of land on November 20, 1984. That was the start of a long, unsuccessful struggle that ended with her death 15 years later. Even before her allotment was demarcated, it was taken over by a landlord, who threatened to kill her if she protested. Undaunted, Summa approached the tehsil revenue court and obtained an eviction order against the landlord. The landlord refused to heed the order. Summa then made an application for demarcation of her plot, but no action was taken. Again she unsuccessfully went to court, which summoned the tehsildar and instructed him to demarcate the plot and ensure possession. Summa wrote an application to the chief minister in 1991. The chief minister's office directed the district collector to take prompt action. But nothing came out. Summa approached the local member of the legislative assembly in 1994. Nothing happed. In 1996 she lodged a police complaint against the landlord, alleging that she was beaten up and mentally tortured. No action was taken. She then approached the scheduled caste welfare department, urging it to take action but again nothing happened.

Some justice was done after her death, when Ekta Parishad presented this case before the district collector in May 2000. The plot, inherited by her two sons, was demarcated, but only partially. The landlord continued to claim possession over an unspecified part of the land.

The above two cases, documented in the study, are an example of near success story. And this story has been constructed by poor women themselves even without questioning the negative forces. However, victims have received limited support from the state and needful support and guidance from the civil society to actualise their land based struggle. The story also narrates that how after dealing with the problem of economic insecurity even in a limited sense, with the help of collective voice, difference can be achieved provided there is constant effort by both the victims and their spokespersons.

But the cases are small in number. It seems that Ekta Parished is also more interested in the distribution of surplus/government land among the marginalised. It is yet to address the question of land rights to women, even among marginalized, in a massive manner.

Institutional Schemes

In order to achieve the land based spirit of Madhya Pradesh policy for women which have been formulated in the light of Articles 14, 15, 16, 39 etc, of Indian constitution some specific efforts have been made. Important among these are:

1. Land distributed by the government under any scheme must contain name of both husband and wife on the land patta. Needless to mention here that under Dalit Agenda more than 5 lakh hectares of land were distributed among landless and near-landless families in Madhya Pradesh of which many of families received land with patta having the joint name of husband and wife (Chaudhary: 2007).
2. Adult women of the villages are also given joint control of all village common lands.
3. Of all the Patwaris which are to be appointed in future at least 30 per cent of them shall be women.
4. According to the new Act (2001) of the Madhya Pradesh Panchayati Raj Adhiniyam (Act) 1993 the quorum of a gram sabha should not be less than one fifth of the total number of members of the *gram sabha,* out of which not less than one-third should be women.
5. It has been decided that persons convicted in cases of violence against women will not be considered for government job. Where such cases are pending and the charges have been framed by the court, appointment of such persons will remain suspended till their cases are finally disposed of.
6. The government has decided to give preference to women's groups in granting of river bed/tank bed *pattas* for growing seasonal fruits and vegetables, thereby enabling them to increase their incomes.
7. The presence of officials from the revenue department in the *Jagriti Shivirs* organized by the Women and Child Development Department and in the information camps organized by other Government Departments has been made mandatory, so that people at large can get full information regarding the provisions of the state government beneficial to women, through these officials.
8. The M.P. Agricultural marketing Act has been amended to increase the representation of women on agricultural marketing bodies/ institutions (Mandi Samatis) to one-third of their total membership.
9. The percentage of women among agricultural extension staff is also being increased. 30 per cent reservation for women has been made on the posts of direct recruitment. For example, out of 105 posts of Assistant Directors, 31 posts have been reserved for women.

No doubt these efforts are radical from the point of view of extending land rights to women and subsequently empowering them in different spheres but in spite of all these efforts only a small number of women have been able to receive land right. Number of studies conducted in the recent past in different parts of Madhya Pradesh also show the lower level of their rights on land.

II

Social Science Insight

While in some studies attempt have been made to know number of women who own land as a pattadhari in other studies emphasis is on engagement of women in farming. So far as the former issue is concerned, in spite of having regional variation, most of the studies conclude that only small number of women own land both at natal as well as at the marital family.

According to Lochan and Lochan (2009) for example, of the total 203208 Khatas in Khargoan district of Madhya Pradesh only 18,314 (9.1%) Khatas have women Khatedars, and there are only 95 Khatas in joint names of both husband and wife. In the same way there are 195190 house owners in the district of which only 6965 (3.57%) women are house owner. Researchers underlined that this state of affair exists in spite of the functioning of two schemes namely free distribution of grazing land to Dalits and tribals as well as house facility under Rajiv Gandhi Ashray Pariyojana. They observed that number of women who have land in their names remains very low, the number of women who have houses in their names is lower still and the number of women who have land or houses in the joint names along with their father or husband is almost negligible. This is so despite the fact that almost half of the women are actively involved in agriculture either as cultivator themselves or as labourers (pp. 159-60).

Chaudhary (2011) conducted study in 12 villages i,e, 6 tribal dominated villages of Sahpur Block and 6 non-tribal dominated villages of Betul Block of Betul district. In all these villages very small number of women own land as a pattadhari. In Sahpur villages only 9 percent women (42) have their single name on land patta in all the 3 villages. In the case of Betul villages also only 10 per cent women (34) have their single name on patta. The situation relating to joint patta is also low. For instance, only 3 per cent women in Sahpur villages (13) and 3 percent (12) in Betul villages have their name on the joint patta. In short, of 831 women in all the six studied villages 101 women (12.5%) have their name on land patta either independently or joint, although most of them are involved in farm activities.

If we see the situation of landownership in all these 12 villages on website of the Govt. of Madhya Pradesh it is obvious that of all the 3907 *khatas* 1078 (28%) *khatas* are owned by women either as a single or joint Pattadhari. This shows wide gap between textual and field view. This may be because women respondents who were interviewed by us, many of them do not know that they are either single or joint Pattadharis as disclosed by the website data. This state has far reaching impact on women from both social justice and empowerment point of view.

Chaudhary (2007) conducted study on the process of distribution of grazing land under Dalit Agenda among landless and near landless Dalit and tribal households and its social and economic consequences. Under this schemes more than 5 lakh hectare of land were distributed free of cost. One of the pre-conditions of this scheme was that names of both husband and wife shall be on the land patta. The study was conducted on 200 beneficiaries households of Sehore district. In course of the study it was found that 74 per cent beneficiaries (150) had received patta with having joint entitlement, in 3 per cent cases patta was issued only to women because there was no adult male member in the family and in the case of remaining 23 per cent cases due to unawareness on the part of family members, absence of women/girl in the family and manipulation done by patwari patta was issued to the male members. So far as participation of women in farm work is concerned, whether women were pattadhari or not, all of them were found to be involved in agricultural activities like their male counterpart.

Kumar and Chaturvedi (2007) studied the question of joint names on land patta with reference to grazing land distributed by the Govt of Madhya Pradesh especially among dalits and tribal of Bundelkhand region. The study was conducted on 182 SC/ST Pattadharis i, e, 50 from Hatta Block of Damoh district and 132 from Shahnagar Block of Panna district. 97 pattadharis were dalit and 85 were tribes. The data reveal that joint patta was issued among all the beneficiaries except the households belonging to Khamtara village of Shahnagar Block of Panna district. Patwari reported that joint patta was distributed in 1980s i.e, much before the formation of Dalit Agenda in 2002. But in all the studied villages women respondents at large were quite unaware about the joint patta scheme. The study concluded that partly because of unawareness among women and partly due to unavailability of other support system, mere name on land patta along with the name of husband was not enough to empower rural women in a meaningful manner.

The study conducted by Verma, Bhardwaj and Tagore (2008) deals with ownership of land by women belonging to Bundelkhand region. The study reveals that in the case of Chinkoe dam, a mass movement was launched by women for their proper rehabilitation. They were allotted land with the joint entitlement. The joint entitlement has empowered them but in most of the cases they are "proxy" owner of the land. Their husbands take decisions relating to land. Level of awareness is very low among these women especially about social and economic importance of land.

All these studies clearly reflect that in spite of proactive role of both state and civil societies only small number of women own land as a pattadharini. Also, many of the joint pattadhari women do not know that they are landowner. This is mainly due to high level of unawareness. Also, one of the historical reasons responsible for low level of landownership by women is the continuation of the culture of patriarchy and different proscriptions and prescriptions introduced as well as legitimised by it.

III

An ideological struggle was initiated by the State in India after independence to change some practices that favour the patriarchal system and male dominance. Needless to mention that patriarchal system has been continuing in our society since ancient days. Among "Hindus" two socio-religious traditions have been flourishing since ancient period. One is *Vedic* tradition, also known as *santanis*. The other is *Tantric* tradition, also known as *Lokayata*. In the Vedic tradition steps began to be taken since the later Vedic period to marginalise women to the rank of *Shudras*. According to Sharma, women and *Shudras* were clubbed together in one cluster and this cluster was deprived of the right to participate in the socio-religious or cultural practices of the males of the upper caste cluster. Women and *shudras* were both prohibited from performing such rites and ceremonies and also from learning the *Vedas* (Sharma: 1966; 29-33). The directives of Vedic tradition institutionalised the isolation of women of all castes and men of non-upper caste from the mainstream of the *Santana* or Vedic socio-religious tradition followed by Upper Caste Males.

So far as *Tantric* tradition is concerned whether it emerged automatically immediately after the emergence of *Vedic* tradition or after a long time gap as an anti-thesis of the doctrines of Vedic tradition, scholars have different views on it but it is said by most of them that women and *shudras* have had access to only one kind of knowledge i.e. *Atharve Veda*. This supplement relates to the *Tantirc Vidya* which is supposed to have been created by non-Aryan i.e. those who did not adhere to the Vedic ideology. Tantric tradition became popular tradition among the women of all caste groups and the males of non-upper caste groups because of the following three factors.

1. Its rituals are mostly related to the issues of the peasant world such as soil fertility;
2. It professes the superiority of feminine power (the shakti cult) ; and
3. It is opposed to the *Varna* order i.e. one of the chief constituents of the Vedic Philosophy (Chattopadhyaya, 1959: 2007-91).

Analysis of these two contradictory traditions reflect that male dominance was not so strongly exercised among the followers of *tantric* tradition and women of non-upper caste groups have not remained subjected to oppression by males of these caste groups to the extent the women of upper caste groups have been exploited and dominated by the males of their caste groups.

However, the dominance of males among non-upper caste groups cannot be ruled out as the patriarchy has continued to exist even among them. The male child particularly in the context of inheritance is, of course accorded preference by them as well. In other words, the patriarchal system exists in spite of the differences in the patterns of life lived in these two sectors. And many of the practices, such as concerning inheritance of family name, lineage identification, *shradha* ceremony etc. started by the Vedic tradition are also followed by the practitioners of *tantric* tradition. But, due to the prevalence of the World View following *Tantric* tradition and ideology, the male dominance is not supposed to be powerful among the non-upper caste groups as that prevailing among the upper caste groups. One may cite examples of female infanticide, dowry deaths, practice of child marriage, practice of *Purdah*, negation of widow remarriage system, lower socio-religious status of widows and divorcees among upper castes, practices of polygamy etc; among upper castes in a massive way incomparison to the lower castes.

Two examples may be cited to support the above narratives.

1. According to one report, it was found that by the death of only 54 Brahmans in 1876, 665 women became widow in Mithila in North Bihar (Jha 1978: 89-90)
2. According to Dr. J.H. Hutton, Census Commissioner, India (1931) in Bhadauria and Tonwar Rajputs of Morena district the sex ratio went down to as low as 634 and 622 females per thousands males respectively, although sex ratio at the district level in these year was 825 (Gazetteer of India: Madhya Pradesh, Morena, reprinted in 1996: 58-59)

In this context one can also see the role of sanskritisation process. Many elements of culture constructed and popularised by the Vedic tradition are today followed by the followers of the *tantric* tradition. Actually family is reproducing patriarchy among all caste groups through socialisation and neighborhood face to face interaction. And the reproductive role of family is supported and legitimised. It is supported by local culture, tradition including elements of civilisation such as religion and language and so on. Role of kinship organisation, Hindi serials and cinemas also perpetuates patriarchy.

Because of the continuation of the tradition of patriarchy with the help of particularistic culture only small number of women are associated with land as an owner in the villages. Even constitutional provisions, land reform measures and civil society organizations and host of other democratic forces are largely failed to extend land rights to maximum number of women. The other inhibiting factors which are both local and non-local also enforces women to remain dependent, deprived and voiceless.

Endnotes and References

Chattopadhyaya, D.P. (1959): Lokayata, A study in Ancient Indian Materialism, New Delhi: People's Publishing House.

Chaudhary, S.N. (2007): Dalit Agenda and Grazing Land to Scheduled Castes and Scheduled Tribes, Delhi: Concept.

Chaudhary, S.N. (2011): Existing State Policies, Women's Access to Land and Women Empowerment with reference to Betul and Murena district of Madhya Pradesh (Mimeo), Bhopal: Rajiv Gandhi Chair in Contemporary Studies.

Desai, S.T. (1982): Mulla Principles of Hindu Law, 15th edition, Bombay: N.M. Tripathy Pvt. Ltd.

Ekta Parishad (2007): Towards a People's Land Policy (Discussion paper), Bhopal.

Hindu Laws (2002): New Delhi: Professional Book Publishers.

Jha, P., A.K. Singh, N.S. Nayak and S. Dayal (2007): Land Reform Experience: Lesions from Across the Globe, Bhopal: Ekta Parishad.

Jha, H. (2009): "Need for an Ideological Struggle: Society and Law in Bihar", in Prem Chowdhary (ed.) Gender Discrimination and Land Ownership, Delhi: Sage.

Jha, J.S. (1978): Report of the Regional Records, Survey Committee, Bihar (1965-76), Patna: Education Department, Govt. of Bihar.

Kumar, Y. and Neha Chaturvedi (2007): "Dalit Agenda and Charnoi Land Distribution among SCs and STs in Madhya Pradesh: Case Study of Dalits and Tribes of Bundelkhand Region" in S.N. Chaudhary (ed.) Dalit Agenda and Grazing Land to Scheduled Castes and Scheduled Tribes, Delhi: Concept.

Kuppuswami, A. (2000): Mayne's Hindu Law and Usage (ed.), New Delhi: Bharat Law House.

Lochan R and M. Rajiv Lochan (2009): "Gendering Land Reforms in Madhya Pradesh", in Prem Chowdhry (ed.) Gender Discrimination in Land Ownership Delhi: Sage.

Marathe, K. (2004): "People's Land Reform Initiatives: A Note on the Bundelkhand-Baghelkhand Area, Madhya Pradesh", in Sumi Krishna (ed.) Livelihood and Gender Equity in Community Resource Management, New Delhi: Sage.

Ramchandran, T.N. (1985): "The Glory that was Vaishali," in Yogendra Mishra (ed.) Homage to Vaishali, Vaishali: Vaishali Research Institute of Prakrit, Jainology and Ahimsa, pp. 128-52.

Sachchidananda and R.P. Sinha (1984): Women's Rights: Myth and Reality, Jaipur: Printwell.

Sharma, R.S. (1966): "Some Joint Notices of Women and Shudra in Early Indian Literature", in R.S. Sharma (ed.) Light on Early Indian Society and Economy, Bombay: Manaktalas, pp. 29-33.

Verma, J., S. Bhardwaj and Anita Tagore (2008): IGSSS Study on Status of Women Land and Housing Rights Work in M.P. (Unpublished report), New Delhi: Indo-Global Social Service Society.

17

Interrogating Social Justice from Gender and Kinship Perspective

Rajatsubhra Mukhopadhyay

In India many kinds of gender disparities and discriminations can be explained by their kinship systems. Indian kinship system offers an important context within which gender based injustice and inequality are well located. The scholars and activists engaged in women studies have not fully realized the importance of kinship as a frame of reference in addressing the problem of social justice from gender perspective. Other than regular institutionalized inequalities as reflected in gender based system of inheritance and resource distribution, socialization, freedom, marriage and conjugal relations, authority and power; the very nature of entitlements to various resources and facilities including food, nutrition, health, education, etc., are often guided by kinship principles and the system gives them legitimacy. Kinship therefore being the most change-resistant institutionalized aspect of social organization appears to contest the question of gender equality and social justice. The present paper intends to examine some of the aspects in a more comprehensive frame.

II

Let me begin with a fundamental question: How could we address the problem of "Gender and Social Justice" sociologically? How biological inequality turns into social inequality through a process of evaluation and starts operating institutionally? Freud's famous remark 'anatomy is destiny' basically addressed that point. The question of biological determinism and concept of 'weaker sex' thus got certain prominence in interrogating Social Justice from gender perspective. According to some feminist critiques the notion of 'weaker sex' is perhaps the most deep rooted obstacle for the analysis of the causes of women's oppression and exploitation in the society.

Structurally gender is understood nothing but as 'biological category'. Thus the organic differences between men and women are differently interpreted and valued. This leads to the growth of two divergent visions of the world and two divergent missions of life. American feminists were the first to employ the word 'gender' to emphasize the fundamental social quality of distinctions based on sex. Gender is also a terminological indicator of the unequal relationship between men and women and the social subjugation of the latter. The word, 'gender' also denotes a 'cultural construction'—the social creation of ideas about the appropriate roles of men and women. Each culture has its own structure of values, which defines and delimits the sex roles.

While the term 'sex' refers both to an act and to a category of person, to a practice and to a gender, the concept of sexuality is almost all encompassing. It includes sexual identities, sexual norms, sexual acts, practices and experiences. But sociologically what is more important, sexuality is socially constructed and is structurally organized into every social institutions, social norms, values and interaction. It becomes a means through which power operates in society. Therefore sexuality is in a vice-like grip of what Foucault calls the 'repressive hypothesis'—where the entire sexual lexicon is carefully administered and managed by select groups in position of social, political, economic and cultural power. In a society, sexuality is being shaped by the social structures, institutions and ideologies.

There is no denying that considerable gender disparity is there in the society. According to a UN report—when women constitute 50 per cent of world's population, do more that 2/3 (60%) of the hours of work done in the world, but they get 1/10 (10%) of the world's income and less the 1/100(1%) of world's property. There are also clear cut gender gaps in the distribution or works, resources and benefits. The declining sex-ratio is a clear pointer of acute gender disparity and inferior status of women in Indian society. Statistics reveal that nearly half of our women population are illiterate, underfed, undernourished, and exploited. There is a sharp fall in the women's work participation rate (WPR) even in the urban areas. But what is more serious that as per the report (Towards Equality) of the Committee on "Status of Women in India" (1971), the dynamics of social change and development had affected the majority of the women adversely, and created new imbalances and disparities. Moreover, the role of women in development had not been fully understood.

In addition to above noted 'visible' markers of gender disparity, there are many invisible discriminations against women followed by stereotyped roles, lack of access to employment/productive activities, education, restricted freedom of leaving domestic space, interaction with opposite sex and social mobility. In our society 'invisible' social values prescribed subordinate productive and reproductive roles of women and where women are handicapped by social customs and usages. In order to control women's sexuality, their dress, behaviour and mobility are carefully monitored by familial, social, cultural and religious codes of behaviour. A range of moral and legal directives restricts the expression of women's sexuality outside marriage. Traditional social idioms portrays women as ideal mothers and dedicated wives who epitomize sacrifice.

Since independence, many constitutional, legal and administrative measures have been taken with an aim at improving the working and living conditions of Indian women and to enable them to actively participate in nation building. Of late it has been realized that empowerment of women is a *sin-qua-non* for bringing about a harmonious, sustainable and equalitarian society. Accordingly the government had declared the 2001 as 'Women's Empowerment Year'.

The importance of gender equality is rooted in Part III (Fundamental Rights) of Indian Constitution. Several Constitutional Articles proclaim the right of women and men to equality and proscribe any discrimination and disability on the basis of sex.

For gender planning in development, in early phase, the women were identified as handicapped by social custom and values and, therefore, some kinds of Social Welfare Services were thought about to rehabilitate them. Gradually there has been a more positive, integrated and comprehensive thinking on women's question in development. However, it was only in the Sixth Plan that a change took place in the policy approach towards women with special reference to their education, employment and health. The Seventh Plan opened a new chapter titled "Socio Economic Programmes for Women". Despite all these progressive gender friendly policies and programmes, a section of social scientists and activists believe that the status of women would not materially alter till such time the mindset of men is radically changed and for this the starting point should be right at the family level.

III

Let me highlight some of the facts which make us anxious about the status and plight of women in India particularly with reference to social justice.

1. The 2001 census showed the unprecendented decline in sex-ratio in 0-6 years age group in the economically progressive states of India. Delhi, Gujarat, Haryana, Punjab and Chandigarh—all have a sex ratio of less than 900 below the age of six. Does it mean economic development and increased wealth brings more infanticides and female foeticides? There is no denying that money and technology have combined to reinforce the most archaic and cruel prejudices in India against girl children. So there is a need to re-examine more critically—why economic development not necessarily always ensures social development?
2. There is considerable gender gap in health and education. Although the female literacy rates have risen, the gender gap in literacy has also increased. A century ago it was 9.2 per cent where as today it is 21.7 per cent. There are 70 districts in the country where the female literacy rate is below 20 per cent. We have largest number of out-of-school girls in the world.
3. In India there are 266 million people in informal sector of whom 90

per cent are women. There are 17 lakhs female domestic workers as against 7 lakhs in case of males. There is acute gender disparity in wages, earning, property rights and right to dispose property. We have the largest number of child prostitutes.

4. The National Bureau of Crime Record shows that only in Delhi, on an average 600 women die in every year from domestic violence. In India 40 per cent of women have experienced violence by an intimate partner [1]. A study of five districts in Uttar Pradesh has revealed that 30 per cent of currently married men acknowledge physically abusing their wives (UNC, 1997). Another survey done by the International Clinical Epidemiologists Network (INCEN) has noted that two out of every five married women reported being hit, kicked, beaten or slapped by their husbands. About 50 per cent of the women experiencing physical violence also reported physical abuse during pregnancy. In Gujarat every 2/3rd of the women were verbally or physically abused only for not preparing meals in time.
5. The incidence of dowry deaths in India is increasing annually at the rate of 8.3 per cent. It is estimated that in every day eight women are killed for non-payment of dowry. It has been reported that at least three girls are burnt for dowry related demands everyday in Karnataka. Dowry related deaths/murders are on rise in economically and educationally advanced regions in Orissa. On the whole it has been reported that in every 12th hour a dowry related death has claimed to have taken the lives of over twenty thousand women across the country between 1990 and 1993.This may be taken as a matter of grave concern, from the point of social justice to women (the prime target/victim of physical torture), as the incidence of the dowry death is one of the typical problems of Indian society.[2]
6. In 1985, when 22,351 Indian women committed suicide, the figure had gone to double in 1995. About 22 per cent of all these suicides were committed by housewives. There were 7,647 cases of women being trafficked in 1984 and it has increased to 11,242 in 2002.

Global intellectual discourses on gender inequality began in early 70s with the appearance of Boserup's work on *Women's Role in Economic Development* (1970). In India NSS data (56th round) reveal that women's participation in labour force in urban areas has declined from 201 per thousand (in 2000-01) to 193 (in 2001-02). There is an apprehension that globalization will increase gender inequality rather than reduce it. It will adversely affect the status of women and the quality of their occupations. This will lead to marginalization of women in unpaid or unorganized labour, exploitation of women engaged in low wage jobs, and impoverishment through loss of traditional sources of income. Women would be the major victim of sex-tourism that has grown rapidly along with globalization and economic liberalization. Culturally the women will tend to lose their identity autonomy to a hegemonic global culture. Western ideals are projecting the very sexuality of women into a marketing device to ensure the acquisition of everything from cars to aftershave lotions, and gratifying the western money culture in a big way. The changing construction of feminity and masculinity in the context of globalization and the role played by the mass media are emerging issues and need sociological investigation.

The term 'sexuality' is certainly connected with sex. It is a historical construction and to be understood in its own specific historical context. Its widespread acceptance has played a crucial role in regulating the social order. In the past, sexuality was considered personal, but today, it has assumed several social forms with the spread of night clubs, parlours, mass media, family planning and diseases like AIDS, etc. Thus sexuality has assumed greater significance in contemporary society. Recently, violence against women has indicated that sexuality is an important issue in producing as well as restricting male violence. Unabashed consumerism and erosion of traditional values, popular culture and media images have greatly contributed to intensify violence against women. Atrocities and violence against women should be viewed against the social mechanism by which women are forced in to subordinate position. Much of the research on sexuality in India thus deal directly or indirectly with exercise of power at the structural level. Development assistance has not done enough to dismantle patriarchal structure of power and to change women's subordination in the domestic, productive and reproductive spheres. Against this backdrop the women of today may certainly ask for 'justice' in social, economic and political spheres of life.

IV

UN Millennium Development Declaration 2000 calls for the promotion of "gender equality and the empowerment of women as effective ways to combat poverty, hunger and disease". But what is more problematic in Indian contest is the social embeddedness of status and role of women in its kinship structure which sets prescribed rules and roles for women and women's subordination both in productive and reproductive roles. In Indian society women are handicapped to a great extent by social custom and values institutionalized through its kinship system. That is why women's position depend on the position of their husbands in the household and the very terms of reference *swami, pati,* or *malik* indicates husband as 'lord' or 'owner' of a married lady. On the part of wife chastity is important in order to ensure the purity of the family bloodline. Women's behaviour and mobility are carefully monitored by familial and kinship codes of behaviour. In recent time the incidences of so called 'honour killing' is a mere reflection of this behaviour. Kinship prohibitions and usages are applied more on women than on men. In the case of women imposition of *parda,* restrictions on food and domestic space are mostly kinship determined, and they all control women's mobility and freedom. Young women in the family are expected to be dutiful and obedient. Self assertion, even in bringing up their own children is blasphemy. That is why many married women now considered nuclear/pair family as a safer matrimonial home for them.

In Indian society the very nature of entitlement to various resources including food, health, nutrition etc., are kinship determined and kinship gives them legitimacy. There is no doubt that entitlement for familial resources are based largely on kinship rules, and in this regard patriliny is unbalanced and works for disadvantage of women.[3] That is why while a son is a permanent member to his father's lineage, a daughter is viewed as a transit or temporary member of this unit. A female child's membership to her father's consanguineal unit is neither permanent nor complete. The boys are considered positive economic assets and supportive kin particularly with reference to the question of old age security. So till date many parents, particularly from rural areas, prefer to give higher education to their sons than to daughters. Mention may be made that there are 70 districts in the country where the female literacy is much below 20 per cent. Considering the economic value of a son, parents desparetely want a first born boy. The status of a newly married bride in her new home (*sasural*) thus largely depend on her ability to bear male children. Incidences of violences against women for her failure to bear a male child thus often occur in our society out of this kinship consideration. In fact the discrimination against women starts the day she is born. Sometimes it also starts when she is in her mother's womb as a foetus. The practice of female foeticides, despite being illegal, is vigorously practised in urban India.[4] It claimed the life of almost two million female babies a year.

In our society property is normally inherited by male heirs and transmitted through them. There is a strong gender gap in the ownership and control of property. It is the most critical contributor to the gender gap in economic well being, social status and empowerment. According to some scholars there are possible links of women's property rights, with control over women's sexuality, marriage practices, and kinship structures.[5] Further, gender equality in legal rights to paternal/own property does not guarantee gender equality in actual ownership, nor does ownership guarantee control[6]. Particularly in rural areas, women face significant barriers in realizing their legal claims on landed property, as well as in exercising control over any land they do get. Further, in absence of conjugal property, a married women is completely dependent on her husband unless she also earns independently and has some control over her income. According to Madan, dowry is a substitute for women's lack of rights of inheritance equivalent to those of men.[7] Our patrilineal system of inheritance restricts rights of women/daughters over productive resources and virtually offers no inheritance rights over landed property. So they are utterly dependent on their husbands. A reason for the origin of dowry could presumably be that the groom and his family had to take up the onerous responsibility of supporting the bride for the rest of her life.[8] Thus lack of command of women over landed property and other economic resources helps sustain the dowry practices in India society.

The patrilocal rule of residence virtually indicates a woman's loss of rights in her natal home and her lack of acquisition to rights over space as such. Under no circumstances she can move back permanently to her parent's home. In this structural condition not many women have enough guts to divorce their husbands and return to their natal family despite considerable mental and physical tortures they faced in their *sasural* or in conjugal family. The lowest divorce rates in India possibly depict so, where only one out of 100 marriages ends up in divorce and it mostly confined to urban areas.

Marriage transfers a woman from her natal home, and her primary or sole duty is towards her husband's family. Anything she earns, should contribute to the upkeep of her new home; and she has no recognized moral right to use it to support her parents or siblings. Only to avoid this patrilocal compulsion,some employed young women in urban areas, and who look after their old parents in natal family often prefer to keep them unmarried. Similarly, a family with single daughter (the only surviving offspring) parents find it difficult to persue their son-in-law to live with them as the *ghar damad* (the resident son-in-law) system of residence after marriage is considered status degrading if not illegal under patrilocal arrangement.

V

Gender discrimination/inequality as being shaped by the social structures, institutions and their ideologies poses many problems relating to the question of social justice in modern India. What the masses of Indian women want today are social justice, economic justice and political justice. In this context the concept of 'empowerment' of women is a *sine qua non* for bringing about a harmonious, sustainable and equalitarian society. However, while devising strategies to bring about changes in social, cultural, economic, political and legal aspects in the interest of women, one needs to understand the limits within which women function, and why certain measures have not succeeded to deliver the expected goods. Here the sociologists could provide necessary inputs from their research, and can show how gender equality could be achieved and where lies the impediments.

India has introduced a series of laws/acts to legally protect the interest of women and in ensuring social justice to them. They are together called 'family laws'. One may locate the enforcement of such laws that began along with the introduction of Sati Regulation in 1829, followed by The Hindu Widow Remarriage Act (1856), Abolition of Female Infanticides (1870), The Child Marriage Restraint Act (1929) etc., to the most recent one, The Domestic Violence Act enacted in 2005. All these legislations /family laws are fair indications of a kind of social justice and protection that Indian women badly required since colonial time. But with reference to the efficacy of many of these legal measures possibly there is a need to distinguish between 'legal' recognition or non recognition of an act and its 'social' recognition, and between recognition and enforcement. For instance a woman may have the legal right to inherit property, but this may remain merely a right on paper if the law is not enforced, or if the claim is not socially recognized as legitimate and family members exert pressure on the woman to forfeit her share in favour, say, of her brothers.[9] In such a situation the question of women's right to equality and social justice as guaranteed under the constitution of India may appear ineffective unless we could challenge old institutional frame within which gender based injustice and inequality are located. In view of continuing failure of the state to ensure social justice to women through legal measures the intervention of civil societies in general and the role of Non Governmental Organizations (NGOs) in particular tend to be effective.

As India does not have any systematic family policy we could hardly redress any gender based discrimination and disparity reinforce by old family/kinship norms, values and usages. On the question of 'gender and social justice' there are significant regional and community wise variations in India as regional cultures, customs and personal laws of different communities subvert women's right to social justice and equality. So there is every justification to endorse the recommendation made by Singh for setting up a Family Policy Council in each State of India to conduct policy analysis, facilitate strategic leadership involvement and influence public opinion.[10] Along with this, we have to also keep in mind that development assistance has not done enough to dismantle patriarchal structures of power as embedded in Indian family and kinship systems, and to change women's subordination in every walks of life. There is a need to properly address women's land, property and inheritance rights in the context of elimination of all forms of discrimination against women. In addition, women have to be provided with health, education and other public facilities particularly in remote and marginal areas. Last but not the least, also there is a need to encourage men to redefine masculinity and power relations at all institutional level.

Endnotes and References

1. J.P. Singh, "Indias Changing Family and State Intervention", *The Eastern Anthropologist*, 63(1), 2010, pp. 17-40.
2. J.P. Singh, "Dowry in India: A Search for New Social Identity, *The Eastern Anthropologist*, 58(2), 2005, pp. 199-220.
3. Leela Dube, *Anthropological Exploration in Gender* (New Delhi: Sage Publications, 2001).
4. J.P. Singh, 2010, *op. cit.*
5. Bina Agarwal, *Gender and Command over Property: An Economic Analysis of South Asia* (New Delhi: Kali for Women,1996).
6. Ibid.
7. T.N. Madan, "Structural Implications of Marriage in North India: Wife givers and Wife takers among the Pandits of Kashmir," *Contributions to Indian Sociology* (n.s.), 9 (2), 1975, pp. 217-243.
8. J.P. Singh, 2005, *op. cit.*
9. Bina Agarwal, 1996, *op. cit.*
10. J.P. Singh, 2010, *op. cit.*

18

Role of Women's Movements in Advancing Gender Justice in India

Sumit S. Srivastava

The article discusses the concept of gender justice in the backdrop of social justice. It focuses on how gender justice is an important constituent element of social justice. It argues that in the absence of gender justice, the agenda of social justice may not be achieved to its optimum. The concept of social justice is intrinsically tied up with the notion of inequality. This inequality leads to the discrimination based on several social variables like age, sex, caste, class, religion among other. In the case of gender, the patriarchal system which is reflected in unequal power relationships between male and female becomes significant. It can be seen as a system of practice where female has comparatively less degree of power and access to opportunity. In this context, the issue of gender justice has become significant. It focuses on the equality of and between gender i.e. male and female. It arrives at the understanding that inequalities between male and female exists and constant initiatives have to be taken so as to bridge the same.

In India, such a process has seen transition from welfare perspective to the woman empowerment perspective. The welfare perspective can be traced from the constitutional provisions and enacted laws and policies for safeguarding the rights of women. The empowerment perspective is reflected in national policy for women empowerment. However, in between is located a vibrant and multilayered practice of women's movements. The core theme of struggle of women's movements have been the issues of violence against women which is reflected in rape, dowry related bride burning, domestic violence and practice of female infanticide among others. The article argues that such a movement has been and still is vital for advancing the practice of gender justice in Indian society so as to realise gender sensitive social development.

INTRODUCTION

In recent times the nature of grand narratives in the centrality of academic discourse are undergoing significant changes. It has resulted in some way or the other in the dominance of certain 'voices' and exclusion of most of the others. However, there is an ongoing struggle by those at the periphery to be included into the mainstream of discussion rather than be left out as they were for centuries. Such continued struggle has been successful to some extent as what we see now that those narratives which were at the periphery of various disciplines have gradually become more visible and significant. The narratives of woman belong to the latter part.

Gender equality which is a key variable in economic and human development of any society or for that matter nation-state has become a major component of visible and significant narratives. Subsequently, the former is continuously in dialogue with notions of women welfare, women empowerment and more recently gender justice. The notion of gender justice is important to realize as the power structure in any society is imbalanced in its nature as it is in relation to social justice. It is based on the notion of social justice which envisages that every individual should have optimum participation in the workings of community and society. Here gender and power structure are entangled with each other. Power structure broadly means how the resources of the society have been distributed or for that matter are disbursed. It brings in to picture the power differentials between men and women. Additively, the availability, affordability and accessibility of the same power resources are of prime concern. Elaborating on this argument it can be said that there are certain resources which are completely denied to the other sections of the society.

In the case of gender, the visibility and mobility of women in the 'public' sphere has been restricted many a times. In this manner, she does not have the resources i.e. resources are unavailable for her as these are outside her purview. Again, even if there is some kind of availability, the issue of affordability comes in to picture. Most of the times, due to her economic dependence on the men, she may not be financially secure to afford that resource. The case of education can be taken here where most of the times girl's education are sacrificed for that of the boy. Thirdly, the accessibility of the resources can also be restricted via traditions and customs of the respective society. In this way, the discrimination of women and the inequality between genders is practiced.

An important design and practice of perpetuating such discrimination is the practice of patriarchy in any given society and more so in the Indian society. Patriarchy, as broadly understood is the system of practices and procedures which positions women inferior to the men and subsequently leads to unequal balance of power between them. It is a system of discrimination towards women. Its bases are primarily inferred from the traditions and customs. Like gender, patriarchy is also a social construct. It does not relate to the biological differences between the sexes. S. Walby (1990) elaborated on the forms of patriarchy. According to her, patriarchy operates both in the private (19th century) and public (20th century) spheres/domains of life. In the private sphere, the dominant structure of patriarchy is household production whereas in the public sphere it is the employment/state. For her the wider patriarchal structures in private sphere household production, sexuality, violence and culture whereas in the public sphere these include employment, state, violence amongst others. Mode of expropriation in private sphere is individual and in public sphere it is collective in nature. For her, the patriarchal strategies also differ.[1]

At the same time, it should not be seen as something which is anti to the women in general. Moreover, sometimes patriarchy draws its strength from the women also. As has been argued that patriarchy "denotes systems of subordinating women—functions simultaneously through coercion or the threat or practice of violence, through making a wide social consensus drawn from and dispersed over many areas of social life and through obtaining in various ways, different degrees of consent from women" (Sangari, 1991:371).[2] It is in the above context that the urgent need for advocating and practicing gender justice emerges. It has to be understood that the true spirit of equality in society cannot be achieved until women are fairly represented and are visible in all aspects of day-to-day activities both in the public and private sphere.

It has been often argued that women do not constitute a homogenous category. Thus, they do not have a universal set of problems and solutions to it. Subsequently, defining gender justice in any context becomes an uphill task. Yet, it "can be defined as the ending of—and if necessary the provision of redress for—inequalities between women and men that result in women's subordination to men. These inequalities may be in the distribution of resources and opportunities that enable individuals to build human, social, economic, and political capital. Or, they may be in the conceptions of human dignity, personal autonomy and rights that deny women physical integrity and the capacity to make choices about how to live their lives. As an outcome, gender justice implies access to and control over resources, combined with agency ... gender justice adds an element of redress and restitution that is not always present in discussions of women's empowerment" (Goetz, 2007:15-57).[3]

GENDER JUSTICE IN DEVELOPMENT FRAMEWORK

Broadly understood, the historicity of gender justice can be traced back to the usages of Women in Development (WID), Women and Development (WAD) and recently the use of the term Gender and Development (GAD).[4] It would be a worthwhile exercise to briefly discuss these concepts. Women in Development (WID hereafter) perspective focuses on the gender dimension in the process of development. It was felt that the developmental paradigm has to be gender sensitive. The developmental agenda has to respond to the specific needs of the women. It can be seen as the offshoot of the modernization process of the 1960s and 1970s regarding development. It argued for devising such strategies and action programmes (action research) so as to minimize gender discrimination. In this perspective it was argued that the developmental process does not have similar impact on men and women. So, the development process has to be critically analyzed keeping women's issues in consideration. Major shortcoming of the Women in Development perspective was that it did not focused at the structural bases of women's subordination to men.

Women and Development (WAD hereafter) perspective grew as the outcome of the critique of modernization theory. In the latter, it was assumed that economic freedom or independence will solve the various problems of women. Yet, it could not do so. Women and Development perspective addresses the gender subordination via locating women intrinsically in the development process. The fine line difference between Women in Development and Women and Development is that the former advocates plans and policies to end women's discrimination whereas the latter sees women located in the community and thus the community has to benefit from the developmental process which will in ultimate scenario benefit women.

Gender and Development (GAD hereafter) perspective emerged in 1980s. It recognizes the agency of the women as a mode of empowerment. At a very broad level it focuses on the gender aspect of woman. The basic difference between woman and gender is that the latter includes the politics of subordination of women to men. It argued for the legal rights of women so as to enable them to be empowered. GAD does not believe in the notion that only women can understand women rather men are also a critical component in understanding the women's problems and trying to resolve them. Some of the basic differences between Women and Development and Gender and Development have been outlined by Kate Young.[5] According to the author, the focus of GAD is not on women per se rather on the gender relations involving both men and women. It argues that women are not passive recipients of the developmental process i.e. top-bottom approach of development rather they are very much a part of this process. State is also responsible for the formulation of policies aiming at minimizing the gender discrimination. Thus GAD has a wider perspective in comparison to WID and WAD.[6]

United Nations Development Programme (UNDP) introduced two new composite indices in its 1995 Human Development Report. The Gender Development Index (GDI) assesses the impact of gender inequality on human development. The Gender Empowerment Measurement (GEM), measures the extent to which there is gender equity in economic and political power. It reflects gender equity in participation in governmental and managerial decision making and professional roles, and economic activity. While the HDI measures average achievement in basic human development capabilities, the

GDI adjusts this to reflect the inequalities between men and women in three dimensions: a long and healthy life, knowledge and a decent standard of living.[7] Focusing on women's opportunities rather than their capabilities, the GEM captures gender inequality in three key areas: political participation and decision-making power, economic participation and decision-making power, and power over economic resources.

Another important set of notions related to gender justice are the practices of gender mainstreaming and gender budgeting. According to the United Nations Economic and Social Council (ECOSOC) (July, 1997), "Mainstreaming a gender perspective is the process of assessing the implications for women and men of any planned action, including legislation, policies or programmes, in any area and at all levels. It is a strategy for making the concerns and experiences of women as well as of men an integral part of the design, implementation, monitoring and evaluation of policies and programmes in all political, economic and societal spheres, so that women and men benefit equally, and inequality is not perpetuated. The ultimate goal of mainstreaming is to achieve gender equality."[8] In the same line of argument, United Nations Development Programme (UNDP) defines gender mainstreaming as "Taking account of gender equality concerns in all policy, programme, administrative and financial activities, and in organizational procedures, thereby contributing to organizational transformation."[9]

With regards to the gender mainstreaming in Indian context, National Policy for the Empowerment of Women (2001) states that, "Policies, programmes and systems will be established to ensure mainstreaming of women's perspectives in all developmental processes, as catalysts, participants and recipients. Wherever there are gaps in policies and programmes, women specific interventions would be undertaken to bridge these. Coordinating and monitoring mechanisms will also be devised to assess from time to time the progress of such mainstreaming mechanisms. Women's issues and concerns as a result will specially be addressed and reflected in all concerned laws, sectoral policies, plans and programmes of action."[10] In this way we can see that gender justice has been included in the vocabulary of the nation-state also.

Gender budgeting is the concept and practice whereby the budget of any nation-state has specific plan outlay for the needs of women. According to—

> "Gender-responsive budgeting (GRB) is government planning, programming and budgeting that contributes to the advancement of gender equality and the fulfillment of women's rights. It entails identifying and reflecting needed interventions to address gender gaps in sector and local government policies, plans and budgets. GRB also aims to analyze the gender-differentiated impact of revenue-raising policies and the allocation of domestic resources and Official Development Assistance. GRB initiatives seek to create enabling policy frameworks, build capacity and strengthen monitoring mechanisms to support accountability to women."[11]

According to the UK-based Department for International Development (DFID), "Gender Budget Initiatives or Gender Responsive Budgets are tools and processes designed to facilitate a gender analysis in the formulation of government budgets and the allocation of resources. Gender budgets are not separate budgets for women, or for men. They are attempts to break down or disaggregate the government's mainstream budget according to its impacts on women and men."[12]

India also has now accepted and has put gender budgeting into practice. According to the Xth Five Year Plan (2002-07) Document, "... the Tenth Plan will continue the process of dissecting the Government budget to establish its gender—differential impact and to translate gender commitments into budgetary commitments ... the Tenth Plan will initiate immediate action in tying up these two effective concepts of Women Component Plan and Gender Budgeting to play a complementary role to each other, and thus ensure both preventive and post facto action in enabling women to receive their rightful share from all the women-related general development sectors."[13]

It is important to note that gender equality and women's empowerment has received commendable thrust in the Millennium Development Goals (MDGs), 2000. It is targeted towards eliminating gender disparity in primary and secondary education preferably by 2005, and at all levels by 2015. It also prescribes indicators of the progress regarding achieving the same. These are ratios of girls to boys in primary, secondary and tertiary education; share of women in wage employment in the non-agricultural sector and proportion of seats held by women in National Parliament.

GENDER JUSTICE AND CONSTITUTION OF INDIA

Various provisions in Constitution aim at empowering women thus practicing gender justice. Some of these are equality before the law (Article 14):

- no discrimination by the State on the grounds only of religion, race, caste, sex, place of birth or any of these (Article 15(1));
- special provisions to be made by the State in favor of women and children (Article 15(3));
- equality of opportunity for all citizens in matters relating to employment or appointment to any office under the State (Article 16);
- State policy to be directed to securing for men and women equally, the right to an adequate means of livelihood (Article 39(a));
- equal pay for equal work for both men and women (Article 39 (d));

provisions to be made by the State for securing just and humane conditions of work and for maternity relief (Article 42) and (Article 51(A)(e)) to promote harmony and to renounce practices derogatory to the dignity of women.

The Factories Act of 1948 provides adequate safeguards to women employees. To enable women who are employed to be able to safeguard the health of the foetus and their own before and after childbirth the Maternity

Benefit Act was passed in 1961. The Indecent Representation of Women (Prohibition) Act, 1986 and provisions in the Indian Penal Code deal with obscenity like Sections 294 and 509. These focus on the question of objectification of women and sexual harassment of women. Some of the traditional practices which are exploitative in character subsequently leading to the subordinate status of women in society have been checked via Commission of Sati (Prevention) Act of 1987, the Immoral Traffic (Prevention) Act of 1986 among others.

The Equal Remuneration Act of 1976 aims to provide for the payment of equal wages to men and women workers. To specifically address the question of female foeticide the Parliament enacted the Pre-natal Diagnostic Techniques (Regulation and Prevention) Act in 1994. It basically criminalizes the use of techniques like ultrasound to determine the sex of the foetus. This Act is supplemented with Medical Termination of Pregnancy Act , 1971. In this way we can see that the principle of gender equality is very much a structural part of the Indian Constitution. It grants women equal rights with men. Additively, it empowers the State to adopt measures of positive discrimination [affirmative action] in favour of women so as to achieve the goal of gender equality and gender justice.

LOCATING GENDER JUSTICE IN WOMEN'S MOVEMENTS IN INDIA

Broadly understood, social movements are "struggles or sustained actions taken by groups of people coming together around an identity, issues or strategies formulated by a partial or developing ideology. These are named after the groups they have been able to mobilize and so we have the women's movement, the gay rights, the displaced, workers, or people for peace, etc. Movements represent their voices, issues and demands as well as formulate their own methodology and organizations" (Gandhi and Shah, 2006:72-76).[14] According to Omvedt (1978:372), "Women's movements are those which arise as conscious, organized efforts of women (often supported by men) to change this system of economic, political and cultural inequality. While women individually struggle against their subordinate position under many conditions, such organized movements have only arisen with the development of capitalism and imperialism, as part of efforts to carry through the democratic revolution. Women's equality movements aim at attaining an equal place for women in social structure whereas women's liberation movements challenge the sexual division of labour itself."[15]

To trace and to provide a brief history of women's movement in post-independent India is very difficult task. Not only India has diverse nature of women population on the basis of caste, class, religion, educational levels, etc. but also the issues of women's movement have different degree of importance for each segment of women population.[16] However, "women's movement in India can be classified into two phases: First, as a part of nationalist struggle—a period of reformist movements, when, first men and later women took up women's issues. Many women's organizations also emerged, spearheading the struggle against social evils, and advancing the cause of female education and female franchise. After a long gap, a second and more militant phase of women's organizations emerged in the 1970s, which directly challenged the patriarchal social order while rallying around issues of violence against women, like dowry deaths and rape cases" (Mehrotra, 2002:63).[17] Thus, addressing and negotiating the issue of violence against women manifested in dowry deaths, rape and rape laws, custodial rapes, female infanticide among others was looming large on the minds of women's movement in post-independent India.[18]

Thus, there are not less than two ways to chronicle women's movements in post-independent India. First is the chronological way and the second one is the theme/issue-based analysis. The former often takes the route of pre and post-independence activities of women movement. The latter focuses on the various women issues related to women like health, education, violence and economic complexities. In here, both the ways are simultaneously taken into account to briefly outline the key features of post-independent India.

As discussed earlier, constitutional provisions safeguarding the women's rights were enshrined in the Constitution. Yet, such a plethora of laws and regulation could not salvage the status of women from obscurity. Reasons vary from 'lethargic attitude towards the formulation and execution of the empowerment policies' to 'traditional patriarchal structure' from time immemorial. The euphoria of independence very soon gave way to the hard realization that even the independence had felt short to fulfill the aspirations of large mass. The battle-lines had to be redrawn and new definitions of 'enemy' had to be evolved as there was "a concern 'with violence against women, although not with the earlier issues of sati and ill-treatment of widows but with rape and wife battering; with marriage, not widow or child marriages but divorce, maintenance and child custody; with legislative reform, not the enactment of more laws but with bringing in amendments that facilitate implementation of existing ones; with education, not only spreading educational facilities but attacking sexist and stereotyped textbooks; with equality, not only equal rights, but equal opportunities to work and with equal pay."[19]

In 1971, the Commission on Status of Women in India (SWI) was constituted by the Ministry of Education and Social Welfare. This move was a response to United Nation's initiative regarding status of women report for International Women's Year in 1975.[20] The committee had to examine "the constitutional, legal and administrative provisions that have a bearing on the social status of women, their education and employment," and to "assess the impact of these provisions."[21] The Committee gave its report in 1974 which was titled *"Toward Equality: The Report of the Committee on the Status of Women in India."*[22] Looking at women's position in the mid 1970s the authors of *Toward*

Equality concluded women's status had not improved in the twenty-five years since independence.

In late 1960s, 'second wave' of Indian feminism emerged focusing on violence in all the forms against women. Patel (1998:198-207)[23] elaborated on following understandings of violence against gender:

- For the liberal activists in the civil liberties groups, sanctity of the individual was an issue of prime concern. Hence any citizen who was violated had to take recourse to Constitutional means of redressal for justice, by approaching the existing judicial system.
- The democratic rights organisations represented the views of the far-left groups and gave a call for direct actions which confronted the state.
- The religious and puritanical groups were perturbed by the violation of 'chastity' and the 'purity' of women.
- The feminists saw violence against women as an outcome of the subordination of women—a weapon to terrorize, intimidate and humiliate women.

During 1980s, the media reported numerous cases of 'burning brides' where newly-wed girls either 'committed suicide' or were 'burnt alive' by the in-laws over dowry disputes. It was the Progressive Organisation of Women in Hyderabad in 1975 which protested openly against dowry for the first time. Later on, these protests spread to Delhi as it was accounting the highest incidents of dowry deaths. Intense mass mobilization along with an attempt to analyze the incidents of dowry deaths brought forth the conclusion that these incidents were not just 'accidents' or issues relate to the private sphere of family and kin groups, rather it was a system of exploiting and victimizing women. Subsequently, there was shift in the understanding from media labeled 'bride-burning' to feminists coining 'dowry murder.' The personal/private sphere was brought into public sphere of dialogue and protest and the early feminist activism protested the deaths of many young women by holding *dharnas* in front of police stations and the houses where the women were burned to death[24]. More significantly, absence of any kind of constitutional remedy was also critiqued.

It resulted in some of the changes oriented towards women like the construction of special Crimes Against Women Cells in select police stations to handle women's complaints and Family Courts. Crimes against women within the institution of marriage were recognized by the law. The Indian Penal Code (Section 498A and 304B) was amended twice during the 1980s, first in 1983 and again in 1986. In 1983, under Section 498A of the Indian Penal Code 'cruelty by husband or relatives of husband' was defined as cognizable offence.

During the same period, two other amendments to the Dowry Prohibition Act of 1961, enacted in 1984 and 1986, made dowry giving and receiving a cognizable offense. A new category of crime named 'dowry murder' or 'dowry death' was covered by Section 304B. Under section 304B, in the case of a 'dowry death', the accused are frequently denied anticipatory, or even regular bail. Later on, the Dowry Prohibition (Maintenance of Lists of Presents to the Bride and Bridegroom) Rules, 1985 [dated 19th August 1985) provided that the lists of presents which are given at the time of the marriage to the bride shall be maintained by the bride.

Another issue was protest against the incidents of custodial rapes and subsequent acquittal of criminals either due to lack of evidence or lack of concrete constitutional remedies. The situation was more exploitative of the victims as the prevalent laws and customs had put the onus of proving the act of rape on the victim herself revealing the patriarchal mindset of law and state machinery (Sarkar, 1994:69).[25] The acquittal of the culprits of Rameeza Bee (1978), Maya Tyagi (1980) and Mathura rape case (1980) by the constitutional bodies intertwined the issues of body and sexuality, gender and caste, gender and communalism, gender and law, morality and law, etc. with each other. It was observed that "...this is the situation we started with in 1980, with how the Supreme Court reasoned, how the Supreme Court thinks of bodily autonomy, the bodily integrity of women. That when there are no injuries, there is no rape" (Agnes, 2005).[26] In a response to unjust judgment on rape cases, activists of women's movement formed Forum Against Oppression of Women (FAOW) which was started as Forum Against Rape in 1979.

At this time, an open letter to the Supreme Court by four lawyers pointing out many shortcomings in the judgment was drafted.[27] Due to such an intense mass mobilization, the government amended the Indian Evidence Act, 1872, the Criminal Procedure Code and the Indian Penal Code and introduced the category of 'custodial rape'. The Law Commission of India in its report on 'Rape and Allied Offences—Some Questions of Substantive Law, Procedure and Evidence' recommended an amendment to Section 155(4) of the Indian Evidence Act, 1872 which allows questions on the past sexual history of the victim only vis-a-vis the accused.

There were various corrective measures taken. Under Section 376(1) of the Indian Penal Code (IPC), a minimum term of seven years imprisonment may be imposed for rape. The Criminal Law (Amendment) Act of 1983 for the first time provided for the offense of custodial rape. Commissioned officers of the paramilitary and military forces are included under Section 376(2)(b) of the IPC and are thus also subject to this mandatory sentence. The Criminal Law (Amendment) Act (1983) also shifted the burden of proof regarding consent to the accused.

Despite such corrective measures Section 155 clause 4 of the Indian Evidence Act, 1872 remained in effect. There were various attempts on part of the government to amend it. Subsequently, the Indian Evidence (Amendment) Bill, 2002 was introduced in the Lok Sabha on November 28 2002. It intended to remove Section 155(4) of the Indian Evidence Act, 1872.

Finally, after more intense mobilization and subsequent recommendations of Law Commission of India and the National Commission for Women, it was only on 3rd January 2003 that it was modified. The Indian Evidence (Amendment) Act, 2003, provided deletion of clause 4 of Section 155 by specifically providing in Section 146.

In recent times, the Indian Evidence (Amendment) Act, 2006 was introduced in the Rajya Sabha on the 12th May, 2006 to further amend the Indian Evidence Act, 1872. It stated that "In the Evidence Act, 1872, after section 114A, the following section shall be inserted, namely 114B: In a prosecution for culpable homicide or murder, as the case may be, of a person by a police officer the court may presume that the death was caused when that person was in the custody of the police, by the police officer having custody of that person during that period after taking into account all the relevant circumstances and facts unless otherwise proved by that police officer."

The women's movement was also instrumental in bringing significant changes in the policy plans and papers of the country. For the first time in country's planning, the Sixth Five Year Plan (1980-85) had a chapter on women and development. It outlined a strategy for women's development. Various issues discussed were i) employment and economic independence; ii) education; iii) health care and family planning; iv) support services to meet the immediate needs of women and v) creation of enabling policy, institutional and legal environment. A separate Department of Women and Child Development was set up in 1985 under the newly created Ministry of Human Resource Development. Thus, the years of 1970s and 1980s were characterized by a plethora of activities aiming at violence manifested in incidents of dowry death and rape (custodial as well as of other nature). In recent times, National Policy for the Empowerment of Women (2001) states that, "The women's movement and a wide-spread network of non-Government Organisations which have strong grass-roots presence and deep insight into women's concerns have contributed in inspiring initiatives for the empowerment of women."[28] Thus there have been achievements such as enacting more stringent laws to punish the culprits as well there were failures as the present scenario starkly reveals that both the issues are far away solved (Flavia, 1992:19-33).[29] Yet, this period was very fruitful for the women's movement.

Another understanding of violence against women during 1980s "was the sharp increase in use of sex determination and sex selection tests with the use of new reproductive technology, which were followed by abortion of female foetuses. By the early 1980s new reproductive technologies like amniocentesis had appeared on the scene" (Mazumdar, 2000).[30] The declining sex ratio coupled with the advent of new technology was a concern with the women's movement. It was found that the states of 'Hindi-belt'/'Cow-belt' laid more premium on the son compared to daughter due to patriarchal social structure. Along with it was the increased prosperity resulting in dowry giving capacity. Thus, daughters became a 'burden' on the family leading to increased incidents of female infanticide.

Various techniques used for such purpose were chorionic villi biopsy, amniocentesis and ultra-sonography (Balasubrahmanyan, 1986:1492; Patel, 1997:19-20).[31] The negative impact of intense use of prenatal diagnostic technology for the purposes of sex determination (SD) followed by use of sex-selection abortion (SSA) is reflected in the declining all-India female/male child ratio in 0-6 age-group (child sex ratio) which was 976/1000 in 1961, 964 /1000 in 1971, 962/1000 in 1981, 945/1000 in 1991 and 927/1000 in 2001. Child sex ratio in 2011 stands at 914 girls, down from 927 girls for 1,000 boys in 2001.

Mumbai was the core of the anti- female infanticide campaign led by women movement activists during 1980-1981 which soon spread to other areas. In 1986, the Forum Against Sex Determination and Sex Pre-Selection was formed in Mumbai to campaign against sex-selective abortions. Another such forum was Doctors Against Sex-Determination and Sex-Preselection Techniques (DASDSP). Under severe pressure, Maharashtra Regulation and Pre-Natal Diagnostic Techniques Act was passed in May 1988. It was for the first time in the country that such a law was formulated. Subsequently, the Pre-Natal Diagnostic Techniques (Regulation and Prevention of Misuse) Act was passed by the Centre in 1994 aiming at registering the users of technologies and to keep a check on doctors violating such act.

The effective implementation of the Act was questioned as the Census data 2001 again showed the decline of female sex ratio. It was then during giving decision on the Public Interest Litigation (PIL) that the Supreme Court strictly directed that states to register all ultrasound centers and to put up notices in ultrasound clinics that sex determination tests were illegal. Later on, the Pre-Natal Diagnostic Techniques (Regulation and Prevention of Misuse) Act was amended in 14th February 2003. The Act became Pre-Conception and Pre-natal Diagnostic Techniques (Prohibition of Sex Selection) Act. Despite formulating such stringent measures for checking the decreasing sex ratio, the 2011 provisional data reflects a very sorry state of affairs as "an analysis of the gender composition of the decline shows that the decline in females is much more than that among males. While there was a decline of 29,91,976 females, the decline among males was only 20,56,132."[32]

The struggle of women's movements to address the issue of domestic violence began in the late 1960s itself. During the struggle for effective laws "Broadly three kinds of definitions of violence and cruelty against wives emerged: a narrow definition which often left out acts which many women consider as violence, as for instance rape within marriage. Second expert or professional definitions of violence, for example those of sociologists and psychologists who often focus on the 'breakdown' of the family, and third, a broader, feminist position which focused not only on the actual manifestations of violence against wives but also the ever present 'fear of violence' through which compliance with the patriarchal family norms is sought. Such a position reveals that across caste and class boundaries there is a continuum of violent practices against wives" (Rege, 1995:235).[33]

After a prolong struggle, it was in 1983 that domestic violence was recognized as a specific criminal offence. Accordingly, Section 498A (Section 304B in 1986) was introduced into the Indian Penal Code dealing with cruelty by a husband or his family towards a married woman. More specifically, four types of cruelty were emphasized like (i) conduct that is likely to drive a woman to suicide; (ii) conduct which is likely to cause grave injury to the life, limb or health of the woman; (iii) harassment with the purpose of forcing the woman or her relatives to give some property, or (iv) harassment because the woman or her relatives is unable to yield to demands for more money or does not give some property.

Thus, "The criminalisation of domestic violence in the form of Sec 498A and 304B (dowry death) sought to increase the certainty and severity of legal responses, thereby correcting historical, legal, and moral disparities in the legal protections afforded to abused women. It sought for the first time to bring the issue of domestic or family violence out of the protected private realm of the family and into the public domain in India" (Kothari, 2005).[34] Yet, even the enactment of such laws were of little help for the victims of domestic violence as "A study covering more than 10,000 women in Chennai, Thiruvananthapuram, Lucknow and Bhopal conducted by the International Centre for Research on Women found that 45 per cent of women have experienced at least one episode of violence (excluding slapping). The National Family Health Survey (NFHS) 2 recorded data on violence acknowledging that suffering domestic violence is a contributory factor in women's ill-being. It found that one in three women over 15 years has experienced some form of violence."[35]

Subsequently, The Protection from Domestic Violence Bill, 2002 was drafted and introduced. According to the Bill, domestic violence constitutes (i) habitually assaults or makes the life of the aggrieved person miserable by cruelty of conduct even if such conduct does not amount to physical ill-treatment; or (ii) forces the aggrieved person to lead an immoral life; or otherwise injures or harms the aggrieved person. It miserably failed to address the issue at hand and thus "attracted criticism from women's groups due to its regressive features such as a narrow definition of domestic violence; a self-defence clause for husbands; mandatory counselling and ill-defined jurisdiction of the courts" (Suneetha and Nagaraj, 2005).[36] As an historic moment for the women's movements in India, a more gender sensitive initiative on domestic violence was witnessed as on 23rd June 2005 the Domestic Violence against Women (Prevention and Protection) Bill, 2005 became a reality. The new law accepts the rights of 'other women' and the multiplicity of domestic violence apart from physical acts of violence.

However, to summarise the 1970s-1980s activities restricted only to issues of rape and dowry will be mistake as "the post-1970s women's movement did not focus on rape and dowry alone—the urban women's groups were actively unionising women, both in established unions like CITU and in new unions such as SEWA for unorganised women's labour. And the rural women's groups actively mobilised rural women, especially landless labour (later some of these groups were to help elect the first women's panchayats in India). Also the mainstream women's groups, those affiliated to the Congress, Left and socialist parties, were very active against rising prices, and on issues like housing and water" (Kumar, 2005).[37] Thus, women's movements in post-independent India addressed various women related issues needed to realize the objective of gender justice.

IN LIEU OF CONCLUSION

The idea of gender justice is inter-linked with the notion of social justice. The latter is more into achieving the social, economic and political equality among the members of any given community or society. Herein justice has to be done as justice as it has an intrinsic value. Undoubtedly, social justice comes from social injustice. Thus, social justice entails distribution of benefits and burden whereas at the same time the identity, recognition, dignity and respect of any individual need not be compromised.

Gender justice, as it spells out is more into unhooking the clutches of social inequalities deeply enmeshed in social structure. The gender inequality in terms of restricting the visibility and mobility of women in particular to the private sphere only is a major concern for achieving gender justice. At the same time, one needs to understand that the question is not only regarding the presence or absence of women's issues in the public discourse, rather the broader questions have to tend to address the issue of availability, affordability and accessibility of the social resources by the women. An obvious corollary to such a scenario is getting together of the like-minded people, to organize and mobilize themselves to make the general public conscious of the discrimination and exploitation of the women. Such a vibrant mobilization in Indian context is widely termed as women's movements.

Though it can be said that the initial phase of women's movements was more a response to the colonial critique of status of women in India, gradually his response matured with time and took up more concrete issues of discrimination and gender inequality. As discussed above, the major concern for women's movements apart from other issues was violence against women in various forms ranging from sexual assault, rape and custodial rapes and domestic violence. One of the significant achievement of women's movements has been the 'naming' of the violence and violent acts. It is so because only when one comes to define any act as violence, it becomes violence otherwise it is seen just as an expression of human behavior. Violence against women severely impedes achieving gender justice as in any just society there is no place for any kind of violence towards any individual.

Thus it can be concluded that the women's movements have played and is still playing a major role in addressing the issues of women. It is very significant to note that the movement in its due course of time had been quite vocal against the gender biased functioning of the state. Yet, the same State in its official policy has applauded the sustained effort in advancing the women's issues. It has not only raised various issues which are very much significant for advancing the practice of gender justice but has in a very vibrant manner contributed in the same also. The opposition to violence against women and subsequent remedial measures has made gender justice within reach for most of us concerned.

Endnotes and References

1. Walby, S. (1990), *Theorizing Patriarchy*, Oxford: Blackwell.
2. Sangari, Kumkum (1999), *Politics of the Possible: Essays on Gender, History, Narratives, Colonial English*, New Delhi: Tulika: 364-409.
3. Anne Marie Goetz (2007), "Gender Justice, Citizenship and Entitlements: Core Concepts, Central Debates and New Directions for Research". In Maitrayee Mukhopadhyay and Navsharan Singh (eds.), *Gender Justice, Citizenship and Development*, Jointly published by Zubaan, New Delhi and the International Development Research Centre, Canada: 15-57.
4. Online Available at: *idl-bnc.idrc.ca/dspace/bitstream/10625/5225/1/34345.pdf.*
5. Online Available at: http://www.eou.edu/socwomen/support/articles/youngGandD.pdf
6. In 1980s the birth of Development Alternatives with Women for a New Era (DAWN) resulted in broader understanding of women's issues. 1990s saw the coming of Women, Environment, and Sustainable Development (WED) discourse. For details see, Bhattacharya, Mohit. 2011. "Gender and Development: Theoretical Perspectives". *Journal of Social and Political Studies*, II(1):12-22.
7. India's HDI rank in 2007 was 134. For India, Gender-related Development Index in 2007 was 0.594. Global Gender Gap Index in 2009 was 0.615. The score of Gender equity index was 40 in 2008. The score of Social Institutions and Gender Index in 2009 was 0.318. For details see *Power, Voice and Rights: A Turning Point for Gender Equality in Asia and the Pacific*. Available Online at: www.undp.org/asia/
8. Online Available at: http://www.ilo.org/public/english/bureau/gender/newsite2002/about/defin.htm
9. Moving From Policy To Practice: A Gender Mainstreaming Strategy For UNDP India. Online Available at: http://arabstates.undp.org/contents/file/IndiaGenderMainstreaming.pdf
10. National Policy for the Empowerment of Women (2001)
Online Available at: http://wcd.nic.in/empwomen.htm
11. Online Available at: http://www.gender-budgets.org/index.php?option=com_content&view=frontpage&Itemid=586
12. *Gender Budgeting*. Helen Leadbetter
Online Available at: http://webarchive.nationalarchives.gov.uk/+/http://www.dfid.gov.uk/aboutdfid/organisation/pfma/pfma-gender-budget.pdf
13. *Women's Empowerment through Gender Budgeting- A review in the Indian context*. Anjali Goyal.
Online Available at: http://www.wcd.nic.in/gbsummary/GBppr_AG.pdf
14. Gandhi, N. and Nandita Shah (2006), "Inter Movement Dialogues: Breaking Barriers, Building Bridges." *Development*, 49:72-76.
15 Omvedt, Gail (1978), "Women and Rural Revolt in India," *The Journal of Peasant Studies*, April, 5(3):370-403.

16. Such issues were raised more than a decade back as pointed out that "Given the diversity of cultures and the complexities of caste and class among women in India, can we actually speak of an overarching women's movement in the country? Or is it that there are a number of fragmented campaigns which do not add up to a movement? How many of these campaigns are urban, middle class and how many rural? Equally how do we define a 'women's' movement: is it one in which only women participate? Or one which raise only women specific issues? How then do we look at women's participation in 'broader mass movements?" (Sen, 1990:3). Sen, Illina. (1990), *A Space Within the Struggle: Women's Participation in People's Movement.* New Delhi: Kali for Women.
17. Mehrotra, Nilika (2002), "Perceiving Feminism: Some Local Responses," *Sociological Bulletin,* March, 51(1):58-79. Also see Mehrotra, Nilika (2005), "Women and Movement Politics: Some Methodological Reflections," *The Eastern Anthropologist,* April-June, 58(2):149-170.
18. The Crimes under the Indian Penal Code (IPC) are (i) Rape (Sec. 376 IPC); (ii) Kidnapping and Abduction for different purposes (Sec. 363 - 373 IPC); (iii) Homicide for Dowry, Dowry Deaths or their attempts (Sec. 302/304-B IPC); (iv) Torture - both mental and physical (Sec. 498-A IPC); (v) Molestation (Sec. 354 IPC); (vi) Sexual Harassment (referred in the past as 'Eve-Teasing') (Sec. 509 IPC) and (vii) Importation of girls (upto 21 years of age) (Sec. 366-B IPC). The Crimes under the Special & Local Laws (SLL) include (i) Immoral Traffic (Prevention) Act, 1956; (ii) Dowry Prohibition Act, 1961; (iii) The Child Marriage Restraint (Amendment) Act, 1979; (iv) Indecent Representation of Women (Prohibition) Act, 1986 and (v) Commission of Sati (Prevention) Act, 1987.
19. Jandhyala, K. (2001), "State Initiatives." *Seminar,* September, 505:31-35.
20. The Commission on the Status of Women (CSW) was established in 1947 at the recommendation of the UN. It prepares reports and recommendations on women's rights and status and serves as the preparatory body for the UN conferences on women. In 1972, the UN General Assembly proclaimed 1975 International Women's Year—IWY. The proclamation called for action to promote equality, the involvement of women in development efforts, and the recognition of the woman's role in strengthening peace and promoting friendly relations among nations. The World Conference of the International Women's Year was held in Mexico City in 1975. *Focus on UN Fourth World Conference on Women.* 7th December 1995.
    Online Available at: http://dosfan.lib.uic.edu/erc/intlorg/conference_women/950712.html
21. Status of Women in India: A Synopsis of the Report of the National Committee (1974-74). National Committee on the Status of Women, *Studies in Family Planning,* 7(12), December 1976, p. 358.
22. Towards Equality: Report of the Committee on the Status of Women in India (New Delhi: Government of India).
23. Patel, V. (1998), "Campaigns against Gender Violence (1977-1993)." In Shirin Kudchedkar and Sabiha Al-Issa (eds.), *Violence against Women: Women against Violence.* Delhi: Pencraft International:198-207.
24. Kumar, Radha (1989), The Women's Movement. *Seminar,* March #355:22.
25. Sarkar, Latika (1994), "Rape: A Human Rights Versus a Patriarchal Interpretation". *Indian Journal of Gender Studies.* VI(1): 69.
26. Agnes, F. (2005), *The Violence Against Women Campaign: Where Have We Failed?*
    Online Available at: http://www.infochangeindia.org/analysis107.jsp
27. This Open Letter to the Chief Justice was written jointly by Lotika Sarkar, Upendra Baxi, Raghunath Kelkar and Vasudha Dhagamwar that critiqued the Supreme Court's decision.

28. National Policy for the Empowerment of Women (2001) Online Available at: http://wcd.nic.in/empwomen.htm
29. Agnes, F. (1992), "Protecting Women Against Violence. Review of a Decade of Legislation, 1980-89." *Economic and Political Weekly*, 27(17):19-33.
30. Mazumdar, V. (2000), *Political Ideology of the Women's Movement's Engagement with Law*. Occasional Paper No. 34. Centre for Women's Development Studies. New Delhi. Online Available at: http://www.cwds.org/OCPaper/PoliticalIdeologyVM.pdf
31. Balasubrahmanyan, V. (1986), "And Now Made to Order Male Babies," *Economic and Political Weekly*. August, 21(32);23. Pp. 1492. Also see, Patel, V. (1997). "Technology in Service of Female Foeticide." *Humanscape*. July. 4(7):19-20.
32. Size, Growth Rate and Distribution of Child Population. Online Available at: http://censusindia.gov.in/2011-prov-results/data_files/india/Final%20PPT%202011_chapter4.pdf
33. Rege, S. (1995), "Feminist Pedagogy and Sociology for Emancipation in India." In *Sociological Bulletin*, September, 44(2):223-239.
34. Kothari, J. (2005), "Criminal Law on Domestic Violence: Promises and Limits." In *Economic and Political Weekly*, November 12-18, 40(46):4843.
35. Women: Discouraging Violence (2002), *Economic and Political Weekly*, October 26-November 1, 37(43):4344.
36. Suneetha, A. and V. Nagaraj (2005), "Adjudicating (Un)Domestic Battles," In *Economic and Political Weekly*, September 17-23, 40(38):4101.
37. Kumar, Radha (2005), 'The Main Point of the Women's Movement was to Gender Human Development'. January. Online Available at: http://www.infochangeindia.org/devp_dictionary_08.jsp

PART V

MARGINALITIES AND JUSTICE

19

Socio-Legal aspects of Migrant Laborers: A Study in Maharashtra

S.N. Tripathy

Migration broadly refers to the movement of people from one country or region and settlement in another country or region. It also includes the change in location periodically, especially by moving seasonally from one region to another. Seasonal migration of rural workers from the traditional agricultural occupations to other rural industries like sugarcane cutting, construction, brick kiln, quarrying and ginning for livelihood in the lean agricultural season is an important characteristic of rural India. Unfortunately, the magnitude and dimensions of the rural-urban migration, the process and problems encountered by these seasonally migrant workers have not been adequately studied.

Maharashtra, with a geographical area of 3,07,713 sq km, consisting 34 districts is the third largest state in India. As per the census of 2001, the state has a total population of 96.8 million, that is, 9.42 per cent of India's total population. Historically known for its industrialisation, the state of Maharashtra has achieved higher economic growth as compared to many other Indian states. The state ranks fourth in terms of per capita income and second in terms of industrial growth during the year 2007-08. Since its formation in 1960, the state per capita NSDP grew at 4.73 percent till 1999-00 and after that the rate has slightly declined to 2.43 percent. A paradoxical feature of high economic growth of India in general and Maharashtra in particular, is the low level of structural transformation in terms of employment.

Around 60 percent of the working population still depends on agriculture for their livelihood. This intense dependence on agriculture leads to all types of deprivation especially in the rural areas. A major chunk of the rural population is in the vicious cycle of poverty, which force them to find alternative jobs. Economic development in the state has been highly polarized toward metropolitans, as about two-fifths of the Net State Income comes from the Konkan region and one-half of the NSDP by the four urbanized districts-Mumbai, Pune, Thane, and Nagpur. Maharashtra suffers from acute regional inequality. The growth of regional economies in the state is mainly led by the tertiary sector. The industrial and service sectors of Maharashtra had attracted the workers not only within the state, but also from other states of India. The state is a migrant state as per the census of India 2001 as well as various survey of NSSO. Heavy dependence on the agricultural sector for employment also generates the need for searching alternative avenues of employment in the lean seasons. A major proportion of the cultivated area in the Vidharbha and Marathwada regions are not irrigated and this adds more trouble and as such, the inter district migration has been a common phenomena in Maharashtra.

In the light of this backdrop, this paper makes an attempt to focus on socio-legal aspects of migrant laborers in the state of Maharashtra with the help of both primary and secondary data.

Inter-State and intra State Migration to Maharashtra

The latest available data at the macro level on migration is the census of India 2001. The results of it with regard to inter state migration are given in Table 1. There are around 77 lakh migrants in the state of Maharashtra. Uttar Pradesh, Karnataka and Gujarat are the states which send maximum migrants to Maharashtra. Nine states together constitute around 90 percent of the interstate migrant to Maharashtra. These workers do migrate not only to the urban centers but also to the rural industries as well. This migration includes only the permanent migrants. The Seasonal migrant workers are kept out of the purview of population census.

Table 1: Inter-State Migrants to Maharashtra (2001)

S. No.	Place of Birth	Migrants	Percentage to total
1	Uttar Pradesh	2172971	28.00
2	Karnataka	1267421	16.30
3	Gujarat	890428	11.50
4	Madhya Pradesh	616059	7.90
5	Rajasthan	463875	6.00
6	Andhra Pradesh	450898	5.80
7	Bihar	386799	5.00
8	Kerala	307676	4.00
9	Tamil Nadu	267477	3.40
	Total for nine states	6823604	88.00
	Other states	932703	12.00
	Total	7756307	100

Source: Migration table, Census of India, 2001.

Due to vagaries of monsoon and heavy dependence on agriculture for job, inter district migration is also prevalent in Maharashtra. Around one third of the migrants are inter-district migrants. The proportion is high among males compared to the females (See Table 2)

Table 2: Percentage Distributions of Migrants by Place of Birth Maharashtra (2001)

Place of Birth	Person	Males	Females
A. Migrants born within the state of enumeration	80.5	72.3	86.1
(i) Migrants born elsewhere in district of enumeration	50.7	40.4	57.6
(ii) Migrants born in other district of the state	29.9	32	28.5
B. Migrants born in other states of India	19	27	13.6
C. Migrants born in other countries	0.5	0.7	0.4
Total Migrants	100	100	100

Source: Migration table, Census, 2001.

The state is also having high incidence of rural to rural migration. 70 per cent of the migrants within the state are from rural areas and among them 50 per cent move to other rural areas only. The seasonal migration within Maharashtra is also expected to follow the general pattern of migration and there is high incidence of migration from rural to rural areas within Maharashtra as well as from rural area of other states. The rural industries do provide some manual job to the agricultural workers coming in the lean season. This is a major interest in our study as well.

Public policy in the state is alarmingly inadequate in terms of recognizing and dealing with migration. These inadequacies cover both, points of origin and destination. Considering the conditions for would-be migrants at their place of residence; there are no official strategies for providing information regarding employment in source areas or assistance in ensuring contract with minimum wages and acceptable work conditions. Further, there are no attempts to ease process of travel—workers left to mercy of contractors or to manage on their own. There is little public consideration for safety of migrants (especially women migrants). Often no basic facilities (housing sanitation, etc) are provided at the destination, for example, construction workers often have to live in tents or temporary homes, arrange their own food, manage without proper sanitation, and so on. Characteristically, for such short-term migrants neither there is public provision of schools, creches or medical services, nor is there anything resembling work protection at the destination; for example there are no public help centres for migrants, no information offices, no complaint cells, indeed no mechanisms to redress any grievances, such as non-payment of wages, bad conditions of work, physical exploitation or violence. Instead, local officialdom in the destination typically views migrants as vagrants or nuisances, and consequently behaves aggressively.

Table 3: Rural and Urban Composition of Internal Migrants by Place of last Residence—Maharashtra (2001)

Place of last residence	Place of Enumeration		
	Total	Rural	Urban
Total Internal Migrants (Within the state)			
Total	34225081 (100)	21265808 (62.1)	12959273 (37.9)
Rural	24089515 (70.4)	17275775 (50.5)	6813740 (19.9)
Urban	7281769 (21.3)	1988464 (5.8)	5293305 (15.5)
In other states of India			
Total	7313139 (100)	1165461 (15.9)	6147678 (84.1)
Rural	4644986 (63.5)	931705 (12.7)	3713281 (50.8)
Urban	2392567 (32.7)	184302 (2.5)	2208265 (30.2)

Note: Figures in parenthesis gives percentages.

Objectives and Data Source

The study is to understand the process involved as well the outcome of the seasonal migration in Maharashtra in selected industries. The specific objectives are:

1. To examine the nature and volume of seasonal migration in selected industries.
2. To analyze the dynamic process involved in seasonal migration.
3. To understand the profiles of trades, services and professions predominantly employing migrant labour.

Census of India and the National Sample Survey Organisation are the two major secondary data base in the area of migration. But these database fails to cover seasonal migration of workers from rural to rural areas. The Census of India, for example, captures only permanent migration, by asking respondents if they had previously lived somewhere else, and how long ago that was. But as the census covers data for a household there is likelihood of some under-enumeration, especially of destitute migrants without fixed address or defined home structures.

The National Sample Survey is better to some extent as it attempts to capture some short-term migration of two months' duration or longer. However, there too are problems in the way the sample is structured, since it is household-based. Further, the nature of the questions asked (migrants must have spent at least 60 days in the previous year away from their place of residence) tends to leave out those who travel on a seasonal basis for shorter periods (say a few weeks or a month in the lean agricultural season) as well as those who commute fairly long distances to work on a regular basis.

This has necessitated for collecting the primary data. Data on various features of migrant workers were collected form four selected industries namely brick making, quarrying, ginning, and construction industry, within the state of Maharashtra. Sample size of 1193 workers was covered in the survey. Field data were collected through interview, questionnaire methods, focus group discussion and quick appraisal technique. Information has also been accumulated from an NGO, Janarth, located at Aurangabad that has been associated with such seasonal migration studies. Selected industries were also identified for survey to capture the nuances of business activities of these industries as well as to cross verify some information, provided by the workers.

The National Commission on Rural Labour (1991) estimated the number of seasonal migrants at 10 million in rural areas alone. The commission pointed out that Census and NSS database are having the limitation of underestimating the severity of seasonal migration. The Commission notes that there are large number of seasonal migrant workers in agriculture, plantations, brick-kilns, quarries, construction sites and fish processing. The National Commission on Enterprises in the Unorganized Sector in India (2007) estimates that the number of seasonal migrants in India could be in the range of 30 million. The report of the commission has suggested various policy measures for the well being of the disadvantaged sections of the workers, including the seasonal migrants. The data limitation has restricted chronological study of the impact of seasonal migration. Because of this, no figures are available for the trends in labour circulation over time. But fortunately, a few scholars like Breman (1985, 1994b, 1996), who had continuously conducted micro level studies all over Gujarat over several decades, has noted that there exist a growth in labour circulation. Some other micro level studies spread over different parts of India also pointed out an increase in labour mobility when all forms of locational mobility are taken into account (Dreze 1997).

Ravi Srivastva (1999) argued that rural to rural migration within India in the recent decades may be specifically seen to be a result of uneven capitalist penetration in agriculture leading to peaking of labour demand in certain seasons and resulting in the rise of mechanisms which source cheap labour over long distances. The tribal districts are the source areas for a large number of migrants to the developed areas. The states of Punjab and Haryana are the pockets of green revolution in other states such as Karnataka. Gujarat and Andra Pradesh are attracting workers from poorer regions (Singh and Iyer 1985). The cultivation of commercial crops on a large scale such as sugarcane in Maharashtra, Gujarat and Karnataka, Tobacco in Karnataka attracts large scale seasonal Migrants.

While studying the migration process, some authors find that labour circulation is not always impelled by labour scarcity but is compatible both with regions of scarce or surplus supply of labour. Brick kilns everywhere, including poorer regions employ a large number of seasonal migrants. Quarrying activity in different states is mostly carried out by migrant workers from underdeveloped regions (Das, 1993).

With regard to the caste composition of the migrants, majority of the studies found that the seasonal migrants are mostly from lower castes like SC, ST and OBC. In recent years, with the depletion of forest based resources, there is increasing migration of tribal population (Tripathy, 1996, 2006).

Wages and Working Condition of Migrant Workers

A number of studies have focused on the working condition of circulatory migrants, but these conditions are also shared by other migrants who operate in the urban or rural labour markets without any employment security. The National Commission on Enterprises in the unorganized sector (2007) has done a detailed review of the various problems faced by the migrant workers in terms of wages and working conditions. The report highlights that many of the industries engaging the seasonal migrant workers are following the exploitative strategy and paying the workers less than the mandatory minimum wages and the working and living condition are pathetic. The rules and regulations on the migratory workers are grossly violated and the contractors act as agents of exploitation. The women and children, who accompany the workers, face all the difficulties and they are deprived of basic health and education facilities. Most of these migrants are not having the ration card, which prevent them from accessing food from the public distribution system.

ILO study noted that, in general, the work migrants, whether in agriculture, industry, construction or forestry, are mostly arduous, low status, and badly paid. Manual workers in rural India are informally contracted, sometimes through intermediaries and, like most rural workers worldwide, they do not have effective collective bargaining mechanisms or legal protections from harsh employment practices (ILO, 1996).

Micro level studies like Singh and Iyer (1985) also noted the long and flexible working hours, combined with low wages. Migrant work is characterized by low wages, often below the level prescribed by minimum wage legislation and those prevailing in the area for local labourers. The modalities of wage payment are such that migrant laborers often remain indebted to the contractors for the entire duration of their employment. The provision of basic facilities and even security to the migrant labourers falls in a no man's land with neither the employers nor the government catering to these requirements (Breman 1996). A majority of the migrants do not have adequate shelter, drinking water or toilet facilities.

Breman (1985) pointed out that the wages in sugarcane harvesting were reportedly lower in Maharashtra than other agricultural activities. Wages in paddy, cotton, sugar cane and tobacco cultivation were generally set at piece rate and implied long hours of work. The same patter is revealed in studies of construction works, quarrying, fish processing, etc (Das 1993). The children of migrant labourers, who often are a part of the labour process, and are on the move with their parents, have little opportunity to go to school. Migrant women are also exposed to the risk of sexual harassment and exploitation (Sardamony, 1995).

The migrant folk mainly consist of poor, illiterate and landless agricultural workers, who do not have adequate income to meet the basic minimum requirements. The seasonality of the agricultural activities makes their life more miserable and they do migrate to better places. The tribes constitute a major chunk of these migrants in all the states. The process of migration is mainly performed through the contractors. They act as the medium of getting workers from the poor regions for work in the industries like brick kiln, construction, sugar cane harvesting, etc. The workers, in general, do experience a lot of exploitation in the hands of agents as well as the entrepreneurs. The minimum wage legislations are violated and they are not better paid off at the work site in terms of any of the standard of living indicator. The condition of women and children, who accompany these workers, is even worse. The overlapping of the migration cycle, with the school calendar makes the study impossible for these children and they end up in the part time work and when grown up become part of the migrant workforce. Hence the generations do the same work again and again and end up in the vicious circle of low education, low capability and low chances of getting employed in the organized sector. The wages and working conditions are miserable and these add to misery in terms of health related issues. The impact of migration on the source areas are limited and it did not lead to any tightening of the labour market and it acts as a safety valve mechanism. At the receiving end there is a competition of the migrant workers with the local workers and this keeps the wage level stagnant.

Even though these problems are there in the migration, still workers are on the move, basically attracted by the better wages and there is no other alternative job available to them. These are mainly distress migration.

Age Profile of Respondents

Age profile of the migrants is important from the demographic and economic point of view as it has impact on labour productivity, fertility, and human capability. The age profile of the male and female respondents indicates that they mainly belong to the working age group of 18-45. The distribution of male workers across industries with respect to various age groups is given in the Table 4. From this table, we can observe that around 85 per cent of the male respondents belong to the age group of 18-45. This clearly indicates their high capability to do the hard manual jobs. The age group varies from 18-77 years with a mean age of 35.39 years. In the construction industry, which mainly involves hard manual work, 90 per cent of the workers belong to the age group of 18-45. The skewed distribution of the respondents towards the age group of 30-45 across industry groups indicates that the prime working age group people are the one who access the opportunity of migration.

Table 4: Age Profile of Male Respondents

Industry	Age group of male respondent				Total
	18-30	30-45	45-60	Above 60	
Road construction	127 (49.0)	104 (40.2)	28 (10.8)	0 (0.0)	259 (100.0)
Construction	117 (50.2)	95 (40.8)	20 (8.6)	1 (0.4)	233 (100.0)
Brick kiln	91 (29.1)	163 (52.1)	56 (17.9)	3 (1.0)	313 (100.0)
Quarrying	116 (37.4)	140 (45.2)	46 (14.8)	9 (2.9)	310 (100.0)
Construction	116 (37.4)	95 (40.8)	20 (8.6)	1 (0.4)	233 (100.0)
Ginning	24 (30.8)	39 (50.0)	12 (15.4)	3 (3.8)	78 (100.0)
Total	475 (39.8)	541 (45.3)	162 (13.6)	16 (1.3)	1193 (100.0)

Note: Figures in parenthesis indicates percentage.
Source: Field study.

The age profile of the female migrants also indicates more or less the same picture and the concentration is in the age group of 18-45 again. The results are given in Table 5.

Table 5: Age Profile of Female Respondents

Industry	Age group of Female respondent				Total
	18-30	30-45	45-60	60 and above	
Brick kiln	134 (43.4)	153 (49.5)	20 (6.5)	2 (0.6)	309 (100)
Construction	118 (58.7)	75 (37.3)	8 (4.0)	0 (0)	201 (100)
Ginning	41 (52.5)	30 (38.5)	7 (9.0)	0 (0)	78 (100)
Quarrying	169 (54.8)	105 (34.1)	33 (10.7)	1 (0.3)	308 (100)
Road construction	139 (58.6)	90 (38.0)	8 (3.4)	0 (0)	237 (100)
Total Count	601 (53.05)	453 (40.0)	76 (6.7)	3 (0.3)	1133 (100)

Note: Figures in parenthesis indicates percentages.
Source: Field study.

Educational Profile

Education is a significant attribute and an asset to an individual. In the present era, education is necessary to obtain gainful, productive and remunerative employment. Lower levels of education among the workers create vulnerability at two levels. It first denies access to 'good jobs' in the organized sector. Secondly, it mostly confines the workers to casual manual jobs. Women workers in rural areas are the worst victims of this double disadvantage. In rural area, illiteracy coupled with extremely low level of education means that the workers remain stuck to the agricultural sector, which is having high incidence of seasonal cyclic tendency. This seasonal character of the agriculture pushes them to migrate to other rural areas, which do have some sort of non-agricultural jobs available.

The education profile of the male and female respondents indicates that majority of them belong to the illiterate class (See Tables 6 and 7). More than half of our male respondents are illiterates. Compared to this, the situation of females is worse; more than 85 per cent of the female respondents are illiterates. This high incidence of illiteracy is a major lacuna of these seasonal migrant workers. This illiteracy restricts them from moving to any good job in the organized sector. They are the group who are forced to migrate from the poor agrarian areas, basically known as distress migration. Only 10 per cent of the male migrants have primary education, 13.7 per cent have upper primary education and 15.7 per cent are having high school education. The mean year of schooling is 3 years for the male and 2 years for females. The range varies from illiterates to the maximum of post graduation in the case of males and graduation in the case of females. The relatively better educated are moving to the construction specifically road construction industry, which

Table 6: Education Profile of Male Respondents

Industry	Education profile of male respondent						Total
	Illiterates	Primary	Upper primary	High school	Higher secondary	Graduation and above	
Brick kiln	195	40	36	33	6	3	313
	(62.3)	(12.8)	(11.5)	(10.5)	(1.9)	(1.0)	(100.0)
Quarrying	190	37	41	37	5	0	310
	(61.3)	(11.9)	(13.2)	(11.9)	(1.6)	(0)	(100.0)
Road construction	114	28	51	54	11	1	259
	(44)	(10.8)	(19.7)	(20.8)	(4.2)	(0.4)	(100.0)
Construction	122	13	26	57	14	1	233
	(52.4)	(5.6)	(11.2)	(24.5)	(6.0)	(0.4)	(100.0)
Ginning	51	8	10	6	2	1	78
	(65.4)	(10.3)	(12.8)	(7.7)	(2.6)	(1.3)	(100.0)
Total	672	126	164	187	38	6	1193
	(56.3)	(10.6)	(13.7)	(15.7)	(3.2)	(0.5)	(100.0)

Note: Figures in parenthesis indicates percentages.
Source: Field study.

require better skills as well as provide higher remuneration as compared to other industries.

The high incidences of illiteracy deprive these migrants from the basic rights at the work site and causes high incidences of exploitation from the employers and contractors. The second generation of these migrants is also deprived of education since these people are moving population and parent's deprivation pass on to the next generation as well.

Seasonal migration is higher in the caste category of Scheduled Caste (SC), Scheduled Tribes (ST) and Other Backward Communities (OBC). There are provisions in the Constitution that allow for reservation of jobs and admissions to higher education for these socially under-privileged groups. A number of other castes have also been identified as backward classes on economic and social considerations, such as the artisan groups. Most of these scheduled communities and backward classes belong to the Hindus.

The caste composition of the respondents is given in Table 7. The caste composition of the respondents shows that a major proportion belongs to Scheduled Caste (SC), Scheduled Tribes (ST) and Nomadic Tribes (NT). Only 15 per cent of them are from general category. One third of the respondents belong to ST category followed by NT and OBC. Scheduled Tribes mainly engage in ginning and brick kiln. The quarrying activity is mainly done by NT, while OBC dominates the construction industry.

Table 7: Caste Composition of Migrants

Industry	Open	OBC	SC	ST	NT	Others	Total
Construction	48 (21.0)	83 (36.0)	26 (11.0)	35 (15.0)	29 (12.0)	12 (5.0)	233 (100)
Ginning	12 (15.4)	9 (11.5)	5 (6.4)	39 (50.0)	9 (11.5)	4 (5.1)	78 (100)
Quarrying	16 (5.2)	27 (8.7)	32 (10.3)	89 (28.7)	131 (42.3)	15 (4.8)	310 (100)
Road Construction	69 (26.6)	35 (13.5)	17 (6.6)	66 (25.5)	53 (20.5)	19 (7.3)	259 (100)
Brick Kiln	44 (14.1)	63 (20.1)	55 (17.6)	118 (37.7)	21 (6.7)	12 (3.8)	313 (100)
Total	189 (15.8)	217 (18.2)	135 (11.3)	347 (29.1)	243 (20.4)	62 (5.2)	1193 (100)

Notes: (i) Figures in parenthesis indicates percentages.
(ii) Others refer to Caste Categories out of Maharashtra.

Source: Field study.

The age group wise distribution indicates that a substantial proportion of them are children, who are accompanying their parents to the work site. This movement highlights the need for school and hospital facilities at the work site.

Table 8: Age-wise Distribution of Migrant Family

Industry	FM					
	Below 15	15 - 30	30 - 45	45-60	60 and above	Total
Brick Kiln	263	101	20	14	3	401
Construction	132	45	7	4	1	189
Ginning	61	20	0	2	0	83
Quarrying	278	151	15	9	4	457
Road Construction	94	33	4	7	0	138
Total	828	350	46	36	8	1268

Source: Field study.

The distribution of our respondents among the various occupational categories is given in Table 9. The migrants were mainly engaged in agriculture and allied activities at their native places. Around 89.6 per cent of the migrants were agricultural workers or directly involved in their farm activities. This implies that they are subject to variations in monsoon and other natural calamities at the source which act as a push factor for migration. The unemployed category also has a significant 8.2 per cent of migrants. We have also collected information on the nature of activity in which the migrants were involved immediately before joining the present job. A high proportion of them has directly come from the villages and joined the present work.

Table 9: Occupation of Respondents at the Source of Origin

Industry	Agricultural workers	Farmers	Others	Unemployed	Total
Brick kiln	252	8	2	51	313
	(80.5)	(2.6)	(0.6)	(16.3)	(100)
Construction	136	84	4	9	233
	(58.4)	(36.1)	(1.7)	(3.9)	(100)
Ginning	32	42	0	4	78
	(41.0)	(53.8)	(0)	(5.1)	(100)
Quarrying	255	29	0	26	310
	(82.3)	(9.4)	(0)	(8.4)	(100)
Road construction	173	71	7	8	259
	(66.8)	(27.4)	(2.7)	(3.1)	(100)
Total	848	234	13	98	1193
	(71.1)	(19.6)	(1.1)	(8.2)	(100)

Note: Figures in parenthesis indicates percentages. Others include Brick Kiln, Business, Driver, Shepherd, Carpenter and Fishing
Source: Field study.

Land Holding and Housing Condition

The housing condition of the workers at their home village also indicates their miserable living condition at the source. Only 11 per cent are having permanent (pucca) house and the rest are living in temporary (kachaa) houses at their native villages. 3.5 per cent of them are not having any house. This again acts as a push factor for migration. The housing condition of the respondents are given in Table 10.

Table 10: Housing Condition at the Source of Origin

Industry	Housing Condition			
	Pakke	Kacche	None	Total
Brick kiln	33	257	23	313
	(10.5)	(82.1)	(7.3)	(100)
Quarrying	33	266	11	310
	(10.6)	(85.8)	(3.5)	(100)
Road construction	30	228	1	259
	(11.6)	(88.0)	(0.4)	(100)
Construction	27	202	4	233
	(11.6)	(86.6)	(1.7)	(100)
Ginning	9	66	3	78
	(11.5)	(84.6)	(3.8)	(100)
Total	132	1019	42	1193
	(11.1)	(85.4)	(3.5)	(100)

Note: Figures in parenthesis indicates percentages.
Source: Field study.

The Pull Factors; Wages and other Benefits

The wage differential between the point of origin and destination acts as a major pull factor in migration decision. In our study also we found that the migrants are daily earning more than 100 per cent of their earnings in the agricultural activities. The wages are higher in the construction activities, which employ more educated and skilled workers. The quarrying and ginning industry have a relatively lower wages, still better than the wages of agriculture as well as the NREGS scheme. The relative comparison of the earnings is given in Table 11.

Table 11: Average Daily Earnings across Industries

Industry	Average Daily Earnings (Rs.)
Construction	143.00
Road Construction	140.44
Brick Kiln	120.00
Quarrying	102.35
Ginning	107.85
NREGS Wages	100.00
Average Agricultural Wages	60-70

Source: Field study.

Weekly distribution of wages is the most prevalent practice. Three-fourths of the workers get weekly wages, which coincide with the weekly market.

In the road construction industry, monthly distribution of wage is the most prevalent practice.

The payment of advance is a strategy mainly employed by the contractors to get a better control over the workers. The workers also have a tendency to accept advances in the lien season to meet the household expenses and for investment in the agricultural activities at the native village. The analysis of the advance payment thus becomes an importance medium of exploitation. We tried to get information from our sample with regard to the practice of taking advance from the contractors or employers as well as the amount of advance.

In our sample a significant proportion of the workers are not taking any advance payments. The practice of advance payments is more prevalent among the brick kiln, quarrying and ginning industry. This is more relevant in the context that the majority of the migrants in these industries are intra district migrants. The inter state migrants who are engaged dominantly in the construction activity do not take advance payments as expected in the light of other studies in this area. Most of the studies have noted that the workers take advance payments and do fell in to the clutches of the contractors and employers and do experience heavy exploitation. But our survey results do not support such vast scale advance payments and related exploitation. The distribution of the respondents as per the amount of advance reveals that majority of the advance recipients take a low amount of less than Rs. 2500 only as advance while three-fourths of the advance recipients take an advance of Rs.5000 (See Table 12).

Table 12: Respondents Receiving Advance Payments

Industry	Received	Not Received	Total
Brick kiln	172 (55.0)	141 (45.0)	313 (100)
Quarrying	197 (63.5)	113 (36.5)	310 (100)
Road construction	210 (81.1)	49 (18.9)	259 (100)
Construction	215 (92.3)	18 (7.7)	233 (100)
Ginning	50 (64.1)	28 (35.9)	78 (100)
Total	844 (70.7)	349 (29.3)	1193 (100)

Note: Figures in parenthesis indicates percentages.
Source: Field study.

In the above illustrations we have attempted to explore the socio economic characteristics of the seasonal migrants. The major results of our analysis follow the conclusion of the general literature in the area. The respondents mainly belong to the poor, illiterate and landless workers from rural areas of Maharashtra and other backward states of India. The backward communities like SC, ST, NT and OBC were the major migrant groups. They migrate with the expectation of higher wages and get it in the rural industries. In our sample survey results, even though a major proportion of the workers are coming through agents, they are not taking any substantial advance payment and they are not in the clutches of exploitation. The facilities available at work site are not up to the expectation of the workers and the majority of them are deprived of school and hospital facilities. Still they are ready to migrate simply because they do not have any other livelihood option. These industries are acting as a safety valve mechanism for distress agricultural workers.

Central Laws for Unorganized Sector Workers

Central laws, which regulate conditions of work in the unorganized sector fall into three groups. The first group applies generally to the unorganized sector. The second group of laws applies to certain groups of workers in the unorganized sector and the scope of application is restricted by the nature of employment, or size of employment. The third group of laws applies mainly to the organized sector workers (viz. factories, establishments, or enterprises employing 10 or more workers), but in certain cases, or by relaxing the employment criterion these laws can (be made to) apply to some sections of workers in the unorganized sector.

First set (Laws which apply to all sections of the unorganized sector labour)
The Equal Remuneration Act, 1976, The Bonded Labour System (Abolition) Act, 1976.

Second set (Laws which apply to some sections of the unorganized sector labour)
Minimum Wages Act, 1948, Child Labour (Prohibition and Regulation) Act, 1986, Dangerous Machines (Regulation) Act, 1983, The Employment of Manual Scavengers and Construction of Dry Latrines (Prohibition) Act, 1993, Inter-State Migrant Workmen (Regulation of Employment and Conditions of Service) Act, 1979, Motor Transport Workers Act, 1961, Sales Promotion Employees (Conditions of Services) Act, 1976, Trade Unions Act, 1926.

Third set (Laws which can be extended to the unorganized sector)
The Beedi and Cigar Workers (Conditions of Employment) Act, 1966, Payment of Wages Act, 1936, The Building and Other Construction Workers (Regulations of Employment and Conditions of Service) Act, 1996, The Contract Labour (Regulation & Abolition) Act, 1970, The Maternity Benefit Act, 1961, Workmen's Compensation Act, 1923, Weekly Holidays Act, 1942.

The Minimum Wages Act, 1948

The Act is applicable to the workers engaged in the scheduled employments and provides for fixing minimum rates of wages in certain employments. It is applicable both to agricultural, non-agricultural and to rural as well as urban workers. The Government may, however, increase the scope of this Act by adding schedules.

Equal Remuneration Act, 1976

The Act is applicable to the women workers and provides for the payment of equal remuneration to men and women workers and for the prevention of discrimination, on the ground of sex, against women in matters of employment. Under the Act, the employer has to pay equal remuneration to men and women workers for same work or work of a similar nature. Same work or work of a similar nature is meant to be the work in respect of which the skill, effort and responsibility required are the same, when performed under similar working conditions. The Act also provides against discrimination made while recruiting men and women workers.

Building and Other Construction Workers' (Regulation of Employment and Conditions of Service) Act, 1996

The Act is applicable to the establishments engaging ten or more building and other constructions workers. It seeks to regulate the employment and conditions of service of building and other construction workers and provides for their safety health and other welfare measures. The establishments engaging less than ten workers are not covered under this Act. The Act provides for fixing hours for normal working days inclusive of one or more specified intervals; provides for a day to rest in every period of seven days, payment of work on a day of rest at a rate not less than the overtime rate, wages at the rate twice his ordinary rate of wages for overtime work. The Act prohibits a person who is deaf or has defective vision to undertake such work. It also provides for adequate drinking water, latrines and urinals and accommodation for workers, crèches, first-aid and canteens. The appropriate government is empowered to make rules for the safety and health of building workers.

Inter-State Migrant Workmen (Regulation of Employment and Conditions of Service) Act, 1979

The Act is applicable to every establishment in which five or more inter-state migrant workmen are employed and to every contractor who employs five or more inter-state migrant workmen. The establishments engaging less than five interstate migrant workmen are not covered under this act. For the purposes of this Act, "workman" means any person employed in or in connection with the work of any establishment to do any skilled, semi - skilled or unskilled, manual, supervisory, technical or clerical work for hire or reward, but does not include any person who is employed mainly in a managerial or administration capacity; or who, being employed in a supervisory capacity and draws wages exceeding five hundred rupees per month.

The Act provides that the wage rates, holidays, hours of work and other conditions of service of an inter-state migrant workman shall be the same as those applicable to such other workman performing the same or similar kind of work and the wage cannot be less that the wages fixed under the Minimum Wages Act, 1948 (41 of 1948) and are payable in cash. It also provides for payment of displacement allowance and journey allowance. The contractor has the liability for regular payment of wages; ensuring equal pay for equal work irrespective of sex; ensuring suitable conditions of work; to provide and maintain suitable residential accommodation to such workmen during the period of their employment; to provide free of charge prescribed medical facilities to the workmen; to provide protective clothing to the workmen; and in case of fatal accident or serious bodily injury to any such workman, to report to the specified authorities of both the states and also the next-of-kin of the workman. The primary responsibility for payment of wages is on the contractor and on his failure, on the principal employer.

Before the enactment of Inter-state Migrant Workmen Act, 1979, the following important points were kept in view.

(i) The Inter-state migrant workmen belong to the lower state of the society.
(ii) The migrant workmen are mostly agricultural labourers. They are illiterate and unable to speak any other language other than Oriya.
(iii) Dealing with provisions of labour laws, the court adopts such procedures which become totally unintelligible to such migrant workmen.
(iv) In the absence of the direct link between the employer and the employee relationship, the workmen can only seek assistance through the sub-contractors.

The inter-state migrant workmen (Regulation of employment condition of service) Act, 1979 aims at regulating the employment of Inter-state migrant workmen and providing them conditions of service and for matters connected therewith, the Act seeks to ensure:

(i) Registration of all principal employers/contractors and licensing of all contractors employing five or more migrant workmen.
(ii) Issues of pass book to every Interstate migrant workmen indicating the name and the place of establishment where the workmen is employed, the period of employment, the proposed rates and the modes of payment of wages and the return fair payable to him on the expiry of the period of his employment or any contingencies, such as resignation or the termination of employment before the expiry of such a period.

(iii) Payment of equal wages to Inter-state migrant workmen doing same type of work in the establishment along with local labourers. In any case the payment of wages fixed under the Minimum Wages Act, 1948 for that kind of work.

(iv) Payment of displacement allowance which is equivalent to 50 per cent of monthly wages payable to the Inter-state migrant workmen. It shall not be refundable and shall be in addition to the wages on other dues payable to him.

(v) The journey allowance of the amount less than the fare from the place of residence of the workmen in his state to the place of work in other state besides payment of wages during the period of his journey.

(vi) Suitable residential accommodation facilities to the workman.

(vii) Prescribed medical facilities to the workman including free charge of hospitalisation.

(viii) Protective clothing to the workmen in cold climate.

(ix) Submission of report to the specified authorities of both the states and also news to the kins of workmen in case of fatal accident or serious bodily injuries to the workmen.

The above provisions as embodied in the law are required to be followed by the contractors recruiting Inter-state migrant workmen. In the event of failure to implement the provisions of the Act by the contractor, the principal employer is required to implement the provisions.

Extent of operation

The act applies, *inter alia*:

(i) To every establishment in which five or more inter-state migrant workmen are employed.

(ii) To every contractor hiring five or more Inter-state migrant worker on any day of the preceding twelve months.

The Act extends to the whole of India.

Establishment (Section 62(1-D) of the Act)

The term establishment means any office or department of the Government or a local authority or any place where any industry, trade, business, manufacture or occupation is carried on.

Principal Employer (G) of the Act

Under this enactment the Principal employer means:

(i) In relation to any office or department of the Government or a local authority or such other officer as the Government or the case may be, may specify in this behalf.

(ii) In relation to a factory the owner or the occupier of the factory and where the person has been named as the manager of the factory under the Factory Act, 1948, the person so named.

(iii) In relation to any other establishment, any person responsible or the supervision and the control of the establishment.

Workmen [Section 2(i) of the Act]

Workman is defined according to the definition of the workman given in the Industrial Dispute Act, 1947. It includes:

(i) Any person employed in connection with the work of an establishment.

(ii) To do skilled, semi-skilled, unskilled, manual, supervisory, technical, or clerical work.

(iii) For hire or reward and the term of employment be expressed or implied.

It does not include any such person:

(i) Who is employed mainly in managerial or administrative capacity.

(ii) Who being employed in supervisory capacity, draws wages exceeding Rs.1600 per mensal or exercises either by the nature of the duties attached to the officer or by reason of the powers vested in him, functions mainly of a managerial nature.

Contractor

The term 'contractor' in relation to an establishment has been defined under Section 2(i)(b) as a person who undertakes as an independent contractor/ agent/employee or otherwise to produce a given result for the establishment. The definition of contractor also includes sub-contractor, Khatadar, Sandar, or agent or any other person who recruit workers.

Definition of Inter-state Migrant Workmen

Section 2(i)(e) of the Act defines an "Inter-state migrant workman as:

(i) Any person who is recruited by or through a contractor in one state.

(ii) Under an agreement or an arrangement.

(iii) For employment in an establishment in another state whether with or without the knowledge of the principal employer in relation to such an establishment.

To satisfy the definition, three conditions are to be followed:

(i) The person should be recruited by a 'contractor' in one state.

(ii) The mode of recruitment may be through an agreement or an arrangement.

(iii) The recruitment should be employment in state other than where the recruitment is done.

The word 'recruitment' has been defined under the Act under section 2(i).

(b) As entering into an agreement or other arrangement for recruitment. Recruitment as per Inter-State Migrant Act means any agreement whether written, oral, expressed or implied. The old people brought from their respective states by the contractors will also be a form of recruitment.

The Bonded Labour System (Abolition) Act is applicable to the Inter-state migrant workmen because in most of the cases the advanced paid to the Inter-state migrant worker before they are brought for work is treated as debt or loan. In most of the cases, they are paid less than the minimum wages. There was a bill introduced in the Rajya Sabha to amend the Act by way of incorporating a provision that a person who had initially been contract labour would be treated as bonded labour for the purpose of release and rehabilitation if it fulfills the criteria of bonded labour system defined in the Act.

The definition of "Inter-state migrant workmen" as given in Section 2(i)(e) of the Act may create a doubt whether it will apply to such employees also who are recruited in an all India or State wise basis for employment in its regular establishment and happen to work in another state. To avoid this confusion an exemption clause has been included in this Act in the form of Section 31 which gives the Government the power to exempt in special cases by way of notification in the official gazette subject to such conditions and restrictions if any and for such specified period or periods from all or any provisions of the Act or rules.

Registration of Establishment of Principal Employers

Similar to the Scheme of contract labour (R&A) Act, 1979 a regulatory provision has been made in this Act also, by way of putting an obligation on the part of the principal employer in whose establishment Inter-state Migrant worker are employed to get his establishment registered with the respective authorities depending on whether establishment is in the Central sphere or the state sphere.

Registering officer

Section 4(i) read with rule 3 requires the principal employer to apply for registration in the prescribed form delivered personally or by Registered post accompanied with treasury Challan showing deposit of required fee and the registering officer shall acknowledge the receipt of such application after noting the date of receipt on the application. Section 4(2) and Section 4(3) and rule 4 of the Act set the limit for Registering Officer within which he has to issue the registering certificate in the prescribed form. Section 4(2) read with the rule 5 empowers the Registering Officer to reject incomplete applications. The Registering Officer can also effect an amendment on receipt of intimation under Rule 4(3) that change has occurred in the particulars specified in the certificate of registration.

Revocation of Registration: Section 5 authorizes the Registration Officer to revoke the registration certificate if he is satisfied that the registration has been obtained by misrepresentation or suppression of material fact or for any other reason, after giving the principal employer an opportunity of being heard and after obtaining prior approval of the appropriate Govt. The order should be in writing and communicated to the principal employer.

Effect of non-registration: Section 5 of the Act prohibits the principal employer to employ Inter State Migrant workmen without obtaining a certificate of registration.

Licensing of Contractor

Section 8 prohibits employment of the Inter State Migrants workmen in an establishment except under or in accordance with a license issued by the Licensing Officer.

Licensing Procedure

Section 9 read with Rule 7 prescribes procedure for making application by the contractor and grant of license by the Licensing Officer. It provides that the contractor is required (i) to submit application in the prescribed form in duplicate (ii) to avail receipt of application on the day of the application itself and grant acknowledgment for granting or refusing license. The Licensing Officer is authorized to take into account matters prescribed under Rule 8. If the licensing officer is of the opinion that license must not be granted, he should provide opportunity to the applicant to be heard. Thereafter, he must convey his decision of rejecting the application by written order giving reasons for such refusal (Rule-10). The term and conditions of the license are prescribed under the rule 11. The license is not transferable and shall be valid for a period of one year which can be renewed after expiry of the period i.e. 31st December of the year in which license has been issued. The procedure and period of renewal of license are prescribed under Rules 14 and 15.

Revocation, Suspension and Amendment of License

Under Section the Licensing Officer on being satisfied can revoke license and forfeit the Security furnished by the Contractor, if (i) the license has been obtained by misrepresentation or suppression of material facts (ii) there has been either non-compliance (without a reasonable cause) or contravention of any of the conditions of the license. The order of the revocation shall be made after the holder of the license has been given reasonable opportunity of being heard. The Licensing Officer is also authorized to suspend the operation of the license, pending such revocation, forfeiture or any other penalty. The licensing officer is authorized to affect an amendment on application of the license holder along with deposit of the prescribed fees by him. In case the Licensing Officer refuses to make the amendment sought, the reasons shall be recorded in writing and conveyed to the applicant. The Registering Officer/Licensing Officer is exercising quasi/judicial functions under the Act. They should give due attention to the details and ensure proper recording of the order following the principle of natural justice.

Security Deposit and Fees

The State Govt., by virtue of notification has specified the security deposit under the sub-section (3) of Section 8. Rules 10 and 17 provides for the procedure regarding adjustment and refund of the security deposits. The security amount may be refunded to license holder on satisfaction of the licensing officer that there is no breach of conditions of license and there is no order for the forfeiture of security. If the license holder does not want the security deposits to be adjusted in respect of his fresh application or does not intend to get license renewed then he has to make an application in the prescribed form to the licensing officer. The fees to be paid for grant of license under section 7 is prescribed under rule 12.

Appeals and Procedure

Section 11 provides a right of appeal to the person aggrieved by an order made under sections 4, 5, 8 and 10. Any appeal preferred against the order or registering license officer shall satisfy following point:

(i) It shall be made within 30 days of the date of communication of the order.
(ii) It shall be accompanied by required Treasury Challan of Rs.25.
(iii) It should be signed by the applicant or his authorized agent.

Responsibility towards Payment of Wages

Section 17 of the Act read with Rules 25 to 35 makes the contractor responsible for payment of wages to the workers employed by him and lays down the procedure to be followed, Section 17(4) makes it obligatory on the part of the principal employer to pay the wages in case the contractor fails to do so. The principal employer is authorized to recover the amount from the contractor by the way of deduction from the amount due to the workers from the contactor's bill.

Responsibility towards Payments of Allowances

Sections 14 and 15 of the Act provides an obligation on the contractor to pay every Inter State Migrant Workmen displacement allowances and journey allowance in addition to the wages payable to him. The period of journey will be included in the period and wages of this period shall be payable by the contractor. Section 18 lays with rule 16 lays down that any allowance payable by the contractor shall be paid by the principal employer on the farmer's failure to do so.

Welfare and Other Facilities

Section 16 read with rules 36 to 45 makes it obligatory on the part of the contractor to provide free medical facilities, protective clothing, drinking water, latrine, urinals, washing facilities, rest room canteens, and residential accommodation. If the contractor fails to do so, it shall be provided by the principal employer.

Rate of Wages

Section 13 read with Rules 25 to 33 requires the contractor to pay the inter State Migrant Workmen Wages in no case less than the rates fixed under the Minimum Wages Act, 1948. If they are engaged in work which are same or similar to the work performed by other workmen in the establishment the rate of wages shall be the same and shall in no case be less than those paid by the principal employer to a workman of lowest category directly employed by him in that establishment. The payment shall be made in cash in presence of authorized representative of the principal employer and shall be made on any working day at the work premises during working hours on a date notified in advance.

Register, Record and Notices

Section 22 read with Rules 48 and 49 every principal employer shall maintain (i) Register of contractor (ii) Register of persons employed as Inter State Migrant workmen. Annual Return in form XXIV shall be submitted to the Registering Officers under Rule 56. Registers/returns to be maintained and submitted by the Contractor are: Register of persons employed, Displacement -cum-outward journey allowance sheet and return journey allowances register, Muster Roll, Register of Wages, Register of fines, Register of deductions, Register of advances, Register of overtime, Half yearly return to the licensing officer.

All registers and records maintained by the principal employer/contractor shall be preserved for 3 calendar year and shall be kept in an office or building in the precincts of the work place so the place specified by the Inspector. Under Rule 55, the notice to be displayed by the contractor/ principal employer are (i) Notices of rate of wages; (ii) Notice of items of work; (iii) Notice of wage period; (iv) Notice of dates of payment of wages; (v) Notices of name and address of the Inspector.

Legal Action

Section 28 of the Act read with rule 60(2) of the rules provides that all offences are timbale by Court of 1st judicial magistrate Metropolitan Magistrate on a complaint made by the previous sanction in writing by the chief Inspector. Section 25 provides that whoever contravenes by provision of this act or of any rules made thereunder shall be punishable with fine or imprisonment which may extend to one year or with both. For continuing offense an additional fine which may extend up to Rs.100 for each day of the period for which such contravention continues after conviction for first such contravention.

Inspecting Staff

Section 20 of the Act empowers the State Govt. to appoint such persons as it thinks fit to be Inspectors for the purpose of this act by notification in official Gazette defining the local limits within which they shall exercise their powers. The Primary duty of the Inspector as described under Section 20 of the Act is to identify the establishments where Inter State Migrant workmen are employed and they should take steps for getting the establishment of the Principal employer registered and covered by the act.

Inspectors have been empowered with the powers of entry, examination, search and seizure and other powers to enforce the Act. The inspectors also have powers to call for any information or statistics in relation to migrant workmen from any contractor or principal employer at any time in writing and such contractor and the principal employer are legally bound to do so (Rule 57)

The technique of Inspections to be carried out under the Act and the Rules will be more or less the same as under Contract Labour (Regulation and Abolition) Act, 1970 and rules made thereunder.

Section 24 of the Act provides for punishment for the person who obstructs an Inspector in discharge of his duties under this Act or willfully neglects to afford the inspector or the authorize person any reasonable facility for making any inspect on, examination, inquiry or investigation etc. the punishment may extend to two years of imprisonment or with fines which may extend to Rs. 2,000 or with both.

Miscellaneous Provisions

Section 21 of the Act provides schedule specifying six enactments namely:-

(1) The Workmen's Compensation Act, 1923.
(2) The Payment of Wages Act, 1936.
(3) The industrial Disputes Act, 1947.
(4) The Employees State Insurance Act, 1948.
(5) The Employees Provident Fund and Miscellaneous Provisions Act, 1952.
(6) The Maternity Benefit Act, 1961.

For the purpose of enactments the Inter-State Migrant Workmen shall be on and from the date of his recruitment the person employed and actually worked in the establishment or as the case may be, the first establishment in connection with work in which he is employed.

Under Section 19, it is the duty of every contractor and every principal employer to ensure that any loan given by such contractor of principal employer to any Inter State Migrant Workmen does not remain outstanding after the completion of the period of employment under the said contractor or Principal employer. The Obligation of inter State Migrant Workmen to repay any debt obtained from the contractor or principal employer and remaining unsatisfied before the completion of such employment be deemed to have been extinguished on completion of the employment. Also no suit or other proceedings shall be made in any court or before any authority for the recovery of such debt or any part thereof.

Under Section 22 all disputes relating to employment, non-employment or terms of employment or condition of labour can be taken up by authorities of the home state of workmen if they have returned after completion of employment and before the expiry of six months at the instance of the workmen. Transfer of proceedings from State to another State is legal and the Central Govt. as the case may be is the appropriate authority on this score.

Section 30 gives an ever riding effect over any other law, agreement or contract of service etc. which are inconsistent with the provisions of this Act. However, if under any other law, agreement or contract of source the Inter State Migrant Workmen are getting more favorable benefits, then these benefits shall continue and the Inter State Migrant Workmen will continue to get other benefits also from this Act.

After the commencement of the Central Act the State Government has appointed Registering Officer, Licensing Officer, Specified Authority, Chief Inspector and Inspector for the purpose of enforcement of provisions of the said Act.

Concluding Observations

While most rural livelihood programmes supported by the government and other development agencies focus on farm and off-farm activities, the needs of seasonal migrants who travel to different parts of a state or to other states in India have not been adequately focused upon. Seasonal migration to both rural and urban areas extends over 4-6 months in a year and even more. Recognizing that migration for wage labour will remain an inevitable reality, there is an increasing concern among government and civil society organisations in India about the living and working conditions at destination sites. These are very often characterized by uncertainty, risk, almost negligible access to health, education and social security services and poor bargaining power for decent work and wages. The present study reveals that policies and services formulated by state governments are mainly for resident populations and the migrant labourers are deprived of any social security provisions, and as such, social justice needs to be provided to such vulnerable sections of population urgently.

Endnotes and References

Acharya, Binoy (1986), Beyond Bricks and Stone, New Delhi: Pria.

Breman, Jan (1985), Of Peasants, Migrants and Paupers: Rural Labor and Capitalist Production in West India, Oxford University Press, Delhi.

____ (1994a), Wage Hunters and Gatherers: Search for work in Rural and Urban Economy of Gujarat, Oxford University Press, Delhi.

____ (1994b), "Capital and Labor in the Cane Fields," in Breman, Jan (1994), Wage Hunters and Gatherers: Search for Work in the Urban and Rural Economy of Gujarat, Oxford University Press, Delhi (originally published in the Journal of Peasant Studies, July 1990).

____ (1996), Footloose Labor: Working in India's Informal Sector, Cambridge University Press, Cambridge.

Das, Biswaroop (1993), "Migrant Labour in Quarries and Brick-kilns: An Overview", Centre for Social Studies (Mimeo), Surat.

Dreze, Jean (1997), "Palanpur 1957-93: Occupational Change, Land Ownership and Social Inequality", in Breman et al. (eds.)

Sardamoni, K. (1995), "Crisis in the Fishing Industry and Woman's Migration: The Case of Kerala", in Schenk-Sandbergen (ed.)

Singh, Manjit and Iyer, K.Gopal (1985),"Migration Labourers in Rural Punjab", in Patnaik and Dingwaney (eds), *op. cit.*

Srivastava, Ravi S. (1999), "Rural Labor in Uttar Pradesh: Emerging Features of Subsistence, Contradiction & Resistance", *Journal of Peasant Studies*, Vol. 26, Nos. 2 & 3, January & April.

Tripathy, S.N. (1997) Migrant Labour in India", Discovery Publishing House, New Delhi

____ (2006) 'Dynamics of Tribal Migration, Sonali Publication, New Delhi.

20

Reservation and the Private Sector

Uma Tripathi

INTRODUCTION

"Reservation is a mechanism of protective discrimination as a social policy of the state enshrined in the constitution to ensure the participation of the traditionally neglected section of the society involving fixation of quota in the electoral, employment and educational institutions."[1]

Reservation is one such part of the system of affirmative action in India that is praiseworthy. William Darity Jr. from the Duke University feels that India has a far more aggressive and well developed system of affirmative action than the USA. He further observes that though the Indian System has not been extended to private sector employment as it has been in the USA, it has included the parliamentary system from the outset, an arena that has never been the purview of affirmative action in the US. The Indian system is a quota system rather than a more timid system of preferential boost of the sort used in America. The Indian system is inscribed in the national constitution precluding the more whimsical status it possesses in the USA.[2]

Marc Galenter renowned sociologist says "The problem of reservational protective discrimination is much dimensional involving formidable burden of policy making and administration in a developing nation. The compensatory or protective discrimination in favour of backward section of society once recognized as unparallel experiment betoking a generosity and farsightedness rare among the nations has developed into one of the most notorious provisions of the constitutions."[3] Now a days reservation is mostly known as 'Discrimination in Reverse' although according to me this is a misnomer. In fact, I feel reservation is nothing but 'Reverse Reservation' a constitutional arrangement for equalizing the unequals in the society. Reservation is upto the level of giving equal platform, it has nothing to do with personal efforts of backwards after that stage. Take the example of a mother who has children one of whom is disabled. She will provide the same food, clothing and other amenities to them without discrimination but for the disabled child she will do the extra effort and help him overcome his disability first. This is exactly why reservation is needed by the backwards and down trodden. Reservation appears to many as reverse discrimination on the face of it but if we observe it along with its background and circumstances in totality it would not be so.

Baba Saheb Ambedkar was the architect of the reservation policy at the All India level although prior to him there were some instances when not only the British but also the rulers of Indian provinces like Kolhapur, Baroda, Travancore and Cochin realized the need to introduce educational and employment rights in 19th and 20th century India for non Brahmins. The social reformer Mahatma Phuley had opened schools for the education of non Brahmins including the untouchables and women in Poona in 19th century.

According to Mulchand S. Rana reservation is not new thing in India. It is present in different ways since times immemorial. Family inheritance right is one such example where upon death of parent a non meritorious son gets the property of the parent and not the more meritorious daughter. He cites another example of how the skilled agriculture labourer does not get land whereas the unskilled absentee landlord living in the city acquires the same land through inheritance.[4]

In businesses where outside shareholders and financial institutions hold the majority stake management would always be by inheritance be it the Ambanis, Birlas or Bajajs.

Management quota in admission to self finance educational institutions is yet another type of reservation based on ability to pay. 85 per cent of all educational admission seats in Government run educational institutes are all reserved for natives domiciled in that state. All these examples according to me are perfect examples of 'Reverse discrimination' whereas reservation for the depressed classes in the educational and political fields is protective discrimination only so that 'people who had none in the past may have priority now.'

In the case of *Akhil Bhartiya Shoshit Karmachari Sangh v. Union of India*[5] Justice Chenappa Reddy said that the backward classes need facility, launching, populism and their needs are their demands, they ask for parity and not charity, so when reservation is provided to them at the stage of initial appointment or at stage of promotion it is in recognition of their undoubted fundamental right to quality of opportunity and in discharge of the constitutional obligation imposed upon the state to secure to all its citizen Justice—Social, economical and political.

Reservation remains a burning topic in India and even the legislature and judiciary seem to be at loggerhead on its many facets but as Mulchand S. Rana says "The reservation provision is one of the measures of putting an unequal with the equal by giving a little push with an ultimate intention of bringing about total equalities in the society. Once this is done when a general situation of equality is established in the nation, the push by way of reservation would be no more required."[6]

Earlier reservation was available in educational institutions either run by or aided out of the Government funds. In PA Inamdar[7] and Pai Foundation Case[8] the Apex court gave a right to decide their own admission polices to self finance educational institutions. 93rd constitutional amendment was passed to nullify the above judgment which had long repercussions due to non availability of reservation in enormously increasing number of self finance institutions. 93rd amendment adds a new clause (5) to Act 15 of the constitution by which laws can be made for providing reservation for backward classes and S.C. and S.T.'s in private run educational institutions but not in minority educational institutions.

Due to the tug of war between the judiciary and legislature regarding recruitment and promotion of SC/ST through reservation a type of stagnation in these matters appeared, only to be revitalized through a few much needed constitutional amendments, much needed because the depressed classes remain so still and I think the Apex Court is wrong in considering reservation only to push the backward on a level plane and not as a punishment for the rest. Why should the society not punish itself by expiation for all the atrocities committed on its weak brethrens? We oppress the weak because it is possible to oppress them. We put forward all the arguments loaded with technicalities, all the justifications loaded with possible dangers to the society when the topic of reservation is raised but were mum for centuries when atrocities were done on one section of the society continuously so that their souls have perished and they have became so down trodden that after over 60 years of the 1st step toward their upliftment they still are on the ground. However hard we help them get up they flounder and slump down.

RESERVATION FOR THE DALITS IN PRIVATE SECTOR

The Maharastra Government had recently passed a bill paving the way for reservation in private sector for Dalits and backwards but due to opposition from many quarters it had to be amended and now reservation will be applicable to only those businesses which are helped or contributed by the Government. Udit Raj a Crusader for Dalit Rights rightfully says, "With the help of reservation in Government jobs and education, Dalits have come to participate in mainstream and everywhere else where there is no reservation made, judiciary, export import, businesses and high skilled technical and professional jobs for instance they are entirely non existent for instance."[9] He compares the Indian dismal situation with that of America where the American Industries on their own provide them with employment keeping in mind their population. To quote Udit, "Their efficiency and meritocracy are not affected by their compassionate move whereas in India without the dalit participation in the private sectors there is not one global Indian brand. In 1982 in US it was discovered that participation of the Afro-American in media was only 2 per cent and at once candidates were searched, trained and employed resulting in their rate of participation shooting upon 7-8 per cent eight years later. Last year in Michigan University a white student getting more marks than a qualified Afro-American failed to get admission in Law school. He challenged the Affirmative Action and lost the case in U.S. Supreme Court which gave the verdict in favor of the policy of reservation which was also backed up by big business educational institutions and philanthropic organisations. Such type of never shaking support to Affirmative Action for the dalits is required in our country too"[10] Udit further says, "The real loss of Indian Industries occurs when MNC's get favorable policies and when agreements are dictated by agencies like World Bank and International Monetary Fund. Indian corporate houses should fight them instead of fighting against reservation for Dalits in private sector. If Dalits get opportunity to get ahead in life the nation as a whole will get ahead. It wont be a benefit which will accrue to outsider. They should help Dalits become entrepreneurs or at least should buy raw materials, products and services from them so that caste based occupation is done away with once and for all."[11]

Himanshu Charan Sadangi strongly supports the demand of Dalit organisations to include the vast private sector within the purview of reservation because though 15 per cent of jobs in state and state supported departments are reserved for the Dalits according to the existing rule considering the population strength of 16.5 (census report 2001). Privatisation of public sector units have already pushed majority of urban Dalits to casual labour with the decline of salaried jobs. Need for reservation in the private sector is a must because we need a level playing field even there too.[12]

Santosh Bhartiya says, "In the private sector they (Dalit) should have adequate share; private sector is not the king of India. They have been given the lands of Dalits; so why should dalits be not made a part of it compulsory? Wherever the Government gives licenses to private sector they should appoint dalits appropriately, dalits should be given representation of opportunities for active participation"[13] Santosh demands reservation in private sectors because there is nothing private about private sector. According to her they get land free of cost or at cheap price, get water and electricity from the Government either free of cost or at cheap price. According to her political democracy can be gained by controlling private sector.

The historic socio-economic exclusion of the scheduled castes and the scheduled tribes has inevitably resulted in their lacking network connection and to make matters worse very few of the private sector companies have transparent hiring policy, so it is necessary to have provision of affirmative action in the form of reservation in the private sector.

"A private enterprise is hardly a private owned entity and major portion of the cost of projects are raised from public equities and working capital financing from financial institutions which are funded either by the Government or the public at large. We all know that the Government provides numerous incentives to boost private sector industrial development, right from allotment of land at concessional rates and providing various types of subsides like capital subsidy, interest subsidy, power subsidy, price difference subsidy, certain budgetary concessions, area specific income tax exemptions, export promotion incentives, selective customs/excise relief's, VAT deferments etc so all these benefits flow out for the private sector from the public exchequer. Raw materials which they use come from natural resource such as land, water, forests, mines, minerals etc which are publicly owned national properties. They are getting required labour from the society and are further abstained from worries relating to law and order which all are managed out of public resources".[14]

Private sector is antagonistic to the idea of reservation in private sector and this stance depicts its immaturity and insensitivity. Should all the affirmative Action to be on behest of the Government, should social justice be not practiced by all the components of the society? Private sectors harp on the factor of merit, can they not do their bit of humanity by giving same additional grooming to a reserved candidate so that he comes up to the corporate expectations just as the media had done in the USA seeing the dismal participation rate of Afro American in the media itself. A little more vigorous and extensive training and care to the reserved category persons will make an useful permanent asset to the institutions. It is surprising that in spite of boasting of a meritorious manpower at their disposal Indian Commerce and Industries does not stand among leaders globally. The picture may become rosy if they throw away their social stigma and adopt the good omen of reservation. Jurist Fali S. Narman feels that the prospect of reservation in private sector is good in theory but extremely difficult to implement and monitor.[15] I do not feel the way he does being an optimistic person by all means. According to me whatever is good in theory can be successfully put in to practice with the aid of determination, hard work and perseverance.

Sukhdev Thorat terms private sector reservation as a remedy against market discrimination. He says, "If the prevalence of economic discrimination is the justification of the reservation in the public sector why can it not be the reason for reservation in the private sector? In Countries like US, Northern Irelands, Malaysia and Latin America affirmative section was developed from very beginning both in the public and the private sector. Therefore it is high time we introduce reservation in the private sector and provide long withheld justice. Economists have now enough evidence to show that markets don't remain neutral but do discriminate against the so called untouchables and other low castes. Some strands in main economics which form the theoretical supportive base for affirmative action polices in the west believe that market discrimination not only brings about unequal income distribution but also adversely affects economic growth by bringing imperfections in the labour market and further by also inducing inter group conflicts. Affirmative action as a remedy for market discrimination is thus justified on the ground of both equity and growth."[16]

Thorat is firm supporter of the opinion that India must enact an "Equal

Employment Opportunity Act' in line with US law so as to provide legal safeguards against discrimination in some categories of jobs and other markets.

Ratan Tata a leading Industrialist favors the introduction of reservation in the private sector. He has written to the Central Government. "Tata Group very well understands their obligations to the society. They give support to the government plea for reservation in the private sector. They are devising a scheme in this regard for being presented to the government."[17] Mr. Tata is a philanthropist in the true sense and realizes his duty towards his society which has raised him to the position in which he has at present. He belies the general private sector perception that it is the sole responsibility of the government for bringing about social justice and correcting the age old social discrimination. He is a gem of a person, a real human being, always trying to feel and solve the problems of the less fortunate and the best examples of this is his 'Nano' car which fulfils the aspirations of such persons who wish to own a car but do not have the adequate financial capacity to do so. He realized their dreams and made it come true for them. Man is selfish by nature and rarely does he try to fulfill the wishes of others, it is only his own dreams which he wishes to come true.

As regards the question of 'merit' and its relationship with the private sector we cannot over emphasize the 'merit theory' because as Mulchand S. Rana says, "Unless economic assets are largely distributed, education is universally and uniformly available and caste prejudices are non existent, the claim of selection on merit is a myth and becomes a process to legitimize preferences of those in power. Merit is more often the name of opportunity given in a particular social set up, natural endowment constituting a subsidiary condition. So long as caste sentiments and social differentiations exist, the test of merit, competition and equal opportunity are eye wash."[18]

Justice Krishna Ayer has rightfully said that the examination system by which we select the so called meritorious person is itself flawed; it has made memory the master of merit and banished creativity into exile. He further says that every new idea has resistance to encounter before reacceptance; every original thought has been branded a heresay[19]. To quote Prof. A.M. Dharamlingam, "Merit cannot be allowed to defeat the principles of democracy and socialism in a welfare state. ... Let us not forget that our freedom movement from 1885 was to free ourselves from British merit and efficiency. The British were talking of us as barbarians divided by castes and religions and enveloped in superstition and ignorance and therefore unfit to self-rule. They felt they had divine sanction to subjugate and rule over us. The attitude of some of our high castes is no less different than this."[20]

Another argument against a reservation system is that the people taken under reservations are inefficient and prevent the resources from being used for the optimal productive use. But on the global front our country is placed at 124th position in the group of 174 countries as per the Human Development Index 2004, only 3 Indian Universities/Institutions rank among the top 500 ones at global level and as per UNESCOs' global Monitoring Report, 2005 India ranked at 106 in the education reach among 127 countries.[21] The poor state of affairs as written above is due to the efficiency or non efficiency of the small fraction of depressed classes in the overall governance we know not.

The relevance of merit is very appropriately mentioned in well known Supreme Court Indra Sawhney Case.[22] To quote the majority judgement "It cannot also be ignored that the very idea of reservation implies selection of a less meritorious person. At the same time we recognize that this much cost has to be paid if the constitutional promise of social justice is to be redeemed." The judgment further states "We firmly believe that given an opportunity, members of the reserved categories are bound to overcome their initial disadvantages and would compete with and may in some cases excel over members of open competition. It is undeniable that nature has endowed it upon members of backward as much as it has endowed it upon members of other classes and that what is required is an opportunity to prove it. It may not therefore be said that reservations are anti-meritarian. Merit is there even among the reserved candidates and the small difference that may be allowed at the stage of initial recruitment is bound to disappear in course of time. These members too will compete with and improve their efficiency along with others".

Lets wipe out completely the illogical notion in our minds that upper castes means merit and lower caste means absence of merit and welcome affirmative action of the Government in the private sector for our down trodden brothers with open arms. Then only can our dream of realizing an egalitarian society be fulfilled and the concept of social justice be revitalized by providing economic justice for all.

Affirmative action is an off shoot of concept of social justice when mobilized in the practical sense. In the case of *Air India Statutory Corporation v. United Labour Union*[23] a three Judges of the Court has explained the concept of social justice in Article 38 of our constitution as follows:

> "Social justice is a dynamic devise to mitigate the sufferings of the poor, weak, dalits, tribals and deprived sections of the society and so elevate them to the level of equality, to live a life with dignity of person. Social justice is not a simple or single idea of a society but is an essential part of complex social change, to relieve the poor etc from handicaps, penury, to ward off distress and to make their life livable for greater good of the society at large. The aim of social justice is to attain substantial degree of social, economic and political equality which is the legitimate expectation and constitutional goal in a developing society like ours. Where there is vast gap of inequality in status and opportunity, law is a catalyst, Rubicon to the poor etc to reach the ladder of social justice. The constitution therefore mandates the state to accord justice to all members of the society in all facets of human activity."

Article 46 of the directive principles enjoins the state to take special case in promoting the educational and economic interests of the weaker sections of the people specially the dalits and to protect them from social injustice and to deprive the dalits to integrate in the immense private sector on whatever whimsical grounds is social injustice at its worst.

Why is there a need for reservation in the private sector for the backward classes specially the dalits?

The huge demand for employment in the government and public sector never warranted for a need of private sector initiative in social cause for the upliftment of the dalits although earlier too the national commission for the scheduled caste and scheduled tribes had recommended for reservation in private sector in its report in 1964 and 1971. As early as in 1978 Mandal Commission had also incorporated similar recommendation for reservation in private rector.

The Prime Minister of India, Dr. Manmohan Singh had rightfully implored, "It is high time for introduction of provisions of reservation in the private sector".[24]

Since this remark comes from a world class economist the prospect of reservation in the private sector would no doubt bring fruitful results for the Indian economy.

In the seventies private sectors started fostering up and due to boom in global exports there was reactionary boom in the employment generating potential in the private sector but parallel to this was the phenomenon of huge employment in public sector institutions due to nationalisation of banks, general insurance etc. The reserved categories were in a comfortable position in such institutions due to the statutory application of reservation provisions.

Nineties saw the core privatisation phase and lions share in employment was generated now by the private sector, the same being further boosted by the private sector expansion, now the time had come when the major job provider i.e. the Government started receding from entire spectrum of its activities. The consequential shrinking of jobs in public sector was inevitable and new employment potential avenues were generated in the private sector to a major extent under new economic reforms popularly known as liberalisation, privatisation and globalisation i.e. L.P.G. It was the effort of World Trade Organisation (WTO) a voluntary global organisation that member countries were brought together at the International forum in 1991 and from thereon global economy kept on converging for the mutual benefits. Due to India's full hearted implementation of the new economic reform the world has started perceiving India now as a giant market of 100 crore consumers.

Liberalisation has loosened to a great extent control of Government over the private sector by discarding unnecessary licenses, inspection formalities and to some extent taxation simplification thus benefiting small entrepreneurs to giant industrial corporates alike.

Privatisation has allowed free entry to private sector industries in all wide spectrums of economic and industrial activities thus giving them full impetus for growth, expansion and diversification. The other fact of privatisation is that it has led to reduction in government role in economic activities and reduction of employment in the government/public sector.

Globalisation has also provided momentum to static Indian economy by allowing entry of multi-national and transnational corporate and industries in our country and vice verse.

The impact of LPG on Indian economy has resulted in negligible rise in the employment absorption in the public sector as compared to the substantial or we may say spectacular increase in the private sector the ratio being 1:4.[25]

Impact of LPG had been fruitful for many segments of the global society barring the poor and backward people one of whom are the scheduled castes, scheduled tribes and other backward classes of India. LPG has resulted in dismantling of jobs in the public sector, and since these jobs in Government sector are reducing day by day scope of representation of SC/ST/OBC in the Government jobs are getting restricted. Government has started withdrawing its stake holding from public sectors through disinvestments and further by privatisation of management of certain essential services such as electricity, telephone communication etc wherein good number of employees belonging to scheduled castes, scheduled tribes and other backward classes got the jobs under the umbrella of reservation provisions. Though the laid down statutory reservation provisions have not been abrogated but the interest of the backward classes are likely to be affected adversely due to emergence of fierce competition in this sector. Due to the new economic reforms the dalits have reduced number of jobs in the public sector and the ever growing and prosperous private sector would not open doors for them so where do they go in this situation where all are in a better and smug position economically except them?

Liberalisation of land allotment and rapid law reforms also carry a danger of acquisition of agricultural lands belonging to dalits, tribals etc by rich farmers not to speak of the new trend of easy land allotment to the corporate sector. The rural economy has suffered due to all these factors.

The Industrial sector whether public or private enjoying liberalisation benefits must voluntarily shoulder some social responsibility by creating job opportunities for the depressed classes keeping in view the national goal of social justice and economic qualities. The corporate sector is reaping the fruits of the policy of privatisation so should it not pay back by shouldering social responsibility towards social justice and social securities for its less fortunate brethrens.

Affirmative Action formulation and implementation can be learnt by following the path of American Affirmative Action where basic quality norms have to be complied by the minority reserved categories. A target lot is taken up from the minorities and a comprehensive arrangement of pre-recruitment training of the so taken candidates is made. A subsequent package aiming at skill up gradation is carefully chalked out and put to implementation during their training phase so that they are trained as per job specifications and skill requirements thoroughly during initial pre-recruitment process. The best thing is that all this is done sincerely and whole heartedly. To quote Mulchand S. Rana, "The industries have admirably witnessed a miraculous positive results also. The whole implementation has been found so successful to produce thousands of minority aspirants to meet with varied and diverse industries expectations. Even the world's best multinational corporates have no cause of complaints regarding levels of efficiency of these minority candidates prepared under the diversity programme. This would not have been perhaps possible but for the strong and honest determination of the industries for the upliftment of those lagging behind in the race of socio-economic development."[26] The world's leading multinational companies like Exzzone Mobiles, Wall Mart, General Motors and Ford have implemented affirmative action earnestly and remain world leaders still. They have adopted a social cause and surprisingly merit and employability has never been a threat in their maintaining their status on the global economic front. Indian private sector is reluctant on the issue of providing reservation to the depressed classes and even without reservation there is not one global Indian brand.

Affirmative action aims at due representation of minorities in the print as well as electronic media in US, the bigger the company the greater responsibility it feels it has to shoulder and hence the agreement known as "Diversity Agreement" which has been entered into by four biggest TV Companies, viz., Fox, NBC, ABC and CBS. This agreement undertakes to give representation to the minorities in various electronic media related roles such as authors, actors etc. As regards the print media 950 out of 1,446 American dailies have accepted the resolution of the American society of Newspapers for giving due representation to the minorities.

One of the most successful experiments on reservation is found in Malaysia. A reservation policy exists there especially for the 'Bhumiputras'[27] designed to weaken the Chinese monopoly. They provide for reservation in educational institutions, awarding of Government contracts, job quota in the private sector and the provision of 30 per cent of new companies to be registered for and owned by the Bhumiputra Malaysian reservation policy is wonderful providing for job assurance in government as well as private sector and priorities to the entrepreneurs. The Bhumiputras who were similar to the oppressed Indians in the 70's got a big fillip with sharing in the economic development of the nation. Their ownership shot up to 23 per cent from a poor 2.3 per cent in thirty years which also resulted in the impressive overall national growth of 6 to 7 per cent.[28] When a developing Asian country like Malaysia wish more of or less the same socio-economic conditions like ours can implement the policy of social justice shedding all inhibitions can we not learn something from it? Just as our Indian Constitution is a product of research and deliberations keeping in view all the best features of the constitutions of the world and we have no hesitance in admitting this could we not follow in the footstep of countries like Malaysia and the USA and formulate and implement a workable Reservation Policy just like them, a policy which does not only work but works wonder?

Coming back to the Indian context suppose there is no affirmative action in the form of positive discrimination, no reservations and no policies of empowerment of the downtrodden in India, all the citizens are treated alike socio-economically and politically. Is this equality according to Article 14 of our cherished constitution? It is not so because as Dr. Jennings puts it "Equality before the law means that among equals the law should be equal and should be equally administered that like should be treated alike ..."[29]

We already know that Article 14 permits classification but prohibits class legislation. It permits reasonable classification of persons, objects and transactions by legislature for purpose of achieving specific ends. Only the classification must be founded on an intelligible differentia distinguishing persons or things that are grouped together from others left out from the group and the differentiation must have a rational relation to the object sought to be achieved by the Act. There should be a nexus between the basis of classification and the object of the Act which makes the classification, so if reservation is provided to the SC/ST's in promotion and in the private sector then Articles 14, 15 and 16 not are offended. Here unequals are not being treated equally but differentially to achieve specific socio-economic aims for the betterment of the nations and if the weaker classes will not be given a preferential treatment in the form of positive discrimination it would indeed be unjust to them and it would as unlikes are treated as likes or unequals as equals. Social justice as a concept emanates from our constitution which is not only a sacred document but an institution of democratic socialism; each and every word of it is permeated with the ink of social justice ... by adhering to the teachings of our constitution we make it sacrosanct.

AN OVERVIEW

Truth is unsavory and this is true that at present majority of those who belong to the so called upward classes cannot judge the reservation policy on the ground of prevailing social realities and the biggest reality is that the caste system is throttling the soul of our nation and also impeding its socio-economic progress. Instead of debating on the topic of reservation or opposing it vehemently we should for once imagine that we are standing in foot of the down trodden or bearing atrocities of the most barbaric types at the hands of the dominant, then only we would feel the pain and trauma which the dalits have faced historically and are still facing. Lets create a spirit of accommodation for the least of our brothers and give them a preferential treatment keeping in view their legitimate aspirations and rightful demands. Almighty God is the creator of each and every living thing on this earth and by showing disrespect to his creations we show disrespect to him I am reminded of a song which I was taught in the primary classes, "Whatsoever you do to the least of your brothers that you do unto me." Keeping in mind these angelic verses lets do our duties.

In the end I would like to remind all that Reservation in Private Sector is not an impossible thing. The two compelling factors to justify reservation in public sector are Backwardness and inadequacy of Representation of the class and these factors are also present when the question of reservation arises in the private sector. With enormous increase in number of self finance institutions (educational) after much debate and deliberations reservations has been provided in such institutions although such was not the position when reservation in Government run or even Government funded educational institutions was provided initially. So this time without that much debate or deliberations lets resolve to give social justice a new meaning- not a theoretical one but a practical one full of life and reality.

Endnotes and References

1. Quoted by Mulchand S. Rana 2008, *Reservation in India—Myths and Realities*, New Delhi: Concept Publishing Company, p. 17.
2. Sukhadev Thorat and Narendra Kumar 2008, Forward to *BR Ambedkar—Perspective on Social Exclusion and Inclusive Policies*, New Delhi: Oxford University Press.
3. Marc Galenter 1983, *Competing Equalities: Law and the Backward Classes*, New Delhi: Oxford University Press, p. 201.
4. *Supra* Note 1 at 27.
5. AIR 1981 SC 298.
6. *Supra* Note 1 at 31.
7. *PA Inamdar v. State of Maharashtra*, AIR 2005, SC 3226.
8. *T.M. Pai Foundation v. State of Karnataka*, AIR 2003, SC 355
9. 'Reservation for Dalits in Private Sector; 22nd Jan 2004' *Counter Current org.*
10. *Ibid*
11. *Ibid*
12. See Sadangi Himanshu Charan (2008), *'Dalit: The downtrodden of India*, New Delhi: Esha Books.
13. Bhartiya Santosh (2008), *'Dalit and minority Empowerment* New Delhi: Rajkamal Prakashan Pvt. Ltd., p. 45.
14. *Supra* Note 1, p. 217 Quoted by Mulchand S. Rana.
15. *'Financial Express'* of 11 June, 2004. p. 1.
16. *'Economic Times'* 26th March, 2004 p. 5.
17. *Ibid.*
18. *Supra* Note 1 at 157.
19. *Supra* Note 5.
20. As cited by Mulchand S. Rana, *Supra* Note 1 at 155.
21. UNESCO 'Global Monitoring Report' (2005).
22. *Indra Sawhney v. Union of India*, AIR 1993 SC 477.
23. AIR 1987 SC 645.
24. *'Sandesh Gujrati Daily'* 24 Oct. 2004.
25. National Sample Survey Statistical Abstract, 2001.
26. *Supra* Note 1 at 325.
27. Bhumiputras are the natives of Malaysia, the children of the soil.
28. *Supra* Note 1 at 329.
29. Ivor, W. Jennings 1943 (3rd Ed) *Law and the Constitution* London: University of London Press, p. 49.

21

Dalits and Social Justice: A Perusal of Electoral Politics

Dhananjay Rai

INTRODUCTION

At the outset, I would like to draw certain nuances of social justice. Throughout the article, social justice has been used as a process not as an end. This formulation extricates social justice from various imposed attributions like as a state-driven mechanism to redress to causes and grievances of dalits, static and passive formulations of empowerment and circumvention of transformative politics. I suggest that social justice has a bigger role, and for this purpose, rigidification of social justice as a sphere *only* for doling out certain resources must be circumvented. There are many areas whereby social justice could assume as transformative role. The underlying theme herein is this: social justice has transformative role and redistribution of resources is one of the components. Exploration of these postulations can easily be located in philosophical landscape of dalit discourse. This article attempts to map out the role of social justice through electoral politics for dalits. In other words, how one should link electoral politics with social justice concerning dalits.

DEMOCRACY AND SOCIAL JUSTICE

Under the rubric of democracy, social justice occupies the kernel place. Due to copious significance of social justice, its perusal has been an intrinsic aspect in political theory. Indeed, social justice has rejuvenated and reinforced the people's movements towards democratic revolution. Thereby, social justice becomes significant for dalits and other oppressed sections. Even in modern India, dalits have been facing apathetic procedural rights. The struggle is to translate it into substantive rights. Besides, ideational aspect of social justice was not only countenanced but also systematically and systemically annulled.

B.R. Ambedkar greatly emphasised and endeavoured to ensure social justice for dalits. For this purpose, there has been a greater emphasis on electoral politics. In fact, to enhance the partaking in democracy thereby changing the nature of democracy were envisaged through electoral politics.

Promise of social justice in democracy takes the recourse of electoral politics. Electoral politics is a vantage point whereby participation on equal footing in terms of voting and choosing decision makers occurs. Hence electoral politics becomes one of the core constituents of social justice. In fact, social justice utilises electoral politics in many ways. To delimit ourselves on two accounts would be fructuous enterprise. In other words, social justice must perceive electoral politics on two accounts. The first account is the maximum participation of dalits in democratic apparatus. The second aspect is transformation of corporeal reality. The first and second accounts can be christened as 'expansion principle' and 'transformative principle' respectively. When social justice takes the recourse of electoral politics, in fact, it emphasises equally on both principles. Both principles work in tandem. Both principles need further explication.

Expansion principle is an assertion of equalitarian principle. It asserts and desires the equal participation of all in democratic process whereby dalits are entitled to elect representatives and acquire mandatory participation rights in the decision making process on equal footing with others. The expansion principle remains conscious about the enhancement of participation in all institutions whereby decisions are chalked out and implemented. Transformation principle encompasses politics of fulfillment and the politics of transfiguration. "The politics of fulfillment envisages that the society of the future attains more adequately what present society has left unaccomplished. It is the culmination of the implicit logic of the present. The politics of transfiguration emphasizes the emergence of qualitatively new needs, social relations, and modes of association, which burst open the Utopian potential within the old" (Benhabib, 1986:13).

In fact, embedded aspect of expansion is transformation. Therefore, expansion cannot be insulated from transformation. Expansion principle and transformation principle through electoral politics has been the omniscient virtue in dalit discourse and were clearly visible in Ambedkar's initiation in form of the Independent Labour Party and the Scheduled Caste Federation. The issue of exploration herein is this: to understand the functionality of expansion principle and transformation principle that is whether both are working in tandem or that the expansion principle has been prioritised over transformation principle. Put differently, social justice via electoral politics emphases on expansion principle and transformative principle. The pertinent question is whether social justice via electoral politics has taken both principles in concert or not.

DALITS, EXPANSION PRINCIPLE AND TRANSFORMATION PRINCIPLE

Expansion principle and transformation principle have taken place in many a ways in democracy. There are constitutional ways through which mandatory participation has ensured thereby creating a podium whereby a slew of transformation can be envisaged. They are equal voting rights and mandatory representation in the Legislature. Expansion of dalits in terms of participation and transformation is galvanised through political parties in the sphere of electoral politics. There are three types of political formation available for dalits in contemporaneous India for the pursuance of expansion and transformation. The first political formation is 'allusive political formation'. Herein, the politics of allusion acquires prominence and becomes the term of reference. The allusion becomes significant, but the transformative issue of Indian societal-economic landscape remains evasive. The political parties, clinging to this standpoint, seek dalits' support, however, they do not offer procedurally or substantially a way out in terms of combating the prevalent malaises. They rely on 'allusion' and conceive of dalits in terms of 'empirical object'. Accordingly, 'empirical object' becomes significant *only* (and due to) in sphere of 'losing-winning syndrome'. Interestingly, expansion could be permitted in this formation but transformation so far has been evaded. Dalits, by and large, have protracted the apathetic distance, at least theoretically and practically wherever alternative is available, with this viewpoint.

The second political formation is 'fellow traveller political formation'. This formation has encompassed innumerable trajectories and historicity. Dalits' association herein suggests an intricate odyssey and thereby a convoluted outcome. Dalits' association has been effective in this standpoint wherever 'universal' and 'specific' have been addressed equally (theoretically and empirically). This association remains void or weaker wherever the universal eclipses the specific in terms of non recognition, theoretically and empirically.

In the third political formation that is the 'core political formation', dalits remain as a core constituent and constituency. In other words, dalits primarily take the responsibility to commence the political party/parties and become the core constituent. After becoming the core constituent, the primary responsibility thereafter has been to reach out significantly amongst dalits. The consolidations of dalits behind the corresponding party/parties also decide the acceptance of particular party as indubitable force resisting the oppressive mechanisms and edifices responsible for the subjugatory practices. The inclusion of other sections is only a subsequent development and non-mandatory. The primary responsibly of expansion and transformation, since Ambedkar days has been entrusted with this formation.

CORE POLITICAL FORMATION AND EXPANSION PRINCIPLE

This article zeroes in on 'core political formation' and understands the expansion principle for dalits through political parties whose core constituents are dalits. The 15th Lok Sabha election unravels and poses various questions and ramifications for the expansion principle in the realm of electoral politics. Though there are innumerable political parties whose constituents and constituencies are confined to dalits, three parties are significant enough to be mentioned: Bahujan Samaj Party (BSP), Lok Janshakti Party (LJP) and Republican Party of India (Ramdas Athavale) (RPI (A)). The 15th Lok Sabha election raises the question about policy and dalit engagement of three parties at both theoretical and empirical levels.

The BSP is one of the seven national parties of India. In 15th Lok Sabha Election, the BSP contested on 500 seats and managed to secure 6.18 per cent of total votes nationally. The party has won 21 Lok Sabha seats, 20 seats from Uttar Pradesh and one seat from Madhya Pradesh. Discussing from the much touted 'social engineering' or 'sarvajan hitay' standpoint, there were 7 Brahmins , 30 OBCs , 18 Dalits, 20 Muslims and 5 Thakurs as candidates in the election fray of General Election 2004 in the state of Uttar Pradesh. The BSP won 19 Lok Sabha seats and in terms of sociology of winners, dalits were five, OBCs nine, Muslims four and Brahmin one in number. The results and social engineering formula pertaining to 15th Lok Sabha election, in Uttar Pradesh (UP), evince significantly a contrasting picture. The BSP's candidates for this election, in UP, were 20 Brahmins, 20 OBCs, 17 Dalits, 14 Muslims, 6 Thakurs, 2 Banias and 1 Punjabi Khatri. The winners amongst the BSP candidates include 5 Brahmins, 4 Muslims, 4 Thakurs, 3 OBCs, 2 Extremely Backward Caste and 2 Dalits. In 2004, out of 17 reserved constituencies of Uttar Pradesh for dalits , the BSP's share was of five MPs in contrast to others' twelve (the Samajwadi Party (SP) seven, the Bhartiya Janata Party (BJP) three, the Congress one and the Rashtriya Lok Dal (RLD) one). In 2009, the BSP's candidates were successful on two seats (Lalganj and Misrikh) and others' candidates on 15 seats (SP nine (Bulandshahar, Etawah, Hardoi, Jalaun, Kaushambi, Machhlishahr, Mohanlalganj, Nagina and Robertsganj), Congress three (Bahraich, Barabanki and Unnao), BJP two (Agra and Basgaon) and RLD one (Hathras)) (Rai, 2009:45-47).

Ram Vilas Paswan headed LJP had four seats (all seats in Bihar) after 14th Lok Sabha Election in 2004. Out of four seats, Hajipur and Roseda were reserved seats whereas Balia and Saharsa belonged to general seats. In General Election 2009, the LJP could not win even a single seat. Ramdas Athavale's RPI(A) in General Election 2009 scored zero in contrast to 14th Lok Sabha election where it had Pandharpur reserved seat (Maharashtra). In Uttar Pradesh, the BSP could take lead only on 100 legislative seats whereas in the State Assembly Election, 2007, it won 207 seats, sufficient for the formation a majority government. In terms of garnering vote percentage in Uttar Pradesh, the BSP is still a leading party with 27.42 per cent (Rai, 2009, 45-47)

One of the intriguing aspects of this perusal is the number of dalits reaching to the Lok Sabha. On this aspect, there is a big decline. In 2004, dalits and non-dalits were 33.33 per cent and 66.67 per cent respectively of total

Lok Sabha seats of these three political parties. In terms of number, there were 24 Lok Sabha members and eight were dalits. In 2009, there are 21 Lok Sabha seats and dalits are only two. In other words, dalits constitute 10.5 per cent of total Lok Sabha seats acquired by these three parties (BSP 21, LJP 0 and RPI(A) 0). The gap between dalits and non-dalits in 2004 was almost 33.37 per cent and it has been widened further i.e., 79 per cent in 2009. It also indicates that expansion of dalit participation through 'core political formation' has reduced significantly (Rai, 2009, 45-47).

RECOVERING EXPANSION PRINCIPLE AND TRANSFORMATION PRINCIPLE

In the backdrop of previously mentioned electoral results, it becomes imperative to discern the expansion principle and transformative principle of core political formation i.e., dalit political parties. In other words, it could be asked whether the decline of expansion principle through three parties, is also the decline of transformation principle! Or these three political parties have given priority to expansion principle over transformation principle! Precisely, does it also symbolise the shrinking of transformation principle? These questions might appear very much uncomplicated but in actuality, they are not due to various factors.

In the historicity of expansion principle and transformation principle, Jotirao Phule (April 11, 1827 to November 28, 1890), B.R. Ambedkar (April 14, 1891 to December 6, 1956) and E.V. Ramasamy Periyar (September 17, 1879 to December 24, 1973) and others had proved that without ideating for social justice and untiring efforts to achieve it, there are hardly any other options. The closer observance of Phule, Ambedkar, and Periyar reveals the untiring effort imbued with singularity that is the social justice and confluence of both 'expansion principle' and 'transformation principle'. In case of Phule, followings are examples extraordinaire of both principles: expansion principle (member of Pune Municipal Council (1876-82) and deposition before the Hunter Commission (May 11, 1888)) and transformation principle (the first school for shudratishudra girls (1848), foundation of two schools (1851), a night school for working people (1855), the household water-tank to dalits (1868), Satyashodhak Samaj (October 19, 1873)). Phule vociferously attacked the religious texts, responsible for the shudratishudra's subjugation and highlighted the issue of alternative religion. The revolutionary aspect of Phule is very much visible in Gulamgiri (Slavery 1873) (Phule, 1991 and Deshpande, 2009).

The confluence of 'expansion principle' and 'transformation principle' reached its zenith in Ambedkar's initiation. The expansion of dalit participation by him was visible in following events: testifying before the Southborough Committee (1919) and the Royal Commission (1925); as a member of the Bombay Legislative Council (1926); introduction of the Hereditary Offices Amendment Bill (1928); participation in the Round Table

Conference (1930) and Joint Committee on Indian Legislative Reform (1933); formation of Independent Labour Party (August 15, 1936); introduction of a Bill against *Khoti* Landlord System (1937) and the Industrial Dispute Bill (1938); launching of the All-India Scheduled Castes Federation (July 18-20, 1942); becoming of a Labour Member in the Viceroy's Executive Council (1942), Chairman of the Drafting Committee (1947) and Minister of Law (1947); introduction of the Hindu Code Bill (1951), and as a member of Rajya Sabha (1952).

The second aspect , transformation principle, encompasses following endeavors: starting of *Mooknayak* (a Marathi Fortnightly, Jan 1920); speech at a Depressed Classes conference (March, 1920); formation of Depressed Classes Welfare Association (*Bahishkrit Hitkarini Sabha,* July 1924); commencement of *Mahad Satyagrah* (1926); beginning of *Bahishkrit Bhara*t (A Marathi Fortnightly, April 3, 1927); initiation of *Samaj Samta Sangh* (September, 4,1927) and *Samata Sainik Dal* (December 1927); address to a second Depressed Classes Conference (December, 1927), *Manu Smiriti* Burning (1927); inauguration of Depressed Classes Educational Society (June 14, 1928), *Samata* (A fortnightly, June 29, 1928) and *Janata* (a Marathi Fortnightly , June 29, 1928); presiding Depressed Classes Congress (1930), the All-Indian Depressed Classes Conference (1932) and Yeola Conversion Conference (1935), commencement of *Prabudd Bharat* (February 4, 1956) and conversion (October 14, 1956). Expansion principle and transformation principle were directed against Brahmanism, casteism, untouchability, fight for social-political-economic democracy, women's rights, legal and constitutional rights, and adherence to the state socialism (Ambedkar, 1989, 1989 and 1990).

E.V. Ramasamy Periyar comprehensively engaged with expansion principle (led the Justice Party (1939) and started Dravidar Kazhagam (1944)) and transformation principle (Vaikom Satyagraha (1924) and (the Self Respect Movement (1925)). Periyar incessantly clung to the anti-Brahmanism, self-respect, rationalism, atheism and self respect marriages (Diehl, 1976: 120-128; Diehl, 1977; and Geetha and Rajadurai, 1998).

There have been divergences in pursuit of expansion principle and transformation principle, and it is also evident in all three. However, there is convergence in terms of aiming for the social justice. Put differently, there is no option but social justice. For social justice, the continuity of struggle against status quo should remain intact or should be intensified. In other words, expansion principle is abortive sans transformation principle. Locating this virtuous ideation and world vision, these three political parties have shown, more or less, elision of transformation principle and greater emphasis *only* on expansion principle. However, expansion of dalit participation has declined significantly through three political parties yet emphasis on expansion principle remains the fulcrum of electoral politics. The strategy could have been to combine expansion principle and transformation principle congruently and electoral battle could have been a testing ground for social justice. The expansion's insulation from transformations leads to focussing primarily on convergence of electoral politics as the realm of former. In a way, the expansion principle displaces the place and vitality of transformation principle. What has happened in the case of expansion principle through electoral politics is that the vantage point and scope of objectivity are confined only with the expansion principle.

Furthermore, various factors categorically highlight that utilising electoral politics only for expansion and bypassing transformation cannot be fructuous. Therefore, it becomes paramount imperative to revive and rejuvenate the transformation along with expansion which would not only reinforce the path towards social justice but also guide the electoral politics analogously, as dreamt and struggled by Ambedkar.

CASTE ANNIHILATION VERSUS CASTE SAMMELAN (CONVENTIONS)

Primarily in Uttar Pradesh, expansion principle gets privileged through caste *sammelan* (conventions) (e.g., Joint convention of Dalits and Brahmins) over transformation principle of which caste annihilation is the desired goal. The divergence between expansion principle and transformation principle has serious implications on the issue of caste. Due to divergence, the primacy of caste has taken a new turn. Theoretical to practical moorings of transformation, especially in Ambedkar, overtly emphasises the annihilation of caste. The justification to annihilate caste and struggle in this vein has been exemplary in Ambedkar and others. Nevertheless, contemporaneous electoral politics for expansion, especially of BSP, zeroes on 'caste parity' in place of caste annihilation. *Jati Jodo Sammelan* (caste conventions) is prioritized over annihilation of caste. The caste conventions have been equalled to the fight against caste. Thereby, the natural culmination of '*Jati jodo sammelan*' is the caste alliance in electoral sphere. This alliance actually bypasses the historicity of caste and its functionality.

In Ambedkar's view, there cannot be any alternative but annihilation of caste. "It is a pity that Caste even today has its defenders. The defences are many. It is defended on the ground that the Caste System is but another name for division of labour and if division of labour is a necessary feature of every civilized society then it is argued that there is nothing wrong in the Caste System. Now the first thing is to be urged against this view is that Caste System is not merely division of labour. It is also a division of labourers. Civilized society undoubtedly needs division of labour. But in no civilized society is division of labour accompanied by this unnatural division of labourers into watertight compartments. Caste System is not merely a division of labourers which is quite different from division of labour—it is a hierarchy in which the divisions of labourers are graded one above the other. In no other country is the division of labour accompanied by this gradation of labourers. There is also a third point of criticism against this view of the Caste System. This division of labour is not spontaneous; it is not based on natural aptitudes.

Social and individual efficiency requires us to develop the capacity of an individual to the point of competency to choose and to make his own career. This principle is violated in the Caste System in so far as it involves an attempt to appoint tasks to individuals in advance, selected not on the basis of trained original capacities, but on that of the social status of the parents" (Ambedkar, 1989:47).

Moreover, "[y]ou cannot build anything on the foundations of caste. You cannot build up a nation, you cannot build up a morality. Anything that you will build on the foundations of caste will crack and will never be a whole" (ibid: 66).The shift from annihilation to *'sammelan'* actually misses innumerable issues around caste like its social and economic functionality and direct link to dalits' 'time and space'. Particularly, the BSP has given primacy to *'sammelan'* over 'annihilation' and corollary to this is the strange mixture of politics of egalitarianism and *'jati sammelan'*. The strange alliance in and of itself has been conceived of the final destiny or reality. The scathe of this discernment has been covertly felt by dalits. They were/are who have suffered the most of this barbaric system and they were/are told that equality is imminent through *'jati sammelan'*.

In aforesaid elections, in Uttar Pradesh, there have been two notable developments. First, a section of dalits has parted with the electoral politics and thereby the BSP could not perform as it was expected akin to State Legislative Election 2007. The expansion aspect sans transformation exhibits disillusionment of dalits with electoral politics. The second development is more vital concerning dalits and electoral politics. The much-touted castes like Brahmins and other upper castes, which were fitting the bill in the schema of electoral-equality, have started deserting the BSP in the context of the Congress revenant. They have had hardly concern for the lessening of dalits' myriad societal-economic hurdles and their entire engagement relies on political partaking.

Unfortunately, in place of cautioning *'jati sammelan'*, various sympathetic and intellectual exercises, representing both 'in' and 'out' streams, did eulogise it and declared innumerable 'Brahmins Sammelan' and 'Kshatriya Sammelan' as sites of social justice and these castes as an agent of transformation . The caste per se and *'sammelans'* became opaque endeavours. In this backdrop, it did not surprise many people that a section of dalits have moved or on verge moving to other political formation. To reverse this trend and to challenge the further strengthening of 'allusive political formation', there has to be a formation of alliance between dalits and poor from other sections. Otherwise, this would weaken the issue of social justice and augmentation of 'allusive political formation'.

CONTINUITY VERSUS STAGNATION

The issue of continuity versus stagnation acquires a contiguous attention. Continuity entails that the exploitation has been incarnated into various forms. There has been a continuity of exploitation. The incessant incarnation of exploitation forces the exploited section to search and construct the rejuvenated postulation to combat the exploitation via struggle. The struggles in context of rejuvenated postulation equip dalits and others towards apt identification of exploitation, thereby corresponding combat.

Of late, expansion principle by way of electoral politics due to insulation from transformation principle has clung to the notion of 'stagnation of exploitation'. In other words, *this* particular politics has been neither engaged with various forms of exploitation nor linked to various forms of exploitation with the state led promulgation of co-option and hegemony. Consequently, the decline of the might of Brahmanism and casteist forces by means of expansion principle via electoral politics has been accepted and endorsed as the empirical truth. In fact, it belies the truth and leads to two diametrical conclusions: first, initiators of this politics do not recognise the continuation of exploitation due to their trust on 'stagnation of exploitation'; and second, since dalits face the direct and brutal assault socially and economically, circumstances force dalits not only to combat their own but also to explore other podium whereby at least exploitation of dalits gets the recognition. In politics of UP, there is, explicitly, a new churning. And it is, furthermore, up to the electoral politics of expansion in terms of responding this churning and combating 'allusive political formation' which has emerged as the dominant force after 15th Lok Sabha Election.

SYMBOL AND MATERIAL

Ambedkar categorically points out three sine qua non aspects of democracy: political, social and economic (Ambedkar, 1986: 39-40). In other words, political democracy in-itself cannot be sufficient ground for amelioration of prevalent 'ills'. The 'social' and 'material' aspect of democracy has to deliver to the people. Therefore, for any progressive endeavour 'symbol' and 'economic' become intrinsic entities. The 'symbol' becomes an important aspect of social. The 'social' decides the method of interaction in everyday life. The method of interaction carries various nuanced meanings. These meanings are not innocent innovation or esoteric comments. They do carry very pertinent meanings. The symbols are significant carriers of meanings. The historicity of symbols in India suggests the invariable dominance of upper castes and justification of dominance ubiquitously against dalits.

Symbols shapes life and public spheres at micro level. In this endeavour, the politics of symbols and construction of symbols by the BSP has a positive and counteractive aspect. In case of 'positivity ', there are, perhaps for the first time, symbols available ubiquitously and each narrates and speaks volumes in terms percolating the message about assertion. In terms of counteractive aspect, it has started to challenge the upper caste's imbued public sphere.

Even so, the symbols are not complete on their own. They could play an important role but not the role. They have to be linked up with material melioration. The significance of symbol becomes greater in associational sense with material. The traverse from symbol to material is a very critical stage. In case of traverse, both become surprisingly illuminating to dethrone the capacious edifice of exploitative forces. In case of non-transformation, 'symbols' may cease to be charming and vivacious meanings. Therefore, the struggle from symbols to material is fundamental in terms of the absolute challenge to casteist forces and respite to dalits.

The unfortunate aspect of electoral politics, especially of the BSP, is its less emphasis on the issue of 'material'. The aforesaid election has shaken the BSP that along with the symbol endeavour, distribution of resources is the fulcrum in terms of combating the concentration and accumulation of resources on the one hand and thereby, extricating dalits from massive prevalent poverty on the other hand. Besides, as of today, it does not seem to becoming primary task of these political parties and government. Despite multifaceted utility of symbol, symbol under the pursuance of only expansion without a transformability vision, does not hold much value. It neither threatens ruling echelons nor brings emancipation of dalits. As soon as expansion principle mixes with transformation principle, a symbol becomes transforming agency. In fact, this is a challenge for transformation. If the struggle could not commence on material front, dalits would be left with no options but exploring those alternatives which are at least promising something though without any roadmap for transformation. Uttar Pradesh is a convoluted example in this regard.

CONCLUSION

In the end, it could be said that without augmenting and strengthening the transformation principle, the future and nature of expansion principle through electoral politics is difficult to discern and predict. Indeed, the weakening of expansion principle nowhere suggests the decline of transformation principle or transformative vigorousness. Conversely, it highlights the significance of vivacious transformation which would think politically that the mere expansion by way of electoral politics spearheaded by existing political parties would be sufficed or time has ripened for the new alternative politics of transformation. Sooner the gap between expansion principle and transformation principle be bridged, it would be better for dalits and other struggling people since the struggle for social justice would be unitedly augmented. Furthermore, due to insulation of expansion principle from transformation principle, it may be replaced by some other political manoeuvres since it does not address the root cause of dalits' exclusion. The commitment deficit of the political class towards sustained transformation eventually strengthens the cyclical nature into electoral politics in form of *mere* expansion whereby upheavals of the socio-material spheres are fleetingly highlighted yet they remain notoriously short lived and ineffective in attaining the purpose of social justice .

Endnotes and References

Ambedkar, B.R. (1986), The future of Parliamentary Democracy. In Barbara R. Joshi *Untouchable!: Voices of the Dalit Liberation Movement* (pp. 39-40), New York: Zed Books.

Ambedkar, B.R. (1989a), *Dr. Babasaheb Ambedkar: Writings and Speeches Volume 1: Castes in India (1916).* (Compiled by Vasant Moon), Bombay: Education Department, Government of Maharashtra.

Ambedkar, B.R.(1989b), *Dr. Babasaheb Ambedkar: Writings and Speeches Volume 1: Annihilation of Caste: An undelivered speech (1935),* (Compiled by Vasant Moon), Bombay: education Department, Government of Maharashtra .

Ambedkar, B.R. (1990), *Dr. Babasaheb Ambedkar: Writings and Speeches, Volume 9: States and Minorities : What Were their rights and how to secure them in the Constitution of free India , Memorandum Submitted on behalf of All India Scheduled Castes Federation (1947)'.* (Compiled by Vasant Moon), Bombay: Education Department, Government of Maharashtra.

Deshpande, G.P. (2009), *The World of Ideas in Modern Marathi: Phule, Vinoba and Savarkar.* New Delhi: Tulika Books.

Diehl, Anita (1976), E.V. Ramaswami Naicker and Hindu Society. In S.D. Pillai (Ed.), *Aspects of Changing India: Studies in Honour of Prof. G. S. Ghurye* (pp.120-128), Bombay: Popular Prakashan.

Diehl, Anita (1977), *E.V. Ramaswami Naicker-Periyar: A Study of the Influence of a Personality in Contemporary South India,* Lund: Scandinavian University Books.

Geetha, V. and Rajadurai, S.V. (1998), *Towards a Non-Brahmin Millennium: from Iyothee Thass to Periyar,* Calcutta: Samya.

Phule, Jotirao (1991), *Collected Works of Mahatma Jotirao Phule, Volume 1: Slavery in the Civilised British Government under the Cloak of Brahmanism.*(Translated by P.G. Patil). Bombay: Education Department, Government of Maharashtra Mantralaya for Mahatma Jotirao Phule Death Centenary Central Committee.

Rai, Dhananjay (2009), Sansadiya Loktantra aur Dalit Rajniti, *Sablog,* June: 45-47.

22

Compensatory Discrimination in Favour of Members of Scheduled Tribes in Panchayats in Scheduled Areas

Anshuman Mishra

India is a land of diversities. For centuries, it has also been a victim of external aggressions, which is one of the basic reasons of neglecting some sections of the society. Under the authoritarian regimes the primary concern of the people was of survival in adverse conditions. It further led to the seclusion of already segregated communities as a whole. However, it did not go unnoticed. Even during the British occupation the great leaders of the nation started fighting for the causes of these communities. Mahatma Gandhi, the father of nation showed us the path of social justice. People also started thinking about how to undo the injustice done to the downtrodden hitherto. One of the measures considered in this regard was discriminative equality. Acharya Vinoba Bhave, a close associate and disciple of Mahatma Gandhi wrote about the discriminative equality in the following words:

> "We want equality tempered with discrimination. The mother does not distribute food among her children on the basis of mathematical equality. To the youngest one she gives only milk, and some bread, and to the grown-ups only bread. In the same way, in society also we will exercise discrimination and take into account the intensity of hunger and the power of digestion of each in the distribution of food. Where equality is brought about by force, all are compelled to conform to the same pattern. We are totally against this kind of regimentation. We aim at spiritual equality based on discrimination."[1]

Acharya Bhave talks about spiritual equality based on discrimination. He clarifies that equality does not mean that everyone should have five acres of land, and the same kind of house, or an equal yardage of cloth. We only want that the things, which are necessary for life, such as air, water and the land, should be equally accessible to all. None will grudge the surplus which may be left over with some after all have had enough of these things.[2] However, the question is- are there any takers of such ideals? Therefore, provisions were made to bring about equality by force- sometimes thoughtfully and sometimes under compulsion. During the British rule in India, the foreign rulers did not take much care of the people but there are examples where they took legislative measures to protect the identity of the weaker sections specially the tribal communities. Special laws[3] were enacted giving them special status and autonomy to regulate their own affairs on the basis of their own convention and traditions. These tribal communities used to elect their respective leaders through consensus or by using other customary methods of selection. The Constitution of India seems to be the first to have expressly provided for affirmative action.[4] Affirmative action means that the State has to take positive steps to lift the socially and educationally backward classes of Indian citizens to a level from where they can enjoy their freedom and liberty on reasonably equal footing. Wider arrangements have been made in fundamental rights' chapter in Part III, the directive principals of State Policy in Part IV and special provisions relating to certain classes in Part XVI of the constitution. Now, affirmative action is no more an exception to the fundamental right to equality but an integral aspect of it. The concept of fairness is inherent in the guarantee of equality under Article 14. The Supreme Court while broadening this concept has held that a law would not only be struck down on the ground of absence of reasonableness of the classification made by it, but conversely a law would be upheld which provides for a 'protective discrimination.'[5] It has been held that the 'protective discrimination' in favour of SCs and STs is a part of constitutional scheme of social and economic justice.[6] In short it may be said that to treat unequal differently according to their inequality is not only permitted but required.[7] The doctrine of positive or affirmative action has been deduced from the 'equal protection' clause of Article 14 of the Constitution.[8]

SCHEDULED TRIBES

Tribes occupy a special position in our Constitution. They are often described as 'untouchables'.[9] They have been receiving ill-treatment for centuries. Article 366(25) of the constitution defines the term 'Scheduled Tribes' thus:

> "Scheduled Tribes" means such tribes or tribal communities or parts of or groups within such tribes or tribal communities as are deemed under Article 342 to be Scheduled Tribes for the purposes of this Constitution.

Article 342 empowers the President of India to specify the tribes or tribal communities or parts of or groups within tribes or tribal communities by means of a public notification. In exercise of the said powers, the President issued the Constitution (Scheduled Tribes) Order, 1950 which has been amended from time to time. By virtue of clause (2) of Article 342, Parliament passed in 1976 the Scheduled Castes and Scheduled Tribes Orders (Amendment) Act, 1976.

Tribe denotes a group of persons forming a community and claiming descent from a common ancestor.[10] 'Adivasis' or 'Tribes' are many in number belonging to different "ethnic, religious and social groups." They reside in India as an integral part of it. Unfortunately, they belong to the most backward areas in India. They are aboriginals or indigenous people. As defined by the United Nations Special Rapporteur[11] to the Sub-Commission on Prevention of Discrimination and Protection of Minorities, Indigenous communities, peoples and nations are "those which having a historical continuity with pre-invasion and pre-colonial societies that developed on their territories, consider themselves distinct from other sectors of societies now prevailing in those territories, or part of them. They form at present non-dominant sectors of society and are determined to preserve, develop, and transmit to future generations their ancestral territories, and their ethnic identity, as the basis of their continued existence as peoples, in accordance with their own "cultural patterns, social institutions and legal systems."

Article 3 of the United Nations Declaration on the Rights of Indigenous Peoples,[12] adopted on 13 Sept., 2007 declares that 'Indigenous Peoples' have the right of self-determination.[13] By virtue of that right they freely determine their political status and freely pursue their economic, social and cultural development. Article 5 of the declaration provides that the indigenous peoples have the right to maintain and strengthen their distinct political, legal, economic, social and cultural institutions, while retaining their right to participate fully, if they so choose, in the political, economic, social and cultural life of the State.

At the outset it should be very clear that the Constitution of India, from the time of its inception itself, recognizes the right of tribal communities. However, it is quite unfortunate to see that people of these communities are up in arms against the Government. Naxalism is on the rise. The condition of law and order situation is changing from bad to worse. Deployment of central Para-military forces in areas dominated by tribal communities is indicative of the alarming state of affairs. Bandopadhyay Committee, constituted in the recent past reported that in more than 100 districts spread over 12 States, there is no rule of the Government. Another Committee, constituted under the chairmanship of Shri Arjun Sen Gupta suggests that 67 per cent of the population is not in position of spending Rs. 20 a day. It means that they do not have the purchasing power at all. The conclusion of the former Committee may legitimately be taken as the logical result of the latter. It is widely believed that corruption, lack of timely action on the part of the administration and developmental laxity are in the root of these problems.

SCHEDULED AND TRIBAL AREAS

When the Constitution of India came into force, Article 244 provided for the administration of scheduled Areas and Tribal Areas. Article 244(1) provides that the provisions of the Fifth Schedule to the Constitution shall apply to the administration and control of the Scheduled Areas and Scheduled Tribes in any State[14] other then the states of Assam, Meghalaya, Tripura and Mizoram. By virtue of clause (2) of Article 244, the provisions of the Sixth Schedule shall apply to the administration of the tribal areas in these States.

Scheduled Areas mean such areas as the President may by order declare to be the Scheduled Areas.[15] These areas are treated differently from the other areas in the country because they are inhibited by aboriginals who are socially and economically backward. Therefore, the whole of the normal administrative machinery operating in a State is not extended to the Scheduled Areas. Para 4 of the fifth schedule states that, there shall be in each state having a "Scheduled Area", a "Tribes Advisory Council" consisting of not more than twenty members of whom, as nearly as may be, three-fourths shall be the representatives of the scheduled tribes in the Legislative Assembly of the state. The duty of such council was to advise the governor on such matters pertaining to the welfare and advancement of the Scheduled Tribes in the State referred to it by the Governor. Para 5 of the fifth Schedule states that Governor of the State may by public notification direct that any particular Act of the Parliament or the Legislature of the State shall not apply to a Scheduled Area or would apply subject to such modifications and exceptions as he may specify. The Governor has power to make Regulations for the peace and good governance of a Scheduled Area after consulting the Tribes Advisory Council.[16] A Regulation may amend or repeal an act of Parliament or of State Legislature applicable to the area in question.[17] A Regulation comes into force only when it is assented to by the President.[18] In *Ram Kirpal v. State of Bihar*,[19] the Supreme Court has observed that this provision confers the "widest" power to legislate on the Governor.

It appears that theoretically everything was going on smoothly but it should actually have been translated into practice. Much is to be performed in a very short period of time to prevent conversion of a social problem into a political one.

THE PANCHAYATI RAJ SYSTEM AND SCHEDULED AREAS

Part IX, 'The Panchayats' was inserted in the Constitution of India by way of the Constitution (Seventy-third Amendment) Act, 1992. Article 243-B of the said Part (Part IX) mandates that there shall be panchayats at the village, intermediate and district levels in accordance with the provisions of Part IX of the Constitution. Article 243-C provides that the legislature of a State may, by law, make provisions with respect to the composition of panchayats. Article

243-D provides for the reservation of seats for scheduled castes, scheduled tribes, women and other backward classes.

However, since "Tribes Advisory Councils" had been constituted for the Scheduled Areas, and further by virtue of Article 243-M(I) of Part IX of the Constitution, Panchayati Raj System, a mandate of Constitution (Seventy-third Amendment) Act, 1992 could not be introduced. Article 243-M(I) of Part IX of the Constitution provides that nothing in this Part shall apply to the Scheduled Areas referred to in clause (I), and the Tribal Areas referred to in clause (2), of Article 244. Clause 4(b) of Article 243-M, however, empowers the Parliament to extend the provisions of Part IX to the Scheduled Areas and the Tribal Areas referred to in clause (I) by making law. Such a law may also be subjected to certain exceptions and modifications.

BHURIA COMMITTEE

After a period of two years of the enforcement of 73rd Constitution Amendment Act, the Union Government appointed a committee of members of Parliament and experts under the chairmanship of Shri Dilip Singh Bhuria to undertake a detailed study to make recommendations about the possible extension of the provisions of Part IX to the scheduled areas. The committee in its report favoured democratic decentralisation in Scheduled Areas. However, the committee made three specific recommendations, viz., (1) Panchayats in Scheduled Areas must have a majority of Scheduled Tribes; (2) Chairman and Vice-Chairman should belong to Scheduled Tribes; and (3) One-third of the seats should be reserved for women.

The committee justified its recommendations on the ground that in course of time, on account of influx of non-Schedule Tribe population, in a few Scheduled Areas, the situation of Schedule Tribe population might have been reduced to a minority but that should not be regarded as having altered the overall character of the Scheduled Area because these areas were notified as such on account of majority of Schedule Tribe population, contiguity, etc. The committee also gave detailed suggestions with regard to powers, functions and procedures of the Panchayati Raj Institutions.

Perhaps the Government was really worried about the prevailing state of maladministration and the ever growing influence of naxalism in these areas.

A Central Legislation on the Lines of Bhuria Committee Report

Parliament on the basis of these recommendations (Bhuria Committee) passed the Panchayats (Extension to Scheduled Areas) Act, 1996 favouring reservations of Schedule Tribe members in panchayats. Section 4(g) of the Act provides that the reservation of seats in the Scheduled Areas at every panchayat shall be in proportion to the population of the communities in that parts IX of the Constitution. A proviso to this sub-section explains that the reservation for the scheduled tribes shall not be less than one-half of the total number of seats. A further proviso makes it mandatory to reserve all the seats of chairpersons of panchayats at all levels for the Schedule Tribes.

Legislation by State to give Effect to the Provisions of the Central Act

Local government including the self governing institutions for the rural areas being exclusive State subject under Entry 5, List II of 7th Schedule to the Constitution, only the State could respond to make law to give effect to the provisions of the abovementioned central law. Therefore, the State Legislature of Jharkhand passed the Jharkhand Panchayati Raj Act, 2001 reserving all the offices of chairperson at all levels for Schedule Tribes and not less than fifty percent seats in panchayats[20] for Schedule Tribes. The Act further provides that in the Scheduled Areas, in Gram Panchayat,[21] in Panchayat Samiti[22] or in Zila Parishad,[23] seats shall be reserved in such number in favour of persons of backward class, proportionate to their population, which, if combined with the seats reserved for scheduled castes and scheduled tribes, if any, shall not exceed more than eighty percent of total seats of that Gram Panchayat, Panchayat Samiti or Zila Parishad respectively.

Legislations Challenged before High Court

Constitutional validity of both the Central as well as State legislations[24] was challenged before the Jharkhand High Court on the ground that second proviso to section 4(g) of the central law whereby all the seats of chairpersons of panchayats at all three tiers in Scheduled Areas were reserved in favour of Schedule Tribes and the corresponding provisions of State law are violative of the provisions of Article 14 of the Constitution.[25] The High Court held[26] the cent per cent reservation of seats of chairpersons of panchayats at all levels in favour of Schedule Tribes unconstitutional and ultra vires. However, on the argument that office of chairperson should be treated a solitary seat, the High Court distinguished the decision in *Janardhan Paswan v. State of Bihar*,[27] keeping in mind that it was decided before the commencement of the seventy-third amendment and Article 243-D of Part IX had contemplated the said reservation policy.

Appeal to the Supreme Court

An appeal from the decision of the High Court was preferred to the Supreme Court. Allowing the appeal the Supreme Court[28] upheld the validity of the impugned provisions of both the Acts viz. Panchayats (Extension to the Scheduled Areas) Act, 1996, a central Act and Jharkhand Panchayati Raj Act, 2001, a State law. The Supreme Court considered in detail about the purpose of inserting Fifth Schedule to the Constitution and came to the conclusion that the primary aim of the Government policy then was to protect the tribal communities from the risk of their agricultural land being usurped by the more civilized section of the population and secondly they were more likely to be victimized by the "wiles of the money lenders." The Court also considered the purpose of introducing Part IX to the Constitution which enables the legislature to take affirmative action in reserving the seats in panchayats.

Doctrine of Compensatory Discrimination

The Supreme Court observed that 50 per cent of reservation in favour of Scheduled Tribes in panchayats at all three levels is a clear example of compensatory discrimination especially in view of the fact that the Scheduled Areas under consideration were completely under a separate administrative scheme as per the fifth schedule to the constitution.[29]

Drawing Analogy between Articles 15(4) and 16(4) and Article 243-D is not correct

The Supreme Court said that an analogy between Article 243-D on one hand and Articles 15(4) and 16(4) on the other cannot be drawn because reservation in Panchayati Raj Institutions has a distinct and independent constitutional basis.[30] The Court[31] approved the decision of Bombay High Court in *Vinayakrao Gangaramji Deshmukh v. P.C. Agrawal,*[32] in this regard where the chairperson position in a panchayat was reserved in favour of a scheduled caste woman.

The Court further said that even for the sake of argument, if an analogy between Art. 243-D and Art. 16(4) is viable, a close reading of *Indira Sawhney v. Union of India,*[33] will reveal that even though an upper limit of 50 per cent was prescribed for reservations in public employment, the said decision did also recognize the need for exceptional treatment in some circumstances, the Court noticed.[34]

The Court found the case of panchayats in Scheduled Areas a fit case that warranted exceptional treatment with regard to reservations. The Court further clarified that under Articles 15(4) and 16(4) the reservation of seats in favour of socially and educationally backward classes is ordinarily done on the basis of proportional representation and an upper ceiling of 50 per cent allows for considerable flexibility in distributing the benefits of higher education and public employment among a wide range of intended beneficiaries. However, for Scheduled Areas compensatory discrimination goes beyond the ordinary standards of "adequate representation" and "proportionate representation."[35]

Approving of the decision of Madhya Pradesh High Court in *Ashok Kumar Tripathi v. Union of India,*[36] wherein the court has gone to the extent of saying that the protective discrimination in favour of deprived sections of the nation and societies in Scheduled Areas can go to the extent of complete exclusion, if the circumstances so justify. The Supreme Court held both the Acts, viz., Panchayats (Extension to the Scheduled Areas) Act, 1996, a central Act and Jharkhand Panchayati Raj Act, 2001, a State law, constitutionally valid.[37]

CONCLUSION

The framers of the Constitution were very well aware of the conditions of tribal communities in India. Therefore, provisions providing for adequate safeguards to preserve their identities have been incorporated in the Constitution since its inception. India as a developing country has always taken care of its population to the extent possible. The directive principles of state policy (Part IV of the Constitution) talk about the positive duties of the state. One of the Articles in Directive Principles Chapter- Article 40 obligates the State to take steps to organise village panchayats and endow them with such powers and authority as may be necessary to enable them to function as units of self-government. 73rd Amendment to the constitution was inserted only in 1992. Was it too late to contain the feelings of unrest among the masses? Further, in States like Jharkhand the process of decentralisation started only in 2001 when the state passed its Jharkhand Panchayati Raj Act, 2001. The condition of the justice delivery system is such that the validity of the impugned Acts could be decided only in 2010, after a period of almost 9 years. Tribal areas are now affected by Naxalism. Naxalism is a problem of poor administration. The question is: When the provisions for separate administration of Scheduled Areas were already incorporated in the constitution why did the tribal population suffer from the problem of poor administration? Moreover, it may be contended that they themselves run the administration. Had there been a problem of maladministration? Why steps were not taken to resolve it. Newspapers report that recently a District Collector Mr. R.V. Krishna, and a junior engineer have been abducted by the Naxalites in Orissa[38] and the government is trying to negotiate with these extremist elements. It is a clear example of the fact that how the law and order situation is deteriorated or it may be said that is on the verge of collapse. As far as reservations in panchayats in favour of Scheduled Tribes to the exclusion of others is not a matter of big concern for them who do not contest elections because the common man is interested only in good governance. In this regard a glaring example is Ms Mayawati Government in Uttar Pradesh where people on its comparison with its predecessor on the basis of situation of law and order find it better. However, the question is whether the cent percent reservation for chairmanship in panchayats in favour of Scheduled Tribes in Scheduled Areas has really changed the situation at ground level and if not, then one has to think about the reasons of failure. Bhuria Committee in its report highlights the ground reality thus:

> "Although, theoretically, there has been difference in the approach after the departure of the colonial masters from tribal areas, in practice, the principles enunciated in Article 39 and other directive principles of state policy have to be followed more rigorously. On account of their simplicity and ignorance, over the decades the tribals have been dispossessed of their natural and economic resources like land, forest, water, air, etc. The dispossession is not confined to that through private

parties. For the purpose of promotion of general economic development projects, the State also has been depriving them of the basic means of livelihood."

Thus deprived of their identity itself what would they do with the decentralisation of power. Here the question is whether the model of development we have adopted is wrong? Was Gandhian model a better one for Indian conditions? It is said that globalisation has benefited only to the middle classes. It may be true to a very great extent. They do not require direct political power because whosoever comes to power will be bound to serve their causes. So even if the chairman belongs to the deprived community, it does not matter much because the experience shows that ultimately favours do restrict to family and close friends. It is humbly submitted that we the people of India as a whole have failed to address the prime need of providing education to all in time which should have been the primary goal of the nation state since beginning and that is the root of the problem in every area—be it of female feticide or of population growth or of environmental degradation.

Another problem is that we talk about justice, liberty and equality but, at the same time, forget about the concept of fraternity enshrined in the Preamble of the Constitution which is nothing but the tool of achieving Acharya Vinoba Bhave's spiritual equality based on discrimination.

ENDNOTES AND REFERENCES

1. Harijan, 20-12-1952. *Source*: Sarvodaya published by Navjeevan Publishing House, Ahmedabad. Fifth reprint, 2008, p. 165.
2. Ibid.
3. E.g. Santhal Parganas and Chutia Nagpur Divisions were created by Act of 1874.
4. See 'The Constitution of India' by Prof. V.N. Shukla, 10th Ed., p. A-47.
5. *D.T.C. v. Mazdoor Union, D.T.C*, AIR 1991 SC 101.
6. *Ashok K. Gupta v. State of U.P.*, [1997] 5 SCC 201.
7. *St. Stephen's College v .University of Delhi*, AIR 1992 SC 1630.
8. *Indra Sawhney V. Union of India*, AIR 1993 SC 477.
9. See 'Constitutional Law of India' by H.M.Seervai, Fourth Ed., p. 574.
10. See the Shorter Oxford Dictionary.
11. Martinez-Cobo, 1984. See file:// F:\ The Rights of Indigenous Peoples. htm.
12. Use of the word 'peoples' cannot be described as a fit one in case of Indian aboriginals. Use of 'Tribes' or 'tribal population' seems to be more appropriate.
13. India ratifies Human Rights conventions like ICCPR with reservations as far as right to self-determination is concerned.
14. The States consisting such areas include Jharkhand, Chhattisgarh and Madhya Pradesh among others. See 'Indian Constitutional Law' by Prof. M.P. Jain, Fifth Ed. Reprint 2007, pp. 467-468.
15. In 2003 Scheduled Areas (States of Chhattisgarh, Jharkhand and Madhya Pradesh) Order was passed. Govt. of Jharkhand passed the Scheduled Areas (State of Jharkhand) Order, 2007 which is in force now. The tribal people of these areas have more or less adopted the culture of the majority of the people, in contrast of the people of Tribal Areas situated in Assam, Meghalaya, Tripura and Mizoram.
16. Cls. 2 and 5 of Para 5 of 5th Schedule to the Constitution.

17. Cl. 3 of Para 5 of 5th Schedule to the Constitution.
18. Cl. 4 of Para 5 of 5th Schedule to the Constitution.
19. AIR 1970 SC 951.
20. See Ss. 17B, 21B, 36B, 40B, 51B and 55B of the Jharkhand Panchayati Raj Act, 2001.
21. Section 17B(2) of the Jharkhand Panchayati Raj Act, 2001.
22. Section 36B(2) of the Jharkhand Panchayati Raj Act, 2001.
23. Section 51B(2) of the Jharkhand Panchayati Raj Act, 2001.
24. Panchayats (Extension to the Scheduled Areas) Act, 1996 and Jharkhand Panchayati Raj Act, 2001.
25. Writ Petitions (Public Interest Litigation) Nos. 2728, 3877 of 2002, 747 of 2001, 1585, 849 of 2002.
26. Order dated 2.9.2005.
27. AIR 1988 Patna 75.
28. In *Union of India v. Rakesh Kumar*, (2010) 4 SCC 50.
29. *Union of India v. Rakesh Kumar*, (2010) 4 SCC 50 at p. 74.
30. Ibid.
31. Ibid, at p. 75.
32. AIR 1999 Bom. 142.
33. 1992 Supp. (3) SCC 217.
34. *Union of India v. Rakesh Kumar*, (2010) 4 SCC 50.
35. Ibid, at p. 77.
36. (2000) 2 MPHT 193.
37. *Union of India v. Rakesh Kumar*, (2010) 4 SCC 50 at p. 80.
38. See *The Pioneer*, Lucknow, February 19, 2011.

23

Health and Human Rights in the Era of Globalisation: An Indian Perspective

Santosh Kumar

The Article 21 of Indian constitution states that every citizen has right to life and liberty. The right to life envisages a decent living condition to meet the minimum physical quality of life (air, water, shelter, sanitation and food) without compromising the personal liberty. The liberty stands for without compromising to fear or favour, infringement or excess, tort or injury, physical or emotional harassment from any quarter. In the era of globalisation, the universalisation of human rights and protection of citizen rights via UN agencies, civil society and government bodies have taken the lead roles. To achieve the constitutional goal of universal human rights to all its citizens in India has faced some structural and contemporary problems. The contemporary issues confronting Indian society today are honor killing, violation of rule of law by *Khap Panchayats*, lack of universal health security, inadequate access of safe drinking water and gender in justice. The rise of non-state actors (MNCs and NGOs), public vs. private and impact of globalisation on health in shaping the human rights are outlined.

INTRODUCTION

The evolution of modern Concept of **Human Rights** can be traced to World War II when its importance for governmental action and accountability was first widely recognized. The Universal Declaration of Human Rights (UDHR) of 1948 described human rights as the rights of individuals, which inhered in individuals because they were human; they applied to people everywhere in the world, and were principally concerned with the relationship between the individual and the state.[1]

The Declaration of Human Rights eloquently upholds the right to life as an inalienable entitlement of all human beings. As the mutually nurturing relationship between health and development becomes increasingly clear, protection of health (as an essential requirement for enabling human beings to develop to their full potential) becomes integral to the mandate of human rights.

As defined in the preamble of the WHO Constitution, health is a "state of complete physical, mental, and social well-being, and not merely the absence of disease or infirmity."[2] This definition illustrates the indivisibility and interdependence of rights as they relate to health, by recognizing that the enjoyment of the highest attainable standard of health was one of the fundamental rights of every human being and that governments have a responsibility for the health of their people, which can be fulfilled only through the provision of adequate health and social measures.

Rights relating to autonomy, information, education, food and nutrition, association, equality, participation and non-discrimination are integral and indivisible parts of the achievement of the highest attainable standard of health, just as the enjoyment of the right to health is inseparable from other rights, whether categorized as civil and political, economic, social or cultural. Thus, the right to the highest attainable standard or health builds on, but is by no means limited to, Article 12 of the International Covenant on Economic, Social and Cultural Rights. It transcends virtually every single other right.[3]

The 1978 **Declaration of Alma-Ata** called on nations to ensure the availability of the essentials of primary health care, including: education concerning health problems and the methods for preventing and controlling them; promotion of food supply and proper nutrition; an adequate supply of safe water and basic sanitation; maternal and child health care, including family planning; immunisation against major infectious diseases; prevention and control of locally endemic diseases; appropriate treatment of common disease and injuries; and provision of essential drugs.[4]

During the modern era of globalisation, **Jonathan Mann** was a central advocate of combining the synergistic forces of public health, ethics and human rights. He theorized and actively promoted the idea that human health and human rights are integrally and inextricably connected, arguing that these fields overlap in their respective philosophies and objectives to improve health, well-being, and to prevent premature death.[5] Mann proposed a three-pronged approach that has appropriately acted as a fundamental explanation of the relationship between health and human rights. First, health is a human rights issue. Secondly (and conversely), human rights are health issue. Human rights violations result in adverse health effects.[6] Thirdly, linkages exist between health and human rights (a hypothesis to be rigorously tested).[7] In 1990, Mann founded the health and human rights organisation Health Right International (initially known as Doctors of the World-USA), as he felt there was a void amongst the health and human rights organisations in the United States and he desired to create a unique organisation whose mission was to create sustainable programs that promote and protect health and human rights in the United States and abroad.[8]

The linkage between human rights and human development is recognized and so is the significance of public health. The primary targets for the year 2015 of the World Bank also include public health issues such as improvement of reproductive health of women, reduction in infant and maternal mortality rates etc. There is a need felt for genuine partnerships between the government, community, NGOs, medical and legal professional with points of entry at policy making, norm setting, professional associations, service delivery area, research and education. The goal of linking health and human rights is to contribute at advancing human well being beyond what could be achieved through an isolated health or human rights- based approach.

Today there is a universal need to reinforce the commitment and capacity of governments to ensure that actions taken by the private sector and other actors in civil society are relevant to health and other aspects of human development. At the same time it should also be made sure that these actions, both within and outside the boundaries of nation-states, are informed and comply human rights principles. The **Ottawa Charter** proposes that the fundamental conditions and resources for health are peace, shelter, education, food, income, a stable eco-system, sustainable resources, social justice and equity.[9]

HEALTH AND HUMAN RIGHTS IN INDIA

The right to health is an integral facet of the right to life. Article 21 of the Constitution of India states that, "No person shall be deprived of his life or personal liberty except according to procedure established by law."[10] This has been interpreted by the law courts as conferring the right to health and medical care as fundamental rights to all citizens. Section 2(d) of the Protection of Human Rights Act, 1993 defines human rights as rights related to life, liberty, equality and dignity of the individual guaranteed by the Constitution or embodied in the International Covenants and enforceable by the Courts in India.[11]

In India, the Constitution recognizes the State obligation in clear terms in Article 47, which provides that raising of the level of nutrition and the improvement of public health are among the primary duties of the State. This is a Directive Principle of State Policy, contained in Part IV of the Constitution, which lays down the principles fundamental in the governance of the country and obligates the State to apply them in making laws.[12] Another Directive Principle is Article 48A which imposes the duty to protect and improve the environment and to safeguard the forests and wild life in the country and which too is related to improvement of public health. Both these articles in Part IV of the Constitution have been judicially interpreted to expand the meaning and scope of 'right to life' guaranteed as a fundamental right in Article 21 of the Indian Constitution. Thus, in India the Constitution elevates the 'right to health of the highest attainable standards' to a guaranteed fundamental right which is enforceable by virtue of the constitutional remedy under Article 32 of the Constitution.[13]

Access to Health Care and Challenges of Public Health

Health and development in various parts of India have progressed unevenly. **Health care** expenditure is the second most common cause of rural indebtedness. The health infrastructure needs to be reviewed, recast and revitalized to ensure its convergence with existing primary health care priorities. Multi-faceted development efforts can improve the health situation. The era of globalisation has led to advancement in health care services thereby giving access to these services to class who can afford them. The Global Health, Fortis, Apollo and Max New York Life are chain of hospitals which lead in providing the world class health care services. India still has high rate of maternal mortality ratio (450/100000), low level of contraceptive prevalence (56/100) and only a few (47/100) births attended by skilled personnel.[14] The government expenditure on health is low beyond expectation; it spends less than 1.5 per cent of GDP and 5 per cent of total expenditure. However, the normal estimated health expenditure for India is 6 per cent of GDP. (Fig. 1)

The public health challenges of safe drinking water, sanitation, right to food entitlement to challenged personnel (HIV/AIDS patients, the old and the homeless, infirm, destitute and street children), malnutrition, tobacco

Figure 1: Access to Improved Drinking Water Sources (per cent)

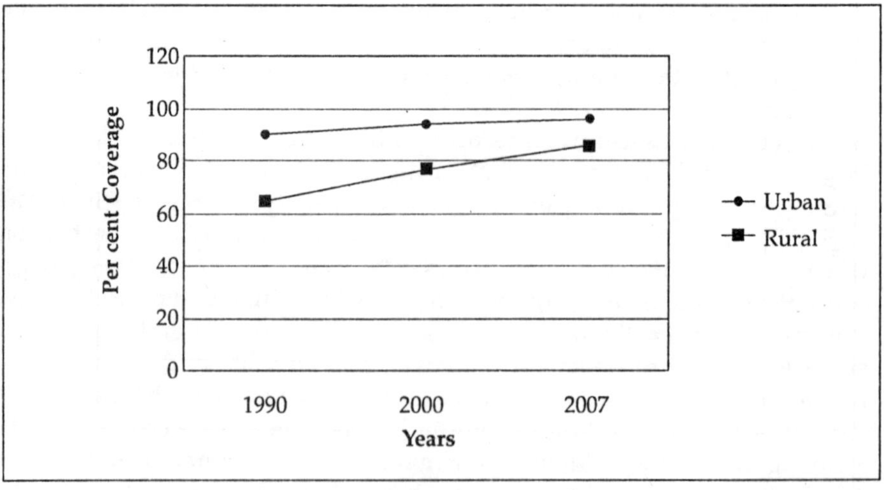

Data Source: World Health Statistics, WHO, Geneva, 2009.

hazard and environment pollution needs attention of the government for the larger well being of the society.

Twenty six years after the Bhopal Gas disaster occurred, and Methyl Isocyanides (MIC) leaked from the Union Carbide plant in Bhopal on December 2-3, 1984, the victims didn't get justice. A Draft Code of Conduct for Corporations was discussed by a group of persons brought together in Geneva by the Office of the High Commissioner for Human Rights on March 30-31, 2001. The First Draft Code envisages social responsibility of corporations, and corporations as human rights watchdogs. In recent years, environmental litigation has been among the visible aspects of contending with pollution. The courts, particularly the Supreme Court, have been accorded primacy in matters concerning the environment, by environmentalists as well as the state. The court has used closure, relocation and cleans up technology as remedial tools and the polluter pays principles and pollution fine as reparative and sanctioning measures. The public health concern has led to the introduction of CNG buses in Delhi. The relocation of industries from within Delhi, and the consequent closure and loss of employment of large numbers in the workforce has emerged from within an environmental context.

Poor sanitation is important risk factor for morbidity, including diarrheal diseases, cholera, worm infestations and hepatitis. Since 1990, the number of people in India using improved sanitation facilities has increased by 140 million. In 2007, 280 million Indian had access to improved sanitation amenities. (Fig. 2)

Fig. 2: Access to Improved Sanitation (per cent)

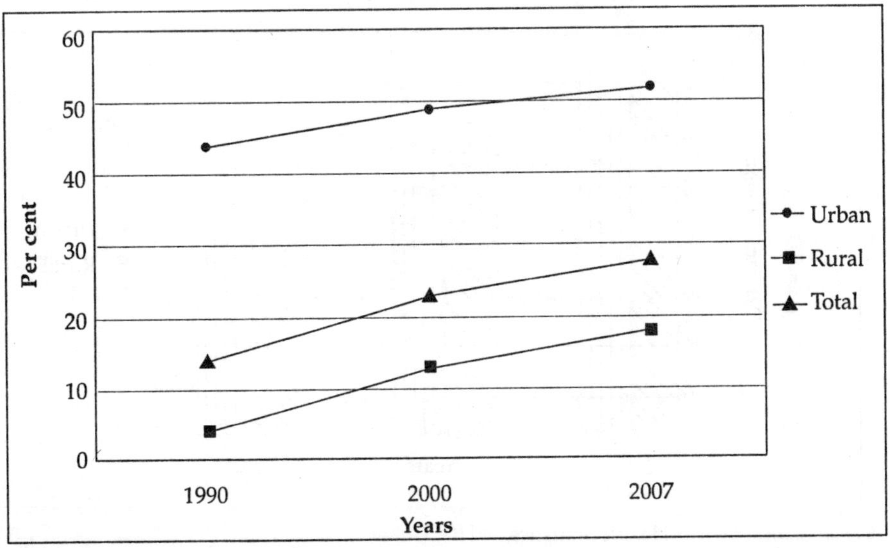

Data Source: World Health Statistics, WHO, Geneva, 2009.

SOCIAL CLASSES, HEALTH AND HUMAN RIGHTS

There are differences in health outcomes among vulnerable groups, women, children, elderly, migrants, disabled, Scheduled Castes and Scheduled Tribes. Infant and child mortality rates are high. Within India the differentials in child mortality is visible across region, gender, class and social groups. Children from Scheduled Tribes (31 per cent) are lowest in terms of immunisation for vaccine preventable diseases as compared to Scheduled Castes (40), Other Backward Classes (41 percent) and Others (53 per cent). Only 30 per cent of children from households with low standards of living are fully vaccinated compared to 65 per cent of children from households with a high standard of living. Children from the scheduled castes (66.0), scheduled tribes (62) and other backward classes (56.0) have higher rates of infant mortality rates than children from the other population (49). Similarly child mortality rates are higher among the SC (23.2), ST (35.8) and OBC (17.3) than among others (11). The infant and mortality rates show quite a variance among those from medium and low standard of living index as against those from the higher standards of living. Rural mortality rates among children are considerably higher than urban mortality rates.[15]

MEDICAL SERVICES, HEALTH AND HUMAN RIGHTS

Some of medical services and research in medical science has been the topic of debate since the ethical, moral and legal protocol needs clearance to work

Fig. 3: Infant Mortality Rate Per 1000 Live Births

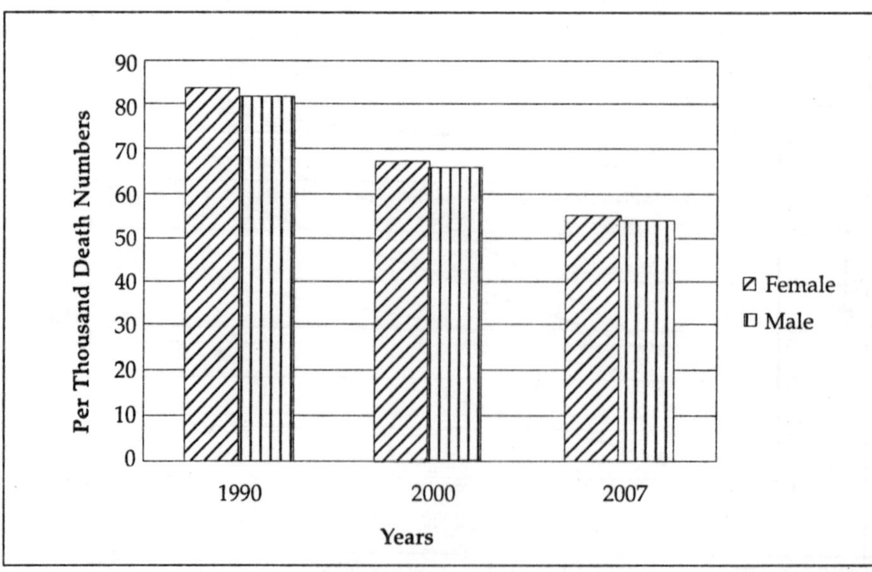

Data Source: World Health Statistics, WHO, Geneva, 2009.

upon, i.e., abortion, invitro fertilisation and gene manipulation or human cloning. Depo Provera, a contraceptive drug, was introduced into the Indian market without conducting Phase IV trials, which meant that the Indian state conducted no specific research amongst Indian users before deciding to introduce the drug in the market. The issue in Phase IV trials of Net-oen was of informed consent. The later Helsinki declaration, we were told, relaxed these rules. And efforts are underway to further relax the notion of informed consent for the greater common good. These efforts have been stalled at the international level. Court battles around banned drugs being sold in the Indian market have sometimes resulted in prospective banning. But the plea of the pharmaceutical company that the stocks be not destroyed, but that they be allowed to transport it to another jurisdiction outside India has been allowed.[16] But ICMR's 'Ethical Guidelines for Biomedical Research on Human Subjects' has been amended in 2000 to allow proxy consent in some cases, such as in epidemiological situations or in the larger public good.

In larger public good and safeguarding human rights, the government of India has made free access of anti-retroviral drugs for AIDS patients in six high prevalence States of India. The States of Tamil Nadu, Maharashtra, Karnataka, Andhra Pradesh, Mizoram and Nagaland have free access of medicine to AIDS patients. (Fig. 4)

TRADE IN HUMAN ORGANS AND VIOLATION OF ETHICAL NORMS

A racket in the sale of kidneys was exposed in Karnataka in the late 1980s and early '90s. There were allegations that the 'donor' was duped and his kidneys were removed and 'donated'; or that the donor had sold his kidneys

Fig. 4: Life Expectancy at Birth (Years)

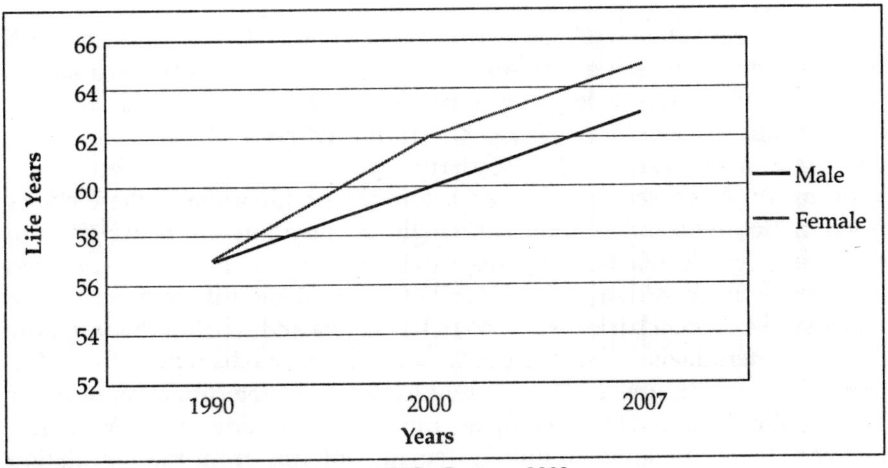

Data Source: World Health Statistics, WHO, Geneva, 2009.

as a commodity may be sold to raise resources—poverty was the characteristic that distinguished the donor. A series of exposés confirmed that there was a pattern to the sale and purchase of kidneys, which implicated, among others, doctors and hospitals. The dust refused to settle, and in 1994, Parliament enacted the Transplantation of Human Organs Act, 1994, which allowed organ donation either only after death, or where the receiver was a near relative of the donor, or it is actuated by 'affection, or attachment towards the recipient.' In the last-mentioned case, an Authorisation Committee has to approve the donation. The Act, in its prefatory text, says it is 'to provide for the regulation of removal, storage and transplantation of human organs for therapeutic purposes and **for the prevention of commercial dealings in human organs.**'[17]

FETICIDE, GENDER GAP AND HONOR KILLING

Female feticide is one extreme manifestation of violence against women. Female fetuses are selectively aborted after pre-natal sex determination, thus avoiding the birth of girls. In India where female infanticide has existed for centuries, now female feticide has joined the fray and is increasing each day. The reasons for this evil are the introduction and proliferation of pre natal diagnostic test/sex determination clinics and cheaper ultrasound machines that help determine the sex of the child before it is born. Dramatic reduction of birth rates in most of India's states contributed toward intensification of son preference in the existing patriarchal society. Even rural families in the states have begun to commit female feticide to satisfy their preference for sons.

In Haryana, residents of upper caste hamlets openly admit to the widespread practice of female feticide. Parents tend to be calculative in choosing the sex of the next child and the decision is based on the birth order, sex sequence of previous children and number of sons. Transfer of reproductive technology to India is resulting in reinforcement of patriarchal values as professional medical organisations seem to be indifferent to ethical misconduct.

Sex determination methods were being used from 1979 onwards in North India to manipulate sex composition of children to have greater proportion of sons. In 10 years, the sex ratio of pre-school children in Punjab dropped from the already low levels (925 to 874 during 1981-91). Sharp declines also occurred in Haryana and Rajasthan, states where female feticide is widespread. A ten year gap ensued before the proliferation of these clinics began in Southern India. In the early eighties, attention was being given to the issue of female infanticide but the activists had not anticipated the problem of female feticide. Although the spread of this problem was initially slower, many taluks even in backward parts of Karnataka and Andhra Pradesh now have sex determination clinics. There were occasional media reports from 1992 onwards about the abuse of ultrasound for fetal sex determination in major cities of Tamil Nadu. However, by the time the magnitude of the problem is realized, there are some 80 million females missing from the population pyramid of India. Moreover, the government has awakened lately to enact the law to check the evil of feticide. The Pre-natal Diagnostic Techniques (Regulation and Prevention of Misuse) Act, 1994 largely came out of the first state law enacted in Maharashtra against sex determination was the Maharashtra Regulation of Use of Prenatal Diagnostic Techniques Act, 1988.[18]

'Honor' killings is not a virulent expression of 'caste' dynamics alone; it has a pan Indian presence with cases reported from various states, regions, religions, and (sub) caste groups. What is important and we need to keep that in mind, irrespective of where it is occurring, such killing is a denial of one's right to 'live' in the name of "honor". Today, things have dramatically changed thanks to the media and civil society. Perpetrated under the garb of saving the "honor" of the community, caste or family, "honor" killings seem to occur almost every day. The largest number of cases is reported in Punjab, Haryana and Uttar Pradesh. It is estimated that Haryana and Punjab alone account for 10 per cent of all 'honor' killings in the country. Significantly, in the majority of cases, the economically and socially dominant castes organize, instigate and abet such acts of retribution. In Haryana and elsewhere, caste *panchayats* (known as the Khaps) have come to play an increasingly important role, especially in situations where political patronage also exists.

Central to the theme of honor and violence is the subordinate position of girls and women in all castes and communities. The Special Marriage Act in India supports couples who choose to marry outside of caste, religion, or against the wishes of their families. A law is also being considered, which besides shortening the 30-day notice period required to getting married, will make 'honor' killings a specific offense.

GLOBALISATION, HEALTH AND HUMAN RIGHTS

Globalisation has the direct impact on health and related aspects of human development by intensifying global flows of money, trade, information, culture and people. Globalisation, and the privatisation of the means of production and services, that can contribute to the advancement of health through the sharing of information, technologies and resources, as well as through the competition it generates to provide more effective, more widely available and higher-quality services Non-state actors are now influencing the health and well-being of people to an unprecedented extent, comparable even to the influence of governments. Governmental roles and responsibilities are increasingly being delegated to non-state actors whose accountability for what they do, do not do or should do about people's health is poorly defined and inadequately monitored. The role of the state is to ensure that all human beings are guaranteed their basic human rights, including the right to the highest attainable standard of health, whether his obligation is fulfilled directly through government-run services or through private intermediaries.

Flip side of globalisation can stimulate the spread of health hazards and disease as a result of intensified population mobility, or through the worldwide marketing of harmful substances, such as tobacco and alcohol. If poorly conceived and monitored, it can contribute to the widening of inequalities by increasing the autonomy and well being of some sectors of the population while producing negative consequences for others without access to safety nets to support the fulfillment of essential needs.[19]

From health and human rights perspective, the desirable forms and extent of responsibility for multinational actors within the international legal system have yet to be defined in ways that help effectively to shape international trade agreements and to ensure their accountability.

CONCLUSION

The linkages between health and human rights are well established by now. The modern age health challenges are intricate with human rights. The role of the state is shrinking against expanding health services but desirably it is more important to give the health coverage for 300 million people in abject poverty in India. The *National Rural Health Mission* is a step in this direction but its goal and efficacy can be realized a few years later from now. The public health consciousness and environment pollution was/is well taken by the courts in India. In this respect, there are a few successes and few challenges remain to be resolved. The justice for Bhopal victims, the eviction of Vedanta from Niyamgiri and entry of Du Pont Chemicals in Hyderabad are some of complex issues that government has to clarify its position for the well being of the common people of India.

During last two decades, world has gone through many changes in technological breakthrough and scientific advancements in fields of medical sciences, information technology and world economic order. However, all the changes were/are not positive. India has realized some social and ethical challenges that have violated the fundamentals of the human rights, e.g., sex selection, feticide, trade in human organs and honor killing are unacceptable in a civil society. The legal protection and enactment of laws to any such challenges are imminent to safeguard the human rights.

The development indicators since 1990 to 2007 have scripted a story of Indian growth. Certain indicators selected in this paper show the steady growth during this period of time. The coverage of access to safe drinking water sources has increased from 71 per cent to 89 per cent. The access to improved sanitation increased 14 per cent to 28 per cent. There is an average increase of 7 years (57 to 64) in life expectancy at birth. The infant mortality rate (0-1, year) declined from 83/1000 to 54/1000. India has well benefited in the era of globalisation but there are still some critical areas that need to be overcome like health, sanitation and well beings of economic impoverished population.

ENDNOTES AND REFERENCES

1. United Nations (1948), *Universal Declaration of Human Rights*, G.A. Res. 217A (iii), UN GAOR, Res. 71, UN Doc. A/810.
2. World Health Organisation (1946), Constitution of the World Health Organisation, adopted by the International Health Conference, New York, 19 June-22 July 1946, and signed on 22 July 1946 by the representatives of 61 States.
3. United Nations International Covenant on Economic, Social and Cultural Rights (ICESCR) (1966), G.A. Rs. 2200 (XXI), UN GAOR, 21st Sess., Supp. No. 16, at 49, UN Doc. A/6316.
4. World Health Organisation (1979), *International conference on Primary Health Care*, 6-12 September 1978, endorsed by 32nd World Health Assembly, Geneva, WHA 32. 30.
5. Gostin LO, Public Health, Ethics, and Human Rights: A Tribute to the late Jonathan Mann. *Journal of Law, Medicine & Ethics*, 2001, 28: 121-130.
6. Schusky RW, Jonathan's Mantle. *Lancet*, 1998, 352 (9145):2025.
7. Mann JM, Gruskin S, Grodin MA and Annas GJ (eds.), *Health and Human Rights: A Reader*, New York: Routledge. 1999:11–18.
8. Institute of Medicine, *Future of Public Health*, Washington DC: National Academy Press, 1988: 1-7.
9. Ottawa Charter for Health Promotion, presented at the First International Conference on Health Promotion, Ottawa, Canada, November 21, 1986.
10. Basu DD, *Introduction to the Constitution of India*, Nagpur: LexixNexix Butterworths Wadhawa, 2010: 111-114.
11. Gostin L, Mann J (1999), Toward the Development of a Human Rights Impact Assessment for the Formulation and Evaluation of Public Health Policies. In *Health and Human Rights, a reader*, Mann J, Gruskin S, Grodin M, Annas G (eds), Routledge, pp. 54-71.
12. Basu DD, *Introduction to the Constitution of India*, Nagpur: LexixNexix Butterworths Wadhawa, 2010: 158-159.
13. ____, *Introduction to the Constitution of India*, Nagpur: LexixNexix Butterworths Wadhawa, 2010: 131-139.
14. World Health Statistics (2009). *Global Health Indicators*, WHO, Geneva: 14-18.
15. National Family and Health Survey (NFHS-3), 2005-06: India (I): 229.
16. Ramnathan, Usha (2001). *Human Rights in India: A Mapping*, Delhi: 24-25.
17. Minisrty of Law, Justice and Company Affairs (1994), *The Transplant of Human Organ Act, 1994*: No. 42, Delhi: 1-13.
18. The Pre-Natal Diagnostic Technique Regulation and Prevention of Misuse, Amendment Act.2002. No.14 of 2003(Revised, PNDT: 1994), (2003): *The Gazette of India: Extraordinary Part II, Section I*, New Delhi. RG.NO.DL.33004/2003.
19. Heggenhougen, K. (1999). Are the marginalized the slag-heap of globalisation? Disparity, health and human rights. *Health and Human Rights*, 4(1), 205-13.

Index